GLOBAL GOVERNANCE AND THE UN

UNITED NATIONS INTELLECTUAL HISTORY PROJECT

Global Governance and the UN
An Unfinished Journey

Thomas G. Weiss and Ramesh Thakur

Foreword by John Gerard Ruggie

Indiana University Press

Bloomington and Indianapolis

This book is a publication of

Indiana University Press
601 North Morton Street
Bloomington, IN 47404-3797 USA

www.iupress.indiana.edu

Telephone orders 800-842-6796
Fax orders 812-855-7931
Orders by e-mail iuporder@indiana.edu

© 2010 by The United Nations Intellectual History Project
All rights reserved

UNIHP

⊗ The paper used in this publication meets the minimum requirements
of the American National Standard for Information Sciences—
Permanence of Paper for Printed Library Materials, ANSI Z39.48-1992.

Manufactured in the United States of America

Library of Congress Cataloging-in-Publication Data

Weiss, Thomas George.
Global governance and the UN : an unfinished journey /
Thomas G. Weiss and Ramesh Thakur ; foreword by John Gerard Ruggie.
p. cm. — (United Nations intellectual history project)
Includes bibliographical references and index.
ISBN 978-0-253-35430-3 (cloth : alk. paper) — ISBN 978-0-253-22167-4 (pbk. : alk. paper)
1. International organization. 2. International cooperation. 3. United Nations.
I. Thakur, Ramesh Chandra, 1948–   II. Title.
JZ1318.W447 2010
341.23—dc22
2009036271

1 2 3   4 5 15 14 13 12 11 10

CONTENTS

BOXES, TABLES, AND GRAPHS

SERIES EDITORS' FOREWORD

We began the United Nations Intellectual History Project (UNIHP) ten years ago to fill a surprising and serious omission, the lack of any comprehensive study of the history of the UN's contributions to economic and social thinking and action. Now, with some satisfaction, we can look back at thirteen published volumes that document the UN's work in these areas. The final three volumes of the series, of which this is one, are in press. The project has unearthed some important findings that are still not adequately recognized: that ideas have been among the UN's most important contributions; that the quality of the UN's work has, at its best, been outstandingly good; that in its intellectual work, the UN has often been ahead of the curve (and ahead of the Bretton Woods institutions); and finally, in terms of impact, that the UN's leading contributions have literally changed history. This is reflected in the title of our capstone volume—a synthesis of the major conclusions of the entire project—*UN Ideas That Changed the World*.[1]

We are pleased that over the last decade, the landscape of UN history has been changing due to the work of others. Books documenting the history of the UN Development Programme; the World Food Programme; the International Labour Organization; UN Educational, Scientific and Cultural Organization; and other UN funds and specialized agencies have been produced or are in the process of being written.[2] The record of the UN's contributions is now more accessible. But though all this is welcome, we should underline that it is no more than what should be expected of all public organizations, especially internationally accountable ones. We look forward to enhanced efforts among these UN funds and agencies to organize, improve, and open their archives so that independent researchers can dispassionately analyze their efforts and achievements. All of this is an essential part of what is needed to improve international cooperation.

The United Nations Intellectual History Project, launched in 1999, is an independent research effort based in the Ralph Bunche Institute for International Studies at The Graduate Center of The City University of New York. We are grateful for the enthusiastic backing from Kofi Annan, the Secretary-General when the project was launched, and of many UN staff. Generous financial support from five foundations and eight governments has ensured total intellectual and financial independence. Details of the project can be found on our Web site: www.UNhistory.org.

The work of the UN can be divided into two broad categories: economic and social development, on the one hand, and peace and security, on the other. Though UNIHP started by focusing on the former, the project grew to encompass three volumes in the areas of peace and security. All the volumes have been or are being published in a series by Indiana University Press. In addition, the project has completed an oral history collection of seventy-nine interviews of persons who have played major roles in launching and nurturing UN ideas—and sometimes in hindering them! Extracts from these interviews were published in 2005 as *UN Voices: The Struggle for Development and Social Justice.*[3] Authors of the project's various volumes, including this one, have drawn on these interviews to highlight substantive points made in their texts. Full transcripts of the oral histories are also available from the UNIHP secretariat in electronic book form as a CD-ROM to facilitate work by other researchers and interested persons worldwide.

There is no single way to organize research, and that is certainly true for such an ambitious project as this one. This UN history has been structured for the most part by topics, ranging from trade and finance to human rights, from transnational corporations to development assistance, from regional perspectives to sustainability. We have selected world-class experts for each topic, and the presentation and argument in all of the volumes is the responsibility of the authors whose names appear on the cover. All have been given freedom and responsibility to organize their own digging, analysis, and presentation. Guidance from us as the project directors as well as from peer review groups is provided to ensure accuracy and fairness in depicting where the ideas came from, how they were developed and disseminated within the UN system, and what happened afterward. We trust that future analyses will build upon our series and go beyond. Our intellectual history project is the first, not the last, installment in depicting the history of the UN's contributions to ideas.

This present volume, *Global Governance and the UN: An Unfinished Journey,* bridges the themes and topics of earlier volumes and seeks to draw them together in terms of the challenges and conclusions for the institutions involved in global norm setting, decision making, action, and monitoring—in short, for global governance. Several chapters present the most concise, complete, and up-to-date account of the most pressing problems of our age.

As explained at the outset by Thomas G. Weiss and Ramesh Thakur, the volume has been long in the making. This in part is a consequence of the difficulties and complications of the topic, especially as seen through the eyes of international relations scholars. Global governance among this fraternity and sorority is generally defined by a critical absence—as global governance without global government. Other disciplines have their own ways to avoid the hardest questions. Many economists have long done it by favoring free market solutions—global governance without the need for government action.

The global financial and economic crisis of 2008–2009—as well as many less serious previous crises—underline the risks, problems, and enormous costs of a global economy without global government—that is, without adequate international institutions, democratic decision making, and powers to enforce compliance. Although countries, especially the major powers, may not yet be ready to accept the need for some elements of global government and the limitations this would impose on their sovereignty, the logic of interdependence and recent developments would seem to place global governance more squarely on the international agenda. Indeed, some of us anticipate that over future decades, a gradual advance of intergovernmental agreements and powers will take place along the lines that most countries have seen nationally over the last century and as Europe and some other areas have seen develop regionally since World War II. Elements of global government will emerge.

Meanwhile, there are still things to do in a world of global governance without global government—and Weiss and Thakur provide a stimulating analysis of what is needed in key areas. They avoid the complacency of accepting the status quo by taking the reader through the actions that are possible and needed to fill the gaps in each of the main areas of the present system. All this is in line with the goals of UNIHP, which expressly committed itself to writing a future-oriented history that draws conclusions about the ways the UN system needs to be strengthened.

The need for improvements in global governance remains urgent. Over the decade of our work, countries, regions, and often the whole world have experienced major crises, setbacks, and difficulties that have shown only too clearly the weaknesses of the international system as it functions at present. These inadequacies have produced war and conflict, weapons of mass destruction, natural and human disasters, and international economic and financial instabilities. All of these have had consequences that have spread far beyond national borders and have had disastrous effects on global instability and human progress. Our project has identified a number of global problems—climate change, growing economic inequality, economic and financial instability, and the risks of nuclear destruction, among other problems—which can only be tackled with stronger agreement and global action by both the major powers and many smaller ones if the world is to survive through the twenty-first century. Global governance with stronger powers, more resources, and mechanisms to ensure compliance will be essential for the longer run, if not in the next few years.

While Weiss and Thakur accept the limits of global governance without global government, they analyze what has been achieved and how things might be improved by strengthening action in five key areas, each at present characterized by an important international gap: in knowledge, in norms, in policy, in institutions, and in compliance. Their core argument is that each of these gaps needs to be filled in relation to the key problems the international system confronts today. By doing so, global governance can be impressively strengthened, even without the stronger powers that global government might bring. For tough-minded realists, this provides a practical agenda for action in the years ahead. For those longing for more robust advances in global governance—including advances toward global government—another volume is still to be written with a subtitle of *Next Steps on the Journey.*

We are persuaded that the UN system needs to be greatly strengthened to meet the challenges of the years ahead. Global governance provides an agenda for all who wish to move forward as well as a wide-ranging overview of the steps already taken and the mechanisms and organization already in place. As former UN Secretary-General Kofi Annan wrote in the foreword to *Ahead of the Curve? UN Ideas and Global Challenges:* "With the publication of this first volume in the United Nations Intellectual History Project, a significant lacuna in twentieth-century scholarship and international relations begins to be filled."[4] With the present volume, another gap in that record is now closed. We are confident that other analysts will now be in a position to use this critical building block to add to the history of UN contributions to global governance.

We hope that readers will enjoy this account, at once a journey through time and an analysis of the strengths and weaknesses of today's attempts to tackle many of the priority issues on the global agenda. As always, we welcome comments from our readers.

LOUIS EMMERIJ
RICHARD JOLLY
THOMAS G. WEISS
New York
December 2008

FOREWORD

Global governance is generally defined as an instance of govern*ance* in the absence of govern*ment*. There is no government at the global level: the UN General Assembly is not a world parliament, and Ban Ki-moon is not the world's president. But there is governance—of sorts. Moreover, as Thomas G. Weiss and Ramesh Thakur indicate, today's desire to improve the functioning of global governance has little to do with wanting to create a world government—though right-wing bloggers and some politicians still try to mobilize their base by fulminating that it does.

Governance is not the same as politics, although they are closely related. Fundamentally, politics is about competition in the pursuit of particular interests, whereas governance is about producing public goods. This is as true internationally as domestically, although the domain of governance apart from politics at the international level is fragile, much thinner, and more fragmented.

Governance, at whatever level of social organization it occurs, refers to the workings of the system of authoritative rules, norms, institutions, and practices by means of which any collectivity manages its common affairs.

The instruments of global governance take the form of treaties, customary international law, formal organizations such as the UN or the World Trade Organization (WTO), embedded norms such as those legitimizing certain uses of force but not others, and habituated practices such as pretending that embassies exist in the home country but not the host country and therefore are not subject to local jurisdiction.

The prevailing state of affairs in global governance at any given time is shaped by an ever-present tension between the need to internationalize rules and the desire to assert and retain national control. The balance between internationalization and state sovereignty may swing back and forth—for large-scale examples, compare the pre–World War I and post–World II eras with the interwar period. Today, powerful forces are pushing in both directions simultaneously, and we simply do not know yet whether reconciliation between the two is possible or how to achieve it.

The modern Westphalian system of global governance—if it can be called "global" at all—had two core features. First, it was a state-centric system. The only *public interest* that had any standing reflected accommodations among different national interests as defined by individual states. States were the sole *decision makers* in this system of governance. States were also the *subjects* of the decisions they made: the rules applied to them and only through them to other actors, such as individuals, companies, or armed factions. And states were the *enforcers* of the rules they made—when they felt like (and were capable of) enforcing them.

Second, in terms of its spatial configuration, this traditional world saw itself as comprising territorially distinct and separate economic and political units that were engaged in *external* transactions. The role of whatever governance arrangements states created was to reduce frictions resulting from those external transactions, largely by helping to manage them at the point of entry or exit between the units.

This template was enshrined in the post–World War II institutions of global governance. In the area of peace and security, for example, the UN Charter rested on the assumption that threats to stability would come from acts of *external* aggression by *states*. It included provisions for helping the victim by mobilizing other states—not an international standing force—to repel the aggression. And so its Article 2.7 stipulated that "Nothing contained in the present Charter shall authorize the United Nations to intervene in matters which are essentially within the domestic jurisdiction of any state."

The same was true in the economic realm. The General Agreement on Tariffs and Trade, the WTO's predecessor, was confined largely to addressing such point-of-entry barriers as tariffs and quotas. The International Monetary Fund's main task was to manage currency exchange rate policies.

And although the UN Charter was drafted in the name of "we the peoples," its sole recognition of actors other than states and intergovernmental organizations was in its provision that the Economic and Social Council could "make suitable arrangements for consultation" with international nongovernmental organizations (NGOs) that were relevant to its work and with national NGOs after consulting their home country governments (Article 71).

Driven largely by the forces of the globalization, the modern system of global governance began to transform slowly but in some respects significantly over the course of the past few decades—not by replacing states but by having its boundaries stretched to encompass novel issues and actors. The result is a postmodern and nonterritorial overlay on the modern system of global governance.

A simple scan of the major issues and actors that now have a broadly legitimate place in global governance indicates how far the modern system has been stretched into "internal" and "universal" directions simultaneously. UN conferences since the 1970s have addressed challenges of the environment, population, human rights, women, children, social development, human settlements, food security, racism, and HIV/AIDS, among others. Until recently, when environmental issues were addressed they tended to be of the "upstream/downstream" externalities variety, whereas climate change, today's most pressing environmental problem, is indivisible and universal.

Proliferating human rights instruments address the most intimate of "internal" political relations, that between a state and its citizens. In the legal realm, there are now more than fifty international courts, tribunals, and quasi-judicial bodies, culminating in the International Criminal Court.

Even the prevalent form of warfare has changed. In the 1990s, over one-third of the world's countries were directly affected by serious intrasocietal warfare, while *inter*state wars have continued to decline. International attention (but less frequently action) has been pulled into the domestic realm as a result.

International organizations remain anchored in the state system, but their activities reflect the expansion of issues on the global governance agenda. Their role in actual enforcement remains tightly constrained by states. But they have become primary vehicles for setting global agendas and framing global issues, creating and diffusing norms, and collective legitimization. International organizations also carry on extensive operational activities in the humanitarian and development fields and in peacekeeping.

Moreover, an array of actors for which territoriality and national interests are not the primary organizing principles has come to occupy positions of prominence in global governance. Civil society actors have moved well beyond advocacy and philanthropic activities. For example, they have become indispensable executing agencies for national and international development assistance and humanitarian programs. They also participate directly in such "collaborative governance" innovations as the Kimberley Process to combat trade in conflict diamonds and the Extractive Industries Transparency Initiative.

The universe of transnational corporations now includes roughly 77,000 firms, and some 800,000 subsidiaries and millions of suppliers and distributors are connected through global value chains. They have been a major force for the privatization and liberalization of markets. In a process that is less visible to the casual observer, they have also assumed a partial international legal personality, a privilege that had been limited historically to states and intergovernmental organizations. For example, under the more than 2,500 bilateral investment treaties in effect, these firms can take host states to binding international arbitration, not only for expropriation without adequate and prompt compensation but also for changes in domestic regulations that adversely affect the investment. The only role of national courts in this process is to enforce the rulings of private international arbitration panels.

Along with expanded rights for transnational corporations have come demands that they accept greater accountability. As a result, a corporate social responsibility movement has emerged, the instruments of which are individual company or industry codes of conduct, multistakeholder initiatives, certification schemes, and the like, which virtually no major transnational corporation can avoid in some measure, if for no other reason than to manage social risks to its brand or business operations. At the same time, a growing number of such companies are finding commercial opportunities in going "green" or in "bottom of the pyramid" business strategies. These new risk and opportunity factors, in turn, can alter the self-interest calculation of companies in relation to public policy issues at the national and international levels, as illustrated by business coalitions that favor climate change policies, HIV/AIDS prevention and treatment, the Millennium Development Goals, and similar social challenges.

In sum, a postmodern overlay on the modern territorial system of global governance has emerged. It is characterized by an extensive transnationalization of issues, transaction flows, and actors that cuts across familiar national jurisdictions, blurs the boundaries between external and internal spaces, and intermingles the public, private, and civic spheres in novel ways.

At the same time, there is a widespread and growing sense that global governance is not working well or even poses a threat. Here are but a few signs.

Elements of "uncivil" society have also gone transnational, most notably criminal networks and, of course, terrorist networks. Cooperation is necessary to deal with the challenges they pose, but it is a form of cooperation that tends to trigger the consolidation or strengthening of state authority in order to protect against outside intrusion.

In a wide range of areas from nuclear nonproliferation to reform of the UN Security Council, everyone acknowledges that the current arrangements are deeply flawed. However, each state's desire for relative gains prevents the collectivity from changing them. We have not yet learned how to conduct global governance effectively in accordance with accountability to broader publics. In the European Union context, this is called the "democratic deficit."

Because of the asymmetries and inequalities that are associated with globalization, particularistic identity politics is on the rise, organized around religion, ethnicity, or economic grievances.

At the normative level, liberal internationalism, of which the United States has been a leading champion, traditionally has served as an animating vision for global governance. But this source of normative capital was seriously eroded by the policies of the George W. Bush administration. Even though American policy will change for the better, the world has not stood still in the interval. Finally, today's emerging global powers do not share this aspirational vision of liberal internationalism in the first place. In economic relations, their state-owned enterprises and sovereign wealth funds are reminiscent of mercantilism, while in the military-political realm their strategies reflect little more than balance-of-power pursuits. In the terrain of global governance, postmodernism collides with a resurgence of nineteenth-century institutional practices.

Thus, we find ourselves at a critical juncture today. Global governance failures, geopolitical changes, and identity politics are pulling global governance back toward more of a statist model. At the same time, human needs as well as the scope of economic activity and the interests of economic actors strive for a more effective organization of transnational spaces. .

Never has a serious book on the United Nations and global governance been more timely. Thomas G. Weiss and Ramesh Thakur take an admirably comprehensive approach, identifying gaps with respect to the role of the United Nations in managing knowledge, developing norms, formulating recommendations, and institutionalizing ideas. Theirs is an empirical assessment, not a normative argument, and it is intended to improve the functioning of this global governance mechanism. Taken seriously, it will do so.

JOHN GERARD RUGGIE
Harvard University
December 2008

ACKNOWLEDGMENTS

Both of us normally write quickly, but we have been struggling with this book for over half a decade. Because "global governance" means so many things to so many analysts, part of our battle was finding a way to make this rather amorphous subject manageable and meaningful. The concept, moreover, covers many topics that are the subject of a book in their own right in United Nations Intellectual History Project, so we had to find a way to distinguish this book from others in the series. After numerous outlines and five complete redrafts, we hope that we have finally found a way to make an original contribution to the study of global governance and to this book series published by Indiana University Press.

In that process, we have accumulated considerable debts of gratitude. On the institutional side, the Centre for International Governance Innovation (CIGI) at the University of Waterloo provided substantial funding and research assistance for this book. CIGI thus joins the other UNIHP donors whose understanding and generosity have made this and other volumes possible: the governments of the Netherlands, the United Kingdom, Sweden, Canada, Norway, Switzerland, and Finland and the Republic and Canton of Geneva; the Ford, Rockefeller, and MacArthur foundations; the Carnegie Corporation of New York; and the UN Foundation.

Since 1999, the UNIHP secretariat has benefited from the congenial surroundings of the Ralph Bunche Institute for International Studies at The City University of New York's Graduate Center. The past and previous presidents, Frances Degen Horowitz and William P. Kelly, have enthusiastically supported these efforts, and on the administrative side, Nancy Okada has helped to ensure the smooth running of a very complicated financial and administrative project with numerous moving parts.

In addition to acknowledging institutional assistance with thanks, we are also grateful to several individuals who provided invaluable help and feedback over the course of writing this volume. First, we should thank two UNIHP directors, Louis Emmerij and Richard Jolly, who kept faith with the authors. Second, we wish to acknowledge Craig Murphy, who along with Louis and Richard valiantly struggled with an earlier, inchoate draft and came back to us with much-needed critical comments. The book is a far better product because of their unstinting and caring professionalism. Third, we would like to express our warm thanks to an expanding corps of research assistants over several years who responded to requests for assistance with good humor and efficiency: Breanne Carter, Anne-Marie Sanchez, and Brodie Ross at CIGI in Waterloo, Ontario; and at the Ralph Bunche Institute in New York, Nomvuyo Nolutshungu, who helped with citations, but most especially to Annelies Kamran, who worked long and hard at the outset to help us accumulate enough information to formulate a framework of analysis that is now reflected in these pages. Fourth, Danielle Zach Kalbacher once again applied her remarkable editorial skills at the finishing stages, and this book simply would not have been as readable or accurate without her careful attention to the final submission.

Finally, we also are grateful that John Ruggie agreed to grace these pages with his foreword. We both have known John for a quarter of a century; and all students of international relations are indebted to his scholarship, as is the United Nations Intellectual History Project for his having served on its International Advisory Board.

We sincerely hope that readers will learn as much from reading this book as we have from writing it. As always, we welcome comments. Obviously, any remaining errors and shortcomings are our responsibility.

THOMAS G. WEISS AND RAMESH THAKUR
New York and Waterloo
December 2008

ABBREVIATIONS

AIDS	acquired immune deficiency syndrome
ARV	antiretroviral
BWC	Biological Weapons Convention
C	Celsius
CD	Conference on Disarmament
CFC	chlorofluorocarbon
CHR	Commission on Human Rights
CIA	Central Intelligence Agency (U.S.)
CITES	Convention on International Trade in Endangered Species
CO_2	carbon dioxide
COP	Conference of the Parties to the Climate Change Convention
CSD	Commission on Sustainable Development
CTBT	Comprehensive Test Ban Treaty
CTC	Counter-Terrorism Committee
CTED	Counter-Terrorism Committee Executive Directorate
CTITF	Counter-Terrorism Implementation Task Force
CWC	Chemical Weapons Convention
DPKO	Department of Peacekeeping Operations
DRC	Democratic Republic of the Congo
ECA	Economic Commission for Africa
ECLA	Economic Commission for Latin America
ECOSOC	Economic and Social Council
ECOWAS	Economic Community of West African States
ECPS	Executive Committee on Peace and Security
EPTA	Expanded Programme for Technical Assistance
EU	European Union
G-7	Group of 7

G-8	Group of 8
G-20	Group of 20
G-77	Group of 77
GATT	General Agreement on Tariffs and Trade
GDP	gross domestic product
GHG	greenhouse gas
GNP	gross national product
HDR	Human Development Report
HIV	human immunodeficiency virus
HRC	Human Rights Council
IAEA	International Atomic Energy Agency
ICC	International Criminal Court
ICISS	International Commission on Intervention and State Sovereignty
ICJ	International Court of Justice
ICRC	International Committee of the Red Cross
ICSU	International Council for Science
IDA	International Development Association
IDP	internally displaced person
IFF	International Finance Facility
IGO	intergovernmental organization
ILO	International Labour Organization
IMF	International Monetary Fund
IOS	International Organization for Standardization
IPCC	Intergovernmental Panel on Climate Change
ITO	International Trade Organization
ITU	International Telecommunication Union
IWC	International Whaling Commission
MCA	Millennium Challenge Account
MDG	Millennium Development Goal
NAM	Non-Aligned Movement
NATO	North Atlantic Treaty Organization
NFWZ	nuclear-weapon-free zone

NGO	nongovernmental organization
NIEO	New International Economic Order
NPT	Nuclear Nonproliferation Treaty
NWS	nuclear weapons states
OCHA	Office for the Coordination of Humanitarian Affairs
ODA	official development assistance
OHCHR	Office of the High Commissioner for Human Rights
OPCW	Organization for the Prohibition of Chemical Weapons
OPEC	Organization of the Petroleum Exporting Countries
P-5	permanent five members of the Security Council
ppb	parts per billion
ppm	parts per million
PSI	Proliferation Security Initiative
R2P	responsibility to protect
SARS	Severe Acute Respiratory Syndrome
SALT	Strategic Arms Limitations Talks
START	Strategic Arms Reduction Treaty
UNAIDS	Joint UN Programme on HIV/AIDS
UNCED	UN Conference on Environment and Development
UNCTAD	UN Conference on Trade and Development
UNDP	UN Development Programme
UNEP	UN Environment Programme
UNESCO	UN Educational, Scientific and Cultural Organization
UNFCCC	UN Framework Convention on Climate Change
UNHCR	UN High Commissioner for Refugees
UNICEF	UN Children's Fund
UNIHP	UN Intellectual History Project
UNITA	National Union for the Total Independence of Angola
UNMOVIC	UN Monitoring, Verification and Inspection Commission
UNODC	UN Office on Drugs and Crime
UNRISD	UN Research Institute on Social Development
UNSCOM	UN Special Commission

UPU	Universal Postal Union
WHO	World Health Organization
WIDER	World Institute for Development Economics Research
WIPO	World Intellectual Property Organization
WMD	weapon of mass destruction
WMO	World Meteorological Organization
WSSD	World Summit on Sustainable Development
WTO	World Trade Organization

GLOBAL GOVERNANCE AND THE UN

INTRODUCTION

The *Problématique* of Global Governance

- • Global Governance: A Sketch
- • Five Gaps in Global Governance
- • The Tsunami and Global Governance
- • The Book

There is no government for the world. Yet on any given day, mail is delivered across borders; people travel from one country to another via a variety of transport modes; goods and services are freighted across land, air, sea, and cyberspace; and a whole range of other cross-border activities takes place in reasonable expectation of safety and security for the people, groups, firms, and governments involved. Disruptions and threats are rare—indeed, in many instances less frequent in the international domain than in many sovereign countries that should have effective and functioning governments. That is to say, international transactions are typically characterized by order, stability, and predictability. This immediately raises a puzzle: How is the world governed even in the absence of a world government to produce norms, codes of conduct, and regulatory, surveillance, and compliance instruments? How are values allocated quasi-authoritatively for the world, and accepted as such, without a government to rule the world? The answer, we argue in this book, lies in global governance.

That said, it is also the case that "normal" periods of calm, stability, order, and predictability are interspersed with periodic bouts of market volatility, disorder, and crisis. At the time we write this, the world is suffering the worst financial crisis since the Great Depression that began in 1929 and continued into the 1930s. In recent times, Latin America suffered a debt crisis in 1982 and parts of Latin America, in particular Argentina, suffered financial turmoil again in the early years of the twenty-first century. The United States experienced a savings and loan crisis in 1980 and again in the early 1990s as well as a crisis in long-term capital management in 1998. Asia underwent a major financial crisis in 1997–1998. Now the spectacular subprime housing loans and banking and financial crisis that began in the United States in September–October 2008 is likely to continue for several years. Where the Asian financial crisis proved the perils of crony capitalism, the 2008 crisis on Wall Street shows the pitfalls of unbridled capitalism. Governments may be fallible, but markets too are imperfect. Both the Asian crisis of a decade ago and the U.S. market collapse in 2008 demonstrate the need for efficient, effective, and transparent regulatory and surveillance instruments and institutions. The state has an essential role to play. Those countries where the state has not abandoned the market to its own supposedly self-regulating devices are seemingly better placed to weather the current crisis of confidence in capitalism.

In other words, these are crises of governance in terms of the proper role of governments and market institutions as well as the appropriate balance in the relationship between them. These are also crises of domestic governance. The causes of the crises lie in imperfect domestic governance, and the solutions entail responses from both domestic governments and the market. The role of global governance institutions is restricted to containing the contagion. This insight will be a recurring refrain in our story: global governance can play a facilitative and constraining role, but it rarely plays a determinant and predominant role. The authority and capacity for the latter is vested almost exclusively in domestic public authorities.

The expectations are greater for global governance on the peace and security side of the ledger, yet here too they may be false or exaggerated. As financial crises periodically occur, armed conflict occasionally breaks out even in the midst of general peace and order. Just in the last decade, we have witnessed large-scale violence and conflict in the Balkans, Rwanda, the Democratic Republic of the Congo (DRC), the Horn of Africa, Iraq, Afghanistan, and Georgia.

Not all emergencies and crises are human-made. The worldwide response to the 2004 Indian Ocean tsunami—which killed 280,000 people —provides us with global governance in microcosm, an illustration of how an enormous transborder problem is addressed in a decentralized world. While it is trite to remark that there is no world government to take charge of international responses, it is less commonly understood why such remarkable assistance was effectively provided to tsunami victims without any central authority.

On 26 December 2004, an earthquake that registered a magnitude of 9.0 on the Richter scale occurred off the west coast of the Indonesian island of Sumatra. The earthquake and the resulting tsunami spread mind-boggling devastation across the Indian Ocean, affecting twelve countries, some as far away as the Horn of Africa. Public opinion was transfixed by the image of waves swallowing islands and cities whole, creating scenes of apocalyptic destruction. The most frequently used adjectives to describe the tragedy were "biblical" and "nuclear."

The globalizing effect of innovations in transportation and communications were in evidence. Thousands of tourists from the West and from around the region were vacationing with video cameras in tow. Their homemade footage began to appear on international television news programs and on the Internet, allowing the scope of the disaster to become clear. The revolution in information technology made global communications instantaneous. It also made it possible to mobilize humanitarian assistance for rescue, relief, assistance, and reconstruction in real time. In the first week after the disaster, experts estimated that as many people would die of disease as were killed by the waves themselves. In fact, help was so effective that the number was close to zero.

Why was the response to one of the worst natural disasters in recent memory as impressive as it was? Is it not puzzling that without a central authority thousands of lives were saved and reconstruction was started? Yes and no. The United Nations can physically deploy humanitarian assistance to people affected by such emergencies anywhere in the world within twenty-four hours, barring any political or bureaucratic hurdles. In addition, it can serve as a magnet that pulls together a host of other private and public actors. The theory and the practice of global governance, of trying to provide international government-like services in the absence of a world government, is the story of this book.

This introduction sketches the details of the concept before presenting our central analytical perspective, that of gaps in global governance. We then revisit the tsunami before presenting an overview of the rest of the book.

Global Governance: A Sketch

As the number of international actors and the frequency and intensity of their interactions have grown, the need for institutionalized cooperation among them has increased. States are likely to remain the primary actors in world affairs for the foreseeable future, and state sovereignty is the bedrock principle on which their relations are based and organized. At the same time, international organizations help states to cooperate in the pursuit of shared goals and manage competition and rivalry in order to avoid conflict and violence. In spite of this reality, seemingly countless threats face the human species—for example, climate change, weapons of mass destruction (WMDs), genocide, and financial instabilities. The *problématique* of global governance in our times may be simply stated: The evolution of intergovernmental institutions to facilitate robust international responses lags well behind the emergence of collective problems with transborder, especially global, dimensions.

States react, cope, and eventually agree under duress to construct institutions in the face of such challenges. Perhaps it has always been the case that too few institutions have developed too late. But in the twenty-first century, the urgent nature of many collective problems suggests that we must build more and soon. We are more than skeptical that the market will graciously provide the kinds of global institutions that the planet so desperately needs to ensure survival with dignity.

If we simplify the business of the United Nations into two main arenas, security and economic affairs—the division of "high" and "low" politics—we can be more specific about the nature of our undertaking. The *problématique* of global security governance consists of the disconnect between the distribution of authority within existing intergovernmental institutions and the distribution of military power internationally. Interestingly enough, the term "international community" is increasingly used by commentators of all stripes to refer to every actor involved in UN efforts, whereas formerly it was used only for the members of the United Nations.[1] In any event, only the most rudimentary collective capacity exists to stem the flow of small arms, conduct WMD inspections, protect populations threatened by genocide, or deploy peacekeeping missions. In UN peace operations, for example, in addition to all the local actors, at least six different sets of outside actors exist with overlapping spheres of activity: those who authorize peace operations in the Security Council, those who contribute military personnel, those who provide funds, those who possess the capabilities needed to enforce security activities, UN humanitarian agencies, and nongovernmental actors in the field. Coordinating the efforts of a multitude of diverse actors—from the local to the global, governmental, intergovernmental, and nongovernmental—is a real challenge.

Economic governance is, for Rorden Wilkinson, "the most advanced and comprehensive dimension of emerging global governance."[2] Yet, as in the security sector, there is a "growing gap between the distribution of authority within existing international institutions and the international distribution of economic power."[3]

There are two verities with respect to the world's financial system. First, while not so long ago finance essentially flowed from corporations based in states with some transnational links, today it is essentially global with some local characteristics. Second, finance is not self-governing. Instead, "stability in financial markets requires the judicious exercise of public authority."[4] Interesting experiments (e.g., the European Central Bank) cannot disguise the reality that (as is the case for security) nothing approaches a global authority in the economic arena, even though the provision of such a global public good could have saved billions in the Asian financial crisis of 1997–1998 or the worldwide recession that was triggered by the collapse of housing and credit markets in 2007–2008.

Moreover, maximizing efficiency cannot be the only goal of international financial and economic policy. Questions of legitimacy and distributive justice are as important as efficacy, currency convertibility, or capital mobility. Practical answers are in short supply because we are still at the stage of summit communiqués, blue-ribbon commissions,[5] and incremental adaptations within existing international intergovernmental financial institutions.[6] This reality is unlikely to change despite the steady stream of reports with substantial proposals that began flowing on the occasion of the UN's sixtieth anniversary.[7] Something gets accomplished (although observers discuss whether the results are palliative or actually ameliorative), and intergovernmental organizations (IGOs) matter in such activities, as do a host of for-profit and not-for-profit institutions. Nonetheless, nothing remotely resembles an overarching authority for global financial governance to help facilitate stability or reduce the social costs of contemporary economic developments and downturns.

At the same time, we repeat our puzzle. Why are there nonetheless elements of predictability, stability, and order despite the absence of a world government? This book examines not only the theory of global governance but the practice and (more especially) the UN's intellectual and operational contributions.

It would be useful to begin with some definitions. "Governance" is the sum of laws, norms, policies, and institutions that define, constitute, and mediate relations among citizens, society, market, and the state—the wielders and objects of the exercise of public power.

"Good governance" incorporates peoples' participation and empowerment with respect to public policies, choices, and offices; the rule of law and an independent judiciary to which the executive and legislative branches of government are subject, as are citizens and other actors and entities; and standards of probity and incorruptibility, transparency, accountability, and responsibility. It also includes the institutions in which these principles and values find ongoing expression. Good governance thus can be considered a normative concept—concerned with standards that most would agree are laudable.

"Global governance"—which can be good, bad, or indifferent—refers to existing collective arrangements to solve problems.[8] Adapting our definition of governance, "global governance" is the sum of laws, norms, policies, and institutions that define, constitute, and mediate relations among citizens, society, markets, and the state in the international arena—the wielders and objects of international public power. Even in the absence of an overarching central authority, existing collective arrangements bring more predictability, stability, and order to transboundary problems than we might expect.

Confusion enters because traditionally governance has been associated with "governing," or with political authority, institutions, and (ultimately) control. Governance in this sense denotes formal political institutions that aim to coordinate and control interdependent social relations and possess the capacity to enforce decisions. In recent years, however, authors such as James Rosenau have used "governance" to denote the regulation of interdependent relations in the absence of overarching political authority, such as in the international system.[9] These may be visible but quite informal (e.g., practices or guidelines) or temporary units (e.g., coalitions). But they may also be far more formal, taking the shape of rules (laws, norms, codes of behavior) as well as constituted institutions and practices designed to manage collective affairs by a variety of actors (state authorities, intergovernmental organizations, civil society organizations, and private sector entities). Through such mechanisms and arrangements, collective interests are articulated, rights and obligations are established, and differences are mediated.

Within the context of the United Nations Intellectual History Project (UNIHP) and in this volume, the focus is on the rise of policymaking arrangements and the intellectual and analytical frameworks behind them at the international and global levels. Both formal and informal mechanisms are key to our understanding of the collective groping toward attenuating global problems.

One of the main conclusions from the project as a whole is a central thread in this volume: a host of actors come together in international attempts to address transboundary problems, namely the three United Nations. Since Inis Claude wrote his textbook over half a century ago, students of international relations have used his lens of two UNs.[10] The first consists of the arena where the UN's 192 member states discuss issues and make recommendations and decisions. The second consists of UN secretariats, or the individuals who compose the international civil service. While analysts do not always make clear which of these two United Nations succeeds or fails, they are aware of the distinctions.

In some ways, our analysis of global governance can be viewed most generally as an attempt to combine the traditional two UNs and to harness nonstate actors—both civil society and market institutions, or what UNIHP has identified as the Third UN.[11] Ideas percolate in UN corridors, regulations are changed in intergovernmental deliberations, and norms are discussed in global forums. In the delivery of development assistance or the monitoring of human rights, global civil society exerts itself frequently and effectively.[12] In the push to create new UN institutions or reform existing ones, nongovernmental organizations (NGOs) are often forces for change.[13]

And so our treatment of the United Nations through the lens of global governance encompasses the numerous actors who are relevant to contemporary global problem-solving. This is one of the strengths of contemporary global governance (as well as one of its weaknesses).

Five Gaps in Global Governance

"The root cause of the business and human rights predicament today lies in the governance gaps created by globalization—between the scope and impact of economic forces and actors, and the capacity of societies to manage their adverse consequences," writes our colleague John Ruggie. "These governance gaps provide the permissive environment for wrongful acts by companies of all kinds without adequate sanctioning or reparation. How to narrow and ultimately bridge the gaps in relation to human rights is our fundamental challenge."[14]

We agree but extend the argument in this book to what we call the five gaps—or what Thomas Kuhn calls the "pockets of apparent disorder"[15]—

that exist between the nature of many current global problems and the feeble nature of the solutions that are currently available. Within each chapter, we emphasize the UN's special intellectual role. It is worth spelling out our conceptualizations of these gaps, as they provide the overall intellectual framework for chapters 2–10.

Knowledge Gaps

The first gap is the knowledge gap. Often little or no consensus exists about the nature, causes, gravity, and magnitude of a problem, either about empirical information or theoretical explanations. And there is often disagreement over the best remedies and solutions to these problems. Two good examples are global warming and nuclear weapons, neither of which was known when the UN Charter was signed. What is the best "mix-and-match" strategy for combating the threat of global warming? Given that the severity and causes of climate change still remain in political if not scientific dispute, which strategy will minimize disruption while also minimizing future risks and damage? Similarly, what is the best strategy for preventing the proliferation of nuclear weapons while also trying to encourage the elimination of existing stockpiles and avoiding their use in the meantime? Another example of a knowledge gap is illustrated in the debate over trade versus aid for developing countries.

Disputed knowledge has direct relevance to international public policy. This is apparent in the paradigm clashes of top-down versus bottom-up approaches, development assistance versus self-sufficiency, and debt-relief versus accountability. Ideological positions exist on each of these issues. However, can we get beyond ideology and let information, data, experience, and science guide us? Civil society institutions—such as universities, think tanks, research institutes, and NGOs—now more than ever are likely to play a crucial role in filling knowledge gaps. The United Nations, however, often provides the stage on which new knowledge can be placed in the limelight, improved, and widely disseminated. Does this division of labor work? If so, where?

The United Nations has played a role in filling two knowledge gaps that are important for contemporary notions of global governance. First, for many global issues, well-defined ideological stances exist and empirical data may or may not be powerful enough to challenge positions that often have been formed and hardened long before information has been gathered and experiences have been registered. An example of such an issue is the role of the state in development. How useful are additional empirical data and theoretical explanations in the face of dominant world views or entrenched ideologies? Can new information and experiences guide policymakers, or are they largely irrelevant?

Second, issues such as population in the 1970s or global warming in the 1990s appear on the agenda because of a previously unknown or underestimated threat about which we do not have sufficient information to make informed decisions (or we have conflicting information). This constitutes a different type of knowledge gap for decision makers but presumably one for which new information can more easily have an impact than it does in the face of rigid ideologies.

At least partially filling the knowledge gap is essential for dealing with the other gaps in global governance—normative, policy, institutional, and compliance. If we can recognize that there is a problem and agree on its approximate dimensions, then we can take steps to solve it. While in a few cases the UN's role has generated new knowledge, more often it has provided an arena where existing information can be collated and collected, a host of interpretations can be vetted, and differing interpretations of competing data can be debated. Depending on the strength of political coalitions and entrenched ideologies, there may be more or less room for an increase in knowledge to make a difference in terms of policy recommendations.

In discussing knowledge gaps, it is important to differentiate between theoretical and factual information. In the past, states and the UN played a relatively more important role both in generating data and in creating and disseminating theoretical explanations than did civil society. States and the UN continue to play these roles, but civil society actors currently are playing a larger role than before in filling knowledge gaps.

Normative Gaps

The second gap is the normative gap. In the decades since 1945, the norms of environmental protection and nuclear abstinence have become firmly established. How were the normative gaps filled? Reaching consensus about universally acceptable norms is enormously difficult. For example, the emerging norm of human rights can be (and has been) culturally deconstructed to cast doubts upon the universality of even long-agreed principles. Here again, civil society is now more likely than ever to be the source of ideas that fill in normative gaps. At the same time, the

United Nations is an essential arena in which states codify norms in the forms of resolutions and declarations (soft law) and conventions and treaties (hard law). The United Nations offers the most efficient forum for processing norms, or standards of behavior, into laws, or rules of behavior. Again, the notion of global governance helps us see how fledgling steps can be taken that foster predictability, stability, and order within the international system despite the absence of overarching global authority.

A norm can be defined statistically to mean the pattern of behavior that is most common or usual—the "normal curve," a widely prevalent pattern of behavior. Alternatively, it can be defined ethically to mean a pattern of behavior that should be followed in accordance with a given value system—the moral code of a society, a generally accepted standard of proper behavior. In some instances, the two meanings may converge in practice. In most cases, they will complement each other. But in some cases, they may diverge.

Norms matter because people—ordinary citizens as well as politicians and officials—care about what others think of them. This is why approbation is often effective in regulating social behavior (as is its corollary, shaming).[16] It is also why the United Nations and its Secretaries-General have often relied upon the bully pulpit. Like Josef Stalin's dismissal of the papacy—"How many divisions does the pope have?"—the power of the UN's ideas and its moral voice is often underestimated, as is the role of the Secretary-General.[17]

We still do not have adequate conceptual tools and enough empirical research for a theory of how international norms emerge, diffuse globally, consolidate to the point of being internalized by members of international society, and embed themselves in international institutions. Nor is there agreement on who can legitimately claim to articulate or pinpoint "global" norms. By definition, collective norms are shared standards of behavior. How many actors of a group must share a norm before we can call it a group norm? How many countries must share a norm before it is a global norm? How important is the power of dissenting states to the emergence of a widely shared norm?

Martha Finnemore and Kathryn Sikkink postulate a three-stage life cycle of norms: a new norm emerges and a norm entrepreneur advocates it; enough actors agree on an emerging norm to create a tipping point, or norm cascade; and actors internalize the new norm so that it becomes taken for granted and norm-conforming behavior becomes routine, requiring no further justification.[18] The United Nations provides an organizational platform for advocacy in the first stage as well as the preferred forum for cascade in the second and for seeking affirmation, reaffirmation, and hopefully compliance in the third and final stage.

In the Ottawa Treaty that banned landmines, for example, norm generation by western middle powers was underpinned by norm advocacy from NGOs. It was also reinforced by norm-promoting standard-setting by the UN Secretary-General when he endorsed the Ottawa process and the convention that resulted from it.[19]

In the third and final stage, once a norm is internalized by most members of international society, it becomes the prevailing standard against which state behavior is measured and against which new norms must arise and struggle for support. Until that happens, however, governments and civil society can appeal to prevailing international norms within the context of domestic policy debates in order to buttress their normative preferences. In fact, many international norms begin as domestic norms and are internationalized through the deliberate actions of norm entrepreneurs. Supporting women's rights is a good example of a domestic norm that became an international norm. The UN's role in promulgating these rights is an example of its function as a norm entrepreneur.

A relatively recent effort at UN norm-building was the Global Compact that grew from the 2000 Millennium Summit. Principle 10 ("Businesses should work against all forms of corruption, including extortion and bribery") attempts to answer the following questions: What is corruption? Why it is wrong? What can be done about it? The search for adequate answers to these questions suggest that filling the normative gap requires first filling the knowledge gap (at least partially) because norms reflect an agreement about the state of affairs as a basis for building a consensus about the most appropriate ways to frame an issue and future action.

As a universal organization, the United Nations is an exceptional forum for seeking normative consensus on how best to deal with global problems. Within the UN, universal norms and approaches are emerging for such activities as reducing acid rain, impeding money-laundering, halting pandemics, and anathematizing terrorism.

At the same time, the UN is a maddening forum because dissent by powerful states or mischief by large coalitions of less powerful states means either that no action occurs or that agreement is possible only on a lowest common denominator. For instance, the avoidance of meaningful action against a white-minority regime in South Africa until the 1990s reflected mainly refusals from the United States and the United Kingdom to agree to resolutions, which they backed by their vetoes in the Security Council. Widespread dissent even by a minority of countries can also slow progress in constructing norms. For instance, cultural differences can complicate the emergence of norms that strike most people in most parts of the world as "no-brainers." The unusual alliance of the Vatican and Islamic fundamentalists against women's reproductive rights is a clear illustration.

The proliferation of actors is vital to our story because the presence and work of civil society is essential in terms of identifying normative gaps and in proposing ways to reduce them. Examples of individuals and institutions come immediately to mind, including Raphael Lemkin's efforts to coin the term "genocide" and his role in the formulation and adoption of the UN Genocide Convention; Henri Dunant and the Red Cross movement in the field of international humanitarian law; Peter Benenson and Amnesty International's pursuit of human rights; and Jody Williams's work on the International Campaign to Ban Landmines.

The main source of ideas that can fill normative gaps is therefore quite likely to be civil society—the Third UN, whose members often affect change by working both with and through the other two United Nations.

Policy Gaps

The third gap is the policy gap. By "policy" we mean an interlinked set of governing principles and goals and the agreed programs of action to implement those principles and achieve those goals.[20] The Kyoto Protocol, the Nuclear Nonproliferation Treaty (NPT), and the Comprehensive Test Ban Treaty (CTBT) are examples of policies designed to combat the threats of global warming and nuclear weapons.

Analyzing policy gaps entails a dual challenge. First, who are the actors, the relevant policymakers? Is "international" policy made and implemented by international organizations or by national authorities meeting and interacting in international organizational forums? Second, there is a disconnect between the numbers and types of actors who play ever-expanding roles in civil, political, and economic affairs within and among nations and the concentration of decision-making authority in intergovernmental institutions. To what extent was the international paralysis over the crisis in Darfur the result of a policy gap rather than an illustration of weak political will among key member states? The source of ideas that can fill policy gaps is likely to be governments and intergovernmental organizations. When policy is made in the absence of institutions, it takes on an ad hoc character. Such an approach can lead to fragmented and incompatible policies that can become incoherent over time. However, is the UN well suited to determine the goals of policy or to guide the processes by which it is made?

A policy necessarily entails both agency and purposive action. Although state actors are policymakers, they usually distinguish public policy from foreign policy, implying a boundary-based separation between domestic and external activities. As two analysts note, "The policy-makers and the policy system therefore stand at these junction points and seek to mediate between the various milieux."[21] Although UN organs such as the Security Council or the General Assembly make policy, the world body cannot be said to make foreign policy, since neither the policymakers nor the policy system of the United Nations are engaged in boundary activities. By definition the whole world is their stage. At the same time, domestic policies often reflect carrots and sticks from international organizations, as when the World Bank or the International Monetary Fund (IMF) requires policy and legal changes as quid pro quo for adjustment loans or grants.

At the domestic level, the civil service may shape and influence policy but is not normally considered to be a policymaker; policymaking is the domain of the political heads of civil service departments, of cabinet ministers individually, and the legislature and political executive collectively. Thus, applying the analogy to the UN, the Secretariat and its officials cannot be described as policymakers. To the extent that in important respects Secretaries-General and such other senior officials as the UN's high commissioners for human rights and refugees can be called independent actors in their own right,[22] on occasion they might be classified as policymakers.

Thus, the policymakers at the UN are actually the world body's principal political organs, the Security Council and the General Assembly. But these are intergovernmental forums. That is, the people making the decisions in the form of adopting resolutions that set out new governing principles, articulate goals, and authorize programs of action to achieve those goals do so as delegates of national governments from the UN's member states. And they make these choices within the governing framework of their national foreign policies, under instructions from their home governments on all important policy issues. Or member states may make the policy choices directly themselves, for example at summit conferences. That being the case, just what might be meant by "United Nations" policy, policymaking, and policymakers?

Moreover, at the national level, policy can also be used to refer holistically to "the entire package of actions and attitudes"[23] (e.g., Indian or U.S. policy) as well as to specific policies toward this or that state in foreign affairs (e.g., Indian or U.S. policy on Israel-Palestinian relations, on the International Criminal Court [ICC], on nuclear proliferation, etc.) or toward this or that issue in domestic affairs (e.g., Indian or U.S. policy on the death penalty, on intellectual property, on immigration).

Policy may also be broken down sequentially into three separate phases: formulation, adoption, and implementation. And its object may be regulative; for example, to regulate services such as transport, telecommunications, public utilities. Its goal may be distributive; for example, to allocate public resources such as housing, employment, scholarships. It may be redistributive; for example, to redress social inequality through welfare programs.[24] The UN is not a federal system like the United States because neither the member states nor the constituent organizations of the so-called system recognize any higher authority. The UN is also not a supranational system like the European Union (EU), in which member states have ceded substantial prerogatives of sovereignty to the common entity. As distinct from state actors, the responsibility for implementation of most "UN policy" (as determined by the First UN) does not rest primarily with the United Nations Secretariat itself (the Second UN) but devolves down to member states. But even UN policy, in the forms of policy resolutions and actions adopted and authorized by the Security Council and the General Assembly or summit decisions made by member states directly, may exhibit regulative, distributive, and redistributive characteristics.

Based on these considerations, some General Assembly resolutions are the equivalent of policy declarations in that they articulate broad principles and goals and call for programs of action to achieve these goals. One of the clearest examples of such a resolution is General Assembly resolution 2922 of 1972 reaffirming apartheid as a crime against humanity.[25] The concept became a staple of UN resolutions over many years—for example, the 1970 Declaration on South Africa in resolution 34/93—until South

Africa was liberated and an elected black-majority government formed by the African National Congress with Nelson Mandela as the first president replaced the apartheid regime. Other examples would be General Assembly resolution 1514 (14 December 1960), the Declaration on the Granting of Independence to Colonial Countries and Peoples, and similar broad and sweeping declarations delegitimizing racism in general.

A second set of "UN policy" documents might be goals, plans of action, and desirable codes of conduct embedded in international treaties and conventions. Good examples include the Convention on the Prevention and Punishment of the Crime of Genocide, the Universal Declaration of Human Rights, the International Covenant on Civil and Political Rights and the International Covenant on Economic, Social and Cultural Rights, the Nuclear Nonproliferation Treaty, and the UN Convention on the Law of the Sea.

It is worth noting a major disconnect in global governance. While the source and scale of most of today's pressing challenges are global and any effective solution must also be global, the policy authority for tackling them remains vested in states.

Institutional Gaps

The fourth gap is the institutional gap. If policy is to escape the trap of being ad hoc, episodic, judgmental, and idiosyncratic, it must be housed within an institution that has resources and autonomy. This gap is especially striking within the UN system because neither powerful global institutions with overarching authority over members nor even flimsy ones with resources commensurate with the size of the transborder problems they are supposed to address exist. Even the most "powerful" institutions such as the Security Council, the World Bank, and the International Monetary Fund often lack appropriate resources or authority or both.[26] The source of ideas about filling institutional gaps is still more likely to be governments and IGOs than nonstate actors. However, the absence of international political will means that many of these organizations are only partially constructed or remain largely on drawing boards with only a small prototype to address gargantuan threats.

The definition of a norm isolates a single standard of behavior, whereas institutions emphasize a collection of rules and practices and do not necessarily capture the "oughtness" of the defined norm. When a problem is relatively well known and a range of policy measures has been agreed upon, what machinery will put such a policy into effect? For example, aid donors may believe that democratic states are less likely to go to war and that increasing their numbers would be valuable in terms of peace. Hence, a policy could be announced to hold elections as part of postconflict peacebuilding efforts in war-torn countries. However, this action would have little meaning unless institutions were also in place such as a local election commission and outside observers to register voters and to arrange for poll workers, polling stations, ballot printing, roll verification, and result tallying.

It would be useful at this juncture to introduce the notion of global public goods. Inge Kaul distinguishes between private and public goods in terms of their tradability in markets.[27] Transactions involving private goods are governed by the price mechanism; they can be bought and sold. Private goods are therefore excludable and rival in consumption. By contrast, public goods, like a street sign or air, are neither excludable nor rival. Rational behavior by private actors encourages free-riding on public goods precisely because they are non-excludable and non-rival: Why should someone pay for something that someone else provides and people cannot be prevented from enjoying its benefits for free? However, free access to public goods can lead to problems of overuse (the so-called tragedy of the commons), underuse, or undersupply. The solution to these problems lies in mechanisms for collective action, the absence of which risks producing "public bads" (as opposed to public goods) such as environmental degradation. Kaul defines global public goods as those goods "whose benefits reach across borders, generations, and population groups."[28] To say that peace is indivisible is to say that it is a global public good: if global peace broke out, we would all enjoy its benefits because no one group or region could be excluded.

Providing for the world's citizens through rules and regulations is needed in such areas as security, health, food and agriculture, weather and meteorology, civil aviation, and maritime law. Economists describe these as international public goods because they are needed by individual countries and their populations and for the efficient functioning of the global system but they are beyond the capacity of the global market on its own to offer, since individual countries lack the incentive and capacity to provide them on the scale required.

This is in part because of the problem of free riders, those who let others pay for their own access to public goods. To ensure that public goods that can exclude no one are available, many specialized organizations would need to be invented if they did not exist already as part of the UN system. Many such specialist institutions were created long before the current generation of post–World War II institutions. For example, the Pan American Sanitary Bureau was founded in 1902 and was made the World Health Organization's Latin American arm in 1948, by then named PAHO, the Pan American Health Organization. The Universal Postal Union (UPU) and International Telecommunication Union (ITU) are perhaps the oldest; their origins lie in the mid-nineteenth century.

Gaps in institutions often exist even when knowledge, norms, and policies are in place. We use "institution" here in two senses: as formal organizational entities as well as regimes—recurring and stable patterns of behavior around which expectations converge. For example, a "coalition of the willing" is a stable pattern even though the membership is variable. It is easier to identify formal institutions that have treaties and budgets, but the informal "messy and political" varieties are just as essential to our analysis of gaps.

Institutional gaps can refer to the fact that there may be no overarching global institution, in which case many international aspects of problem-solving may be ignored. An example is the control of nuclear weapons. Or it may be impossible to address a problem because key states are missing; for example, the World Trade Organization (WTO) before China entered or the League of Nations without the United States.

One of the most obvious explanations for institutional shortcomings, or gaps, is simply that the resources allocated are not commensurate with the magnitude of a problem. This applies to most planetary-wide problems. Inadequate financial support is often a reason why too little progress is made. Examples include inadequate funding for activities to improve the lot of women, who constitute half the world's population, or the funding for human rights protection, which currently constitutes about 2 percent of the UN's regular budget.

This is an appropriate point at which to note a second major disconnect in global governance. The capacity to mobilize the resources necessary to tackle global problems also remains vested in states, thereby effectively incapacitating many international institutions.

International institutions exist that deal reasonably well with a specific problem area, and the most effective of these often deal with specific issues and operate on the basis of well-embedded norms and consensus among member states. Examples include the International Atomic Energy Agency (IAEA), the UN Children's Fund (better known by its acronym,

UNICEF), the ITU, and the World Health Organization (WHO), to name but four. Positive examples thus should figure in contemporary discussions along with laments about those that fall short, for example the late Commission on Human Rights (CHR).

Part of the explanation for why institutions may work well is because they focus on specific problems and are functional. According to David Mitrany, a functional institution deals with one of the growing number of technical issues.[29] These issues are not seen as having political salience—they do not threaten a state's vital interests and thus would not lead to conflict. Therefore, these issues can safely be turned over to experts for resolution.[30] To political scientists, of course, everything is political, and Mitrany's characterization, although it is useful, has obvious limitations. Even technical activities—for instance, the IAEA's monitoring of Iran or North Korea or the WHO's monitoring of SARS in China or AIDS in South Africa—impinge on state interests and are contested.

More contemporary expert-group approaches in international relations scholarship include Peter Haas's work on epistemic communities,[31] Peter Hall's on the impact of Keynesian economists,[32] and Ernst B. Haas's on knowledge[33] as well as Keck and Sikkink's on transnational networks of activists.[34] Expert consensus has been central to efforts to restructure the UN system and to the creation of new institutions to meet newly recognized needs. States set up institutions and pay the bills (sometimes), but networks of experts pushed by activists in civil society are usually the driving force behind their establishment.

A significant body of literature examines the role of intellectuals in creating ideas and the role of technical experts in diffusing ideas and making them more concrete. Networks of knowledgeable experts influence a broad spectrum of international politics through their ability to interact with policymakers irrespective of location and national boundaries. Researchers working on HIV/AIDS or climate change can have an impact on policy by clarifying an issue. They can help frame the debate and narrow the terms of international negotiations. They can introduce standards of action. These networks can help justify alternatives and often build national or international coalitions to support chosen policies and advocate for change. In many ways, and as mentioned at the outset, this approach to change builds on Thomas Kuhn's work on the nature of scientific revolutions.[35]

It is important to keep in mind the extent to which current expectations about global governance contain rather feeble notions of contributions by intergovernmental institutions in comparison with past visions. At Bretton Woods in 1944, John Maynard Keynes and the British delegation proposed a monetary fund equal in value to half of annual world imports, while Harry Dexter White and the American side proposed a smaller fund worth one-sixth of annual world imports. As Hans Singer sardonically notes: "Today's Fund is only 2 per cent of annual world imports. Perhaps the differences between Keynes's originally proposed 50 per cent and the actual 2 per cent is a measure of the degree to which our vision of international economic management has shrunk."[36] If this is the case for the IMF, which is regularly lambasted in many development circles for its power and the conditionalities it imposes, what kind of adjectives should be used to describe the disconnect between demonstrated and supposedly agreed needs, norms, and policies, on the one hand, and the resources available to such institutions as the Office of the High Commissioner for Human Rights (OHCHR) or the UN Environment Programme (UNEP)? How much would the institutional gaps vis-à-vis human rights or the environment shrink if we applied the expectations of Keynes or even White about global governance to these two issues?

In our discussion of such gaps, some institutions fall between those that seem to work well in many ways on at least certain issues and those that can be considered so weak as to constitute a near-total gap. We illustrate with examples from both the security and economic arenas. (As always, subjective judgment enters into the picture.) How, for instance, should we categorize the practice of establishing international tribunals simply because it is generally agreed that judicial proceedings are the way to go?[37] The Security Council's establishment of ad hoc international criminal tribunals for the former Yugoslavia in 1993 and Rwanda in 1994 sought legal justice for those responsible for war crimes, crimes against humanity, and genocide. Subsequently, in 2002 the council convened a special court and a fact-finding commission in Sierra Leone, in 2003 it created a special court in East Timor, and in 2005 it established another hybrid court (part national and part international) in Cambodia to try members of the former Khmer Rouge regime who were responsible for the "killing fields." What about the ICC, based on the Rome Statute signed in 1998 that came into force in 2002? How substantial is the gap when three permanent members of the Security Council—the United States, Russia, and China—have not ratified the Rome Statute?

Although confronting pandemics is certainly an agreed-upon human security norm and knowledge about how do so is growing, a substantial international institutional gap exists when it comes to implementing effective policies. The WHO's budget and capacity for dealing with SARS or HIV/AIDS are woefully inadequate for the scope of the challenge. As another example, although substantial evidence about global warming has existed for some time and experts and policymakers generally agree that something should be done and a treaty should be concluded about this issue, an institutional gap exists without the participation of key states such as the United States, which has refused to enter into the Kyoto Protocol.[38]

Compliance Gaps

The fifth and final gap is the compliance gap. Compliance measures must include mechanisms to identify defections and defectors from agreed-upon norms and commitments in the realm of international governance as well as incentives that reward cooperation and disincentives that punish defection (including the use of force to bring those who have not complied back into line). Our approach to analyzing compliance gaps has three facets: implementation, monitoring, and enforcement. Recalcitrant or fragile actors may be unwilling or unable to implement agreed-upon elements of international policy, for example a ban on commercial whaling or the acquisition of nuclear technology and material. Even if an institution exists or a treaty is in effect or many elements of a working regime are in place, the political will to implement an agreement or even to provide resources for established institutions or processes is often absent. Also, it is not clear who has the authority, responsibility, and capacity to ensure that commitments that have been made and obligations that have been accepted are being implemented and honored. How do we monitor the implementation records of states who have signed on to the Kyoto Protocol and the NPT? In addition, when clear evidence exists that one or more members of the collective group is out of compliance, the group may lack the strength of conviction or commonality of interests to enforce the community norm. How do we enforce treaty obligations on signatory states and norms on non-signatory states, not to mention nonstate actors who lie outside the jurisdiction of any formal normative architecture?

What can be done to persuade or force a party to comply? U.S. president Andrew Jackson is widely reported to have sneered in response to the U.S. Supreme Court's decision to uphold Cherokee property claims in

Worcester v. Georgia, "Mr. Justice Marshall has made his decision, now let him enforce it." Enforcement is a subset of compliance and is especially difficult at the international level in an anarchic society of sovereign states. The source of ideas for filling enforcement gaps is mixed: governments and intergovernmental organizations are just as likely to provide ideas as civil society is. The source of monitoring is as likely to be civil society actors (for example Human Rights Watch) and states (for example the United States vis-à-vis Iran's and North Korea's compliance with NPT obligations) as it is to be international organizations (for example the IAEA). The source of implementation is also likely to be mixed. The past sixty-five years of UN history are the story of the never-ending search for better compliance mechanisms in the absence of an overriding central authority.

With the exception of the Security Council, UN bodies can only make "recommendations." Hence, publicity of information about noncompliance mixed with the use of the bully pulpit has been a central dynamic in efforts to secure compliance. One of the main tactics used in the face of these constraints has been to embarrass those who do not comply. This tactic is used when UN secretariats or NGOs generate and publicize information and data about noncompliance.

The challenge of filling global governance gaps is demonstrated by the extreme difficulty in ensuring compliance. Indeed, no ways exist to enforce decisions and no mechanisms exist to compel states to comply with decisions. This generalization may be limited because influential organizations (especially the WTO, the IMF, and the World Bank) can make offers to developing countries that they dare not refuse. The more relevant and typical examples of compliance gaps, however, are in the area of international peace and security. Even though the UN Charter calls for standing UN military forces, no such forces exist. The UN has to beg and borrow troops, which are always on loan, and there is no functioning Military Staff Committee (as called for in Charter Article 47). Perhaps even more tellingly, the UN has no capability for responding rapidly to crises. This is not because of a lack of ideas or policy proposals—former UN Secretary-General Trygve Lie's proposal for a small standing UN force was first made in 1947 and the latest proposal came from the Brahimi report in 2000. When Tehran thumbed its nose at the IAEA and the Security Council in 2006–2008, the compliance gap was more than evident.

In the area of human rights, often neither hard law nor soft law has the capacity to enforce agreements. Although ad hoc tribunals and the

International Criminal Court have led to some indictments and convictions, there is precious little enforcement capacity in this arena. For example, knowledge, norms, and institutions about genocide have been universally accepted since 1948. Alas, without an enforcement mechanism, genocide still occurs; in fact, forensic evidence uncovered by the International Commission for Missing Persons indicates that those who are bent on committing genocide are far more furtive than in the past and make more attempts to hide physical evidence.[39] We will see later how assiduous efforts to monitor and publicize mass atrocities have (on occasion at least) secured an enforcement response from the Security Council in the forms of imposing collective sanctions, activating international judicial bodies, and even using military force.

In the area of international trade and finance, the WTO is considered a relatively effective enforcement mechanism although it is among the youngest of IGOs. While the WTO is undoubtedly a step in the right direction in comparison to its predecessor, the General Agreement on Tariffs and Trade (GATT)—that is, it has some teeth—international trade disputes are still largely regulated bilaterally. Monitoring by the Second and the Third UNs has led to changes in policy and implementation by some governments and corporations—that is, voluntary compliance by good citizens.

And finally, in the area of environment and sustainability, the 1997 Kyoto Protocol created binding emission targets for developed countries, a system whereby developed countries could obtain credit toward their emission targets through Clean Development Mechanisms, emissions trading (trading the "right to pollute"), and providing the finances for energy-efficient projects in less-developed countries (known as "joint implementation"). Backtracking, however, began almost before the ink was dry on the signatures. As the world hurtles toward an irreversible tipping point on climate change, there is no way to ensure that even the largely inadequate agreements on the books are being respected. Here is probably the most obvious illustration of the limits of using public shaming and bully pulpits in the hope of promoting widespread voluntary compliance.

We highlight the compliance gap by examining the lacunae in the international system's ability to ensure a modicum of compliance even when knowledge appears sufficient and relevant norms, policies, and institutions are in place. In each case, we tell a story of hesitant and insufficient progress toward ensuring compliance with agreed objectives. This progress has been easier to see in the areas of human rights and trade. In the areas of security and the environment, regimes are in flux and progress is more difficult to ascertain.

As we finalize this chapter in the midst of a global financial meltdown, we return to our point of departure—namely that the planet will remain hard pressed to respond to current and future challenges without more robust intergovernmental institutions. Try as we might, the sum of many governance instruments, inadequately resourced and insufficiently empowered to enforce collective policies as they are, cannot replace the functions of a global government.

The Tsunami and Global Governance

Revisiting the example of international responses to the tsunami illustrates the gaps that we have sketched: gaps in knowledge, norms, policies, institutions, and compliance. Prior to the December 2004 catastrophe, for example, there was local knowledge about tsunamis in East Asia—what causes them, what the warning signs are, and what the damage could be—that was not known in Southern Asia. While we still lack the capacity to predict earthquakes and prevent the death and destruction caused by tremors directly, our predictive knowledge about tsunamis is common and reliable. We can ascertain whether or not to expect a tsunami following an earthquake, where and when a tsunami will occur, and how powerful it will be. An early warning mechanism exists for the Pacific Ocean—the Pacific Tsunami Warning System, which is integrated into the UN system and operated by the U.S. National Oceanic and Atmospheric Administration.

After the tsunami occurred, no one questioned the notion that there was a responsibility to protect individuals or the notion that if governments could not manage the disaster and its consequences, outsiders should exert pressure and come to the rescue. For decades the United Nations has preached the culture of prevention with regard to disasters, natural disasters as well as those caused by ecologically damaging patterns of human and social activity, as much as it has done so with regard to conflicts. In his millennium report, the Secretary-General noted that the cost of natural disasters in 1998 alone had exceeded the cost of all such disasters in the 1980s.[40] Governments around the Indian Ocean rim, however, had not internalized the norm of disaster prevention.

As a result a critical policy gap existed in this region. Policymakers faced competing priorities: Should they divert resources to cope with a once-in-a-century tsunami or invest in preparations for dealing with floods and earthquakes that occur more regularly? Should there be a tsunami warning system in the Indian Ocean (which rarely experienced tsunamis) or would the money be better spent elsewhere? The point is not that the lower policy priority given to tsunami warning and response systems is incomprehensible. Rather, given the existing state of knowledge in other countries and within the UN, policymakers consciously chose not to invest in adequate early warning systems and response mechanisms.

The fact that such a warning system is in place for the Pacific points to the critical institutional gap for the Indian Ocean. Institutionally, the UN is not the main avenue for implementing disaster relief and prevention, which is still seen as the primary responsibility of states and civil society. However, the tsunami highlighted the fact that the UN is the institution of choice for coordinating the international response to a disaster of such enormity.

The UN, through its Office for the Coordination of Humanitarian Affairs (OCHA), orchestrated the relief effort across the twelve affected countries. Its daily situation reports contained such useful information as country-by-country situation summaries; a breakdown of aid provision by sector, agency, and dollar amount; a description of UN efforts; and a description of national responses. Through the ReliefWeb Internet site, OCHA was able to inform the world about survivors' immediate needs, what was being done to meet those needs, and what help aid workers required, such as transportation and communications equipment. The relief effort showed the UN's centrality and ability to convene and foster processes involving multiple constituencies and its ability to provide global leadership.

Finally, we highlight dimensions of compliance. The mobilization of political will to provide immediate and longer-term assistance to affected countries was instantaneous. Ordinary citizens in some countries dipped into their pocketbooks more generously than their governments,[41] which then were shamed into increasing their pledges. But there were operational failures, or implementation gaps, and aid agencies often competed with one another.[42] The disaster also highlighted the potential for another major and recurring gap, namely between pledges and delivery of the promised funds and resources. There simply is no enforcement mechanism for holding governments or other donors to their word. One of the strongest methods of enforcing compliance seems to be the UN's moral authority to call down shame on niggardly or uncooperative actors.[43] Indeed, OCHA made publically available on its Internet site, ReliefWeb, a record of pledges to the tsunami appeal and other humanitarian appeals to hold donors accountable.

In short, and despite its shortcomings and the absence of any overarching authority or established pool of financial and relief resources, ideas and experiments that had circulated for years resulted in a strange patchwork of responses that impressed even the UN's harshest critics. Our task here is to understand how global governance works and determine whether we can build on such foundations in the future. The tsunami provides a rich vein of examples.

The UN's response to the disaster showed what the United Nations could do in terms of filling gaps in global governance. The Intergovernmental Oceanographic Commission of the UN Educational, Scientific and Cultural Organization (UNESCO) is coordinating the development of tsunami monitoring and warning systems in the Pacific, the Indian Ocean, the Mediterranean, and other regions. Because the world organization had standing relationships with almost all governments, civil society actors, and other organized groups, not only was it able to fill the gap in knowledge about what happened and what was needed, but UN agencies were also well placed to coordinate the disaster response. The UN thus helped fill the institutional gap by guiding the relief efforts of a multitude of agencies operating on the ground.

The UN also filled other gaps. Normatively, donors exhibited a marked preference not just for coordination but more specifically for UN coordination. The world organization also filled the policy gap: ReliefWeb documented the priorities where food, water, and medical care was most needed and later provided information about setting priorities in recovery efforts such as rebuilding housing and infrastructure.[44] The enforcement gap, as is the case all too often for transborder problems, was glaring as agencies competed for turf. However, overall the moral imperative to overcome suffering attenuated the gap. Funding was abundant, and by the end of April 2005, OCHA had reported that some 91 percent of all flash appeal pledges from official donors had been converted into contributions or commitments.[45]

In short, the various moving parts of humanitarian global governance meshed better than one would have expected when looking at the reality of an extremely decentralized delivery system—including the UN system's major players (the United Nations High Commissioner for Refugees, UNICEF, the World Food Programme, the United Nations Development Programme [UNDP], and OCHA) literally hundreds of international and thousands of local NGOs, and the civilian and military components of outside and local governments.[46] Emergency assistance was dispensed and lives were saved (the speculation that another 250,000–300,000 deaths would occur was proven wrong), and reconstruction began almost immediately.

So how full or empty is the global governance glass? While the reader is undoubtedly already sated with our reminders that nothing like a world government exists, the collective international response to the December 2004 tsunami illustrates the current system's value, however many and obvious its shortcomings might be. It also suggests the need for the United Nations—the First, Second, and Third—to redouble efforts to address the gaps in knowledge, norms, policies, institutions, and compliance.

The Book

In chapters 2–10, we provide an in-depth examination of these gaps and historical efforts to fill them. First, however, chapter 1 explores the origins of the idea of global governance. We probe the evolution of global governance with special emphasis on the last two decades, when the term became a central part of the public policy lexicon.

The five types of disconnects between transborder problems and existing global capacities provide the backbone for our substantive discussions. While there is unevenness across sectors, we see the generation of ideas about attenuating all five kinds of gaps as an essential task of the United Nations. Indeed, generating ideas is the comparative advantage of the world organization.

It would be misleading to organize the narrative of this intellectual history in a linear fashion. Instead, our story is told through historical examples that provide, in our subjective judgment, the best illustrations of the gaps by issue area. Each chapter begins with a brief presentation of landmarks since 1945 in a particular substantive area in order to provide the context for the analysis of gaps that follows. In many ways, these antecedents indicate some of the gaps that have been filled so that readers can better understand the gaps that remain. We end each chapter with a forward-looking conclusion, spelling out what we see as likely developments over the next decade as well as the developments we would most like to see.

The substantive illustrations and analyses in the book span what in our view are the most pressing contemporary problems for international public policy across the UN system's three major areas of interest. Part 1 explores the crucial issues of international security under three headings: "Use of Force: War, Collective Security, and Peace Operations" (chapter 2); "Arms Control and Disarmament" (chapter 3); and "Terrorism" (chapter 4). Part 2 analyzes three central challenges of development: "Trade, Aid, and Finance" (chapter 5); "Sustainable Development" (chapter 6); and "Saving the Environment: The Ozone Layer and Climate Change" (chapter 7). Part 3 probes three crucial perspectives on human security: "Generations of Rights" (chapter 8); "Protecting against Pandemics" (chapter 9); and "The Responsibility to Protect" (chapter 10).

Chapter 10 also serves as a rather personal conclusion for the volume as a whole. Rather than repeating the final sections from each chapter, we thought it not only more intriguing but also more creative to illustrate how the United Nations has helped move toward improved global governance with a concrete example. Human protection in conflict contexts is an issue that we know intimately and have been involved with as both analysts and practitioners. Given such ongoing crises in Darfur, the DRC, and Myanmar, the failure to provide protection to noncombatants in conflict situations also bluntly demonstrates the limits of global governance in 2009.

In each chapter we ask the following questions: When did the issue appear on the agenda and why? What caused the differences? And what was the role of the UN in this process? In other words, how many of the gaps or solutions came from within the UN system? We examine the least and the most substantial examples of gaps related to the subject of each chapter and ask: what is the relationship between the UN's current work and these gaps?

It is time for us to embark on the unfinished journey.

1

Tracing the Origins of an Idea and the UN's Contribution

- Global Governance: The Idea
- Governance without Government
- Globalization
- An Historical Perspective
- Identifying and Diagnosing Problems
- The UN's Ideational Role: This Book and the UNIHP Series

This chapter explores three themes: the idea of global governance itself, the UN's ideational role in framing this idea, and the anomalies in the international system that have provided openings for the spread of this concept. The UN's "ideational role" is fancy new packaging for the world organization's intellectual or creative capacities in global governance—its efforts to understand problems and address them by formulating norms or policy recommendations.[1]

We identify gaps or disconnects in order to examine the search for new solutions—including new combinations of actors—to address challenges that are beyond the capacities of states. The essential challenge in contemporary global problem-solving is the fact that no central authority exists to make global policy choices and mobilize the required resources to implement these decisions. Consequently, only second- or even third-best solutions are feasible at present. The United Nations has been more effective in filling gaps in knowledge and norms than in making decisions with teeth and acting upon them.

Global Governance: The Idea

While we spelled it out earlier, another way to think of governance is as purposeful systems of rules or norms that ensure order beyond what occurs naturally. In the domestic context, governance is usually more than government and implies a shared purpose and goal orientation as well as formal authority or police powers. In international politics, what little organizational structure exists is amorphous, even morally suspect for some. It is important to make clear the differences between national and global governance.

The *Human Development Report 1999* argued that "governance does not mean mere government."[2] In a domestic context, this is correct because governance is government plus the additional mechanisms required to ensure order and predictability in problem-solving. For the planet, however, governance is the whole story because there is no central authority. In many instances, the UN's network of institutions and rules provides the appearance of effective governance but these mechanisms do not produce the actual desired effects. International organizations sometimes function in a quasi-governmental fashion and try to exercise social control by promulgating norms and laws. The United Nations, not unlike national governments, represents a structure of authority that rests on institutionalized practices and generally accepted norms.

The starting point for thinking about international public policy is that governance for the planet is weak. Readers should keep in mind that global governance is not a supplement but rather what the French would call a *faute de mieux,* a surrogate for authority and enforcement for the contemporary world in the absence of something better. No matter how strong the contributions of informal and formal networks are, no matter how plentiful the resources from private organizations and corporations are, no matter how much goodwill from governments exists, the striking reality is that there is no central authority. While vast improvements are plausible and desirable in contemporary global governance, we must continually ask a sobering question: Can we ever get good global governance without something that looks much more like effective world government? Can global governance without a world government actually address adequately the range of problems faced by humanity?

As noted earlier, some would argue that all efforts to solve problems beyond state borders since the nineteenth century are part of the history of global governance, but the birth of the term "global governance" reflects an interesting marriage between academic and policy concerns in the 1990s. It replaced an earlier exploration of what was called world order studies, which some critiqued as overly top-down and static, failing to capture the variety of actors, networks, and relationships that characterize contemporary international relations. At the end of the Cold War, scholars believed that the collapse of the bipolar system created an opportunity for a substantially new world order—one achieved not by some sort of consensus among different cultural and political traditions but a U.S. or at least a classical liberal world order. When the multiple perspectives in the work done by world order scholars started to look a little old fashioned, James Rosenau and Ernst Czempiel published their theoretical collection of essays *Governance without Government* (1992).[3] In 1995, the policy-oriented Commission on Global Governance's report *Our Global Neighbourhood* was published[4] and the first issue of the journal *Global Governance,* whose subscribers are both scholars and practitioners, appeared.

In addition to interdependence and a growing recognition of problems that defy solutions by a single state, the other explanation for the emergence of concept of global governance stems from the sheer growth in numbers and importance of nonstate actors (such as NGOs and transnational corporations), which also are conducting themselves in new ways. Indeed, this was the logic behind the creation of the Global Compact at the Millennium Summit of 2000, which characterizes the private sector—both the for-profit and the non-profit species—as a necessary partner with states and intergovernmental organizations.

Society has become too complex for citizens' demands to be satisfied solely by governments. Instead, civil society organizations play increasingly active roles in shaping international norms, laws, and policies. Civil society provides additional levers that people and governments can use to improve the effectiveness and enhance the legitimacy of public policy at all levels of governance. However, both governments and civil society actors face challenges of representation, accountability, and legitimacy. In an increasingly diverse, complex, and interdependent world, solutions to problems that require collective action are often unattainable by state actors alone. Instead, on many issues partnerships form between different types of actors.

The growth in the number and influence of nonstate entities as well as technological advances and increasing interdependence necessarily mean that state-centered structures (i.e., IGOs, especially those of the UN system) find themselves sharing the governance stage with a host of other actors. Civil society actors participate in global governance as advocates, as activists, and as policymakers in many instances. Their critiques and policy prescriptions have demonstrable consequences in the governmental and intergovernmental allocation of resources and the exercise of political, military, and economic power. Paradoxically, IGOs seem marginalized at exactly the moment when enhanced multilateralism is so sorely required.[5] Coordination and cooperation are increasingly complex and problematic as a result of the growing number of actors and the existence of decentralized and informal groupings.

Depending on the issue area and geographic location, vast disparities in power and influence exist among states, IGOs, multinational corporations, and international NGOs. Consequently, today's world is governed by a patchwork of authority that is as diffuse as it is contingent. In particular, the IGOs that collectively underpin global governance are too few in number, have access to too few resources, do not have the requisite policy authority and capacity to mobilize resources, and are sometimes incoherent in their separate policies and philosophies.

According to Anne-Marie Slaughter, the glue that binds the contemporary system of global governance is government networks, both horizontal and vertical.[6] Horizontal networks link counterpart national officials across borders, such as police investigators or financial regulators. This was demonstrated vividly when a terror plot being hatched in London was foiled in August 2006.[7] Vertical networks are relationships between national officials and a supranational organization to which they have ceded authority, such as the European Court of Justice. For those who dismiss the idea of a world government, the solution to the weaknesses of global governance lies in strengthening existing networks and developing new ones that could create a genuine global rule of law.

Unlike many in earlier generations of analysts of international organization, most contemporary proponents of global governance do not seek to create a world government.[8] Some rule it out as undesirable, while others do not believe it to be feasible within the foreseeable future. The quest for global governance remains an unfinished journey because we are struggling to find our way and are nowhere near locating a satisfactory destination. Global governance is incoherent, and its separate parts often move at different paces and in different directions.

We define global governance as the sum of laws, norms, policies, and institutions that define, constitute, and mediate transborder relations between states, citizens, intergovernmental and nongovernmental organizations, and the market. It embraces the totality of institutions, policies, rules, practices, norms, procedures, and initiatives by which states and their citizens (indeed, humanity as a whole) try to bring more predictability, stability, and order to their responses to such transnational problems as warfare, poverty, and environmental degradation that go beyond the capacity of a single state to solve and that are increasingly recognized as such.

Governance without Government

The long tradition of criticizing the existing state system and seeking to replace it with a universal government began with Dante's *Monarchia* at the beginning of the fourteenth century.[9] Harold Jacobson noted that the tapestries in the Palais des Nations in Geneva—the headquarters of the League of Nations and now the UN's European Office—offer a fitting image for the older view of world government. He observed that they "picture the process of humanity combining into ever larger and more stable units for the purpose of governance—first the family, then the tribe, then the city-state, and then the nation—a process which presumably would eventually culminate in the entire world being combined in one political unit."[10] Along the same lines, a contemporary theorist, Alexander Wendt, suggests that "a world state is inevitable."[11]

However desirable, such an eventuality appears fanciful. While we agree with E. H. Carr that a mixture of utopia and power is required to avoid stagnation and despair, we also note that he (appropriately) wrote, "Any real international government is impossible so long as power, which is an essential condition of government, is organized nationally."[12]

We certainly are not complacent about what is at stake and are not satisfied that global governance can accomplish what a world government could. That should be clear by now. Rather, our approach is based on our judgment about how to best use our analytical energies in this volume, although we proceed differently in other publications.[13]

Our aim with the bulk of the analysis is to understand efforts to enhance order in international relations and improve, as the UNDP's *Human Development Report 1999* put it, "the framework of rules, institutions and practices that set limits and give incentives for the behavior of individuals, organizations and firms."[14] We are specifically interested in actions that aim to be comprehensive and are not merely piecemeal social engineering; in actions that are multisectoral, democratically accountable, and include members of civil society in the shared management of a troubled and fragile world order; and in actions that are possible to imagine as being implemented over the next decade.

That said, we emphasize how best to realize a stable, peaceful, prosperous, and well-ordered international society of the type that international relations scholar Hedley Bull sought—the maximum in the absence of a unifying global authority.[15] Improved global problem-solving may or may not involve creating more powerful global institutions in the immediate term; our emphasis will be on UN ideas that explore the need for such entities in the medium term. This is not to say that we are disinterested in the critical longer-term problems of more democratic forms of global governance; such voices as Martha Nussbaum and David Held raise critical issues regarding social justice, representation, and participation that obviously are the topics for entire books.[16]

There is no guarantee that the supply of global public goods will follow the growing demand for them. Better and more effective global governance will not simply materialize. For us, concerted action is essential. Craig Murphy encourages us: "The longer history of industry and international organizations indicates that the task of creating the necessary global institutions may be easier than many of today's liberal commentators believe."[17]

We realize that states and state-centric institutions do not have the capacity to adequately address all the challenges of an increasingly globalized world. Several of these challenges expose the limited ability of states to control outcomes through self-help. How can we improve the provision of essential global public goods in an anarchic society? To date, the system of global governance has not met the test that "it must channel behavior in such a way as to eliminate or substantially ameliorate the problem that led to its creation."[18] How do we develop "the capacity to get things done"[19] in the absence of international institutions with enforcement capacity and in the absence of prospects for their creation on the horizon?

We have not abandoned hope that satisfactory (or at least better) answers can be found for these questions, which provide the impetus for the concluding section of each chapter. Even without a world government, there is much room for more initiatives from governments and groups in power and better incentives and initiatives from secretariats and civil society—in short, better mobilization and use of the three United Nations in better governance for the planet.

Globalization

The other key concept in our analysis is "globalization," which we define as a process of increased interconnectivity throughout the world. The term has become the focus of some controversy and a considerable analytical industry.[20] Many regard it as both a desirable and irreversible engine of commerce that will underpin growing prosperity and a higher standard of living throughout the world. Others recoil from it as the soft underbelly of corporate imperialism that plunders and profiteers on the basis of unrestrained consumerism. There is also the dark side of globalization with many interconnections between the disparate elements of the underworld trafficking in drugs, arms, and humans.[21] Some observers have argued that globalization has been occurring since the earliest trade expeditions (e.g., the Silk Road), and it is true that the process itself is not fundamentally new. For example, Amit Bhaduri and Deepak Nayyar point out that as a proportion of total production in the world economy, international trade was about the same in the 1980s as it was during the last two decades of the gold standard (1890–1913).[22] But others have suggested that the current era of globalization is unique in the rapidity of its spread and the number of interactions in real time.[23]

The primary dimension of globalization concerns the expansion of economic activities across state borders, which has produced increasing interdependence through the growing volume and variety of cross-border flows of finance, investment, and goods and services and the rapid and widespread diffusion of technology. Other dimensions include the international movement of ideas, information, legal systems, organizations, and people as well as cultural exchanges.

A few caveats and clarifications are in order. First, even in this age of globalization, the movement of people is still restricted and strictly regulated, even more so in the aftermath of 9/11. Second, growing economic interdependence is highly asymmetrical: the benefits of linking and the costs of delinking are not equally distributed among partners. Industrialized countries are highly interdependent in their relations with each other, but developing countries are largely independent in their economic relations with other developing countries and highly dependent on industrialized countries. Third, compared to the postwar period, the average rate of world growth (including growth in China) has steadily slowed during the age of globalization: from 3.5 percent per capita per annum in the 1960s to 2.1, 1.3, and 1.0 percent in the 1970s, 1980s, and

1990s, respectively.[24] Fourth, there has been a growing divergence—not convergence—in income levels between countries and peoples and widening inequality among and within nations.[25] Assets and incomes are more concentrated. Wage shares have fallen while profit shares have risen. The mobility of capital coupled with the immobility of workers has reduced the bargaining power of organized labor. Increased unemployment has generated an excess supply of labor, and the intensification of jobs in the informal sector has depressed real wages in many countries.

Thus, globalization creates losers as well as winners and entails risks as well as provides opportunities. As an International Labour Organization (ILO) blue-ribbon panel noted, the problems lie not in globalization per se but in the "deficiencies in its governance."[26] The deepening of poverty and inequality—prosperity for a few countries and people, marginalization and exclusion for many—has implications for social and political stability, among as well as within states.[27] The rapid growth of global markets has not created a parallel development of social and economic institutions to ensure that they will function smoothly and efficiently, labor rights have been less assiduously protected than capital and property rights, and the global rules on trade and finance are unfair to the extent that they produce asymmetrical effects in rich and poor countries.

An Historical Perspective

For many analysts, global governance overlaps with the rise of formal international organizations, which began in the mid-nineteenth century. These institutions, in Craig Murphy's words, are customarily seen as "what world government we actually have."[28]

It is useful to explore a bit of the history of such terms. A genuine world government would imply an international system with at least some of the capacities and powers of what we customarily associate with functional national governments—notably powers to control or repel threats, raise revenues, allocate expenditures, redistribute incomes, and require compliance from citizens as well as ensure their rights. While such distinguished commentators as Nobel laureate Jan Tinbergen and the World Bank's former president Robert McNamara have declared the need for the UN system to have some of these powers, such a goal remains elusive, highly contested, and very far from being accepted politically, even as a distant objective.

For this reason, most students of international relations now prefer the term "global governance," which came into widespread use in the

1990s and refers to the formal and informal systems and networks that with all their imperfections and limitations provide some measure of international order in the absence of a world government. In this system, states pursue their own national interests and cooperate when they perceive that doing so will serve their goals. Though some still believe that a vision of global government must remain the long-term answer in an ever-more-globalizing world, realists argue that this is doubly misleading—a vastly exaggerated and idealistic vision of what will be possible or desirable over the next few decades and, worse, a chimera that presents a serious distortion of the elements of global governance to which we should strive during the nearer future. Naysayers include right-wingers afraid of any intrusion by supranational authorities as well as left-wingers who see current actions by the Bretton Woods institutions and the WTO as a top-down conspiracy of the rich against the poor.

This said, the existing structures of global governance are anything but static. Rules, regulations, institutions, and requirements have evolved considerably since the UN was established, sometimes increasing in strength, sometimes moving backward. Even critics would agree that in a number of technical areas—such as agreements on rules and regulations for shipping and international air flights, the standardization of weather systems, and the mapping of epidemiological trends—global governance has demonstrated its value and has had positive outcomes. Indeed, some of these arrangements date back to the nineteenth century, when the need for technical coordination of areas such as telecommunications and postal services became obvious. By 1914, over thirty such institutions had been created, and hundreds more had been created by the end of the twentieth century.[29]

What happened in the nineteenth century? International institutions emerged as sovereign states made new arrangements for the increased interactions brought about by the industrial revolution. In *Swords into Plowshares,* Inis Claude identified three major streams of institutional development. At the beginning of the nineteenth century, the first concert system of multilateral, high-level political gatherings such as the Congress of Vienna was devised, which established "diplomacy by conference" among the European powers.[30] Echoes of this system can be seen in the structure of the UN Security Council. At the end of the nineteenth century came the second strand in the form of the Hague system, the goal of which was a universal membership conference system that would meet regularly to build a peaceful world politics based on law and reasoned deliberation as well as to consider specific problems or crises. The UN General Assembly has its roots in the Hague type of system.

The third strand, which generated the longest-lasting institutions, created public international unions or administrative agencies. As Claude explains, "Whereas both the Concert and The Hague reflected the significance of the quest for security and the importance of high political issues, this third phenomenon was a manifestation of the increasing complexity of the economic, social, technical, and cultural interconnections of the peoples of the modern world."[31] Examples include the International Telegraphic Union, founded in 1865 (now the International Telecommunication Union), and the Universal Postal Union, established in 1874.

Claude emphasizes the evolutionary character of such institutions. They were not planned and "represented adaptation, not innovation; it was less the work of idealists with schemes to advance than of realists with problems to handle."[32] These institutions expanded the subject matter of international relations beyond war and peace. Furthermore, they were new not just in function but also in form; decisions in these agencies were made by public and private experts in subject areas rather than by diplomats, ministers, and heads of state.

Thus, the human species has moved in many ways, particularly during the UN's lifetime, that were hardly imaginable when the efforts to improve navigation on the Danube in the nineteenth century began this experiment in international regulation. And even in comparison with the League of Nations period, many services—including the regulation of the skies and seas, Internet traffic, and mail—occur in a way that our forefathers and mothers would find mind-boggling.

While it is true that the antecedents and growing components of a working system of global governance can be found in the previous two centuries, many of the life-threatening problems we discuss in these pages—from nuclear proliferation to climate change, from poverty to human rights abuse—require solutions that appear to exceed our current global institutional capacities. We must be careful not to indicate too much continuity with the past. Murphy's work on formal international organizations could be considered somewhat outmoded since it ignores the kinds of informal networks and groupings that are part of contemporary international relations. At the same time, such observers as David Kennedy and Tim Sinclair would undoubtedly judge our emphasis on the

UN system as old-fashioned in another way because we stress the state-centric and static UN construct when so many other bodies—the EU, NGOs, multinational corporations, and so on—are not only central to contemporary global governance but have more potential for adaptation in the future.[33] Even so, the United Nations provides a fulcrum for our analysis as the most universal and most legitimate organization with the greatest potential for expansion. This does not mean that we are uncritical of the UN, though, and our book should demonstrate that.

Rorden Wilkinson notes that there is much to be gained by analyzing international organizations and global governance, "but the synonymity with which these two phenomena are treated does not enable the qualitative dimensions of contemporary global governance to be fully captured." Wilkinson specifically points to the importance of analyzing the diversity of global governance actors and "the way in which varieties of actors are increasingly combining to manage—and in many cases, micro-manage—a growing range of political, economic and social affairs."[34] Global governance entails multilevel and networked governance—what Jan Aart Scholte calls "an emergent polycentric mode of governance"[35]—to deal with the linkages across policy levels and domains. The United Nations cannot displace the responsibility of local, state, and national governments, but it can and should be the locus of multilateral diplomacy and collective action to solve problems shared in common by many countries. "Good" global governance implies not exclusive policy jurisdiction but an optimal partnership between the state, intergovernmental, and nongovernmental actors operating at the national, regional, and global levels.

In the introduction, we specifically refrained from characterizing global governance as a new international relations paradigm to replace the existing paradigm of state sovereignty. Although it is clear that more and more anomalies cannot be explained by looking through Westphalian lenses, global governance is less a world view and more a halfway house that provides additional and necessary insights as we attempt to understand the contemporary world and identify new ways of approaching ongoing and future global threats.

In spite of the ringing rhetoric of "We the peoples" in the UN Charter's opening lines, the stark reality is that the world organization and other parts of the UN system and the Bretton Woods institutions are composed of states. While they remain the main actors on the world stage, states themselves and their creations in the form of the current generation of

IGOs are inadequate to meet many of the challenges of the twenty-first century. Indeed, this was a key assumption behind the reports prepared for the world organization's sixtieth anniversary in September 2005 by the High-level Panel on Threats, Challenges and Change and by the Secretary-General.[36] To use one example, the recent merging of development with security and human rights points toward a more holistic treatment of the UN's role in global governance that reflects the increasingly dense network of other institutions that facilitates the world organization's efforts to make a difference in international and global problem-solving.

Before going further, we should be clear about two terms. "International" is an adjective that refers to state-based or territory-based units. Hence, the North Atlantic Treaty Organization (NATO) is an international intergovernmental organization and Oxfam is an international nongovernmental organization; the former refers to state members whose geographical boundaries are defined, while the latter refers to an institution composed of individuals that operates across the boundaries of states. "Global" is an adjective that refers to universal and worldwide coverage. In this sense, the UN is both international and global and other institutions are international but not global. Many problems are global in reach but currently are defined as international in scope (that is, requiring cooperation from states and units that are incorporated in states).

Identifying and Diagnosing Problems

In this book we adopt a holistic approach to gaps in knowledge, norms, policies, institutions, and compliance. A critical hole in any of the five stages can cause the entire problem-solving endeavor to collapse. The United Nations plays four essential roles in its intellectual capacity of identifying and diagnosing problems: managing knowledge, developing norms, promulgating recommendations, and institutionalizing ideas.

Managing Knowledge

The world faces problems today that are global in scope and require multilateral efforts to solve them on a global basis. These problems simply could not have been imagined at the time of the signing of the UN Charter in San Francisco in June 1945. For example, the atomic age began with the bombing of Hiroshima and Nagasaki two months after the San Francisco conference that founded the UN. How to control the atomic genie now that it is out of the bottle has been a major item of concern to the international policy community ever since. Issues such as climate change and HIV/AIDS were unknown until decades later.

How is knowledge of new problems and issues acquired or created? How is it transmitted to the policy community? And how do solutions get formulated and adopted? The first step in eventually addressing a problem that goes beyond the capacity of states to solve is recognizing that a problem exists. The next step is collecting solid data that challenge the consensus about the nature of the problem in order to diagnose its causes; in short, explaining the problem. To stay with the medical metaphor, the final step is providing medicine and a prognosis—prescribing solutions.

A generation ago Raymond Aron, an influential French theorist, argued that "the *diplomat* and the *soldier* . . . *live* and *symbolise* international relations which, insofar as they are inter-state relations, concern diplomacy and war."[37] This mainstream understanding changed dramatically over the decades (beginning especially in the 1970s), and the United Nations—its member states, officials, accredited NGOs, and media contacts—began to identify and diagnose problems and keep them in the limelight. Today, multinational merchants, international financiers, World Bank technocrats, UN peacekeepers, and NGO humanitarian workers jostle for space alongside diplomats and soldiers on the increasingly crowded international stage.

Basic research is done in universities, not in the United Nations. Yet the UN is a knowledge-based and knowledge-management organization, and it has its own research unit called the United Nations University. Identifying issues and keeping them in front of reluctant governments are quintessential UN tasks. As Gert Rosenthal has summarized: "It is usually a cumulative process, where some seminal ideas which tend to be discussed among a very limited group of people sort of bursts into the public consciousness through media, through word of mouth, through documents. And all of a sudden, maybe two, three, five years after the document [comes] out, everyone is repeating some of its main points as if they were gospel."[38] The vehicles through which such idea-mongering occurs include expert groups, panels and study groups that include eminent persons, and of course the global ad hoc conferences that were especially prominent in the 1970s and 1990s.[39]

One underappreciated advantage of the United Nations is its capacity to convene groups and to mobilize power to help funnel knowledge from outside and ensure that it is discussed and disseminated among governments. UN-sponsored world conferences, summits of heads of government, and blue-ribbon commissions and panels have been used to frame issues, outline choices, make decisions; to set, even anticipate, the agenda; to frame the rules, including the rules for settling disputes; to pledge and mobilize resources; to implement collective decisions; and to monitor progress and recommend midterm corrections and adjustments. Once a threat or problem has been identified and diagnosed, the next step is to solidify a new norm of behavior. It is to this UN task that we now turn.

Developing Norms

Human social interaction is viewed through normative lenses, from bilateral relations between two individuals to relations between national leaders. Rules and norms help simplify choices; they impart rationality by specifying the factors that must be taken into account in the process of coming to a decision through deliberation and reflection. Moreover, laws and norms do more than just shape decisions; they permit human beings to pursue goals, challenge assertions, and justify actions.[40]

Once information has been collected and knowledge that a problem is serious enough to warrant attention by the international policy community has been acquired, new norms need to be articulated, disseminated, and institutionalized. For example, once it became known that HIV / AIDS was transmitted through unprotected sexual activity, health care workers and organizations promoted the norm of safe sex. Or as we gain information about the sexual activities of UN personnel deployed in the field, the norm of no sexual contact between them and local populations might be articulated by the UN Secretariat.

In spite of the obvious problems of accommodating the perspectives of 192 countries, the First UN is an essential forum for the expression and eventual coagulation of official views from around the planet on international norms. International society is not homogenous regarding human rights and humanitarian concerns, and no unifying normative architecture exists on this topic. The variations in norms attest to the existence of a polymorphic international society. This is why even though the concept of "Asian values" has been disruptive for human rights discourse (and one should not ignore the obvious self-serving nature of some official views), norms that purport to be "universal" require inputs from around the world and differences in views, priorities, and interpretation are to be expected. Similarly, in spite of the obvious problems of running a secretariat with a multitude of nationalities, cultures, languages, and administrative norms, the Second UN is also an ongoing bureaucratic experiment in opening the range of inputs to include views other than Anglo-American ones.[41]

The most effective form of regulating behavior is a system where rules (or laws) and norms converge, for example with regard to murder. In international relations, epochal shifts in the generally accepted standards of state behavior mean that institutions such as slavery and colonialism are today proscribed in law. Conversely, regulating behavior is most problematic when there is near-total dissonance in cases where a practice has been outlawed without a change in the underlying societal norm; two examples would be the dowry system and the caste system in India. The result is a total disconnect in which the law is continually flouted. This weakens the rule of law.

The reason for the dissonance lies primarily in different moral frameworks of social behavior. At the international level, one of the most likely arenas for normative dissonance is that of human rights, precisely because alternative moral frameworks exist that define and locate the rights and responsibilities of individuals, communities, and the state vis-à-vis one another. Again, international law has moved ahead of norms and practices in large parts of the world—examples include human rights norms against the honor killings that still take place in the Middle East, the caste and dowry deaths that are still common in South Asia, the continuing practice of female genital mutilation in Africa, and the flouting of international criminal justice by the United States.

The crucial question is how contested norms become institutionalized both within and among states. This involves a process of institutionalization at the national, regional, and global levels. International norms can be transmitted down into national politics when they are incorporated into domestic laws or into the policy preferences of political leaders. International norms can be integrated into domestic standards only through state structures. Diffusing international norms is not, therefore, about the state withering away. Indeed, the United Nations has promulgated norms with the consent of most member states with a view toward sustaining—not eroding—the prerogatives of sovereigns.

Formulating Policy Recommendations

Once norms begin to change and become widespread, a next step is to formulate a range of possibilities about how governments and their citizens and IGOs can change behavior. When an emerging norm comes close to becoming a universal norm, it is time to address specific approaches to problem-solving, to fill the policy gap. The policy stage refers to the statement of principles and actions that an organization is likely to take in the event of particular contingencies. Thus, UN policy might promote awareness about the gravity and causes of HIV/AIDS, encourage educational campaigns, and declare zero tolerance of sexual exploitation by UN peacekeepers. Clearly, as new problems emerge and new norms arise, they will highlight gaps in policy that also need attention. The UN's ability to consult widely plays a large part in its ability to formulate operational ideas—recommendations about specific policies, institutional arrangements, and regimes. This is a function that is in the job descriptions not only of member states but also of the Second UN, the staff of international secretariats, who are often complemented by trusted consultants, NGOs, and expert groups from the Third UN. The discussion of and dissemination of new norms often occurs in public forums and global conferences.[42]

Perhaps the best way to illustrate this process is to explore recent developments regarding a topic that is at the heart of global governance itself, namely civil society, to understand better how the UN plays this intellectual role. In February 2003, Secretary-General Kofi Annan established the Panel of Eminent Persons on United Nations–Civil Society Relations, chaired by the former president of Brazil, Fernando Henrique Cardoso. The panel took seriously the injunction to consult; they met with members of civil society, the private sector, parliamentarians, UN staff, and others in a series of meetings, workshops, and focus groups on three continents as well as at large international gatherings such as the WTO Ministerial Conference in Cancún, Mexico. In 2004 the panel issued its report, *We the Peoples: Civil Society, the UN and Global Governance.*

With a starting point that "governments alone cannot resolve today's global problems,"[43] the panel focused on the following trends: the widening democracy deficit in global governance, the growing capacity and influence of nonstate actors, and the rising power of global public opinion. The panel sought ways to ensure the UN's continued relevance to central issues of global governance.

Of course, civil society in the form of NGOs had been with the United Nations since the signing of the Charter—Article 71 provides for their participation. However, the role for NGOs was essentially peripheral at the

UN for many decades. During the Cold War, some states, especially those of the socialist bloc and Third World, routinely attempted to marginalize nonstate voices, which they perceived as threats to their sovereignty. By the twenty-first century, however, the situation had altered considerably and such voices were more numerous, diverse, and loud—hence much harder to ignore.

The report offered thirty concrete proposals for the evolution of the UN's role in the world. These included fostering processes that include multiple constituencies, investing more in partnerships with civil society; keeping the focus on the country level; including members of civil society in Security Council meetings; engaging with elected representatives; streamlining and depoliticizing the accreditation of civil society organizations; making recommendations for changes in UN staff, resources, and management to enhance the impact of the proposals; and providing moral leadership to urge coordinated approaches to global civil society, which "refers to the associations that individuals enter into voluntarily to advance their interests, ideas and ideologies."[44] The words of the report are pertinent for students of global governance and of the Third UN:

a) Multilateralism no longer concerns Governments alone but is now multifaceted, involving many constituencies; the United Nations must develop new skills to service this new way of working;

b) it must become an outward-looking or network organization, catalyzing the relationships needed to get strong results and not letting the traditions of its formal processes be barriers;

c) it must strengthen global governance by advocating universality, inclusion, participation and accountability at all levels; and

d) it must engage more systematically with world public opinion to become more responsive, to help shape public attitudes and to bolster support for multilateralism.[45]

Recommendations and proposals from many blue-ribbon panels and secretariats wither and die because member states, not the authors of the recommendations, are responsible for the next steps. However, such reports are sometimes under discussion when a crisis arises that facilitates action. As fate would have it, many of the recommendations from the 2004 Cardoso report were implemented almost immediately in the response to the Indian Ocean tsunami. The findings of the report met a demand. The relief effort showed the UN's ability to convene and foster multiconstituency processes, its ability to catalyze networks, and its capacity to exercise global leadership. However, now that the sense of urgency is gone, the recovery effort will be a more severe test of the world organization's ability to carry out the rest of the report's operational proposals concerning global governance and civil society.

The Cardoso report notes the "democratic deficit" and offers suggestions for increasing accountability through the United Nations. According to the report, the world organization works through two personas: "the norm-setter with its global deliberations and the practical fixer with its country operations."[46] Internally, the UN can encourage two-way communication between these two personas. Externally, policymaking tends to be top down, and the UN should encourage more communication from countries and civil society to the global deliberation level.

Finally, the Cardoso report pinpoints global public opinion as an emerging and powerful force in setting priorities and shaping policies.[47] While this is a positive development, public opinion still lacks the mechanisms to ensure accountability, transparency, and responsiveness. In particular, global public opinion lacks reliable sources of information. While the UN has been a leader in generating ideas, norms, and recommendations, it has been less successful in competing for time in the mass media, particularly in the United States. The Internet has made the communications part of the UN's job easier; information is now readily available and cheaper to transmit. But too often recommendations remain in reports and filing cabinets rather than on the desks of parliamentarians and decision makers.

Institutionalizing Ideas

Institutions are another example of the impact of ideas. Six-and-a-half decades into the UN's history, multiple global institutions are working on many key issue areas. Actors in world politics can and do cooperate, and they do so more often than they engage in conflict. The problems involved in cooperation include difficulties due to the lack of reliable information about what other actors are doing. Actors form institutions to mitigate collective action problems by sharing information, reducing transaction costs, providing incentives for concessions, providing mecha-nisms for dispute resolution, and establishing processes for making deci-sions. Institutions can facilitate such problem-solving even though they do not have any coercive powers. In particular, intergovernmental insti-tutions can increase the number of productive interactions among their member states; this in turn can help build confidence and bridges for other relations. Once they are created (and because they promise benefits in one arena of technical cooperation), organizations formed by states can sow the seeds of additional cooperation—in short, they can take on a personal-ity and life of their own.

John Ruggie has explained that "international regimes have been defined as social institutions around which actor expectations converge in a given area of international relations"; these regimes create "an inter-subjective framework of meaning."[48] They consist of accepted principles, norms, and policies. Regimes are important because material power alone cannot predict the type of international order created. Ruggie argues that change can come from shifts in power or from shared social purpose (or sense of legitimacy) and that most change is gradual, consisting of a change in rules and procedures, rather than changes in norms and prin-ciples. He writes that regimes enhance continuity because the normative framework of regimes may remain stable even when the power distribu-tion changes. Robert Keohane explains that just as with more formal insti-tutions, "international regimes alter the relative costs of transactions."[49]

State policymaking processes have been internationalized and globalized—meaning that individuals, NGOs, and companies are involved in lobbying, gathering information, and other forms of participation. Although our focus is on global policymaking and universal institutions, this generalization applies not just to UN member states but also to virtu-ally every kind of professional association.

However, problems involved with collective action have not been eliminated. While we have witnessed more practice in international coop-eration, globalization has introduced additional layers of complexity and potential for conflict. In our framing, the creation of institutions requires that the knowledge, normative, and policymaking gaps be at least par-tially filled. When they are effective, however, institutions also help fill existing gaps—in other words, they have recursive effects. They can also uncover new ones. For example, an institution can gather statistical data, which can help fill the knowledge gap. Based on new information, new

. norms might develop, leading to new policies and institutions, but then a new gap or problem appears (or is uncovered)—for example, how to put a value on the informal sector, where many women in developing countries work—which then necessitates additional work.

Judith Goldstein and Robert O. Keohane explain that ideas can affect policy in three ways: by becoming road maps that point actors in the right direction, by affecting actors' choices of strategies, and by becoming embedded in institutions.[50] An overview of UN history suggests that the source of ideas to fill international institutional gaps is more likely to be states and intergovernmental organizations than civil society. Institutions can extend the life of an idea because they can outlast the individuals who first had the idea. And institutions that attack global problems require substantial financing and backing, which makes them the kind of concrete step that governments can initiate as an indication that they are taking an issue seriously. Once in existence, institutions are staffed by people and interact with entities with a vested interest in their continuance.

Institutions embody ideas but can also provide a platform for challenging existing norms and received wisdom about the best approaches to problem solving. For instance, the generalized system of preferences for less industrialized countries—which was hardly an item on the conventional free-trade agenda—grew from both the UN Conference on Trade and Development (UNCTAD) and GATT. The need to find ways to supply inexpensive drugs to AIDS patients in developing countries is now on the agenda of the World Intellectual Property Organization (WIPO).

However, institutions can also become a place where ideas get trapped and fossilize. Enrique Iglesias, for one, described as "ECLA's Talmud" the ideas about protecting infant industries and commodities that Raúl Prebisch had promulgated and that had outlasted their utility.[51] As former director of the International Institute for Labour Studies Robert Cox explains, "It is the rigidity of existing institutions that leads to the idea that if you want to start something new, you have to create another institution. . . . An institution that has become successful in its routine becomes, in some ways, a prisoner of its success and goes on doing the same thing in the same way because it has worked. But if it no longer is really dealing effectively with the issues that you can now perceive, then maybe it needs to be changed."[52] Former executive secretary of the UN Economic Commission for Africa (ECA) Adebayo Adedeji extends the caution: "If all ideas were institutionalized, you would have too many institutions around. There is no doubt that once you establish an institution, in this society of ours in the world in which we live today, they are like cemeteries. You can't remove the graves."[53]

That said, the institutionalization of governance through the UN system and such other multilateral organizations as the European Union, the Organization of the Petroleum Exporting Countries (OPEC), NATO, and the Economic Community of West African States (ECOWAS) is quite advanced in comparison to nineteenth-century public international unions.

Once knowledge has been acquired, norms have been articulated, and policies have been formulated, an existing institution can oversee the implementation and monitoring of the new norms and policies. The outbreak of swine flu in Mexico in April 2009 demonstrated once again the importance of an international institution capable of and responsible for global monitoring. "After all, it really is all of humanity that is under threat during a pandemic,"[54] said WHO director-general Margaret Chan when she increased the threat level to orange at the end of April. While the strain of the virus ended up being less virulent than feared, the WHO warning system is based on how far and quickly a virus spreads, not on its lethality. The H1N1 virus quickly spread across the planet. Following the outbreak of SARS in 2003, states adopted rules in 2005 that authorized the WHO director-general to demand information about threats to global health rather than merely requesting cooperation from indulgent states. At the same time, one of the main reasons why the swine flu did not become a deadly killer in large numbers around the globe was the swiftness and scale of response by Mexican public health authorities at the epicenter of the outbreak. They quickly shut down schools, businesses, and sporting events in a successful effort to quarantine the infected population, provide medication, and test suspected cases. That is, the current ideal partnership for "global governance" consists of vigorous national action and monitoring, surveillance, and precautionary advisories by global public authorities.

But if the problems that generated the new norms and policies are distinctive enough from other problems, are cohesive in their own cluster of attributes, and are of sufficient gravity and scale, the international community of states might well consider creating a new IGO (or hiving off part of an existing one) dedicated to addressing this problem area. This is what happened when the Joint UN Programme on HIV/AIDS was set up in Geneva in 1996. A resolution of the WHO's World Health Assembly outlined the need for it in 1993, and the Economic and Social Council (ECOSOC) endorsed the idea the following year in resolution 1994/24. The program is meant to be the main advocate for global action on HIV/AIDS; its mandate is to lead, strengthen, and support the worldwide response aimed at preventing the transmission of the disease, provide care and support to those suffering from it, reduce the vulnerability of individuals and communities to it, and alleviate the impact of the epidemic.

Complications and shortcomings might appear during the implementation of a new policy. The zero tolerance policy toward sexual exploitation by UN soldiers has been in existence for some time, yet the problem has continued.[55] Inevitably, even with full knowledge, adequate norms, and policy and operations to back them up, some individuals or groups will always challenge and defy the norms and laws of the broader society and community. This is why all societies have mechanisms in place to detect violators and outlaws, subject them to trial, and punish convicted offenders. The goal is both punishment of outlaws so justice is seen to be done and deterrence of future violations. For these goals to be achieved, the modalities and procedures for enforcing compliance with community norms and laws must be efficient, effective, and credible.

The UN's Ideational Role:
This Book and the UNIHP Series

While two books in this project's series deal with preventive diplomacy and human security, UNIHP's main focus has been on economic and social development (including human rights). We, however, approach the notion of global governance and the UN's role in this topic across the entire gamut of the organization's activities.[56] This volume is thus a different kind of synthetic volume in the project's book series. It is framed by the anomalies (or disconnects, disjunctures, or gaps) between perceived problems and threats and readily available solutions. It includes both socioeconomic as well as military-security dimensions of global governance and the UN's intellectual contributions in these areas.

In the chapters that follow, we discuss the UN's intellectual and operational roles across selected issues. For us, the relevant ideas about global governance concern attempts to think through collective efforts to identify, understand, or address global problems that individual states cannot solve. Not all intellectual efforts since 1945 qualify; if they did, we would be writing a history of every idea in the world organization's vocabulary and every acronym in its alphabet soup.

Two important features distinguish global governance from earlier UN thinking about collective responses to international peace and security, human rights, and development. First, when the UN was founded and during the organization's early years, many saw international cooperation and law as more effective than unilateral efforts and the law of the jungle. But it was still typical for a state to solve most problems on its own or at least to insulate itself from many problems that emanated from outside its borders. While it is true that high politics and events such as the assassination of Archduke Francis Ferdinand and Adolf Hitler's occupation of the Sudetenland engulfed much of the world, many other problems could be addressed by single states. Eradicating malaria within a geographical area and preventing those with malaria from entering that area thus is different from halting money-laundering by terrorists or acid rain, or what Kofi Annan called "problems without passports."[57] Over time, starting in the 1970s, the reality of interdependence has meant that a growing number of problems are clearly recognized as without passports and, as such, require the globalization of the policymaking process—finding solutions without passports.

Second, earlier conceptual efforts emphasized state-centric notions and only grudgingly admitted the presence and capacities of other actors. But starting in the 1980s (and earlier in some cases), the UN recognized that nonstate actors (both civil society and market-oriented ones) were growing in importance and reach. It began to embrace them more systematically, and they became an increasingly integral part of comprehensive solutions that the UN and many of its member states either promulgated or actually undertook. It has become commonplace to recognize, for instance, that international human rights monitoring would not function without Human Rights Watch and Amnesty International.[58] Similarly, the UN considers foreign direct investment, which now dwarfs the amount of official development assistance (ODA) that comes from states or international institutions, in its statistics and development programs.

Moreover, it became increasingly difficult to maintain that the existence of problems without passports or the increase in nonstate actors and their influence were exceptional. For one-off problems, ad hoc solutions are acceptable. But several decades after the recognition of many types of interdependence, cobbled-together solutions and ad hoc coalitions seem increasingly tenuous. Today's recurrent problems obviously require predictable and institutionalized responses. This volume tells the story of collective efforts to generate such responses.

The UN's traditional role of improving government policy and formulating intergovernmental policies thus is giving way to new emphases. In view of the increasingly transnational character of many problems and the importance of nonstate actors, the UN's conceptualization of global governance has expanded to encompass both transnational market forces and civil society as a regular bill of fare instead of an occasional snack.

As a result, the operative concept is improving governance for the globe and dropping any pretense of moving toward world government. The strict hierarchy of international action involving states is being replaced by global efforts that involve both states and nonstate actors. Paradoxically, the proliferation of actors and problems enhances the potential role of the United Nations as a clearinghouse and coordinator even if it remains very distinctly not a world government.

As an "intellectual actor" on the topic of global governance, the UN has made three distinct contributions: identifying and diagnosing problems, developing norms, and formulating recommendations. Somewhat less successfully institutionalizing ideas. The book discusses how the UN has filled (or not filled) these functions in various historical cases for our five types of gaps: in knowledge, norms, policies, institutions, and compliance.

For each of these intellectual roles, we endeavor to identify the roles of the three United Nations as an arena for state decision making, for the professional secretariats, and for civil society. And we ask a set of questions: How does the United Nations and the current system of global governance compare with national models? How substantial are the gaps for the globe's current capacities to address life-threatening problems?

Our unfinished journey begins in part 1 with the UN's intellectual contributions to international security and then continues in parts 2 and 3 with its contributions to development and human rights.

PART 1

International Security

2

The Use of Force: War, Collective Security, and Peace Operations

- Antecedents: Taming the Use of Military Force
- Knowledge Gaps: Still as Many Questions as Answers
- Normative Gaps: Trying to Regulate the Use of Force
- Policy Gaps: Ad-Hocism Has Its Advantages
- Institutional Gaps: Lacunae Filled, Lacunae Remaining
- Compliance Gaps: The Limitations of Chapter VII
- Culture of Prevention and the Role of International Commissions
- Multiple Levels and Multiple Actors in Global Governance: The Contemporary Reality
- Conclusion: Looking Ahead

Given the UN's central mandate to maintain international peace and security and its creation from the ashes of World War II, it is appropriate that this book's first substantive chapter begin with the topic of security. Contrary to general perceptions, the number of conflicts between and within states, the number of terrorist incidents, and the overall number of people killed in battle has declined in recent years.[1] During the 40-year "Long Peace" of the Cold War,[2] the number of armed conflicts within states increased each decade until the early 1990s but then began to drop. By the end of that decade, wars and lesser armed conflicts had declined by a third to a half, depending on the definitions and the dataset chosen. The cost in lives has declined to an even greater degree.[3] One of the main explanations for these trends is the success of the UN's efforts to fulfill its security mandate.

This chapter begins with a brief overview of important developments before the birth of the UN and over the UN's lifetime as a prelude to a

discussion of the five gaps. It then explores the recent emphasis on prevention rather than reaction and the contribution by two international
commissions. A concluding section discusses the multiple layers of actors
and actions needed for the contemporary global governance of the use of
force.

Antecedents: Taming the Use of Military Force

Establishing the UN was a small but symbolically crucial step in taming the use of force as a means of settling quarrels among different members of the human family scattered across the globe. Violence is endemic
in human relations at all levels of social organization. War between states
has been a feature of the current international system since its inception
in 1648, following the Peace of Westphalia. But military aggression is an
affront to international norms regarding peace and security.

War has traditionally performed certain functions in international
relations from three points of view. From the perspective of states, it has
served as an instrument of policy, a means to a desired end. Thus, in
Vietnam during the 1960s, the opposing sides shared one belief: that war
was the most effective instrument for solving the dispute. From the perspective of the international system, war has determined the shape of
the international order. It has been the arbiter of the creation, survival,
and elimination of actors in the system; of the ebb and flow of political
frontiers; and of the rise and decline of regimes. From the viewpoint of
international society, war is both a manifestation of disorder that threatens the survival of the society and an instrument to enforce community
values and goals. In the first sense, war is dysfunctional; in the second
sense, it is the functional equivalent of a municipal police force.

The problem of peace and order is not new. At the Congress of Vienna
in 1814, major European powers established the Concert of Europe system, transforming a military alliance for the single purpose of defeating
Napoleon into a longer-term loose political organization whose goal was
to prevent one power from dominating Europe. The Concert of Europe
was an innovative attempt to construct new machinery to maintain the
peace among the great powers.

The Hague Conferences of 1899 and 1907 signaled the broadening of
international relations, in terms of both the number of participants and the
international agenda. They both pointed to an emergent extra-European
international system in which the lesser powers would demand a say. In
addition, with their emphasis upon mediation, conciliation, and inquiry,

the conferences demonstrated a rationalistic and legalistic approach to international disputes.

The outbreak of world war in 1914 and 1939 discredited the old balance-of-power system that relied on the central role of the great powers. The two major international organizations of the twentieth century were created after world wars. People who were horrified by the destructiveness of modern war created the League of Nations and the United Nations to avoid a repetition of such catastrophes.

By signing the League Covenant, member states signified their "acceptance of obligations not to resort to war" (Preamble). To that end, they agreed to submit disputes to arbitration or judicial settlement and to refrain from going to war until three months after arbitration or adjudication (Article 12).

The League was prepared to condemn Japanese aggression in Manchuria in 1931, a significant normative advance even though there was no prospect for any collective action. The Italian invasion of Ethiopia in 1935 presented the League with its moment of greatest triumph: for the first time, the international community of states, acting through institutionalized channels, condemned aggression, identified the aggressor, and imposed sanctions. For the first time, the ideal that the international community of states can take joint coercive measures against outlaws was advanced. However, Ethiopia stands as the symbol of the League's failure to realize these high hopes because Italy secured its ends through the means of its choice—forceful military occupation.

An important step in the development of the idea that an international community has both the right and a responsibility to prevent armed conflict between its member states was the Pact of Paris of 1928 (also known as the Kellogg-Briand Pact), in which signatories condemned "recourse to war for the solution of international controversies, and renounce[d] it, as an instrument of national policy in relations with one another."[4] The facts that the pact was not enforceable and that the signatories insisted on qualifications—for example, the extension of self-defense to include a state's colonies—eroded the practical significance of the agreement. Yet the declaration of principle, that war was henceforth to be treated as an illegitimate method of dispute settlement, was of symbolic significance even if it fell well short of being a contractual obligation.[5]

Although the League of Nations failed to prevent another world war in 1939, the UN resurrected the cause of securing peace from the ashes of World War II. The fact that the UN was closely modeled on the League was testimony to the fact that while the League had failed, people still had faith in the *idea* of an umbrella international organization to oversee world peace and cooperation. U.S. president Abraham Lincoln spoke of the "scourge of war,"[6] an apt description that found its way into the UN Charter, the Preamble of which begins with the clarion call: "We the peoples of the United Nations determined to save succeeding generations from the scourge of war, which twice in our lifetime has brought untold sorrow to mankind."

The UN seeks to replace the balance of power with a community of power and represents the dream of a world governed by reason and the rule of law. The UN vision replaced the League's efforts to abolish war with a Charter that included a provision that states could use military force collectively. The intention was that negotiations and the rule of law would replace the unilateral use of force and that collective security would guarantee the sovereignty and territorial integrity of all states. The Charter invested the Security Council with the authority to authorize military action to restore the peace, and only when the Security Council failed to act were individual countries allowed to use force in self-defense.

Thus, collective decision making was the means of outlawing war and mobilizing the international community of states to deter, apprehend, and punish international lawbreakers. Especially significant were the Charter provisions that outlawed the use of force in Article 2 (4) unless it was authorized by the Security Council and that outlawed the use of force except in self-defense as spelled out in Articles 39–51. A cynic will be quick to indicate that this article is breached as frequently as it is respected, but the creation of a legal basis for calling miscreants (other than the five permanent members and their close allies) to task is a step forward.

However, the persistent reality of numerous interstate, transregional, and internal armed conflicts; the frequent collapse of peace agreements and relapse into armed conflict; and the continual rise of fresh conflicts discourages pacifists and conflict managers. While the Charter's version of collective security has never been realized—with the possible exceptions of actions taken during the Korean War and the 1991 Gulf War—and the autonomous forces required to keep the peace have not materialized, nonetheless the United Nations has made important contributions. Unarmed UN military observers and lightly armed UN peacekeepers have made a difference since their first deployment in the 1948 Middle East War and the 1956 Suez crisis, respectively. Both continue to maintain the peace in conflict-ridden parts of the globe where neutral and impartial armed forces are required. The UN has continued to adapt peace operations to include important multifunctional duties, from monitoring elections to humanitarian action. In short, the absence of a world military force to ensure the peace has not meant that elements of global governance are not present.

One more antecedent is critical for an understanding of the intellectual history of the United Nations with respect to warfare. The organization's single most important and consequential member is the United States, and its single most important and influential group is the European Union. The political culture of the respective attitudes of these two entities toward warfare, which have been conditioned by sharply contrasting historical experiences and collective memories, is a source of occasional friction in UN diplomatic circles. While other major twentieth-century combatant states suffered heavy military and civilian casualties, American military casualties were surprisingly light and its civilian deaths negligible. While Britain, France, and Germany lost between 1 and 2 million soldiers each in World War I, the United States lost fewer than 120,000. While China, France, Germany, and the Soviet Union lost between 2 and 11 million soldiers in World War II, only about 420,000 U.S. soldiers died. The total U.S. civilian deaths from the two world wars combined was less than 2,000, compared to the deaths of half a million Yugoslavs and between 2 and 16 million Germans, Poles, residents of the Soviet Union, and Chinese.[7] Robert J. Rummel estimates that 217 million lives have been lost in wars, pogroms, genocides, and mass murders during the twentieth century.[8] And of course this figure does not include the many more uncounted who have lived diminished lives as refugees, internally displaced persons, detainees, widows and widowers, orphans, and paupers.[9]

The human and collective national toll of these cold statistics is worth a moment's reflection. For victors and defeated alike in Europe, wars meant displacement, destruction, deprivation, privation, invasion, occupation, and mass murder. Europeans have a shared memory of war as a terrible human-made calamity. Would France really want to repeat its "victories" in the two world wars? Moreover, most countries were increasingly militarized during the two world wars and their sense of society and community badly fractured, as Tony Judt tells us: "States and societies seized . . . by Hitler or Stalin . . . experienced not just occupation and exploitation but degradation and corrosion of the laws and norms of civil society. . . . Far from guaranteeing security, the state itself became the leading source of insecurity." That is, he continues, "War—total war—has been the crucial antecedent condition for mass criminality in the modern era."[10]

By contrast, the United States today "is the only advanced democracy where public figures glorify and exalt the military."[11] This partially explains the dramatically contrasting moods of triumphalism in the United States and relief in Western Europe at the end of the Cold War. And it is at least a partial explanation for the UN's failures to bring human warfare to an end. Its most powerful member state, which has virtual control over many security issues, believes in the efficacy and morality of the use of force while rejecting that same logic when others use it.

Knowledge Gaps: Still as Many Questions as Answers

Armed conflict is as old as the human race. How can there still be holes in our knowledge about it? By knowledge gap we mean either one or both of two interrelated shortfalls: gaps in the empirical base of facts and in the linkages between events and decisions (correlations), on the one hand; and gaps in understandings of the causes and consequences of armed conflict, on the other. Both types of gaps characterize our ignorance about war and peace.

Not everyone agrees about what constitutes war, a war casualty, aggression, self-defense, preemption, preventive war, terrorism, hot pursuit, and war crimes. Was Israel's 2006 war against Lebanon waged in self-defense in response to an unprovoked attack by Hezbollah? Was it a preplanned escalation waiting for an opportune moment? Was it a war of aggression because the scale was far out of proportion to Hezbollah's provocation?[12]

Even statistical methodology is highly disputed. How can one get an accurate assessment of the total casualties in Iraq since 2003? Should "excess deaths" form part of the casualty count under the catchall phrase "conflict-related" deaths? When an independent, non-UN team carried out a survey in Iraq after the 2003 invasion to determine the total casualty figure through the standard methodology of "excess deaths" (as opposed to deaths that were the direct result of fighting) and published the results in the respected medical journal *The Lancet,* London and Washington severely criticized the findings.[13] The media then either stopped using these figures or qualified them by describing them as controversial. Yet the media reported a comparable study in January 2006—also published in *The Lancet*—that estimated the total death toll in the eight years of war in the Democratic Republic of the Congo as 3.9 million (currently the figure is 5.5 million).[14] Only the recklessly courageous dare to enter the political and emotional minefield of trying to get an accurate measure of the number of Jews killed in the Holocaust: significantly downsizing the total could be career-threatening in the West while increasing the total could provoke hostility in parts of the Islamic world. Will Japan, Korea, and China ever agree on the number of people killed by Japanese imperial forces in East Asia in the first half of the twentieth century?

There is no disagreement about the existence of the long cold peace in Europe after 1945. But the explanation for this is variously ascribed to nuclear deterrence, the democratization of Western Europe (the democratic peace thesis), or the integration of Western Europe. Even if the explanation lies in a combination of these three factors, analysts will still differ on the relative weight of each explanatory variable.

Interpretations, explanations, and narratives about all these examples are anything but free of subjective influences, both individual and national-societal. The past continues to shape the present through the intense emotions people have experienced during particular historical episodes and events.

And what about examining types of wars? In 1945 the literature focused on interstate conflict, not on intrastate or nonstate conflict. By the 1980s, the issue of civil war was becoming more pressing.

To build peace, we must understand the nature and causes of conflict. Microtheories trace the causes of aggression to individual behavior: particular personality traits, the tendency toward cognitive rigidity by key decision-makers in times of crisis, the displacement of frustration-induced hostility to foreign targets, an innate biological propensity to engage in aggressive behavior, and socialization into ritual aggressive behavior.[15] The attempt to root war in human behavior falls into the trap of biological pessimism that rests on five propositions: human beings have inherited a tendency to make war from animal ancestors; violent behavior is genetically determined; aggressive behavior has acquired an evolutionary ascendancy over other types of behavior; the human brain is violent; and war is caused by human "instinct." The leap from an analysis of individual behavior—which exhibits good as well as evil traits—to an explanation of the group phenomenon of war is reductionist but nonetheless widespread.

Macrotheories of conflict postulate an even more bewildering array of causes: arms races, alliances, balance-of-power politics, military-industrial complexes, fascism, capitalism, communism, military dictatorships, militant religions, even the dialectics of international crises. The most elegant and parsimonious explanation of warfare is international anarchy—that is, the absence of restraints upon unbridled national behavior.

The plurality of possible causes indicates a multiplicity of potential remedies: because we do not know which remedy will work and how effective various remedies will be, we try them all. Historians,[16] political theorists,[17] political philosophers,[18] and policy analysts study issues of war and peace from different perspectives and with a variety of methodological tools.[19]

The United Nations has not been at the forefront of advancing knowledge on the subject of war and peace. If we think of just a few of the iconic long-running and protracted conflicts—in Kashmir, Palestine, Cyprus—it becomes immediately obvious how deep national passions and pride run and how difficult it is for the world organization to study or discuss them dispassionately. Politics—rather than science and scholarship—are likely to guide the UN's approach to generating knowledge about conflict. Most key analytical studies have been carried out by social scientists in universities and other research institutions. Their objective is to generate theories about patterns of violent international behavior that can be tested and refined and thus become commonly accepted as valid.

Conscious of its limitations, the UN sometimes commissions or encourages others to undertake studies that will fill critical gaps. For example, the organization encouraged the International Peace Institute to undertake a major project on economic agendas in civil wars.[20] More recently, aiming to combine the authoritative presentation of the most reliable and current data held inside the UN Secretariat with analytical capability and editorial independence, the UN has collaborated with New York University to produce annual reviews of UN and non-UN peace operations.[21]

The inaugural *Human Security Report* was a mix of original research and the collation and synthesis of existing knowledge about civil wars and other forms of political violence based on an extensive array of research from around the world. It concluded that a prima facie case can be made that the much-maligned UN—despite inappropriate mandates for peace operations, inadequate resources, lack of political commitment by key players, and many other problems—has made a difference in reducing the risk of war. Some of its information came from inside the United Nations. Its lead author, Andrew Mack, was a scholar but also had been the first director of the Strategic Planning Unit within the Executive Office of the Secretary-General, which was established in 1998 by Kofi Annan. And much of its analyses and recommendations were targeted at the UN policy community.[22]

Normative Gaps: Trying to Regulate the Use of Force

Until the end of World War I, which was prematurely labeled the "war to end all wars," violent conflict was an accepted part of the international system and had its own distinctive rules, norms, and etiquette. In that Hobbesian world, the only protection against aggression was countervailing power, which increased both the cost of victory and the risk of failure. Since 1945, the UN has spawned a corpus of law designed to stigmatize aggression and create a robust norm against it. Over the decades, the norm of using peaceful rather than forceful means to resolve conflicts between states has become firmly entrenched. It relies on the concept that each member of the international community of states has a stake in avoiding war and that this justifies its involvement in bilateral disputes between member states.

The techniques used to peacefully settle disputes (Chapter VI of the Charter) range from bilateral negotiations between the disputants to formal adjudication by third parties. Chapter VII of the Charter provides military teeth to enforce collective decisions when the five permanent members of the Security Council agree (or at least do not stand in the way) and a total of at least nine of the fifteen members agree. A multitude of additional actors works to delegitimize the resort to war as a means of solving internal and international disputes; this group includes individual states, coalitions of states, civil society organizations, and non-UN international organizations.

That most people and countries sought a Security Council imprimatur before specifically authorizing the use of force against Iraq in 2003 as a prerequisite for their support for the war is testament to the norm against wars that are not waged in self-defense or under UN authority.[23] This legitimacy function remains a substantial political asset and one to which we will return in other contexts as well.

BOX 2.1. The Difficulty of Reaching Consensus about the Nature, Causes, and Consequences of Major International Events: The Case of Iraq

Under modern conditions, the real-time access journalists and academics have during international events is greater than ever before in history. The abundance of factual information and evidence notwithstanding, the "knowledge" bases—a broadly shared interpretation of why, what, how, and with what result—often remain as fiercely contested as ever. In the case of the Iraq war, major disagreement exists about three key issues: the reasons for the war; what the immediate, long-term, and broader consequences of the war will be; and what impact the war will have on the UN's role in maintaining international peace and security.

Cause of the Iraq War

Many years after the U.S.-led invasion of Iraq, there is still confusion about the mix of personal, geopolitical, and military-technological motives for going to war. The George W. Bush administration gave six reasons for initiating the 2003 war on Iraq: the threat posed by the proliferation of weapons of mass destruction; the threat of international terrorism; the need to establish a beachhead of democratic freedoms in the Middle East; the need to promote the rule of law; the need to bring Saddam Hussein to justice for the atrocities committed by his regime; and the duty to be the enforcer of international decisions.

Critics in the United States and elsewhere pointed to other possible reasons for the Bush administration's decision to wage war: the U.S. need for oil; geopolitics; the influence of the Israeli lobby; the need to test new high-tech weapons; George W. Bush's need for revenge for Saddam Hussein's failed attempt to assassinate his father; and the need of senior officials who had served in the George H. W. Bush administration for revenge against Saddam for his actions in the first Gulf War.

Consequences of the Iraq War

The Iraqi people are free of Saddam Hussein's tyranny—that is a decided benefit. But the balance sheet must also include the damaging effects of the war.[1] No consensus exists about the extent or severity of these effects, which include the number of casualties among coalition soldiers, Iraqi insurgents, and Iraqi civilians; the impact on international norms about wars of choice as an instrument of unilateral state policy; the relationship between the UN and the United States; trans-Atlantic relations; the impact on European unity; the toll on the role of the United States as a global leader; the impact on the credibility of the United States in the Islamic world; the impact of the credibility of the United States as a champion of human rights, civil liberties, and political freedoms; the erosion of U.S. soft power; the polarization of U.S. society; the erosion of the credibility of the media; the impact on the international space in which humanitarian actors can operate; the degree to which the war has enriched and empowered Russia and Iran; the degree to which the war has exacerbated the Sunni-Shia divide across the Middle East; and the degree to which the war has intensified the threat of international terrorism.[2]

Iraq's Implications for the UN

Four opinions about the UN's actions regarding the Iraq war exist. President George W. Bush famously implied that by refusing to support the war, the UN had in effect rendered itself irrelevant.[3] A second group countered with the point that the vigor of the worldwide debate showed how central the United Nations still is to the great issues of war and peace, noting also that the failure of the United States to obtain a UN resolution authorizing the war robbed the war of legitimacy and legality. A third group that was comprised of strict constructionists argued that the Security Council had worked as the Charter was intended—that is, when one of the P-5 disagrees, no decision is possible or desirable. A fourth group went even further, insisting that if the Security Council had been bribed and bullied into authorizing an unjustified war, the UN would have been complicit in a war of aggression. So the United Nations—First, Second, and Third—was powerless to make the regime in Baghdad or the administration in Washington behave according to the rules. Alternatively, it could be argued that it worked exactly as it was supposed to and even that it continued to occupy the high ground.[4]

1. The damage the war has wrought is discussed in more detail in Ramesh Thakur, *The United Nations, Peace and Security: From Collective Security to The Responsibility to Protect* (Cambridge: Cambridge University Press, 2006), 222–243.

2. National Intelligence Estimate, *The Terrorist Threat to the US Homeland* (Washington, D.C.: Government Printing Office, July 2007).

3. See David E. Sanger and Elisabeth Bumiller, "U.S. Will Ask U.N. to State Hussein Has Not Disarmed," *New York Times,* 14 February 2003, available at http://www.nytimes.com/2003/02/14/international/middleeast/14IRAQ.html (accessed 11 August 2009). See also President George W. Bush's speech before the UN General Assembly on 12 September 2002; transcript available at http://www.cbsnews.com/stories/2002/09/12/national/main521781.shtml (accessed 11 August 2009).

4. See Thomas G. Weiss, "The International Political Costs of the Iraq War," in *Balance Sheet: The Iraq War and U.S. National Security,* ed. John S. Duffield and Peter J. Dombrowski (Palo Alto, Calif.: Stanford University Press, 2009), 106–131.

Policy Gaps: Ad-Hocism Has Its Advantages

The world organization's overarching policy goal is securing international peace, first by preventing the use of military force as an instrument of unilateral state policy and second by requiring UN member states to use military force when the Security Council directs them to do so in response to a threat to international peace and security. The trend toward narrowing the permissible range of justification for a unilateral resort to force has been matched by the movement to broaden the range of international instruments available to states for settling their disputes by means other than war.

Given that the attainment of a reliable system of collective security is not in the foreseeable future, the UN's instrument of choice for avoiding and containing conflict in the contemporary world is peacekeeping. Terms like "peacekeeping," "peace support operations," and "peace operations" are used generically to refer to missions and operations that fall short of military combat between clearly recognizable enemies. Peacekeeping has been one of the most visible manifestations of the UN's role in international peace and security—indeed, it is one of the most important of the world organization's policy inventions.

Peacekeeping is a surprisingly good example of the two-track advances in global governance that we postulate in this book. The first advance is *policy adaptations* to cope with new and unexpected challenges and requirements within the existing broad policy framework, the equivalent of auxiliary hypotheses designed to reinforce the existing paradigm of state sovereignty rather than replace it. The second advance is *policy innovations* to cope with challenges that cannot be accommodated within the existing framework but require a fresh approach, the equivalent of a new paradigm that emerges to explain major anomalies.

As is commonly observed, the word "peacekeeping" does not appear in the Charter and does not fit conceptually elsewhere in that document. Thus, peacekeeping is often jocularly referred to as being grounded in "Chapter VI and a half." Evolving in the gray zone between the two categories of pacific settlement of disputes (Chapter VI) and collective enforcement (Chapter VII), peacekeeping grew side by side with preventive diplomacy as practiced and articulated by Secretary-General Dag Hammarskjöld.[24] The United Nations aimed to keep new conflicts outside the sphere of confrontations between the West and the Soviet bloc during the Cold War. The technique of preventive diplomacy was to be used to forestall the competitive intrusion of these rival power blocs into armed conflicts that were either the result of or the potential cause of a power vacuum in the Third World. Preventive diplomacy was a policy designed to contain a peripheral war, to achieve a kind of disengagement before the fact. It was implemented by inserting a thin wedge of UN soldiers in blue helmets between belligerents.

One of the originators of the UN Emergency Force (UNEF) in the Sinai, then Canadian foreign minister Lester Pearson, aptly characterized a UN peacekeeping force as "an intermediate technique between merely passing resolutions and actually fighting."[25] Pearson worked closely with Hammarskjöld to resolve the Suez crisis in 1956 (and was awarded the Nobel Peace Prize for his efforts). More relevantly for our present purposes, Hammarskjöld quickly wrote the principles that were to guide this uncharted type of UN operation, and those notes stand the test of time for defining the essential points of peacekeeping as the characteristic UN policy for managing interstate conflicts. On 4 November 1956, the General Assembly asked him to produce a plan for UNEF within forty-eight hours. He submitted a plan the same day,[26] and the assembly adopted it on the following day. In a follow-up report two days later, he proposed that the force be under UN command and be comprised of troops from countries other than the council's permanent members and that its main mission be to secure and supervise the cessation of hostilities. It would not be "a military force controlling the territory in which it was stationed."[27] In other words, although they were made up of military soldiers, UN peacekeeping troops were prohibited from using military force to secure UN objectives.[28]

More than two-thirds of UN member states have contributed personnel to UN peacekeeping operations since that time, suggesting a burden-sharing and consensus about peacekeeping forces that could not have been predicted when the mechanism was invented in 1956. In 2008, approximately 120,000 UN peacekeepers (soldiers, police officers, and civilian personnel) from 118 countries—over half the total UN membership—were deployed in eighteen missions around the world.[29]

The United Nations thus has considerable experience with peacekeeping, and the organization has learned over the years.[30] Awareness of the conditions for success has grown. The tenets of classical UN peacekeeping came under a sustained challenge with the end of the Cold War, and in 2000 Secretary-General Kofi Annan appointed a high-level international panel to make recommendations for changes in UN peacekeeping.

The so-called Brahimi report that resulted was unusual in the candor of its analysis and recommendations.[31] It came to the sound overall conclusion that "when the United Nations does send its forces to uphold the peace, they must be prepared to confront the lingering forces of war and violence with the ability and determination to defeat them." In the final analysis, "no amount of good intentions can substitute for the fundamental ability to project credible force if complex peacekeeping, in particular, is to succeed."[32] Mandates have to be guided by pragmatic and realistic analysis and thinking, the report concluded. The UN Secretariat "must not apply best-case planning assumptions to situations where the local actors have historically exhibited worst-case behaviour."[33] The Brahimi report also argued that the UN needs to develop a culture of providing advice that is sound, is based on a thorough assessment of options, is independent of what might be politically popular or might fit the preconceptions of the decision makers, and is free of fear of consequences for politically neutral officials—all elements of a professional civil service. The report urged the Secretariat to tell the Security Council what it needs to hear, not what it wants to hear.[34] In situations in which impossible missions have been approved because of confused, unclear, or severely underresourced mandates, the Secretariat has to say "No" to the Security Council.

Institutional Gaps: Lacunae Filled, Lacunae Remaining

In our exploration of institutional gaps for UN military operations, it is useful to examine an institution that exists but has no purpose (the Military Staff Committee) and the organic growth of an institution that was not imagined in the Charter (the Department of Peacekeeping Operations, DPKO). Looking at three institutional lacunae is also helpful: the UN still lacks an effective body for postconflict peacebuilding, an intelligence analysis unit, and rapid reaction capability. Something was recently done about one of these gaps when the United Nations Peacebuilding Commission was created in 2006. The other two remain on many drawing boards: an intelligence analysis unit and a rapid reaction capability.

The military teeth for collective decisions were supposed to come from the bite of the major powers whose chiefs of staff would sit in the Military Staff Committee, the functions of which are spelled out in Article 47. But this idea never became reality, largely due to disagreement among the P-5. Indeed, the Military Staff Committee, which is usually comprised of military advisers from the P-5 countries, meets once a month for lunch but has no real role.

The Department of Peacekeeping Operations is responsible for planning, preparing for, and conducting UN peacekeeping operations in accordance with mandates provided by member states, usually through Security Council resolutions. The DPKO was created in 1992, but it was preceded in functions and inspiration by the Department of Special Political Affairs, the first two heads of which were paragons of international civil servants—first Ralph Bunche and then Brian Urquhart. Indeed, the Department of Special Political Affairs provided administrative support for both military and political analyses. The Department for Political Affairs, which now provides such support for political analysis, is seriously underresourced, and the tragedy of the Rwandan genocide of 1994 flowed in part from this gap. In August 1993, Brigadier-General Roméo Dallaire—who would later be the force commander of the UN peacekeeping mission in Rwanda during the genocide—headed a reconnaissance mission to Rwanda to determine the needs of the proposed UN mission. He recalls that the DPKO-based UN military adviser, Major-General Maurice Baril, told him, roughly, that "This thing has to be small and inexpensive, otherwise it will never get approved by the Security Council."[35] In other words, in a pathology that the First UN imposes on the Second, the mission must fit the budget instead of the budget being constructed to meet the needs of the work.

UN approaches to peacekeeping need to reflect the multifaceted nature of UN action in countries afflicted by mostly civil wars. This means promoting both the rule of law and economic recovery by integrating the military, policing, institution-building, reconstruction, and civil administration functions of peace operations to a much greater degree than in the past. Following the Brahimi report, a number of changes were made at the UN regarding its peacekeeping operations. The staff complement of the DPKO in New York was increased to provide better support to field missions. Military officers and police advisers were bolstered. The old and not-so-well-regarded Lessons Learned Unit of the DPKO was restructured into the Best Practices Unit. The DPKO's logistics base in Brindisi, Italy, received funding to acquire strategic deployment stocks. The UN Standby Arrangements System was reorganized and was mandated to provide forces within thirty to ninety days of a new operation.[36] Another set of modifications was made amid some controversy during the first months of Secretary-General Ban Ki-moon's administration.[37] But these all amount to technical tinkering. The chief determinant of whether a mission will succeed or fail remains the quality of decisions of member states, especially the P-5, and the willingness of member states to provide military personnel.

A recent illustration of institutional growth to meet felt needs was the creation of the Peacebuilding Commission.[38] Few conflicts end neatly. "Post-conflict transition" refers to a complex set of interconnected changes in political, social, and economic relations that is neither smooth nor linear; achievements are offset by reverses. The United Nations has not generally been able to move from initial stabilization, infrastructural reconstruction, and the reestablishment of local governance institutions to the more demanding task of leaving behind self-sustaining state structures that can implement rapid economic growth and social transformation. Peacebuilding—efforts to reduce the risk that conflict will resume and to create conditions most conducive to reconciliation, reconstruction, and recovery—is still a work in progress.

In response to the call of the High-level Panel on Threats, Challenges and Change (HLP) for a new institutional architecture for peacebuilding,[39] the 2005 World Summit approved the creation of a new Peacebuilding Commission, backed by a Peacebuilding Support Office, to fill this critical institutional gap for maintaining international peace and security. General Assembly resolution 60/180 created the Peacebuilding Commission and the office to service it. It is meant to be the central node for promoting peacebuilding strategies both in general terms and in country-specific situations. The commission is currently working to coordinate efforts across the UN system in Burundi and Sierra Leone, and Guinea Bissau and Côte d'Ivoire are on the agenda.

The Brahimi report's fifth recommendation called for the creation of an Executive Committee on Peace and Security (ECPS) and an Information and Strategic Analysis Secretariat that would support the information and analysis needs of all members of the ECPS. The Brahimi panel argued that there was a need for a professional system in the UN Secretariat "for accumulating knowledge about conflict situations, distributing that knowledge efficiently to a wide user base, generating policy analyses and formulating long-term strategies."[40] The International Commission on Intervention and State Sovereignty (ICISS)[41]—two of whose members, Klaus Naumann and Cornelio Sommaruga, had been members of the Brahimi panel—repeated this recommendation. Because of political sensitivity, however, the recommendation that an Information and Strategic Analysis Secretariat be created continues to gather dust, and the UN remains dependent on the largesse of member states whose willingness to share information with the international organization is constrained by fears of compromising their intelligence sources and shaped by their own political agendas.

Finally, the standard operating procedure for the UN is to pass a begging bowl when it needs troops. On numerous occasions—and never more poignantly than in April 1994 when no troops were available as 800,000 Rwandans were murdered—the need for an independent UN institutional capacity to respond to violence has appeared. Indeed, as Brian Urquhart has pointed out, the idea for a rapid reaction force was originally floated by the first Secretary-General, Trygve Lie, in 1947.[42] It was discussed by Lester Pearson ten years later.[43] After the Rwandan tragedy, a veritable cottage industry arose after Dallaire claimed that he could have virtually halted or at least slowed down the Rwandan slaughter if he had had access to 5,000 troops on the ground.

Whether that number would have been adequate remains disputed,[44] but there is no dispute about the fact that the UN Secretariat is required to have a response capacity. Over the years, such countries as Canada and Norway have raised the idea of a lean and autonomous UN rapid reaction military force that would provide the Secretary-General with a contingent that he could deploy quickly in the face of a felt need. In 2000, interest was rekindled when Representative Jim McGovern introduced H.R. 4453 in the U.S. Congress, which called for support for the creation of a 6,000-person UN Rapid Deployment Police and Security Force. Unfortunately, though he introduced a similar bill in 2001 (H.R. 938), neither came to fruition.

In 2005, UN emergency relief coordinator Jan Egeland announced an analogous idea to establish a rapid reaction force of 100 aid workers, another proposal that went nowhere.[45] Most recently, a group of scholars have come forward to support the idea of a United Nations Emergency Peace Service composed of 12,000–15,000 personnel of various backgrounds ready to be deployed in case of emergency.[46]

Compliance Gaps: The Limitations of Chapter VII

The concept of collective security is predicated on the proposition that war can be prevented by the deterrent effect of overwhelming power being brought to bear against any state contemplating the use of force. It entails the use of diplomatic, economic, and military sanctions against

international outlaws. Article 42 of the Charter authorizes the Security
Council to "take such action by air, sea or land forces as may be necessary
to maintain or restore international peace and security" and in Article 43,
member states agreed to make available such "armed forces, assistance,
and facilities" as may be necessary for the purpose.

The closest the UN has come to engaging in collective enforcement
action was in Korea in 1950. Yet its collective security activity was heavily qualified. In essence, the United States responded to North Korea's
invasion of South Korea, and the UN responded to the immediate U.S.
reaction. That is, the UN action in Korea was made possible by a temporary marriage of convenience between collective security and collective
defense[47] and by a rather fortuitous combination of circumstances, namely
the absence of the Soviet Union, which was temporarily boycotting the
Security Council to protest Taiwan's presence in that body instead of the
People's Republic of China. Moscow quickly returned to the Security
Council to limit the damage, thus ending the experiment with collective security when the debate and authorizations for action moved to the
General Assembly under the "Uniting for Peace" resolution of November
1950.

Four decades later, another ambiguous collective security operation
took place after Iraq illegally seized neighboring Kuwait in 1990. After
comprehensive sanctions authorized by Chapter VII were imposed, the
Security Council made a decision in resolution 678 to enforce its decision
to reverse Iraqi aggression. The situation was a textbook case anticipated
by the Charter's framers, but the conduct of the enforcement military
effort was not. Indeed, the council crossed a conceptual Rubicon by authorizing the enforcement of sanctions and the eviction of the aggressor by
troops that were not even nominally under UN command. As in Korea in
the 1950s, the advantage of the procedure was that it allowed the UN to
approximate the achievement of collective security within the clear chain
of command necessary for large-scale military operations. The cost was
that the Persian Gulf War of 1991, like the Korean War, became identified with U.S. decision making over which the organization exercised little
control.

As we have just seen, classical peacekeeping was a creative and useful
invention but certainly was not a substitute for collective enforcement.
Brian Urquhart—who probably personifies the theory and practice of UN

peacekeeping more than any other individual—argued that "it is precisely because the [Security] Council cannot agree on enforcement operations that the peacekeeping technique has been devised, and it is precisely because an operation is a peacekeeping operation that governments are prepared to make troops available to serve on it."[48]

When many complex humanitarian emergencies broke out at the end of the Cold War, the UN could not continue to ignore the need for its own peace operations to use force. The Brahimi panel concluded that the need for impartial peacekeeping should not translate automatically into moral equivalence among the conflict parties on the ground: in some cases local parties consist not of moral equals but of obvious aggressors and victims.[49] The panel argued that political neutrality has too often degenerated into military timidity, the abdication of the duty to protect civilians, and an operational failure to confront openly those who challenge peacekeeping missions in the field. Impartiality should not translate into complicity with evil. The Charter sets out the principles the UN should defend and the values it should uphold.[50] Hence, impartiality should be seen in terms of the fair application of UN mandates, not as an excuse for moral equivocation between victims and perpetrators.

The United Nations suffers from a pronounced tendency to look to fresh legislation as the solution to problems of implementation. There is probably no better region to illustrate this than the Middle East. It would not be a simple matter—and it would certainly be a controversial exercise —to try to compile the number of resolutions that Israel has failed to implement. Security Council resolutions 242 (1967) and 338 (1973) are at the core of the many "new" solutions for conflict in the Middle East. More recently, Israel pointed to the failure of the Lebanese government to implement resolution 1359 of 2001, which required Hezbollah to disarm completely.

In the buildup to the Iraq War in 2003, the United States and its two main co-belligerents, Australia and Britain, pointed to the twelve-year history of Saddam Hussein's defiance of UN resolutions and his deceitfulness in concealing that defiance. A reader might well ask what value resolutions have if they are not enforced. As the war began, many people and countries questioned the relevance of the United Nations if it could not prevent an unprovoked attack on and conquest of a member state by a major power. If the Iraq War was indeed illegal, as most scholars of international law (although by no means all) argue, what should the

United Nations do to ensure compliance with the law by the three belligerent countries?[51]

Culture of Prevention and the Role of International Commissions

In many ways, the old adage "a stitch in time saves nine"—the norm that prevention is better than the cure—could well be considered the foundation stone of the United Nations. The desire to avoid a third world war or a repetition of the cataclysmic economic consequences of the Great Depression motivated the Allied powers during their wartime gatherings to plan postwar organizations. Indeed, the Bretton Woods institutions (the World Bank and the IMF) as well as the Food and Agriculture Organization were established prior to the end of the war in Europe, and the San Francisco conference occurred with the ashes still smoldering in Europe and before Japan's surrender.

So prevention was a key notion for the framers of the Charter on both the development and security sides of the international agenda. Chapter I spells out one of the key purposes and principles of development: "to achieve international co-operation in solving international problems of an economic, social, cultural or humanitarian character." And Chapter X details the responsibilities of one of the six principal organs, the Economic and Social Council, which is expected to oversee the work of the specialized agencies working in their functional areas. The framers saw development as important in and of itself, but they also viewed it as an important way to improve the underlying economic and social conditions that so often lead to armed conflict.

Chapter VI outlines the various measures for the pacific settlement of disputes. And the variety of measures used by successive Secretaries-General—negotiation, fact-finding, mediation, conciliation, arbitration, judicial settlement—are the bread and butter of old-fashioned as well as contemporary prevention. Peacekeeping is widely recognized as a UN invention; that is why UN peacekeepers were selected as the recipients of the 1988 Nobel Peace Prize. Keeping belligerents from returning to armed conflict is a central task of prevention. And of course Chapter VII of the Charter, "Action with Respect to Threats to the Peace, Breaches of the Peace, and Acts of Aggression," was specifically designed so the Security Council could decide when and whether to ratchet up diplomatic, economic, and military sanctions designed to halt aggression.

While prevention itself is thus an old idea, the need to put it back at the center of state calculations—what Secretary-General Kofi Annan called "the culture of prevention"[52]—was revived as a result of the turbulent 1990s and the intellectual work of many. Our real story begins here because the end of the Cold War opened new possibilities for more vigorous multilateral action, including prevention. Two developments triggered a new cottage industry as scholars and analysts sought to redefine what constitutes a "threat to international peace and security": the expanding definitions of what constitutes a threat to international peace and security and the collapse of member states.

Since 1945, there has been a noticeable broadening of what constitutes a sufficient threat to international security, and the scope of Security Council activity has increased as well. For example, in 1995 the Commission on Global Governance proposed that the UN Charter be amended so that humanitarian crises could be so considered.[53] In the early 1990s, many member states and analysts viewed Security Council resolutions that authorized the protection of Kurds in northern Iraq as an exceptional extension of the council's authorization, the first Chapter VII UN action since Korea. Similarly, they viewed the UN's 1992 intervention in Somalia as a unique case, given that the country was essentially a failed state.[54] As Security Council decisions to respond to civil wars and the rapid succession of humanitarian crises in the 1990s became commonplace, however, the commission's recommendation became moot. Alongside the internationalization of what were previously considered domestic issues, such topics as AIDS and climate change were also introduced on the Security Council's agenda in the twenty-first century.

The concept of failed states did not exist in 1945; it is the product of several decades of disappointing performance on the part of postcolonial governments, especially in the Horn of Africa, Sub-Saharan Africa, and South Asia.[55] Although a host of more politically correct labels have appeared, "failed state" quite accurately captures the reality that the institutions of government no longer work and the state is no longer seen by its citizens as the custodian of legitimate authority. The clearest effect of a failed or failing state is that it severely compromises the physical security of its citizens, especially when the instruments of the state are hijacked by one group for the purpose of preying on another. Another effect is that a failed state upsets the (often delicate) balance of neighboring states through the flow of refugees, arms, and combatants. And a third effect is that small groups of warlords and other kleptomaniacs are able to channel state resources into their own pockets.

Genocide in Rwanda

For almost three decades, the dynamics of Cold War efforts of each superpower to keep tenuous states from falling into the camp of the other actually prevented the implosion of weak states. The new reality was first unmasked in Somalia after the fall of the Berlin Wall and the breakup of the Soviet Union. However, the possible scope of disintegration in weak states and the impact on international peace and security truly became evident in 1994 when Rwanda, a small Central African country formerly ruled by Belgium, was the site of Africa's worst mass slaughter in recorded history.

The Charter and the vast bulk of the laws of war concern interstate and not intrastate armed conflicts. But the dramatic and real-time media exposure of the murder of some 800,000 Rwandans jump-started a new debate about the need for prevention. Part of the logic was a legal imperative to stop the horror of genocide, which had supposedly been outlawed with the General Assembly's adoption in 1948 of the Convention on the Prevention and Punishment of the Crime of Genocide. But part of the logic was also more pragmatic: Would earlier military intervention not have been cheaper as well as more humane? Why were the same countries that refused to foot the bill for a military intervention to prevent or halt atrocities willing to spend much more on reconstruction, rehabilitation, and war crimes tribunals?

Major outbreaks of ethnic violence in 1963 and 1988 between Hutus and Tutsis foreshadowed the slaughter of 1994.[56] The genocide in Rwanda was the result of many factors that had been festering for decades. During its colonial history, first under Germany and then Belgium, the smaller Tutsi ethnic group (about 14 percent of the population in 1994) was favored for advancement over the larger Hutu ethnic group (about 85 percent of the population).[57] Social, political, and economic inequality began increasing in the mid-1980s. Meanwhile, Rwanda's demographic explosion following independence exerted severe pressure on available cultivatable land,[58] and the repatriation of refugees from Uganda and Burundi, falling prices for cash crops, and progressive deforestation exacerbated matters. Added to the witch's brew was a failed political system that was authoritarian, corrupt, and prone to create and manipulate ethnic tensions.

Rwanda was one of the most heavily aided countries in the world; nearly a quarter of its gross national product (GNP) came from outside financing. Ironically (or perhaps predictably), most of this aid went to development projects that benefited the elite and intensified rather than mitigated ethnic tensions, as Peter Uvin has demonstrated.[59] It was against this background that Hutu extremists slaughtered some 800,000 people in less than three months. From its base in Uganda, the Tutsi Rwandan Patriotic Front invaded Rwanda in the beginning of April 1994 and made steady gains; by July it controlled the country. During the violence, over 2 million refugees, both Hutus and Tutsis, fled into neighboring countries, overwhelming relief workers. The Security Council's late and incomplete response—which was essentially subcontracted to France under Opération Turquoise—despite the advance warning helped nudge the international community of states toward revisiting the notion of prevention and the principle of nonintervention in so-called domestic affairs.[60]

The logic of prevention gained an additional international dimension in 1995 and 1996. The violence spread into Burundi and eastern Zaire (now the DRC), killing thousands more and virtually destroying the economies of all three countries. Since 1998, some 5.5 million people have died in the DRC as a direct or indirect result of war.[61] After Rwanda, it was harder for the UN to ignore questions about acting sooner rather than later to prevent mass atrocities.

International Commissions: Processing Ideas into Global Norms and Policy

Blue-ribbon international panels and commissions are a favored UN mode of transmitting ideas into the norms, laws, and institutions of global governance. The Brandt, Palme, and Brundtland commissions; the Commission on Global Governance; the Brahimi Panel on United Nations Peace Operations; the International Commission on Intervention and State Sovereignty; and the High-level Panel on Threats, Challenges and Change are some of the most prominent milestones in the evolution of global governance since 1945. As one study concluded, these panels and commissions "have been central to international agenda setting."[62]

In examining the relevance of panels and commissions, it is helpful to trace the origins of their conceptual contributions, their political origins, and the context surrounding their establishment. In the case of the Brundtland Commission, for example, the backdrop included a series of

high-profile environmental accidents and disasters across several continents: the Three Mile Island nuclear reactor accident in 1979 in the United
States; the accident at the Union Carbide plant in Bhopal in India in 1984;
and the Chernobyl nuclear reactor accident in 1986 in Ukraine (then part
of the former Soviet Union). Linked to these events was increasing evidence of a growing hole in the earth's protective ozone layer that led to
the negotiation of the Montreal Protocol in 1987, the same year that the
Brundtland report was published. During this period, many environmental NGOs were created. (We return to this topic in chapter 6.)

Two independent international commissions contributed to providing better intellectual frameworks for establishing a norm and culture
of prevention: the Carnegie Commission on Preventing Deadly Conflict,
which began in 1994 and published its final report in December 1997;[63]
and the International Commission on Intervention and State Sovereignty,
which began in 2000 and published its report in December 2001.[64] With
the context of the genocide in Rwanda (as well as other horrors in northern Iraq, Somalia, Haiti, and the Balkans) in mind, what did these commissions produce that improved the culture of prevention?

Before examining their ideas about prevention, it would be useful to
say a few words about such commissions, which constitute part of the
Third UN. These commissions serve as a nexus between the UN, NGOs,
and the private sector; many are sponsored by foundations and think tanks
and are part and parcel of contemporary public policymaking.[65]

Such independent commissions combine the knowledge and expertise of many eminent individuals from outside the UN system who have
worked for or with the UN system over extended periods of time: Lakhdar
Brahimi, chair of the Panel on United Nations Peace Operations, is a good
example of such individuals; he had longtime experience as a diplomat
and minister for Algeria and had undertaken numerous special missions
on behalf of the Secretary-General. The primary target audience of such
individuals is the UN community in New York and Geneva. They bring
political visibility and a spectrum of opinion and nationalities as they
explore new ideas, norms, and options. Acting in their private capacities,
they are able to take positions and make compromises that would not be
feasible in an intergovernmental forum. Their job description, in short,
is to break new intellectual ground and sell the results. Thus, they can be
assets in filling normative gaps because they can provide a new way to
frame a challenge and its response, and they have sufficient political cred-

ibility and clout to raise the visibility of an emerging norm on the global agenda.

Their reports are intended to be consumed and digested by the First UN and the Second UN—the forum of member states and the international civil service—as well as by members of civil society and the private sector. The importance of such commissions is a central finding that has emerged from the oral histories in the United Nations Intellectual History Project. According to *UN Voices*, "the three functions of such commissions that emerged from the interviews are increasing awareness and raising consciousness, advocating for particular ideas, and lending legitimacy to programs and ideas." However, "the way reports from high-level commissions are received and used usually depends on factors that are impossible to control, including changes in the world economy, domestic politics, and elections in major powers."[66]

What were the contributions of these two commissions to the continually emerging norm of prevention? The Carnegie Corporation of New York established the Carnegie Commission on Preventing Deadly Conflict in May 1994, half-way through the Rwandan genocide.[67] Its president was David Hamburg, who headed the foundation from 1982 to 1997, and its co-chair was former U.S. secretary of state Cyrus R. Vance. The sixteen-member group also included familiar Third UN names, such as Gro Harlem Brundtland, Gareth Evans, and Shridath Ramphal.[68]

The Carnegie Commission's brief was broad: to explore the principal causes of lethal ethnic, nationalist, and religious conflicts as well as the conditions that foster or inhibit them. It surveyed the tools the international system would need to prevent such armed conflicts. It identified three broad aims of action: prevent the emergence of violent conflict; prevent ongoing conflicts from spreading; and prevent a relapse into violence. It recommended "an early reaction to signs of conflict . . . a comprehensive, balanced approach to alleviate the pressures that trigger violent conflict," and "an extended effort to resolve the underlying root causes of violence."[69] The report identified general strategies that outsiders could employ to head off violence—both operationally in the case of immediate crises and structurally to address core foundations of conflict. In many ways, these points were already generally well known to specialists, but they certainly were invisible on the international public policy agenda.

The report introduced a new concept for prevention: universal responsibility. It assigned responsibility for preventing violent conflicts not only to states and their leaders but also to the institutions of civil society (NGOs, religious leaders and institutions, the scientific community, educational institutions, the media, the business community, and the public), the United Nations, international financial institutions, and regional arrangements. "The lack of a response—particularly by states that have an obvious capacity to act—will encourage a climate of lawlessness in which disaffected peoples or opposing factions will increasingly take matters into their own hands," argued the commissioners. "The effort to help avert deadly conflict is thus a matter not only of humanitarian obligation, but also of enlightened self-interest."[70] Underlying this assertion of responsibility were three assumptions. First, not all conflict is zero-sum. Second, while conflict appears to be inherent in human relations, not all conflict need be deadly. And third, outsiders can take steps to mitigate a conflict.

One of the lasting legacies of the Carnegie Commission is its contribution to knowledge: it has produced twenty-seven reports, twelve books, and seventeen other major publications financed by a related program.[71] The International Crisis Group (see box 2.2), which is devoted to monitoring and publicizing globally the warning signs of armed conflict, was an interesting and crucial institutional offshoot of the project. Such monitoring is an essential component of filling institutional gaps, and in this case a respected member of the Third UN is better positioned to be outspoken than the Second UN.

The politics of acting sooner rather than later, however, defy the straightforward logic of prevention, which is why one of us called it a "pipe-dream" and Stephen Stedman called it "alchemy."[72] Indeed, the international community of states desperately requires a new strategy that stresses proactive rather than reactive thinking. Early action is problematic because prevention leads to finger-pointing when the evidence is unclear or rests on uncertain extrapolations and controversial analysis. The paradox of prevention is that it is hard to muster either the money or the political will for it, while generating the will for intervention, even though it is far more expensive, is relatively easier. It is easier still to mobilize resources to mop up. Without a full-blown humanitarian crisis, it seems, there is little incentive to mobilize domestic or international political will.

The year 1999 was the annus horribilis for prevention; international myopia was obvious in two cases that year. After East Timor voted for independence in a UN-mandated referendum, the occupying power, Indonesia, watched from the sidelines as armed militias backed by

Indonesian troops unleashed mass killings and destruction on unarmed civilians. Then Kosovo became the last of a series of humanitarian disasters in the Balkans. Both events were clearly predictable. Indonesia had routinely repressed its captive population since 1975 and an estimated 100,000 Timorese had died in the process. And Slobodan Milosevic had routinely demonstrated his intentions, especially in the province where he had launched his pursuit of a "Greater Serbia" in 1989. But the First UN ignored the warning signs in these countries. Afterward, both countries were targets of major and costly humanitarian military operations followed by a substantial armed presence to keep the peace, which today remains shaky and expensive.

Once again, demand arose for a new conceptual "hook" on which to hang the activity of prevention. Again, the motivation was the dramatic suffering that resulted from a failure to act early. Moreover, while in Rwanda the Security Council had done too little too late, in Kosovo it was unable to act at all because Russia and China threatened to veto resolutions authorizing intervention.

Against this international backdrop, the Canadian government established the International Commission on Intervention and State Sovereignty in 2000. The twelve-person group formulated its recommendations in less than a year. Given the supposedly wide disparity of views across the North-South divide, it was co-chaired by Gareth Evans (Australia) and Mohamed Sahnoun (Algeria).[73] The new twist for independent commissions of this type was the behind-the-scenes role of a sympathetic government, Canada. This model, which actively promoted the report and provided financial resources for a secretariat to engage in follow-up efforts, has subsequently been replicated for other commissions that sought to ensure that key topics were not relegated to coffee tables and bookshelves.

We pursue the evolution of "humanitarian intervention," as it was called then, later in the book, but here we emphasize prevention. That is, building on the work of the Carnegie Commission, ICISS's thinking in *The Responsibility to Protect* made concrete recommendations about preventing both the root causes and the direct causes of armed conflict, outlining when it was most useful to employ a particular measure. The commissioners believed that defining strategies that could be used prior to the use of military force was an essential component of a comprehensive logic of the international responsibility to protect human beings. The report argued that "prevention is the single most important dimension of

Box 2.2. The International Crisis Group

The International Crisis Group is an exceptionally good example of a civil society organization of the Third UN that helps fill knowledge, normative, and policy gaps in its niche area of operations. In 2005, *Time* honored it as a "change agent," a "problem solver," and an organization whose voice is "heard, and heeded, where it matters most: among the world's power brokers."[1] There is no other entity—governmental, intergovernmental, or nongovernmental—that comes close to matching the authority, impartiality, and credibility of the International Crisis Group in timely evidence-based analysis and on-the-ground reality-based prescriptions. The high regard in which it is held at the UN is illustrated by the fact that it was the only NGO to be asked to formally address a meeting of the UN Peacebuilding Commission in New York on 25 July 2007.

The roots of the International Crisis Group lie in its members' dissatisfaction with—and disaffection from—the international community's highly visible failures in the humanitarian tragedies of Somalia, Rwanda, and Bosnia. Begun in 1995 with two people, the International Crisis Group now has a highly skilled, dedicated, and professional staff of almost 150 from some fifty countries and an annual budget of $14.5 million. In less than a decade, the International Crisis Group has successfully positioned itself as the world's leading source of definitive analysis of conflicts (including early warning) and authoritative prescriptions for the prevention and resolution of deadly conflict.

The 100 or so detailed reports and briefing papers that the International Crisis Group produces annually are among the best available diagnoses and prognoses of international and internal conflicts from inside or outside government agencies and intergovernmental organizations. Resting on field-based analysis and sharp-edged policy prescriptions that are made without fear or favor, the reports are indispensable to practitioners and analysts alike. The group has unparalleled access to senior policymakers in governments and international organizations, including the United Nations. This access is facilitated by the fact that both its senior management and its advisory board include people highly experienced in government (which also adds gravitas and realism to the organization's work).

The International Crisis Group has worked in Afghanistan, the Balkans, the Caucasus, Central Asia, the Korean Peninsula, Iraq, the Middle East, the Congo, Somalia, Sudan, and Zimbabwe. Although its international headquarters are in Brussels, it has other advocacy offices in Washington, New York, London, and Moscow. The organization operates fifteen field offices and has analysts working in over seventy crisis-affected countries and territories across four continents. Governments, charitable foundations, companies, and individual donors fund the organization.

Its virtue and value lie in its fresh approach to the age-old problem of how to prevent and manage conflicts. Existing approaches had clearly proven inadequate to the magnitude of this task. Governmental and inter-governmental modalities, while they are more authoritative, suffered from the politicization inherent in their identity. NGOs have greater freedom and flexibility but have traditionally suffered from lack of access to policymak-ers and the fact that many governments do not take them seriously. The International Crisis Group has the authority matching that of governments and the freedom and agility of NGOs, and its work has instant credibility and relevance with policy actors and decision makers.

Gareth Evans, one of Australia's longest-serving foreign ministers, was its president and chief executive between January 2000 and mid-2009 when he turned the organization over to former UN High Commissioner for Human Rights Louise Arbour. Evans has become a regular member of the Third UN; he has been a co-chair of the International Commission on Intervention and State Sovereignty, a member of the Carnegie Commission on Preventing Deadly Conflict, and a member of the High-level Panel on Threats, Challenges and Change. In 2008–2009, he co-chaired the International Commission on Nuclear Non-Proliferation and Disarmament, which revisited the efforts of the Canberra Commission and worked to identify the next steps to prevent nuclear proliferation and promote nuclear disarmament. He thus personifies the International Crisis Group as an organization with one foot in the formal United Nations and one foot in civil society.[2]

1. "International Crisis Group: The Problem-Solvers," *TIMEasia,* 3 October 2005, available at http://www.time.com/time/asia/2005/heroes/icg.html (accessed 11 August 2009).

2. Information drawn from International Crisis Group, "About Crisis Group," March 2009, available at http://www.crisisgroup.org/home/index.cfm?id=208&l=1 (accessed 11 August 2009).

the responsibility to protect." It emphasized that "less intrusive and coer-cive measures [should] be considered before more coercive and intrusive ones."[74]

The Responsibility to Protect also made the important point that it was necessary "for the international community to change its basic mindset from a 'culture of reaction' to that of a 'culture of prevention.'"[75] For UN member states, this means recognizing straightforwardly that the core responsibility to preserve international peace and security under Chapter VI and Chapter VII of the Charter will sometimes trump the noninterven-tion principle enshrined in Article 2 (7).

Secretary-General Annan sought to mainstream prevention as a recurring theme in his sermons from the bully pulpit, beginning shortly after the Carnegie Commission issued its report. His *Facing the Humanitarian Challenge,* which endorsed the idea of cooperation among state and non-state actors, clearly influenced ICISS. Noting that using prevention strategies more often and more effectively was much less expensive than acting after a conflict had begun, the Secretary-General also noted that prevention would not bring a political payoff: "Building a culture of prevention is not easy, however. While the costs of prevention have to be paid in the present, its benefits lie in the distant future. Moreover, the benefits are not tangible; they are the wars and disasters that do not happen."[76]

Prevention was also a major theme in the High-level Panel's report, *A More Secure World* (2004), which reaffirmed the problem that prevention poses in an age of transnational threats to collective security. The report observed that the "primary challenge for the United Nations and its members is to ensure that, of all the threats in the categories listed, those that are distant do not become imminent and those that are imminent do not actually become destructive."[77] In his 2005 report *In Larger Freedom,* the Secretary-General focused again on prevention. Again, he hammered home the importance of prevention despite differences in perceptions of what constitutes a threat: "Depending on wealth, geography and power, we perceive different threats as the most pressing. But the truth is we cannot afford to choose. Collective security today depends on accepting that the threats which each region of the world perceives as most urgent are in fact equally so for all." He explained the selling point behind the comprehensive packaging of threats: "In our globalized world, the threats we face are interconnected."[78]

Finally, in September 2005 the heads of state and government at the World Summit acknowledged the importance of prevention, noting that "we are living in an interdependent and global world and that many of today's threats recognize no national boundaries, are interlinked and must be tackled at the global, regional and national levels in accordance with the Charter and international law."[79] And the emphasis on prevention and state capacity also became the primary focus for paragraphs 138–139 of the *World Summit Outcome,* which deal with the responsibility to protect.

Multiple Levels and Multiple Actors in Global Governance: The Contemporary Reality

Partnerships between state, intergovernmental, and nongovernmental actors have become the norm rather than the exception in preventing, managing, and resolving conflict. An excellent illustration of this phenomenon is the so-called quartet for addressing the Middle East conflict, which includes the United States, Russia, the EU, and the UN.

As explained earlier, "good" global governance does not imply exclusive policy jurisdiction by any one actor but rather a partnership among a variety of actors. Structured, systematized frameworks for collective action at the regional level can offer an alternative to unilateralism at the state level and multilateralism at the global level. Neither states by themselves nor the UN as their universal collective forum and sometimes operational coordinator can substitute for regional governance. Within Africa, the Americas, Asia, and Europe, countries share certain policy problems and approaches on a regional scale that they do not hold in common with all countries on a global scale. At the same time, however, regional governance cannot substitute for the United Nations, particularly in promoting security, human rights, sustainability, and development in the world. One crucial task is therefore to build effective partnerships between regional organizations (e.g., NATO, the African Union, the Inter-American Development Bank) and global agencies.[80]

Although the world organization has from its beginnings been based on state membership, regional groups are also pervasive in its deliberations and operations. For example, regional considerations figure in the composition of UN organs and the appointment of UN personnel at all levels. States often caucus at the United Nations through regional groupings. The established convention is for the office of Secretary-General to rotate between the different regional groups. In addition, the UN maintains regional commissions and economic regional substructures. Several regional governance bodies such as the Caribbean Community and the League of Arab States have obtained observer status at the UN. And of course an entire section of the Charter, Chapter VIII, is devoted to regional arrangements and their relationship to the global body. These relationships corroborate the claim that regional-scale governance, far from being incompatible with UN goals, is integral to the makeup and functioning of the organization.

In 1992 Secretary-General Boutros Boutros-Ghali's *An Agenda for Peace* called for greater involvement by regional organizations in UN peace and security activities. His proposed division of labor envisioned using regional arrangements for different mechanisms such as preventive diplomacy, peacekeeping, peacemaking, and postconflict peacebuilding. Since then, formal cooperation between regional organizations and the UN has been improved if not yet adequately consolidated. Between 1993 and 2005 Secretary-General Annan convened six high-level meetings on security matters with regional organizations from all the continents. These discussions considered challenges to international peace and security, including the role of regional organizations in peacekeeping and peacebuilding activities.

The Security Council also has given more attention to regional organizations. In July 2004, after the second meeting between the council and regional bodies, the council invited regional organizations "to take the necessary steps to increase collaboration with the United Nations in order to maximize efficiency in stabilization processes, and encouraged enhanced cooperation and coordination among regional and sub-regional organizations themselves, in particular through exchange of information and sharing experience and best practices."[81]

Not surprisingly, the High-level Panel discussed the UN's relationship to regional organizations.[82] Its report urged the Security Council to be more active and effective in preventing and responding to threats by utilizing Chapter VIII provisions more frequently and productively. The report advised the UN to promote the establishment of such regional and subregional groups, particularly in view of the important contributions these groups have made to peace and security. Most crucially, the High-level Panel explicitly recognized that regional organizations can be a more vital part of a thriving multilateral system. Their efforts neither contradict those of the UN nor absolve the United Nations of its primary responsibility for maintaining international peace and security. Rather, the critical requirements for regional action are that it be organized within the framework of the Charter and be consistent with its purposes and principles and that regional organizations and the UN should work together in a more integrated fashion.

Kofi Annan accepted the broad thrust of this analysis.[83] At the sixth high-level meeting between the UN and regional organizations in July

2005, he affirmed that strengthening UN relations with regional and other intergovernmental organizations is a critical part of the effort to reform the multilateral system. The aim is to create "a truly interlocking system that guarantees greater coordination in both policy and action" with partnerships that "build on the comparative strengths of each organization."[84] The meeting also endorsed the HLP's call for the establishment of regional and subregional groupings in highly vulnerable parts of the world where no effective security organizations currently exist.

The 2005 World Summit acknowledged the special contribution of regional organizations to peace and security, the importance of partnerships between the United Nations and regional organizations, and the special needs of Africa. In this context, the conference endorsed efforts by the EU and others to develop rapid deployment capabilities, standby and bridging capacities, and a ten-year plan to build capacity in this area for the African Union. More generally, the summit declaration advocated a stronger relationship between the UN and regional and subregional organizations within the framework of Chapter VIII; urged more consultation and cooperation between them through formalized agreements and the involvement of regional organizations in the work of the Security Council; encouraged regional organizations with peacekeeping capacities to place these at the disposal of the United Nations through standby arrangements; and promoted economic, social, and cultural cooperation.[85] In a report issued in July 2006,[86] the Secretary-General accepted the broad thrust of these recommendations, which are still being considered by the administration of Ban Ki-moon.

Conclusion: Looking Ahead

Wars are cataclysmic events. Out of the destruction of major wars emerge new fault lines of international politics. Yet, surprisingly for a category of human behavior that is as old as the human species, we lack agreed-upon, reliable, and robust knowledge about the causes and consequences of war and how best to control and limit it.

Wars have performed many functions throughout history,[87] including sculpting the contours of international systems. The capacity to wage and win wars defines major powers and determines the international power hierarchy. Major powers have the greatest capacity to destabilize a given international order or contribute to its stability. The Concert of

Europe system in the nineteenth century recognized this dual potential. The assigning of permanent membership to world powers in the League of Nations Council and the UN Security Council marked a structural continuity of this duality.

But the international power hierarchy is dynamic and is constantly readjusting, while the permanent membership of the UN Security Council has been static. This major anomaly continues after inconclusive and bitter clashes during discussions of major reform initiatives on the occasions of the UN's fiftieth and sixtieth anniversaries in 1995 and 2005. The fact that the P-5 represent the victorious powers of 1945 while current economic giants such as Brazil, Germany, India, and Japan are not even guaranteed seats represents only one anomaly. The P-5 retain their vetoes, and developing countries are underrepresented.

We defined global governance as norms and practices that define and constitute relations between different categories of actors across many levels. Religion is among the many factors influencing the interpretation of the laws of war.[88] The norm that defines interstate relations is no war except in self-defense or under UN authorization. When Russian military forces marched into South Ossetia in August 2008 to repel attacks on the breakaway province by Georgian troops, many commentators noted that Washington and NATO were reaping what they had sown in Kosovo and Iraq by flouting agreed-upon rules—no matter how disagreeable—governing the use of force in world affairs.[89]

A common understanding of and policy on the use of force is necessary for revitalizing the UN's role in the twenty-first century. This means not only renouncing force as an instrument of national policy but also making national forces available for international duty as and when determined by the Security Council. The gap on both points continues to be wide. Warfare remains an option to settle disputes. Michael Glennon makes this point in his pertinent critique of the High-level Panel's report.[90] He differentiates between the Charter regime of treaty-based law and the actual practice of states as custom-based law, noting that between 200 and 680 instances of the use of force (depending on who does the count how) by states took place between 1945 and 1989, as cited by the HLP itself.[91]

On the institutional front, the Peacebuilding Commission will have to establish its relevance and effectiveness, the UN will need to create a unit to collate and analyze intelligence, and some sort of an international ready-reaction capability will have to be established. Moreover, if the Security Council is to retain its authority as the arbiter of the international use of force by nations individually and collectively, its structure and procedures will have to be changed. This should include the "Gulliverization" of the five (and, perhaps after reform, all additional) permanent members through pragmatic modifications in the council's working methods aimed at enhanced transparency and accountability. In recent years, many significant advances have been made in the global governance of international criminal justice, but this concerns the conduct of hostilities during armed conflicts and does not deal with the lawfulness of and justification for initiating hostilities in the first place. As one would expect, major powers tend to be heavily involved in armed conflicts. But five of the major powers also constitute the P-5. The one possible solution to this conundrum in terms of holding the belligerent conduct of the P-5 to account is to broaden the scope and compulsory jurisdiction of the International Court of Justice (ICJ) instead of relying on the Security Council. Legal mechanisms for handling world affairs are woefully inadequate and underutilized. Enhancing their role in regulating the resort to armed conflict would be a good start toward rectifying the gap.

Until then, clearly, institutional and compliance gaps for international security remain stark and significant. Some of the most innovative ideas for these advances in global governance will most likely come from the Third UN. For example, a coalition of civil society actors has been advocating the creation of a UN emergency peace service as the solution to the absence of an adequately resourced ready reaction force.[92] Yet the actual decisions in the end will have to be made by member states—the First UN, while the Second UN—international civil servants—will play the major role in implementing these ideas in the field.

3

Arms Control and Disarmament

- Antecedents: The Slow Move Back from the Brink
- Knowledge Gaps: A Portrait since Hiroshima
- Normative Gaps: Moving beyond the CTBT
- Policy Gaps: Step by Step, with or without the Major Powers
- Filling Institutional Gaps: the CD, the IAEA, the OPCW, and UN Headquarters
- Compliance Gaps: How Full Is the Glass?
- Conclusion: Tipping Point?

The nuclear arms control regime—centered on the 1968 Nuclear Non-proliferation Treaty—is under challenge on many fronts. In some quarters of the international community of states and civil society there is exasperation about the failure of an accelerated timetable of nuclear disarmament by the five NPT nuclear powers (the United Kingdom, China, France, Russia, and the United States, the so-called N-5). In western circles, there are worries that some nonnuclear signatories will fail to keep their NPT obligations, especially North Korea and Iran. Analysts are divided about whether the nuclear cooperation deal between India and the United States, the Indi-U.S. Civilian Nuclear Agreement of 2008, marks an advance or a setback for the nonproliferation agenda. Almost everyone is concerned about the potential that terrorists will acquire and use nuclear weapons and worries about the safety and security of Pakistan's nuclear arsenal amid grave political crises and turmoil.

Although this chapter focuses on nuclear weapons, it is worth noting that in 2007 the authoritative Stockholm International Peace Research Institute reported that world military expenditures had reached $1.2 trillion, a figure that was higher in real terms than at any time since the 1940s (see Table 3.1). Spending by the P-5 and India accounted for the bulk of the expenditures (and by the United States alone for about half),which meant that some eighty or so developing countries were spending less than they had two decades earlier (and in terms of a percentage of GNP considerably less than previously).

Against this backdrop, on the one side, there was fresh interest in the long-standing goal of abolishing nuclear weapons by a surprising coalition of influential heavyweights from the U.S. strategic community as well as President Barack Obama.[1] As Ivo Daalder and Jan Lodal tell us, "This vision of a world free of nuclear weapons . . . has been endorsed by no less than two-thirds of all living former secretaries of state, former secretaries of defense, and former national security advisers."[2] On the other side, a group of former NATO generals issued their own call for a commitment to the option of the first use of nuclear weapons by the West in order to prevent undesirable actors from acquiring them and threatening to use them.[3] However, the United Nations largely was "missing in action" in this post-9/11 debate.[4] This is especially surprising given the world organization's early engagement with the issue and the fact that in 2004 the UN's High-level Panel warned that "we are approaching a point at which the erosion of the non-proliferation regime could become irreversible and result in a cascade of proliferation."[5]

But we are getting ahead of the story. First, we need to briefly summarize some landmarks since the UN was established and discuss the five gaps that emerge from our consideration of nuclear arms control and disarmament.

Antecedents: The Slow Move Back from the Brink

Analysts and policymakers have long been interested in regulating the tools and weapons of warfare as a means of limiting deaths and injuries during armed conflicts as well as lessening the temptation to go to war because of the ready availability of an abundant supply of weaponry. As an old saying has it, to one who has a hammer, the world looks like a nail. At the same time, however, states have believed that to protect themselves from becoming the victims of the use of force by others, they had to be adequately armed themselves. This would increase the chances of defeat for any hostile state contemplating aggression and, even if victorious, raise the cost of victory.

The First Hague Peace Conference (18 May–29 July 1899) was convened at the initiative of Czar Nicholas II of Russia "with the object of

TABLE 3.1. World Military Expenditures, 1950–2005 (in millions of U.S. dollars)

YEAR	UK	UNITED STATES	USSR/ RUSSIA	FRANCE	CHINA	WORLD TOTAL	P-5 AS PERCENT OF WORLD TOTAL
1950[1]	3,568	17,733	9,208	1,987	2,750	4,7618	74.0
1955	5,031	44,428	11,888	2,977	2,500	8,4013	79.5
1960	4,639	45,380	10,333	3,908	2,800	8,8964	75.4
1965	4,925	48,618	14,222	4,293	5,500	10,7783	72.0
1970	7,673	89,065	63,000	8,835	27,200	254,130	77.0
1975	8,794	75,068	61,100	9,903	27,300	268,220	67.9
1980	26,767	143,981	131,800	26,428	42,700	567,050	65.5
1985	30,573	204,896	146,200	28,035	30,000	663,120	66.3
1990	60,696	457,648	171,349	57,340	13,153	1,136,000	66.9
1995	50,818	357,382	21,683	52,812	14,994	855,000	58.2
2000	47,778	342,172	19,141	50,205	23,778	875,000	55.2
2005	60,003	503,353	28,492	52,917	44,322	1,113,000	61.9

1. While SIPRI has recorded world military expenditures data since 1950, their collection methods have improved since 1988. Because of this, figures reported prior to 1988 may be subject to different criteria.

Source: Data drawn from the Stockholm International Peace Research Institute (SIPRI) Military Expenditure Database, available at http://www.sipri.org/databases/milex.

seeking the most effective means of ensuring to all peoples the benefits of a real and lasting peace, and, above all, of limiting the progressive development of existing armaments."[6] The representatives of the twenty-six governments that attended failed to reach agreement on this primary objective.

The next major international attempt to control arms was embodied in the League of Nations Covenant. Article 8 required "the reduction of national armaments to the lowest point consistent with national safety and the enforcement by common action of international obligations." The League's Council was given the task of formulating plans for such reduction, "taking account of the geographical situation and circumstances of each State." States also agreed to a full and frank exchange of information on their armaments. Article 9 stipulated that a permanent commission would be constituted to advise the council "on the execution of the provisions of Articles 1 and 8 and on military, naval and air questions generally." Article 9 was never implemented, and the caveats—about national safety, international obligations, geographical situation, and the individual circumstances of each state—continue to bedevil efforts in the areas of arms control and disarmament.

Reflecting the conventional wisdom of the 1940s that pacifism had contributed to the unchecked rise of fascism, the UN Charter downgraded the importance of arms control and disarmament in comparison with the importance of these topics in the Covenant of the League of Nations. Article 26 stipulates that the Security Council shall be responsible for formulating "plans . . . for the establishment of a system for the regulation of armaments." Article 47 (1) called for the establishment of a Military Staff Committee to advise and assist the Security Council on the military requirements for the maintenance of international peace and security, including "the regulation of armaments, and possible disarmament."

Just weeks after the Charter was signed in San Francisco on 26 June 1945, the United States conducted the world's first nuclear test at the Alamogordo Air Field in New Mexico on 16 July. Just weeks later, on 6 and 9 August, it detonated the first atomic weapons in Hiroshima and Nagasaki. The enormous destructiveness of nuclear weapons produced five major strategic changes. First, modern delivery systems mean that there is no protection against nuclear bombs because the only defense is to destroy every enemy missile and bomber. Such certainty is unavailable today and unlikely in the foreseeable future. Second, nuclear weapons make old-fashioned defense impossible. They also destroy the gallantry that pitted soldier against soldier and left noncombatants alone (if not in peace). The presence of nuclear weapons completed the historical trend toward blurring the line between military and civilian sectors that was already in evidence in the two world wars. Third, the destructiveness of nuclear weapons and the speed of their delivery mean that wars no longer are necessarily protracted affairs. Nuclear war could be over in days or even hours, denying leaders a chance to rethink strategy and change their minds. Fourth, because of the speed of nuclear war, a country can no longer afford to mobilize fully only when the onset of hostilities is imminent. Nations must keep their nuclear forces in a state of constant readiness at full strength. Finally, where in previous wars the belligerent countries could destroy one another and affect other states to varying degrees, an all-out war between two adversaries heavily armed with nuclear weapons would destroy everyone else and most of the planet's life systems as well.

It could be argued that the cumulative impact of these changes makes nuclear weapons devoid of any military use whatsoever; their only purpose can be deterrence. But here too strategists are confronted with a fundamental paradox. If one side seeks to deter war by creating the fear that it will use nuclear weapons, it must convince the opponent of its determination to use them in certain circumstances. If, however, the weapons are used and produce a like response, then the side that strikes first is very much worse off than if it had abstained. A country that poses an unacceptable risk to the enemy therefore necessarily poses the same risk to itself. To prepare to fight a nuclear war is to impose on a nuclear equation the logic of pre-nuclear strategy; the circle cannot be squared.

As the disquieting implications of this paradox seeped into public consciousness, many people made their unhappiness felt to their governments and organized into national and transnational groups to lobby against nuclear weapons.[7] The numbers and types of actors engaged in the different layers of global governance grew. Moreover, *all* governments—nonnuclear and nuclear as well as allies, adversaries, and neutral parties—became stakeholders in peace and demanded a voice in the governance of the nuclear order, in effect insisting that there be no annihilation without representation. The UN provided a global platform for articulating this demand. In addition, several governments of nonnuclear states decided to draw "red lines" by creating nuclear exclusion zones on their own. The nuclear powers tried to enhance transparency and regulate aspects of the nuclear arms race (for example with respect to testing) that then also required institutional and compliance mechanisms. In other words, all the aspects of global governance as framed in our story came into play, from growing knowledge to instituting norms, formulating policies, building institutions, and ensuring compliance.

The sheer destructiveness of the new type of weaponry had a profound impact on world leaders from the start of UN deliberations. The very first General Assembly resolution in January 1946 called for the newly established United Nations Atomic Energy Commission to make proposals to eliminate atomic weapons and other weapons of mass destruction.

Several giant normative steps forward have marked the UN's history since that time. Not surprisingly, Moscow and Washington as the two superpowers led the way both in advances and setbacks. The United States presented the Baruch Plan for the international control of atomic energy as early as June 1946, which led eventually to the establishment of the

International Atomic Energy Agency. The Soviet Union tested its first device in 1949, and Ethel and Julius Rosenberg were executed in New York in 1953 during the hysteria of the McCarthy era for having passed information about the atomic bomb to Moscow. While the first proposal for a "standstill agreement" on nuclear testing came from Indian prime minister Jawaharlal Nehru in April 1954, the western allies submitted a working paper to the United Nations in August 1957 that advocated a halt to nuclear testing and weapons production and the initiation of a reduction in nuclear weapons stockpiles as well as in general armaments.[8]

Of greater import were a series of bilateral nuclear arms control agreements following the Strategic Arms Limitations Talks (SALT I) that began in Helsinki in November 1969. The superpowers signed SALT I documents limiting strategic offensive arms in Moscow in May 1972; the agreement expired in October 1977. They also signed the Anti-Ballistic Missile Treaty in May 1972, limiting strategic anti-ballistic missile defenses, followed by the SALT II treaty, which was signed in Vienna in June 1979 but was withdrawn almost immediately from U.S. Senate consideration after the Soviets invaded Afghanistan in December of that year.

The real momentum for dramatic reductions in nuclear stockpiles and preparations came under Soviet and American presidents Mikhail Gorbachev and Ronald Reagan. The Intermediate Range Nuclear Forces Treaty of December 1987 was the first arms control agreement to ban an entire class of nuclear weapons. The Strategic Arms Reduction Treaty (or START I) of July 1991 committed the United States and the Soviet Union to halving their long-range nuclear forces. Before the year was out, Washington had unilaterally withdrawn all U.S. land- and sea-based tactical nuclear weapons from overseas bases and operational deployments and Moscow had stood down all Soviet strategic bombers on day-to-day alert status, plus other measures. That same year, the U.S. Congress passed the Soviet Nuclear Threat Reduction Act to help Moscow destroy nuclear, chemical, and other weapons. George H. W. Bush and Boris Yeltsin signed the START II Treaty to reduce intercontinental ballistic missiles even further in January 1993. In the meantime, however, other P-5 countries were joining the nuclear club. The United Kingdom tested its first nuclear device in Australia's Montebello Islands in 1952, France in the Sahara in 1960, and China at Lop Nor in 1964.[9]

Many multilateral initiatives and achievements were recorded in parallel with the bilateral efforts of Moscow and Washington. Twelve states, including the United States and the Soviet Union, signed the Antarctic Treaty, which demilitarized and denuclearized the uninhabited continent, in 1959. The NPT, which was signed in 1968 and has been in force since 1970, established a robust norm of nonproliferation and a weaker norm against nuclear weapons. But even after its entry into force, the "five nuclear powers" according to the NPT, which were also the Security Council's five permanent members (China, France, the Soviet Union, the United Kingdom, and the United States), conducted a large number of atomic and nuclear tests both in the atmosphere and underground. The Partial Test Ban Treaty of 1963 outlawed atmospheric, space, and underwater nuclear testing. The preamble to the NPT recalled the determination expressed in the Partial Test Ban Treaty "to seek to achieve the discontinuance of all test explosions of nuclear weapons for all time. In 1974, the Threshold Test Ban Treaty outlawed underground tests with more than a 150-kilotonne yield. But underground testing below this threshold continued, for example in Moruroa in French Polynesia; the last test was conducted on 27 January 1996."[10]

The 1996 Comprehensive Test Ban Treaty (CTBT), even though it has not yet entered into force, brought the end of the nuclear arms race to a close through an international legal convention. As such, it is the embodiment of the world's abhorrence of these weapons of mass destruction. But its practical utility was shown to be wanting within two years with nuclear tests by India and Pakistan, followed by North Korea. The 1993 Chemical Weapons Convention (CWC) did the same with respect to chemical weapons. The NPT was extended indefinitely and unconditionally in 1995, and the NPT Review Conference of 2000 had an ambitious forward-looking agenda, although it stalled with the advent of the George W. Bush administration and its distinctive and dangerous agenda for remaking the world to its neoconservative liking.

U.S. president Barack Obama and Russian president Dmitry Medvedev began discussions in July 2009 about drastic reductions in their military arsenals as a step back toward a nuclear-free world. The worldwide hopes for change were reflected in the Nobel Committee's October decision to award the Nobel Peace Prize to Obama, specifically mentioning his "vision of and work for a world without nuclear weapons."

Knowledge Gaps: A Portrait since Hiroshima

Past predictions from experts about the development and acquisition of arms have been notoriously inaccurate; the proliferation field was once rather aptly called "the sky-is-still-falling profession."[11] Today, the empirical data on nuclear weapons is relatively sound and clear, especially compared to the data about other weapons. The data that has been collected is quite dependent on U.S. sources of information, but it is reliable.

We know the full details of the inventories in the nuclear arsenals of the five NPT-licit nuclear powers. But we can only make informed guesses about the two self-declared possessors of nuclear weapons, India and Pakistan (which tested devices in 1974 and 1998, respectively); and we can make even less-well-informed guesses about the deliberately ambiguous non-NPT nuclear power, Israel. The situation becomes decidedly murky with respect to suspected and potential NPT violators such as Iran and North Korea. The same is true of nonstate actors that pursue the development or acquisition of nuclear weapons. For example, the existence and extent of Dr. Abdul Qadeer Khan's underground nuclear bazaar—which came to light in 2003 only because Libya renounced the nuclear option, came back into the NPT fold, and began cooperating in the verified dismantling of its clandestine infrastructure—caught everyone by surprise. Conversely, most western commentators had assumed that Saddam Hussein had some level of nuclear weapons capability and were subsequently proven wrong when U.S.-led occupation forces did not uncover any evidence of an ongoing nuclear program.

The other two classes of weapons in the WMD trinity—biological and chemical weapons—are easier to conceal and more difficult to detect. For example, when the Chemical Weapons Convention entered into force, the inventory of some states such as India came as a surprise. Similarly, with conventional weapons, heavier armaments are easier to trace and monitor (many independent research institutes publish annual statistics), while light weapons are often the subject of guesswork, no matter how informed or scholarly the guesses might be.

The main international repositories of information for nuclear and chemical weapons are the UN Secretariat, the IAEA, and the Organization for the Prohibition of Chemical Weapons (OPCW). Similarly, the UN Register of Conventional Arms aims at the most authoritative data collection. It has the merits but also the shortcomings of relying on official reports from member governments. Additional sources include standard compilations from the Bonn International Center for Conversion, the International Institute for Strategic Studies (London), and the Stockholm International Peace Research Institute. An op-ed on small arms in the

New York Times, for example, used data from the *Small Arms Survey,* the International Action Network on Small Arms, the *CIA World Factbook,* and other sources,[12] illustrating well our point that a multitude of actors at different levels constantly interact in the web of global governance.

The psychology and the logic of political leaders of proliferating states and of nonstate networks and groups trying to acquire nuclear weapons are distinctive. Yet they remain relatively unknown, another topic for future research.[13]

Because the definitions, causes, and consequences of armed conflict are intensely contested (as we saw in the previous chapter), it is hardly surprising that the instruments of violence also excite much controversy. The first difficulty, again not surprisingly, is about how to define key concepts. "Arms race" is one of those glib phrases that has gained wide currency internationally but is uncommonly difficult to define. The metaphor does not sit well with the facts. Rarely do rivals "race" each other regarding the numbers or quality of weapons or the amount they spend on weapons; these are three different metrics that may or not be congruent across countries.

The more important factors that define the size and content of weapons stockpiles seem to be economic pressures or opportunities, political latitude, regime needs, and the lobbying leverage of military-industrial-scientific complexes. The advantages to politicians and to captains of industry from arms races clearly range across all cultures, political systems, and time periods. From Krupp to Halliburton and from the Soviet Union to North Korea, waving the flag during arms buildups has clear beneficiaries. Even when arms proliferate in absolute numbers, the numbers do not necessarily increase relative to the expansion of actors in the international system, to the gross world product, or to increased international trade flows. The historical results are illustrated in graphs 3.1, 3.2, and 3.3.

The argument that arms buildups cause wars is not easily sustainable by the historical record. Indeed, the conventional wisdom about World War II is that the failure of Britain and France to engage in an arms buildup in time was at least partly responsible for the onset of the war. Hence, we can see the validity of the claim *si vis pacem para bellum:* "If you want peace, prepare for war." If actions speak louder than words, the vast majority of the world's countries would seem to subscribe to this theory.

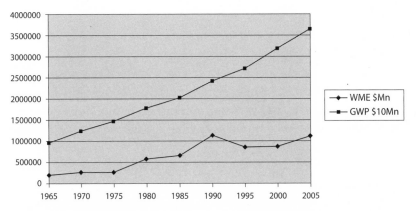

GRAPH 3.1. World Military Expenditures and Gross World Product, 1960–2005. *GWP in Constant 2000 U.S. Dollars. *Sources:* The Stockholm International Peace Research Institute (SIPRI) Military Expenditure Database and World Development Indicators. While SIPRI has recorded world military expenditures data since 1950, their collection methods have improved since 1988. For this reason, figures reported prior to this date may be subject to different criteria.

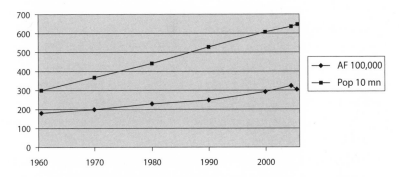

GRAPH 3.2. World Military Personnel and Population, 1960–2005. *Sources:* World Development Indicators and United Nations Population Division.

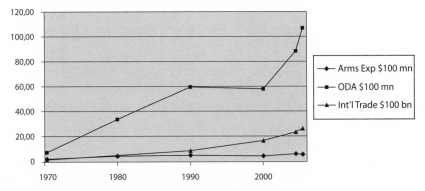

GRAPH 3.3. World Arms Exports, ODA, and International Trade, 1970–2005. *Sources:* World Development Indicators, UN Comtrade.

Conflicts and arms races can have a mutually reinforcing effect; tension can be as much a cause of an arms race as the other way round. The empirical evidence suggests that three separate propositions are justified about the relationship between arms races and wars: an arms race can result in a war; an arms race can be terminated peacefully without resulting in war; and wars may occur even in the absence of any discernible arms race. The first proposition leads to the policy prescription that disarmament should be pursued with unremitting vigor. The second imbues efforts toward arms control and disarmament with the hope of success. The third proposition suggests that arms control and disarmament may be necessary conditions of peace but are by no means sufficient.

The comments on arms buildups and conflict in general acquire particular urgency with respect to nuclear weapons, the central thread in this chapter. Nuclear weapons are arguably the most alarming technological development of the twentieth century. Unfortunately, some of those whose scientific work led to the development of nuclear weapons awoke to its possible dangers too late to stop it. They were also ambivalent about it in the context of the grave Nazi threat and the fear that Hitler's Germany might acquire the bombs first. In the words of Albert Einstein, "I made one great mistake in my life . . . when I signed the letter to President Roosevelt recommending that atom bombs be made; but there was some justification—the danger that the Germans would make them."[14]

One way to lessen the alarm while acknowledging the sense of threat is to regulate the numbers, quality, and types of armaments. The United Nations has been good at collecting empirical information and has often attempted to link military expenditure to drags on development, but it has been considerably less good at analytical studies that establish causal relationships between arms control and security. In part, the world organization has been hampered by political correctness. How could arms be considered to be anything other than a threat to international peace and security?

The UN's role has been rather more substantial in expanding the knowledge base by collecting data about nuclear weapons than in providing testable propositions about the relationship between nuclear weapons and security. Examples of the UN's contributions to the knowledge base include reports by the Secretary-General on various subjects—for example, clearing mines and reducing or eliminating stockpiles[15]—that are widely used as relatively neutral and unbiased sources. In addition, the Department of

Disarmament Affairs publishes the *UN Disarmament Yearbook,* a quarterly update, and occasional papers on a range of topics such as small arms, the UN arms register, and the NPT. Although there is no consensus on the requirements for a nuclear-weapon-free zone (NWFZ), the closest approximations to widely acceptable criteria are contained in two comprehensive expert studies conducted under UN auspices in 1975 and 1985.[16]

The United Nations also tries to fill gaps through compiling and disseminating information. In November 2000, the General Assembly, acting on the advice of the Secretary-General's Advisory Board on Disarmament Matters, adopted resolution 55/33, "United Nations Study on Disarmament and Non-Proliferation Education," without a vote. In this resolution, the assembly requested the Secretary-General to prepare such a study, with the assistance of a group of qualified governmental experts, and to report to the assembly on the question at its fifty-seventh session (2002).[17] The resolution left follow-up action to member governments, and (predictably) it has not been robust.

Normative Gaps: Moving beyond the CTBT

Charles Perrow classified nuclear weapons as "dread risks," those that are characterized by lack of control over an activity, fatal consequences if a mishap of some sort occurs, high potential for catastrophe, feelings of dread, inequitable distribution of risks and benefits (including transfer of risks to future generations), and the belief that risks are increasing and are not easily reducible.[18] Because of the horrible effects of nuclear weapons, one of the most powerful norms since 1945 has been the taboo against their use. There have been many occasions since 1945 when nuclear weapons could have been used without fear of retaliation but were not, even at the price of defeat in a conflict.[19] Norms, not deterrence, have anathematized the use of nuclear weapons as unacceptable, immoral, and possibly illegal—even for states that have assimilated such weapons into military arsenals and integrated them into military commands and doctrines.

Three high-profile independent international commissions have reaffirmed and attempted to strengthen international norms related to weapons of mass destruction. The Canberra Commission on the Elimination of Nuclear Weapons, which the Australian government established in 1995, argued that the case for eliminating nuclear weapons was based on three propositions: their destructive power robs them of military utility against other nuclear weapons states (NWS) and renders them politically and morally indefensible against non-NWS; it defies credulity that they can be retained in perpetuity and never used either intentionally or inadvertently; and the fact that some states have them stimulates others to acquire them.[20] Its argument has been amply vindicated.[21] The 1999 Tokyo Forum for Nuclear Non-Proliferation and Disarmament sounded the alarm on nuclear dangers, saying: "To deal effectively with international security problems in the twenty-first century, Security Council reform, new normative principles, operational arrangements, financial compliance and new sources of financing are urgently needed."[22]

The Weapons of Mass Destruction Commission, launched in Stockholm in 2003 under the chairmanship of Hans Blix and the sponsorship of Sweden, addressed the issue of WMDs in the context of the changing international security environment. Its report, which it formally presented to Secretary-General Kofi Annan in June 2006, is more likely to be remembered for reinforcing the norm against the use of WMDs than for new policy recommendations.[23] The ideas for the commission, which was chaired by an eminent former UN official, was suggested by two serving UN officials in 2002 following the successful example of the International Commission on Intervention and State Sovereignty.[24] In 2008 a follow-up commission to the Canberra Commission and Tokyo Forum, the International Commission on Nuclear Non-Proliferation and Disarmament, was announced. It was jointly sponsored by Australia and Japan and was co-chaired by former foreign ministers Gareth Evans and Yoriko Kawaguchi. The commission aims to strengthen the Nuclear Non-Proliferation Treaty that is up for review in 2010, but it will also focus explicitly on nuclear disarmament and nonproliferation.[25]

The unique legitimacy of the United Nations, especially of the General Assembly, is the chief explanation for why so many declarations and resolutions were first adopted in the UN before producing conventions and treaties in the UN and elsewhere; this is an example of norms followed by laws. Even treaties that are negotiated outside UN forums are often submitted to the UN machinery for formal endorsement. This process has no bearing on the legal standing of a treaty but substantially enhances its moral weight. This has been true, for example, of the treaties creating various regional NWFZs.

Over the course of the 1980s and 1990s, Australia and New Zealand pursued the goal of a total ban on nuclear testing with particular urgency and mobilized growing international support for their CTBT resolution at the UN, which they presented annually. Increased momentum on arms control initiatives reflected the changing world climate after the implosion of the Soviet Union and the collapse of the communist threat. In the fall of 1992, the U.S. Congress adopted path-breaking legislation that imposed a moratorium on testing and looked forward to a comprehensive, mutually agreed test ban within ten years. The Conference on Disarmament (CD), the Geneva-based multilateral disarmament negotiating forum, decided in August 1993 to begin negotiations on a comprehensive test ban. Later that year, a CTBT resolution in the General Assembly was co-sponsored by 156 states and was supported by the N-5; the assembly adopted it by consensus.

Gradually support grew in large segments of the international community of states for proscribing nuclear testing in a universal treaty that included all testing at all levels in all countries and that would be verifiable.[26] This amounted to promulgating a new global norm against nuclear testing as a subtext of the norm against the use of nuclear weapons. While the CD was used as the forum for negotiating the Comprehensive Test Ban Treaty, its procedural obstacles prevented it from adopting the treaty's text. The General Assembly was then used as the forum to stamp the CTBT with the imprimatur of international legitimacy. In 1996, when India vetoed the final product in the CD in Geneva, Australia used a constitutional maneuver to move the text from the CD in Geneva to the General Assembly in New York. On 10 September 1996, the General Assembly approved the text of the CTBT by a vote of 158 to 3. Only Bhutan and Libya supported India in rejecting it.

Policy Gaps:
Step by Step, with or without the Major Powers

A large number of treaties and conventions—that is, statements of international public policy—regulate the use and spread of armaments. Nuclear, chemical, and biological weapons are regulated by the CWC, the Biological Weapons Convention (BWC), the NPT, the CTBT, several regional NWFZs, and a series of bilateral and multilateral treaties and agreements. Nuclear weapons were the first of the classes of weapons usually grouped together as weapons of mass destruction to be subjected to an international regime. The CWC, signed in 1993 and in force since 1997, was the jewel in the crown of global treaties regulating the three categories of WMDs. Other agreements impose controls on conventional weapons, including, for example, the Convention on the Prohibition of the Use, Stockpiling, Production and Transfer of Anti-Personnel Mines and on Their Destruction (sometimes called the Ottawa Convention), which has the distinction of banning a class of weapons that is in widespread use.

The United Nations has not been the chief policy architect for arms control and disarmament. Most of the key treaties and regimes were negotiated outside the UN framework. This includes multilateral regimes like the NPT, the CWC, the BWC, and the various regional NWFZs as well as the bilateral treaties signed by the Soviet Union and the United States during the Cold War on intermediate range and strategic forces.

Yet this truth masks a deeper underlying reality. First, the United Nations has often been the forum for negotiating new international instruments and the depositary organization for many treaties negotiated outside the UN framework even when the architects were non-UN actors. The General Assembly can adopt resolutions that initiate new negotiations on arms control and disarmament. It can also adopt treaties negotiated in the CD, as with the CTBT. The NPT was negotiated outside the UN framework, but its conceptual origin lies in a resolution Ireland introduced in the General Assembly in 1958. Over the next three years, Ireland annually sponsored resolutions (1380 in 1959, 1576 in 1960, and 1665 in 1961) that called for a nonproliferation treaty. In 1965, the Soviet Union presented a draft treaty to the assembly that adopted resolution 2028, which outlined five principles of nonproliferation submitted by eight nonaligned countries. Resolution 2346A of December 1967 asked the Eighteen-Nation Committee on Disarmament (the predecessor of the CD) for a full report on the NPT negotiations. After receiving this, General Assembly resolution 2373 commended the draft text of the NPT in June 1968, and the NPT was opened for signature on 1 July 1968 in London, Moscow, and Washington (the capitals of the three designated depository countries).[27] The treaty entered into force on 5 March 1970, when the IAEA established its safeguards system for NPT parties.[28]

Second, the ideas behind many of the existing regimes were often funneled through the UN system. For example, India proposed a total cessation of nuclear testing at the General Assembly in December 1954.[29] In January 1957, the United States submitted a five-point plan to the General Assembly proposing an end to the production of nuclear weapons and testing. During the 1980s through the mid-1990s, pressure for a comprehensive test ban was channeled through the General Assembly.[30] Similarly, the idea of negotiating a South Pacific NWFZ was submitted to the General Assembly for endorsement in 1975 under the joint sponsorship of Fiji, New Zealand, and Papua New Guinea, and the 1985 treaty links the regional verification system for the South Pacific to the global IAEA inspections regime within the UN system.

The United Nations has thus historically been the funnel for processing arms control and disarmament proposals, and this role continues today. The New Agenda Coalition (Brazil, Egypt, Ireland, Mexico, New Zealand, South Africa, and Sweden), which cuts across traditional regional groups, has used the world organization as the forum for advancing the twin agendas of nonproliferation and disarmament. The basic policy positions are agreed among the New Agenda Coalition countries and then taken to the wider international community of states through UN structures.

Regional NWFZs

Perhaps no subject so clearly illustrates these kinds of dynamics for policy gaps as the concept of nuclear-weapon-free zones. The closest approximation to a widely acceptable definition of this concept was contained in a 1975 report by a group of experts commissioned by the General Assembly.[31] The report defined it as a treaty-based zone established by a group of states to ensure the total absence of nuclear weapons from the zone and an agreed system of verification and control to guarantee compliance. NWFZ participating countries must not manufacture, acquire or test nuclear weapons or permit any outside states to store or deploy them in zone territory. The last requirement distinguishes a NWFZ from the NPT. States that do not possess nuclear weapons can adhere to the NPT and still accept a stationing of nuclear weapons on their territories as long as they do not exercise control over the weapons. NWFZ status prohibits such stationing of nuclear weapons.

Rooted in intellectual traditions of liberalism and pacifism, the NWFZ concept seeks to insulate specific geographical regions from the specter of future nuclear warfare. The Antarctic Treaty mentioned above is an example. Another example is the Outer Space Treaty of 1967, which prohibits nations from putting nuclear weapons or other WMDs in orbit around the earth or on celestial bodies or in outer space. However, outer space has remained open for ballistic missiles carrying nuclear warheads. The Seabed Arms Control Treaty of 1971 prohibits nuclear weapons on the seabed or the ocean floor beyond a twelve-mile coastal zone. The impact of this treaty is limited, however, by the fact that it allows "the use of the seabed for facilities servicing free-swimming nuclear weapon systems."[32]

Achieving unequivocal and permanent NWFZ status has thus been problematic even in uninhabited areas; creating NWFZs in populated and politically defined regions has, not unexpectedly, proven rather more difficult. The first substantial NWFZ proposal was the so-called Rapacki Plan. In a speech to the General Assembly in October 1957, Poland's foreign minister Adam Rapacki proposed that a NWFZ be created by treaty among Poland, Czechoslovakia, and the two Germanys that prohibited the manufacture, possession, or stationing of nuclear weapons in those nations.

The Rapacki Plan failed because NATO countries believed that it would give a global strategic advantage to the Warsaw Pact with its numerical superiority in conventional arms and troops. But the Rapacki proposals inspired Sweden's foreign minister, Östen Undén, to present his own plan at the General Assembly in 1961. The Undén Plan shifted the focus from a regional multilateral treaty to unilateral decisions by states against acquiring nuclear weapons. The Undén Plan also failed, but like the Rapacki Plan, it inspired yet another proposal. In three successive waves in 1962–1965, 1972–1975, and 1978, Finland's president Urho Kekkonen suggested, without success, that Denmark, Finland, Norway, and Sweden create a Nordic NWFZ by mutual proclamation.

The Treaty of Tlatelolco established the first internationally recognized NWFZ in a densely populated region of the world by prohibiting nuclear weapons in Latin America. Signed on 14 February 1967 and endorsed by the General Assembly on 5 December 1967, the Treaty for the Prohibition of Nuclear Weapons in Latin America and the Caribbean came into force in April 1968. The next great wave of interest in regional NWFZs spread across the Southern Hemisphere as such zones were established in rapid succession in the South Pacific by the Treaty of Rarotonga (1985), in Southeast Asia by the Treaty of Bangkok (1995), in Africa by the Treaty of Pelindaba (1996),[33] and in Central Asia by the Treaty of Tashkent (2006).[34] Not only were all reported to and endorsed by the United Nations, but in some respects the international organization was the intellectual and political force behind the initiation and conceptualization of these treaties, it provided financial backing during negotiations, and it helped bring the negotiations to successful conclusions. In the words of one African analyst, "Without doubt, the UN was the fundamental force behind the establishment of a NWFZ in Africa. Since the 1960s, it provided the political impetus which gave legitimacy to African initiatives in addition to its own resolutions."[35]

Nonproliferation versus Disarmament

The biggest tension in the policies of arms control regimes is between nonproliferation and disarmament. As the foreign ministers of the New Agenda Coalition noted, that which does not exist cannot proliferate.[36] The NPT contains a triangular linkage between verified nuclear nonproliferation, cooperation in peaceful uses of nuclear energy, and nuclear disarmament. It is difficult to convince others of the futility of nuclear weapons when some demonstrate their utility by hanging on to them and developing new doctrines for their use. The pursuit of nuclear nonproliferation is doomed without an accompanying duty to disarm.

Secretary-General Annan's 2005 report, *In Larger Freedom,* argued that "progress in both disarmament and non-proliferation is essential and neither should be held hostage to the other." The unique status of the nuclear weapons states "also entails a unique responsibility," Annan said, and they must do more, including making further and irreversible reductions in nonstrategic nuclear arsenals, reaffirming negative security assurances, swiftly negotiating a fissile materials cutoff treaty, and maintaining the moratorium on nuclear testing until the CTBT enters into force.[37]

Despite Annan's pleas for progress, the NPT review conference in May 2005 collapsed. The first half of the conference was dogged by wrangling about procedures, and the second half was equally rancorous. The exercise ended with recriminations over where to place the primary blame for the lost opportunity to bolster the NPT. The 2005 World Summit similarly failed to come to any agreement on nonproliferation and disarmament, a failure that Kofi Annan described as "inexcusable" and "a disgrace"; he blamed it on posturing that got in the way of results.[38] A January 2008 speech by Secretary-General Ban Ki-moon echoed these sentiments; he declared that he was "deeply troubled" by the "impasse over priorities" at the Conference on Disarmament, which was "in danger of losing its way."[39]

Unlike nuclear weapons, both biological and chemical weapons have been outlawed under universal international conventions. The BWC, which was opened for signature in 1972 and has been in force since 1975, prohibits the development, production, stockpiling, acquisition, and retention of toxin and biological weapons.[40] The CWC was signed in 1993 and entered into force in 1997. It is the first multilateral treaty to ban an entire category of WMDs, provide for international verification that these weapons have been destroyed and the facilities that produced them has been

BOX 3.1. Policy Gaps and the World Court Project

The Nuclear Nonproliferation Treaty was a bargain wherein nuclear-weapons-states agreed to eliminate their nuclear weapons eventually in return for the non-NWS foreswearing the nuclear weapons option. But the bargain was asymmetrical and unequal. The nonproliferation obligations are concrete, binding, subject to IAEA verification, and enforceable by the Security Council. The disarmament clause is vague, declaratory, and is not timetabled, verifiable, or enforceable—at least until the International Court of Justice, more commonly called the World Court, filled this particular gap.

The ICJ has two types of jurisdiction: contentious and advisory. The first concerns disputes between states. Article 96 of the Charter authorizes the General Assembly or the Security Council to seek advisory opinions from the ICJ "on any legal question." Advisory opinions, although not binding, are considered to be authoritative interpretations of the law at the time they are delivered. Their political significance lies in the nature of the ICJ as the supreme authority for interpreting international law.

In October–November 1995, the ICJ—at the request of the World Health Organization in 1993 and the General Assembly in 1994 to render an advisory opinion—heard oral arguments on the legality of the use or threat of nuclear weapons. This case had four interesting features: it attracted the widest participation of any case in the ICJ's history; it originated in civil society rather than with national governments or UN agencies; its targets were the five NWS; and instead of creating new law by treaty or convention, the case sought to hold the five NWS to existing norms.[1]

The World Court first had to decide whether it had the competence and authority to render an advisory opinion on the nuclear issue. The NWS argued that whether a state possesses or deploys nuclear weapons are questions of national security. As essentially political, not legal, questions, they were outside the scope of the ICJ's authority. Moreover, intrusion by a judicial organ into political-security questions would have the perverse effect of stalling progress on disarmament negotiations. The non-NWS, a larger group, insisted that a determination of the legal question by the ICJ would facilitate, not impede, strategic disarmament. The World Court ruled that it did indeed have the authority to render an advisory opinion.

The second jurisdictional question was whether the WHO, which has a mandate to improve the net health of humanity, had the competence to request an advisory opinion from the ICJ on a legal question concerning weapons of war. The World Court ruled that it did not.

On the substantive question—the legality of the use or threat of nuclear weapons—the NWS noted the absence of any treaty or convention comparable to the biological and chemical weapons conventions that banned states from possessing and deploying nuclear weapons. Against this, the anti-nuclear advocates who banded together in the World Court project countered that in cases not specifically covered by international treaties or agreements, civilians and combatants are still protected by customary international law, the laws of war, and international humanitarian law. The principles of proportionality in the use of force and distinction between combatants and civilians were especially applicable to nuclear weapons. The NWS also argued that the NPT legitimized the possession of nuclear weapons by the five NWS. The non-NWS responded that the NPT merely recognized a fact of international life but simultaneously signaled the increasing illegitimacy of nuclear weapons by requiring the NWS to begin good-faith negotiations toward nuclear disarmament (Article 6 of the NPT).

The ICJ delivered its opinion on 8 July 1996. It found that there is no specific authorization for (14–0) or a comprehensive and universal prohibition on (11–3 vote) threatening to use or using nuclear weapons in customary or conventional international law. On the central question before it, the court was split 7–7. The ICJ president, Judge Mohammed Bedjaoui of Algeria, cast the deciding vote in favor of the opinion that threatening to use or using nuclear weapons would generally be contrary to the rules of international law, in particular international humanitarian law. However, the World Court could not conclude definitively whether threatening to use or using nuclear weapons would be lawful or unlawful in an extreme circumstance of self-defense in which the very survival of a state was at stake.

The opinion thus strengthened the normative structure of restraints on possessing, threatening to use, or using nuclear weapons and so contributed to delegitimizing these weapons. The court emphasized the unique characteristics of nuclear weapons, in particular their destructive capacity, their capacity to cause untold human suffering, and their ability to cause damage to generations to come. In view of these unique characteristics, the ICJ observed that using such weapons was scarcely reconcilable with respect for the requirements of the laws of armed conflict. The opinion significantly altered the nature of disarmament obligations of the NWS. Under Article 6 of the NPT, the NWS committed to pursue nuclear disarmament negotiations in good faith. The ICJ concluded, unanimously, that these states have an obligation to pursue in good faith *and bring to a conclusion* negotiations leading to nuclear disarmament.

How to enforce the authoritative policy is a different matter.

1. Saul Mendlovitz and Peter Weiss, "Judging the Illegality of Nuclear Weapons: Arms Control Moves to the World Court," *Arms Control Today* 26, no. 1 (1996): 10–14.

converted to peaceful purposes, and involve the global chemicals industry in the verification regime. The CWC also promotes cooperation among countries in the peaceful uses of chemicals and provides for assistance and protection to signatories under chemical weapon threat or attack. The principles of universality, equality, and nondiscrimination have secured near-total adherence to the CWC. States parties to the convention represent 98 percent of the world's population and 98 percent of the world's chemical industry.[41]

A Promise Unfulfilled

Although nuclear, biological, and chemical weapons have usually been lumped together as weapons of mass destruction, in real life the true weapons of mass casualty are light arms and antipersonnel land mines. Small arms result in hundreds of thousands of deaths each year around the globe in countries at peace and at war. Since 1990, an estimated 2 million children have been killed with small arms.[42] Since the 1980s, fatalities and injuries resulting from land mines have numbered in the hundreds of thousands, according to the International Campaign to Ban Landmines. By the end of the 1990s, land mines and unexploded ordnance were causing 15,000 to 20,000 casualties annually, and most were civilians in peacetime.[43]

The success of the civil society–led Ottawa process leading to the Mine Ban Treaty, which 133 countries signed in December 1997, was evidence of mounting frustration with the painfully slow rate of progress on this issue in the state-based Conference on Disarmament. Nevertheless, treaty negotiators were careful not to isolate themselves from the international organization; they integrated treaty review, reporting, and depository processes with the UN system.

The four countries most active in the Ottawa Convention process— Austria, Belgium, Canada, and Norway—are members of the CD and played an active role in taking the negotiation out of the CD. The states parties to the Ottawa Convention were careful not to organize intersessional meetings or the meetings of states parties along UN lines. They were keen to establish a modus operandi in which states, NGOs, and international organizations can work in partnership with no barriers in terms of legitimacy and the right to speak. Although the treaty is integrated within the UN system, the states parties set up an Implementation Support Unit that operates under the wing of the Geneva International

Centre for Humanitarian Demining (an independent foundation) rather than within the United Nations.

The success of the Ottawa process demonstrates why, in the view of Jessica Matthews, the standard static model of UN-sponsored agreements—"years of negotiations leading to a weak final product"—should be replaced by a fluid and dynamic model—"a rolling process of intermediate or self-adjusting agreements that respond quickly to growing scientific understanding."[44] The strategic partnerships forged between NGOs, governments, and international organizations during the land mine ban campaign facilitated negotiations and the treaty's subsequent implementation.

The United Nations also serves as a forum for a number of other disarmament-related processes such as the 2001 United Nations Conference on the Illicit Trade in Small Arms and Light Weapons in All Its Aspects, which adopted a Programme of Action to combat the problem at the national, regional, and global levels. That same year, the General Assembly adopted the Protocol against the Illicit Manufacturing of and Trafficking in Firearms, Their Parts and Components and Ammunition, which supplements the United Nations Convention against Transnational Organized Crime of 2000. Here, as elsewhere, we have a long distance yet to travel.

Filling Institutional Gaps:
the CD, the IAEA, the OPCW, and UN Headquarters

In spite of difficulties and limited resources, three fledgling UN institutional mechanisms partially fill institutional gaps. Several international bodies within the UN framework are part of the implementation mechanism for treaty regimes: the IAEA (in Vienna), the OPCW (in The Hague), and the Preparatory Commission for the Comprehensive Test-Ban-Treaty Organization (also in Vienna). The United Nations Monitoring, Verification and Inspection Commission (UNMOVIC)—previously the United Nations Special Commission (UNSCOM)—was charged with disarming WMDs in Iraq under Security Council resolutions 687, 715, 1284, and 1441, among others. This is a surprisingly dense UN network that, among other things, suggests a more active role for the world body in the future.

Conference on Disarmament

Although it is not formally a UN body, the CD, which is based at the United Nations Office in Geneva, is intimately linked to the world organization. The final document of the First Special Session on Disarmament in 1978 described the CD as the world's "single multilateral disarmament negotiating forum." Its origins lie in the Ten-Nation Committee on Disarmament of 1960 (five members each from NATO and the Warsaw Pact), which was subsequently expanded to include eight neutral and nonaligned countries and then further enlarged to its present strength of sixty-six when the number of independent states increased. The CD is in the paradoxical position of being the UN's sole disarmament legislative forum while not being a true UN body. Nevertheless, its budget is included in the UN budget, its meetings are serviced by the UN, its secretary-general is the director-general of the United Nations Office in Geneva, its deputy-secretary-general is the head of the Geneva branch of the UN Department for Disarmament Affairs, and its reports go to the General Assembly.

However, the CD does not follow UN rules and procedures. For example, the CD operates by consensus only; there is no voting procedure. Consequently, every treaty is hostage to the veto of any one of its sixty-six members. Since the completion of the CTBT in 1996, the CD has been unable to begin negotiations on a ban on fissile materials or any other issue. To many outside the inner disarmament circle, it seems bizarre that at a time of international crisis the CD cannot get down to business and deal with one of the key issues at the heart of that crisis—weapons of mass destruction—or even agree on a program of work. In the process the CD is bringing the entire multilateral disarmament process into disrepute.

The CD has been in stalemate for about a decade due mostly to its consensus rule, which essentially says that "if everything is not agreed, nothing is agreed."[45] Three blocs of states want the CD to commence negotiations and not merely continue discussions on a range of issues: many, but certainly not all, members of the Non-Aligned Movement (NAM) want to negotiate a nuclear disarmament treaty; Russia and China want a treaty to prevent an arms race in outer space; and the United States and other NATO members want negotiations on a fissile material treaty. To complicate matters, Pakistan believes that a treaty on fissile material should apply not just to present and future production but also to stocks. In addition, a host of other disagreements concern how to define what types of "fissile material" should be included in the treaty and whether and how such a treaty should be verified, and the George W. Bush administration, in fact, argued against verification. Indeed, it is difficult to imagine the number of divisions on the fissile material treaty issue alone—including a gap between those who want negotiations to begin without preconditions and those who think some parameters must first be agreed so that negotiations can be possible.

So who are the main culprits? Depending on the issue, almost all member states figure in one of the above categories; there are more than enough foot-draggers to go around. Some say "Eliminate the consensus rule," but that will not solve the problem. And if negotiations are moved outside the CD, opposition from the same states will arise. For example, what purpose would it serve to get a treaty on fissile materials without the agreement of the states that produce the most fissile material?

There is a widespread sense that the UN has become dysfunctional and moribund as a forum for negotiating arms control and disarmament treaties. Kofi Annan, for one, acknowledged openly that the CD "faces a crisis of relevance resulting in part from dysfunctional decision-making procedures and the paralysis that accompanies them."[46]

The International Atomic Energy Agency

With a secretariat of 2,200 professional and support staff, the IAEA is the centerpiece of international efforts to combat proliferation from within the NPT regime. Although it is autonomous, it is a member of the UN system and reports annually to the General Assembly on its work. It pursues a three-pronged strategy to combat nuclear risks: preventing illicit and military use of nuclear material; detecting any efforts to use nuclear material for military purposes in a timely fashion; and making swift and decisive recommendations to the Security Council when nuclear risks are apparent. It also has three main areas of work: verifying safeguards that nuclear material and activities (such as power generation) are not used for military purposes; protecting people and the environment from radiation; and developing and promoting peaceful applications for nuclear energy.

Although its roots extend farther back in postwar American nuclear policy, the IAEA's birth in 1957 is often attributed to U.S. president Dwight D. Eisenhower's 1953 "Atoms for Peace" speech, which "marked the end of the postwar U.S. nuclear policy of secrecy and denial [internationally] and provided the framework for future U.S. policy on peaceful nuclear trade, cooperation and nonproliferation."[47] The Atoms for Peace proposal also marked a substantial contribution to filling the knowledge gap on nuclear issues by providing publicly available information to member states—nuclear powers, aspiring nuclear possessors, and non-nuclear countries.

According to former director David Fischer, perhaps the IAEA's chief claim to a place in history will be as the body that pioneered the practice of international on-site inspection, in states that have nuclear weapons as well as those that do not. It thus helped prepare the way for major advances in chemical and conventional as well as nuclear disarmament. The IAEA also facilitated U.S.-Soviet cooperation through the rigors of the Cold War.[48]

The Achilles' heel of the IAEA has always been the policy gap. How can policy be formulated without a consensus about what constitutes possession of nuclear power? When the IAEA has been allowed to operate, it has been remarkably successful. The decision to "aim" the IAEA at a particular state is taken by other states. The case of Iraq is illustrative. "While the national intelligence services were getting it wrong, UN inspectors were getting the picture largely right," Jessica Tuchman Mathews points out. "In 1991–1998, UNSCOM and the IAEA—while facing unrelenting Iraqi opposition and obstruction—successfully discovered and eliminated most, if not all, of Iraq's unconventional weapons and production facilities."[49] As Jean Krasno and James Sutterlin have demonstrated, the IAEA "defanged the viper,"[50] which should have removed one of the justifications for the decision of the United States and the United Kingdom to go to war in Iraq in 2003.

The IAEA has become an institutional expression of a double standard on proliferation that seems to serve the interests of the five NPT nuclear powers and to be unable to deliver on the NPT non-nuclear-weapons states' rights to civilian nuclear assistance. The issue of selectivity, for example, arose in 2005–2008 with respect to the Islamic Republic of Iran. A member of the NPT, Iran had repeatedly proclaimed its right to pursue nuclear technology for peaceful purposes by enriching uranium. A number of countries did not believe that Iran's nuclear technology would be used only for peaceful purposes and repeatedly demanded that the UN take action to halt Iran's activities. In July 2006, the Security Council instructed Iran to suspend uranium enrichment and reprocessing. When Iran did not comply with the resolution, the council imposed a number of sanctions in December 2006 and widened them in March 2007. Yet the IAEA repeatedly criticized the United States for making unwarranted allegations against Iran, and a February 2008 report stated that it had clarified all outstanding issues with respect to the scope and nature of Iran's enrichment program with the exception of the "alleged weaponization studies that supposedly Iran has conducted in the past."[51]

Although IAEA director-general Mohamed ElBaradei and the agency were jointly awarded the Nobel Peace Prize in 2005, critics of the institution have been numerous.[52] Others emphasize the meager returns after years of UN disarmament efforts.[53] This is not the place to apportion blame, but certainly the First United Nations of states—and especially the permanent members of the Security Council (which, for a time, were the only nuclear powers)—must be faulted for the lack of any real movement (See table 3.2). This was especially the case during the Cold War, when the standoff between the superpowers virtually paralyzed the world institution. As the nuclear club grows, the number of UN member states that are at loggerheads and willing to impede progress in the IAEA has grown. At the same time, the IAEA's support for the Security Council's authorization of an intrusive inspections regime in Iraq suggests the importance of having an independent and technical institutional capacity that can be called upon once knowledge, norms, and policies are in place.

The Organization for the Prohibition of Chemical Weapons

Unlike the NPT and the BWC, the CWC established an implementing secretariat, the Organization for the Prohibition of Chemical Weapons, which is required to oversee and verify the total destruction of all declared chemical weapons, inactivate and destroy or convert to peaceful purposes all facilities that formerly produced chemical weapons, and inspect the production and (in some cases) the processing and consumption of dual-use chemicals and receive declarations of their transfer in order to ensure that they are used exclusively for peaceful purposes.[54]

Unlike the BWC, the CWC contains rigorous state-of-the-art provisions on monitoring and verification. For example, its monitoring procedures routinely reach into the private sector to a depth and breadth neither contemplated before nor emulated since. Consequently, the OPCW was required to develop procedures that enabled it to monitor the stocks and destruction of chemical weapons and facilities without compromising proprietary knowledge of legitimate chemical industry activities. It provides technical assistance to countries across a broad spectrum that is custom-tailored to the individual requirements of each. The OPCW has developed a certified and peer-reviewed analytical database

TABLE 3.2. Number of Nuclear Warheads in the Inventory of the Five NPT Nuclear Weapons States, 1945–2005

YEAR	UNITED STATES	USSR/ RUSSIA	BRITAIN	FRANCE	CHINA	TOTAL
1945	6	0	0	0	0	6
1950	369	5	0	0	0	374
1955	3,057	200	10	0	0	3,267
1960	20,434	1,605	30	0	0	22,069
1965	31,982	6,129	310	32	5	38,458
1970	26,662	11,643	280	36	75	38,696
1975	27,826	19,055	350	188	185	47,604
1980	24,304	30,062	350	250	280	55,246
1986	24,401	45,000	300	355	425	70,481[1]
1990	21,004	37,000	300	505	430	59,239
1995	12,144	27,000	300	500	400	40,344
2000	10,577	21,000	185	470	400	32,632
2005	10,295[2]	17,000[2]	200	350	400	28,245

1. Peak year globally.

2. Slightly less than half of U.S. and Russian stockpiles are considered operational; the balance is in reserve, retired, or awaiting dismantlement.

Source: Hans M. Kristensen and Robert S. Norris, "Nuclear Notebook: Global Nuclear Stockpiles, 1945–2006," *Bulletin of the Atomic Scienctists* 62, no. 4 (2006): 64–67, using data from the Natural Resources Defense Council. Of the non-NPT nuclear weapons states, Israel is estimated to have 60–85 warheads, India and Pakistan about 110 between them, and North Korea could have around 10. Altogether, more than 128,000 nuclear warheads are estimated to have been built since 1945, with the United States and the former Soviet Union/Russia accounting for 55 and 43 percent of them, respectively.

with information on over 1,500 compounds related to chemical weapons. In addition, a network of protection experts consults on a regular basis on the means to improve the capacity to respond to chemical weapons attacks and protect civilian populations.

By the end of 2009, 188 countries had joined the OPCW. All declared that their chemical weapons production capacity had been deactivated and that two-thirds of their declared facilities had either been verifiably destroyed or converted for peaceful purposes. The inventory of all declared stockpiles of chemical weapons had been completed and verified, but less than one-third of the declared 8.6 million chemical weapon munitions had been verifiably destroyed. Of the 70,000 tons of declared chemical weapons agents, just over one-third had been verifiably destroyed. Over 5,000 industrial facilities around the world are liable to inspection; the OPCW had conducted over 3,600 inspections at over 1,600 military and industrial sites in eighty-one countries.[55]

UN Headquarters

The First Committee of the General Assembly is charged with considering disarmament and international security. Each year, member states gather to discuss resolutions put forward by one or more states. The resolutions cover the gamut of disarmament and security issues—land mines, small arms, terrorism, biological weapons, information technology security, and nuclear weapons. Many resolutions are repetitions of the resolutions of previous years, but new resolutions are also introduced and serve as a gauge of progress or lack of it. These resolutions are weathervanes of current international thinking on disarmament and international security. Voting is by a simple majority. Resolutions may be adopted by acclamation, without objection, or without a vote or the vote may be recorded or taken by roll call. After the committee has completed its consideration of items and submitted draft resolutions, the General Assembly passes resolutions in it plenary meetings, usually toward the end of its regular session. However, unlike Security Council resolutions, General Assembly decisions are not legally binding.

The United Nations Disarmament Commission is the body where all member states come together to set the framework for disarmament. This deliberative body, an intersessional organ of the General Assembly, is mandated to consider and make recommendations in the field of disarmament and to follow up the decisions and recommendations of the UN's First Special Session on Disarmament in 1978. Unlike the First Committee, the disarmament commission does not pass resolutions. It focuses on a limited number of agenda items to allow for in-depth discussions. Yet its work too has become moribund.

Originally established in 1982 upon the recommendation of the General Assembly's Second Special Session on Disarmament, the Department for Disarmament Affairs functioned as a department within the Secretariat until 1992. From 1992 until the end of 1997, it was a center under the Department of Political Affairs. In January 1998, as part of the

BOX 3.2. The Revolving Door of Personnel for the Three UNs

Understanding the interactions among the three United Nations is crucial in the analysis of global policy processes, but the task is challenging because of the increasing ease with which talented people who contribute to UN deliberations and actions move from several vantage points during their careers. A few examples illustrate how difficult it is to clearly identify the role of UN personnel in global policymaking, since staff members have often also served in national governments and have been members of the Third UN.

We begin with an example with direct relevance for this chapter. As a government official, Jayantha Dhanapala was the president of the NPT Review and Extension Conference in New York in 1995, which extended the NPT indefinitely. In an earlier stage of his career, he served as the director of the UN Institute for Disarmament Research in Geneva. He also served as the UN under-secretary-general for disarmament (1998–2003). He is currently an independent researcher working on nuclear issues, the president of the Pugwash Conferences on Science and World Affairs, and chair of the UN University Council.[1]

Other examples illustrate the importance of the revolving door for other issues of global governance. Adebayo Adedeji was a junior academic working on UN issues before he became a government minister. He subsequently became the head of the Economic Commission for Africa, and after retiring from the commission's secretariat in Addis Ababa, he established his own UN-related NGO in Nigeria. The late Bernard Chidzero was a junior academic before becoming the first black African UNDP resident representative and later served as UNCTAD's deputy secretary-general and after Zimbabwe's independence became a member of parliament, minister of economic planning and development, and then senior minister of finance.[2] The late Julia Taft's work as director of the UNDP's emergency program was preceded by a period where she played the dual roles of the CEO of InterAction (a consortium of some 165 U.S. development and humanitarian NGOs) and a member of a UN committee to coordinate emergency operations. Before that, she headed the U.S. State Department's Bureau of Population, Refugees, and Migration.[3] Boutros Boutros-Ghali was a professor of international law and a government minister in Egypt prior to spending five years as UN Secretary-General; he subsequently headed two NGOs in Europe.[4] Ellen Johnson Sirleaf, who was elected president of Liberia in 2006—the first woman head of state anywhere in Africa—had previously served as assistant minister and then minister of finance in Liberia, vice-president of a regional branch of Citibank in Africa, and director of the UNDP's regional bureau for Africa.[5]

1. See "Jayantha Dhanapala: Under-Secretary General for Disarmament Affairs," available at http://disarmament.un.org/dda-jdbio.htm (accessed 11 August 2009).

2. For Adedeji and Chidzero, see Thomas G. Weiss, Tatiana Carayannis, Louis Emmerij, and Richard Jolly, *UN Voices: The Struggle for Development and Social Justice* (Bloomington: Indiana University Press, 2005), 435 (Adedeji) and 438–439 (Chidzero).

3. Yvonne Shinhoster Lamb, "Julia Taft; Crisis Manager Helped Resettle Refugees," *Washington Post,* 19 March 2008, B7.

4. Weiss, Carayannis, Emmerij, and Jolly, *UN Voices,* 437–438.

5. "Biographical Brief of Ellen Johnson Sirleaf," available at http://www .emansion.gov.lr/content.php?sub=President's%20Biography&related=The%20 President (accessed 11 August 2009).

Secretary-General's program for reform, it was reestablished as a department. However, in 2007, Secretary-General Ban Ki-moon proposed a reorganization of the department. In the end, it was renamed the United Nations Office for Disarmament Affairs but its staff, organizational structure, and mandate remain the same.[56]

Compliance Gaps: How Full Is the Glass?

Nuclear arms control faces a four-part crisis: some NPT states are engaged in undeclared nuclear activities, other states have failed to honor their disarmament obligations, some states are not party to the NPT, and some nonstate actors seek to acquire nuclear weapons. Faced with this four-pronged pressure that challenges the norms and laws governing the acquisition, production, transfer, and use of such nuclear arms, the P-5 may have to resort to coercive measures ranging from diplomatic and economic to military measures. However, the P-5 proved utterly unable to cope with Israel's policy of deliberate ambiguity about whether it possessed nuclear weapons in the 1960s and 1970s. They have also been ineffectual in their response to India's "peaceful nuclear explosion" in 1974 and the pursuit of nuclear weapons by both India and Pakistan since then. In 1981, the council's failure to take action to halt Iraq's nuclear program led Israel to unilaterally bomb the Osirak reactor, in response to which Saddam Hussein drove his nuclear weapons and other WMD acquisition programs underground. The nonproliferation norm became potentially enforceable in January 1992, when, in the context of the discovery of an advanced clandestine nuclear weapons program in Iraq and threats and defiance from North Korea, the Security Council declared proliferation to be a threat to international peace and security.[57]

In the meantime, after the Gulf War of 1990–1991, the United Nations was tasked with ensuring that Iraq disarm its WMDs. Despite incredible hurdles, UNSCOM and the IAEA were successful in determining the extent of the Iraqi WMD program and in disarming Iraq even without the cooperation of the Iraqi government. Following a 1998 attack on Iraq by U.S. cruise missiles, damning revelations that UNSCOM was "infiltrated and fatally compromised" by American and British intelligence brought about its downfall. (The intelligence gathered had been used to choose targets for the 1998 airstrikes.)[58] UNMOVIC was established as a clean slate, a newly mandated inspection body for Iraq.

A few things are now clear about Iraq that have important implications for the future of the United Nations and disarmament. First, UNSCOM did a very good job. Despite all the obfuscation, subversion, and evasion by Iraq, UNSCOM found and destroyed most of the weapons of mass destruction in Iraq's possession between 1991 and 1998. Second, it appears that UN sanctions and national export controls may have worked better than expected to prevent Iraq from purchasing, acquiring, and developing WMDs. Third, UNMOVIC's painstaking analysis of all the UNSCOM data carried from 1999 to 2002 paid off. UNMOVIC found evidence of WMDs in a few months of in-country inspections between November 2002 and March 2003 with very little useful intelligence information and very limited cooperation from the Iraqi government. The failure of the American-led Iraq Survey Group to find WMDs after the 2003 war is a testament to UNSCOM and UNMOVIC's success. In its final report to the U.S. Congress in September 2004, the Iraq Survey Group stated that it had not found any substantive evidence of large-scale programs for WMDs in Iraq and that because of sanctions, Iraq did not have the ability to recreate its nuclear program after it ended in 1991. (However, it mentioned Saddam Hussein's intention to rebuild Iraq's nuclear capability.) The Iraq experience shows the enormous difficulty of enforcing compliance with international norms and commitments. After 1998, the international community of states was unable to agree on the appropriate response to one of the world's most odious regimes that had been pursuing some of the world's most destructive weapons. Moreover, there is an inherent tension between the IAEA's mandate for promoting peaceful nuclear energy use and the overall strategic goal of nonproliferation. This is best illustrated by the fact that India and Pakistan, which are outside the NPT regime, are on the IAEA's Board of Governors. The IAEA's promotion of peaceful uses of nuclear energy is increasingly problematic because more and more nuclear technology, materials, and equipment have dual uses.

It is particularly necessary to call on the moral authority of the United Nations to ensure that states comply with global norms and implement global policies when behavior considered to be unacceptable is not in fact proscribed by any treaty to which a state may be party. In May 1998, India and Pakistan conducted nuclear tests. In doing so, they broke no treaty, for neither had signed the NPT, but they violated the global norm against testing nuclear weapons and were roundly criticized for doing so. However, the Security Council was in a bind. The P-5 are caught in a particularly vicious conflict of interest with regard to nuclear nonproliferation in that they are also the NPT-defined nuclear weapon states. In these circumstances, the Security Council's condemnation of the 1998 Indian and Pakistani tests—when not one of the over 2,000 previous tests by the P-5 nuclear powers had ever been so condemned by the council—predictably inflamed opinion on the subcontinent.[59]

To monitor compliance with nuclear norms, regional NWFZs typically set up regional monitoring, reporting, and compliance procedures as well as obligations and organizational machinery—for example, the Agency for the Prohibition of Nuclear Weapons in Latin America and the Caribbean. These tend to be more stringent than international obligations associated with the NPT regime; withdrawal clauses, for example, are stricter than their counterparts in the NPT regime, thereby raising confidence about their efficacy compared to that of the NPT.

While the international institutional architecture is complete and effective with respect to chemical weapons, many critical components of the inspections regime remain untested and efforts are lagging for achieving universality of the convention, monitoring of dual-use exports and imports, and ensuring effective verification and enforcement. The OPCW has yet to refer a case of possible noncompliance to the Security Council. The curious oddity of a distinctively strong challenge inspection system that has never been used may indicate that the convention's deterrent effect has been perfect. But one could just as easily question the effectiveness of the system until such time as it has been tested. Perhaps we need an intermediate mechanism between a routine industrial inspection and the politically charged challenge inspection system.

If the international challenge system was not backed up by national legislation, it would amount to nothing. Strengthening treaty regimes means national legislation and measures to criminalize proliferation activities; effective protection of proliferation-sensitive personnel, materials, and equipment; control and accounting systems to monitor materials and stocks; and regulation and surveillance of dual-use transfers. In these respects, the OPCW shows the way for the NPT and the BWC by emphasizing national implementation of the Chemical Weapons Convention to address proliferation threats. The CWC global treaty has been reinforced by national implementation legislation, and the implementation of Article 7 obligations under the CWC creates an environment of enforceability. Yet states have lagged behind in the CWC-mandated destruction of chemical weapons stocks. The OPCW has verified the destruction of only one-fifth of declared weapons agents. At this rate, the convention's goal of complete destruction of all chemical weapons stockpiles by the agreed extended deadline of 2012 will not be met.

Within the constraints of the NPT, a nonnuclear country can build the necessary infrastructure to provide it with the capacity to upgrade quickly to nuclear weapons. Nonstate actors are outside the jurisdiction and control of multilateral agreements. Recognizing this, a U.S.-led group of like-minded countries launched the Proliferation Security Initiative (PSI) to interdict illicit air, sea, and land cargo linked to weapons of mass destruction. Its premise is that the proliferation of such weapons deserves to be criminalized by the civilized community of states. Questions remain about the legal basis for searching and interdicting ships in international waters. It runs the risk of being seen as a vigilante approach to nonproliferation by a self-appointed world sheriff at the head of a self-selecting posse. Even so, the PSI signals a new determination to overcome an unsatisfactory state of affairs through a broad partnership of countries that will coordinate actions to halt shipments of dangerous technologies and matériel, using their own national laws and resources. The High-level Panel encouraged all states to join the PSI,[60] and the Secretary-General welcomed the voluntary initiative.[61] Unilateral approaches have greater flexibility to formulate more precise responses to meet specific situations, while multilateral solutions are likely to prove more enduring and stable. Of course, multilateral products depend on national implementation.

Conclusion: Tipping Point?

The UN's strengths and assets in arms control and disarmament are research, advocacy, norm building, and networking. It has established procedures and forums for sustaining annual debates and discourses; it provides a rare channel for nonnuclear countries to network with one another and exert pressure on the nuclear states that have not yet joined the NPT; it tries to coordinate global regimes and regional initiatives; and it undertakes analytical, empirical, and problem-solving research. Its universality provides a legitimizing capacity that is a precious resource.

The world organization's weaknesses are that it uses antiquated procedures by which holdouts and recalcitrants can block any initiative; it devotes meager resources to the gravest threats to international security; and the most powerful enforcers of peace (the Security Council's permanent members) are the worst offenders in terms of military arsenals and sales. Given its nature and structure, the United Nations will continue to achieve progress in articulating normative restraints on arms acquisitions and use, be the clearinghouse for information on conventional and WMD arsenals, and be the forum of choice for condemning proliferation activities, but it will be seriously handicapped in reining in the conventional and nuclear stockpiles and doctrines of the N-5 that are also the P-5.

The United Nations has played three linked but analytically distinct roles:[62] it is a funnel for processing ideas into norms and policies and for transmitting information from national sources to the international community; it is a forum for discussing and negotiating common international positions, policies, conventions, and regimes; and it is a source of international legitimacy for the authoritative promulgation of international norms, appeals for adherence to global norms and regimes, and coercive measures to enforce compliance with them. These three roles should be strengthened in the years ahead.

The General Assembly houses the divided fragments of humanity, but when it is united speaks authoritatively with the collective voice of the international community of states. This is what makes it the arena where contested norms can be debated and reconciled, the unique forum of choice for articulating global values and norms. There is no substitute for the United Nations as a source of international authority and legitimacy. This was illustrated in the way that the campaign to ban land mines was careful to keep in touch with the United Nations.

The core of the international law enforcement system with respect to nonproliferation and disarmament is the Security Council. When faced with a challenge to the norms and laws governing the acquisition, production, transfer, and use of arms, the P-5 undoubtedly will increasingly resort to coercive measures that range from diplomatic and economic to military. Because the General Assembly has little substantial power and the Security Council is often deadlocked, the weight of UN initiatives frequently falls on the Secretary-General. He may be ignored, but he is not easily delegitimized. However, the Secretary-General is not in the best position to issue judgments and edicts against member states regarding armaments and weapons platforms that involve national security unless they have violated specific and binding obligations.

Unlike the topics in most other chapters in this book, the way forward on arms control and disarmament—in particular with respect to nuclear weapons—has been extensively signposted already. The gaps in implementation and compliance in the arms control and disarmament regime include the lack of verification machinery and compliance mechanisms for the disarmament obligations (Article 6) of the NPT, the lack of a credible and binding inspections regime for nonproliferation, and the lack of agreed criteria to assess proliferation threats.

The normative gaps in the arms control and disarmament regime are clear. They include the fact that the NPT has not been signed by all UN member states, the lack of a basis in international law to enforce nonproliferation norms for states outside the treaty regimes, and the inapplicability of norms and regimes to nonstate actors. It is imperative that three policies be implemented: reduce nuclear inventories among the nuclear weapons states, strengthen controls over nuclear stocks and materials, and minimize the attractiveness of nuclear weapons to states that do not have them.

The main policy gap in the arms control and disarmament regime is the lack of a nuclear weapons convention outlawing the possession and use of nuclear weapons by all actors. Perhaps here the battle lines between the three United Nations are more distinct than they are in other areas. Governments, especially the nuclear powers, are the main actors and constantly drag their feet. Secretaries-General and other senior officials carefully make statements but face enormous constraints in challenging orthodoxy. And the members of the Third UN often outspokenly campaign and press hard for more vigorous action.

Because of weaknesses in its verification system (a reflection of the scientific state of the world in 1972), the BWC has not prevented the proliferation of biological weapons. The need to rectify this lacuna is urgent.

Regarding light arms, the Ottawa Treaty has yet to be ratified by the significant producers and users of antipersonnel land mines, even though the normative barrier set up by the treaty has not been breached by any state. In 2008, ten years after the treaty was signed, the Oslo Process replicated its success with the signing of the Convention on Cluster Munitions.

To move forward from where we are today, the High-level Panel's prescriptions accurately identified four layers:

- Demand reduction. This would require NWS to restart nuclear disarmament and de-alert strategic nuclear weapons, and it would require the Security Council to make explicit pledges to take collective action if a non-NWS is attacked by nuclear weapons.

- Restrict supplies. This would require states to recognize the IAEA's Model Additional Protocol as the international gold standard and it would require the IAEA to act as the guarantor for the supply of fissile material to civilian nuclear users. It would also require states to agree to a voluntary moratorium on constructing any more enrichment or reprocessing facilities, to convert highly enriched uranium research reactors to proliferation-resistant reactors, and to promptly negotiate a fissile material cut-off treaty.

- Enhance enforcement. This would include biannual reporting to the UN Security Council by the directors-general of the IAEA and OPCW.

- Improve public health defenses, especially against biochemical warfare.

To fill institutional gaps, the High-level Panel recommended that the implementation committee of Security Council resolution 1540 on the prevention of nuclear, chemical, and biological weapons proliferation establish permanent liaison with the IAEA, the Nuclear Suppliers Group, and the OPCW; that the directors-general of the OPCW and IAEA be invited by the Security Council to report twice yearly on the status of safeguards and verification processes and on any serious concerns they have short of actual treaty breaches; and that the council be prepared to deploy inspection capacities for suspected nuclear and chemical violations, drawing on the OPCW and IAEA. In addition, the High-level Panel noted that the NPT could be strengthened by making the IAEA Additional Protocol mandatory for all states parties, strengthening or even eliminating the exit clause, and making clear that withdrawal from the NPT would be treated as a threat to peace and security. But these measures are inadequate without also addressing gaps on the disarmament side of the NPT and reform in the composition, procedures, and working methods of the Security Council.

The problems of states who have not signed the NPT and nonstate actors could be addressed by accepting the suggestion that the fruitless search for universal membership should be replaced by "universal compliance" with the terms of arms control regimes. The Carnegie Endowment for International Peace lists a set of "six shared obligations that involve all states" to make this a reality: make nonproliferation irreversible; devalue the political and military currency of nuclear weapons (which would have to include the steady and verified dismantlement of nuclear arsenals); secure all nuclear materials using robust standards for monitoring and accounting for fissile materials in any form; institute enforceable prohibitions against efforts by individuals, corporations, and states to assist others in secretly acquiring the technology, material, and know-how for nuclear weapons; make a commitment to resolve conflict; and persuade India, Israel, and Pakistan to accept the same nonproliferation obligations as the NWS signatories to the NPT.[63]

Because much of the program of action for disarmament agreed at the First Special Session on Disarmament in 1978 remains to be achieved— including banning the production of fissionable material for weapons purposes, phased elimination of nuclear weapons, a NWFZ in the Middle East, a convention on radiological weapons, measures to prevent an arms race in outer space, and limitation and reduction of conventional arms— comprehensive review of the disarmament program and machinery has met with fierce resistance. A number of states want to reformulate the disarmament agenda in the light of political developments since the end of the Cold War, while others fear that dearly held and hard-won ambitions could fall prey to the revisionists and the goal of nuclear disarmament could be undermined. Consequently, the proposal to hold a fourth special session of the General Assembly devoted to disarmament in order to update the disarmament program and machinery in the UN has not, as yet, led to anything.[64] It needs to happen.

The prospects for the successful convening of such a special session improved dramatically with the election of Barack Obama as president of the United States. As IAEA director-general Mohamed ElBaradei reminds us, the number of potential nuclear weapons states could more than double in a few years unless the major powers take radical steps toward disarmament. The next wave of proliferation, he said in an interview, will most likely involve "virtual nuclear weapons states" that can produce plutonium or highly enriched uranium and possess the technical knowhow to make warheads, but stop short of assembling a weapon. That is, they remain technically compliant with the NPT yet are within a couple of months of making, deploying, and using a nuclear weapon.[65]

President Obama noted a strange turn of history in a major speech in Prague in April 2009: while the threat of global nuclear war has gone down, the risk of a nuclear attack has gone up. He recommitted the United States to the goal of a world eventually free of nuclear weapons. In the meantime, he also outlined a series of practical, tangible steps to reestablish U.S. credibility as a responsible arms control and disarmament leader: ratification of the CTBT; the pursuit of a verifiable fissile materials cut-off treaty; urgent resumption of negotiations with Russia on new strategic arms reduction talks and treaties to reduce nuclear warheads and stockpiles; explore a new framework for civil nuclear cooperation, including an international fuel bank so countries can access peaceful power without increasing the risks of proliferation; and a new international effort to secure all vulnerable nuclear material around the world within four years.

Two further items are worth noting on the basis of good news and bad news. Obama's speech came shortly after the Central Asian Nuclear-Weapon-Free Zone—the first to require states parties to comply fully with the CTBT—came into existence on 21 March 2009.[66] And the morning of Obama's speech, halfway around the world, North Korea launched a long-range missile over Japan and the Pacific, which was followed by a second underground nuclear test on 25 May. Although described as a failure by U.S. experts, it was nonetheless a sobering reality check for the optimistic assumptions underlying Obama's new nuclear-free agenda. The 2009 Nobel Peace Prize attempts to alter the odds in favor of a world without nuclear weapons.

4

Terrorism

On 11 September 2001—now usually referred to as 9/11—global terrorism struck at the symbolic headquarters of global power and globalization. This was followed over the next five years by other horrific terrorist attacks in such locations as Bali, Madrid, Beslan, Tel Aviv, London, and Mumbai.[1] Iraq witnessed more acts of terrorism than anywhere else in 2004–2008; there, the preferred modus operandi of large-scale car bombings was complemented by the kidnapping and beheading of foreigners. These examples confirm that terrorism is indeed, in the words of a 2002 UN report, "an assault on the principles of law, order, human rights and peaceful settlement of disputes on which the . . . [UN] was founded."[2]

A major difficulty the United Nations faces in trying to fill normative, policy, institutional, and compliance gaps on terrorism is the familiar refrain about one country's or group's terrorist being another's freedom fighter.[3] This is not mere empty sloganeering, as conceptual labeling carries considerable political implications. Many western leaders initially accepted the branding of Nelson Mandela as a terrorist by the apartheid South African regime; today he is internationally revered. Conversely, how many western countries would accept Palestinians using the same tactics against the Israelis that the Kosovo Liberation Army employed successfully against the Serbs? Successive U.S. administrations have had links to numerous unsavory regimes in Latin America that have ruled by terror and sometimes also to opposition groups that have committed terrorist acts against governments hostile to U.S. interests.[4]

This hot contemporary topic has a shorter history within the United Nations than the security issues discussed in the previous two chapters. Nonetheless, this chapter examines significant antecedents and the five gaps and suggests that more UN involvement would benefit efforts to halt this scourge.[5]

Antecedents: Putting 9/11 into Context

International efforts to confront terrorism predate the United Nations. The League of Nations drafted a convention for the international repression of terrorism in 1936. The twenty-first century thus was foreshadowed by efforts to bring national laws into harmony in order to cope with "the use of criminal violence for political ends."[6]

Until the 1990s, the General Assembly debated terrorism almost entirely as a general problem of international law rather than one relating to specific events or conflicts.[7] The thirteen existing UN conventions[8] related to terrorism identify particular forms of outlawed action but contain no definition of terrorism per se.[9] The lack of consensus among member states about how to define terrorism exposes a rift in the world organization that also explains why the UN has been a marginal actor in this issue area.

Reaching broad transnational agreement on the definition of terrorism is no easy matter. Some states may find it useful to oppose the *terrorisme du jour* but also want to preserve their freedom to choose similar force in the future. There always have been two main sticking points. First, many developing countries justify armed violence that includes attacks on civilians by those fighting for national liberation—as did American colonists fighting the British and French *résistants* fighting Nazi occupiers. Second, "state terrorism" arguably should be included in any definition,[10] but for many, the use of force by Israeli and more recently by U.S. forces is hard to mention in the same breath as suicide bombers in the London tube or at Madrid's central station.[11] Yet the historical fact remains that some Jewish groups perpetrated acts of terrorism in their armed national liberation movement against British rule in the Middle East, and the same is true of India's struggle for independence from the British.

While western states sought to delegitimize and criminalize terrorism by pointing to its horrific *consequences*, countries who participated
in the Non-Aligned Movement, particularly when armed national liberation movements were fighting colonialism, tried to soften UN responses
by emphasizing its underlying *causes* such as misery, frustration, despair,
grievances, and foreign occupation. Similarly, while western states highlighted acts of terrorism perpetrated by nonstate actors against innocent
individuals, NAM states pointed to examples of state or state-sponsored
terrorism that targeted groups. That is, for western countries terrorism
was principally a humanitarian problem, whereas for many of the NAM
countries it was primarily a political problem.

Nevertheless, several points are clear. International humanitarian law,
specifically the Geneva Conventions of 1949 and the Additional Protocols
of 1977, prohibits attacks on civilians who take no active part in hostilities.
Various other treaties prohibit attacks on diplomats, interference with civilian aircraft, and so forth. Thus, the international community of states can
and has reached agreement on which targets of violence should be prohibited, which gets around some of the difficulties in defining terrorism.

The United Nations can provide the enabling legal regime and the
normative weight of all three UNs, speaking as one in condemning all
forms of terrorism, no matter how just the cause may be. Implementation
of international treaties is still dependent on states' acting individually and
collaboratively through enforcing national laws, providing policing and
intelligence capacity, implementing judicial and penal machineries, providing cooperation between border control agencies, and so on. The primary UN contribution has been the establishment of international norms
against specific types of terrorist acts and their codification into international law through a crime-by-crime approach. The failure to agree on a
definition of terrorism is primarily political and, as such, not an insuperable
impediment to the elaboration of a legal regime. Rather than be stymied
by the difficulty with definitions, the organization has slowly but surely
built up an impressive record of addressing specific acts of terrorism on
which there is general international agreement, including the attack at the
Munich Olympics in 1972, the the Lockerbie bombing in 1988 sponsored
by Libya, and the terrorist attacks on U.S. soil in September 2001.[12] The
United Nations began by building a set of global anti-terrorism norms
in the 1970s. During the 1980s and 1990s, the UN's response evolved into
stronger institutional enforcement of those norms. And after 9/11, the

norms and the institutions in which the norms are embedded were codified into a reasonably robust legal regime.

The UN's interest in terrorism increased in the 1990s, when proportionately more attacks were directed at U.S. targets, the casualty rate per incident rose, networks of terrorists globalized, the fear that terrorists would acquire and use weapons of mass destruction increased, and states continued to play roles as sponsors and supporters of international terrorism. In the early 1990s the Security Council focused on terrorism, primarily at the instigation of the United States and in response to specific events: several attacks against aircraft, including the downing of Pan American flight 103 over Lockerbie, Scotland, in 1988; the attempted assassination of Egyptian president Hosni Mubarak in 1995; and the bombings of two U.S. embassies in East Africa in 1998. In each case, the Security Council responded by imposing sanctions against certain states: against Libya and Sudan for refusing to extradite suspects and against the Taliban regime in Afghanistan for supporting terrorist groups and refusing to extradite Osama bin Laden. While sanctions helped curb state terrorism, they were ineffective in altering the behavior of groups—such as the Taliban and Al Qaeda—"that situate themselves outside of the international system and reject its institutions and norms."[13]

The Security Council responded to Libya's downing of Pan Am flight 193 and UTA flight 772 in resolution 731 of January 1992. This was the first time the United Nations had implicitly accused a member state government of complicity in an act of terrorism and demanded the extradition of its citizens to stand trial in another country—a conceptual breakthrough in overriding the sacrosanct principle of state sovereignty. This was followed on 31 March by resolution 748, which imposed mandatory sanctions on Libya under Chapter VII of the UN Charter, the first time the Security Council had condemned an act of terrorism as a threat to international peace and security. These resolutions proved a welcome exception to the general inefficacy of sanctions; the economic and diplomatic costs to Libya proved painful enough to bring it back into line with international norms. Libya progressively severed ties with terrorist acts, and the UN eventually lifted the sanctions.

The Security Council's approach changed abruptly in the aftermath of 9/11. Whereas many states had experienced terrorism in the past, this time the remaining superpower had been attacked. Because all national diplomats posted to UN headquarters reside in or in the vicinity of New

York (usually with their families), 9/11 was very personal for them. The council's responses are noteworthy. Resolution 1368, passed on 12 September 2001, recognized "the inherent right of individual or collective self-defense," thus approving the U.S. invasion of Afghanistan. This was the first time that the right to self-defense outlined in Charter Article 51 was formally recognized as a legitimate response to nonstate violence. A few weeks later, the Security Council passed resolution 1373, a comprehensive list of measures states should take to "prevent and suppress" terrorist acts, including changes to national legislation. The resolution also established the Counter-Terrorism Committee (CTC) to monitor member states' implementation of these measures. The council decreased the domain of domestic affairs by subjecting national legislation (in this case, laws involving taxes and contributions to charities) to international monitoring and mandates.

The Secretary-General also became active on the issue, establishing the High-level Panel on Threats, Challenges and Change in 2003 to generate policy ideas to confront terrorism and other security issues of the twenty-first century. Its 2004 report articulated a definition of terrorism and asserted that "attacks that specifically target innocent civilians and non-combatants must be condemned clearly and unequivocally by all,"[14] which the Secretary-General agreed "has clear moral force."[15] At the 2005 World Summit, further progress was made: while the summit's final text lacks a definition of terrorism, for the first time in UN history the heads of state and government issued an unqualified condemnation of "terrorism in all forms and manifestations, committed by whomever, wherever and for whatever purposes."[16] The final text eliminated draft language that had asserted that the targeting of civilians could not be justified, even for movements resisting occupation, but the summit's condemnation of terrorism is a step forward that is fully consistent with the laws of war. Moreover, it places the UN near the center of the fight against terrorism—certainly in terms of important international norms and policies and in terms of operational decisions related to better global governance in the security arena.[17]

Knowledge Gaps: Confronting Alternative Hypotheses

Studies of the UN's responses to terrorism are sparse. On the one hand, the problem of terrorism has been peripheral for most UN analysts and analyses; on the other, the organization has been peripheral to most students of terrorism.[18] Moreover, by their very nature terrorists rely on secrecy and confidentiality. And to the extent that terrorism is distinct from criminality in its political content, public statements by those engaged in terrorist activity or those speaking on their behalf may be designed primarily for public relations rather than to disseminate accurate information.

As a result, there is much we do not know about terrorism. For example, what causes and motivates terrorism? In particular, to what extent do poverty, wealth, and education facilitate the development of terrorist leadership? What methodology should analysts and policymakers use to investigate these issues? How confident can we be about the answers to such questions?

A particular manifestation of the problem of lack of knowledge is the controversy surrounding the so-called root causes of terrorism, especially poverty and deprivation. As *In Larger Freedom* argues, "While poverty and denial of human rights may not be said to 'cause' civil war, terrorism or organized crime, they all greatly increase the risk of instability and violence."[19] To describe terrorism as an *understandable* response does not make it a *legitimate* response. Explanation is not justification; to try to understand is not to seek to condone, let alone to endorse. But because the argument about root causes is deeply connected to the global fault lines on terrorism, it has been summarily dismissed as implying that the United States had provoked or somehow deserved 9/11.

An equally emotionally laden controversy concerns calls to talk to and negotiate with terrorists. The instinctive response of tough-minded government leaders is "We don't talk to or negotiate with terrorists, we kill them." The counter to this is threefold. First, it is precisely with enemies and rivals that one should negotiate in earnest. Second, by definition, terrorism differs from mere criminality in its political content. That being the case, it is necessary to understand the political basis of the grievances and resentments that motivate mainly young people to commit acts of terror so that a solution by political means can be sought. Third, breaking the link between terrorist perpetrators and their wider support base is often a key task. That is more easily achieved when the broader population or community believes that "we" are making a genuine effort to understand and redress their grievances than if they feel ignored and rejected.

A dialogue among civilizations is a necessary if insufficient step in promoting intercultural communication and defusing hate-based terrorism, and the UN arena is a unique place to conduct such conversations.[20]

Talking to representative groups of Muslims might be helpful in drawing moderates away from extremists and in understanding that not all Muslims are terrorists and not all terrorists are Muslims. Islamic terrorism is fundamentally misleading and comparable to the lumping together of such "European terrorists" as Euskadi Ta Askatasuna (ETA) in Spain, the Red Brigades in Italy, the Baader-Meinhof gang in Germany, and the Irish Republican Army in Ulster. More subtlety is required.

After 9/11, some sought to resurrect the vacuous and discredited thesis of the clash of civilizations.[21] Individual terrorism should not provoke mass intolerance. Just as there coexist many ways of thinking and many different value systems within the "West," so are there many who daily honor Islam and a tiny minority who sometimes dishonor it.[22] Islamic terrorists are no more representative of Islam than any terrorists are of their broader community, such as Protestant and Catholic Irish terrorists or fundamentalist Christian anti-abortion terrorists or the Hindu terrorists who destroyed the Babri Masjid in Ayodhya in 1992.[23]

A positive step would be to work harder to close the knowledge gaps and discuss alternative views honestly. Indeed, a provocative contribution by the Human Security Report Project at Simon Fraser University, a member of the Third UN, argued that Islamist terrorist violence decreased during the period 2004 to 2006 even if the intentional killing of civilians in Iraq is counted.[24] As should be obvious, members of all three UNs have roles to play in filling knowledge gaps, just as they do in improving the normative basis for anti-terrorism, to which we now turn our attention.

Normative Gaps: Democracy, Human Rights, and the Elusive Definition

Good governance and the rule of law constrain capricious behavior and the arbitrary exercise of power by rulers, mediate citizen-state relations, and absorb the strains and stresses of political contestation. The campaign against terrorism must be anchored in the norms of accountability, the rule of law, and the upholding of core human rights and civil liberties, including life, liberty, and due process. Democracy legitimizes the struggle for power, and its absence drives dissent underground.[25] Terrorism flourishes amid frustration with repressive, inept, unresponsive, and dynastic regimes that spawn angry and twisted young men and women who take recourse to lethal violence.[26] Sometimes religious institutions are the only alternative rallying point in autocratic regimes.

Terrorism has an impact on human rights in three ways. First, it is an extreme denial of the most basic human right—namely the right to life—and it creates an environment in which people cannot live in freedom from fear and enjoy other rights. Second, governments can use the threat of terrorism to justify enacting laws that strip away many civil liberties and political freedoms. One simple but popular technique is to reverse the burden of proof: those accused of terrorist activities or sympathies or even of guilt by association based on accusations by anonymous people are presumed to be guilty until they can prove that they are innocent of unspecified charges. And third, without necessarily amending laws or enacting new ones, governments can use the need to fight terrorism as a justification for stifling many legitimate forms of dissent and criticism and imprisoning or threatening domestic opponents.

The United Nations has tried to fill both ends of the normative gap—by encouraging the growth and consolidation of democracy as a mechanism of governance for preventing and diluting terrorism, on the one hand; and by trying to protect democratic norms in the "war against terror," on the other. Security Council resolution 1456 of January 2003 obligates states to ensure that counterterrorism measures comply with obligations regarding international human rights, refugees, and international humanitarian law. Kofi Annan urged all countries to create special rapporteurs who would report to the Commission on Human Rights (now the Human Rights Council [HRC]) on whether counterterrorism measures were compatible with international human rights.[27] The UN can provide technical assistance in drafting model counterterrorism legislation. The Office of the High Commissioner for Human Rights has published advice on how counterterrorism can be balanced with human rights standards and norms.[28]

The UN has pursued a rather comprehensive approach to promoting democracy, good governance, human rights, and the rule of law. It is the single best font of authority for promulgating the international rule of law and the most effective forum for building global respect for democracy and good governance. Kofi Annan affirmed the right of peoples "to choose how they are ruled, and who rules them," noting that the UN gave support to elections in a number of countries and lamenting that it was a little-known fact that "the United Nations does more than any other single organization to promote and strengthen democratic institutions and practices around the world."[29]

At the same time, the struggle against terrorism, as Secretary-General Annan argued, "must not take place at the expense of the fundamental freedoms and the basic dignity of individuals. Success in defeating terrorism can come only if we remain true to those values which terrorists eschew."[30] In resorting to the lesser evil of curtailing liberties and using violence in order to defeat terrorism, we should be careful not to succumb to the greater evil of destroying the very values for which democracies stand.[31] Governments should justify all restrictive measures publicly, submit them to judicial review, and circumscribe them with sunset clauses to guard against the temporary becoming permanent. Safeguards to protect basic human rights are especially important because history suggests that most people, even in mature democracies, privilege the security of the majority over the harm done to minorities who are deprived of their rights in the name of national security.

After 9/11, U.S. priorities shifted to subordinate human rights to victory in the "war" against terrorism. President George W. Bush's declaration that detainees in the war on terror were not covered by the Geneva Conventions was a deliberate tactic to reduce their chances of making successful legal claims against the government. The U.S. Department of Defense adopted stress and duress techniques that violated both international humanitarian law and the U.S. Constitution and were questionable in their effects. As the conditions of detention of suspected foreign terrorists in American prisons became widely known in the Muslim world, they contributed to a hardening of the *jihad* through *shahid* (martyrdom), for, as Nasra Hassan's study of suicide bombers uncovered, "death is preferable to Guantánamo Bay."[32]

Two issues merged in the public debates: determining which legal regime should apply to prisoners in this particular war and abuses in the treatment of prisoners. The fact that the United States designated prisoners as "enemy combatants" and confined them at Guantánamo Bay, Cuba, where they were abused and questioned using torture, raised serious questions about the commitment of the United States to the right to a fair trial and impartial justice.[33] Only a minority of prisoners held by the United States were abused, but like the gulags in the erstwhile Soviet system, they were integral to the war and provided unbecoming worldwide publicity.[34] In a validation of Hannah Arendt's thesis on the banality of evil, most ordinary U.S. citizens went about their daily business while all this was being done in their name.[35] Many other democracies—including

Australia, Canada, and the United Kingdom—joined the United States in shifting the balance of laws and administrative practices toward state security. And the distasteful practice of "rendition" also developed, a sub-contracting arrangement that sent prisoners back to their home countries or to third countries that are known to practice torture as part of their interrogation routines.

It is critical that civil liberties, political freedoms, and the rule of law be protected in efforts to defeat terrorists. An opinion piece in the *Washington Post* asked: "How can President Bush preach to the world about democracy, about transparency, about the rule of law, and at the same time disregard national and international law at will? What message can Vladimir Putin be hearing? Or the dictators in Beijing? Or the mullahs in Tehran?"[36] The robustness and resilience of the commitment of the United States to human rights norms and values will be judged, in the final analysis, not by the breaches in the aftermath of 9/11 but by the reversal and attenuation of the breaches through domestic judicial and political processes as well as the pressures of civil society.[37] These converged with the election of Barack Obama as U.S. president. Obama ordered an unequivocal and immediate halt to such practices as waterboarding that the Bush administration had euphemistically relabeled "enhanced interrogation techniques" but which most observers and many Americans recognized as torture.

The most glaring normative gap is the lack of a universally accepted definition of terrorism. The High-level Panel on Threats, Challenges and Change tried its hand at defining terrorism as "any action . . . that is intended to cause death or serious bodily harm to civilians or non-combatants, when the purpose of such an act, by its nature or context, is to intimidate a population, or to compel a Government or an international organization to do or to abstain from doing any act."[38] The High-level Panel's focus on the nature of the acts breaks the link with causes and motivations. It affirms that "terrorism is never an acceptable tactic, even for the most defensible of causes."[39] That the Palestinian people have a just cause and a justified grievance does not mean that blowing up a busload of school children or a pizza parlor is just. International acceptance of the proposed definition could remove the ideological edge from the debate and mute the charges of inconsistency and double standards.

Recalling that existing normative instruments for the use of force by states are well developed and robust, the High-level Panel called for similar measures against nonstate actors.[40] International relations scholar Tom

Farer points out that for decades it has been common to use the word "terrorist" to describe regimes "that kill, torture and make people disappear in order to terrify the rest of the population." The High-level Panel and the Secretary-General tried to alter this powerful moral discourse, especially as the moral effects of shaming "are likely to be greater where state officials fall within the definition of terrorist than when private actors do."[41]

In his report released in preparation for the World Summit, the Secretary-General noted that terrorism is "neither an acceptable nor an effective way to advance" a cause and called for a comprehensive convention "based in a clear and agreed definition."[42] The draft outcome document at the 2005 summit reiterated the strong condemnation of terrorism "in all its forms and manifestations," no matter what the cause, and endorsed the call for a comprehensive convention.[43] But the heads of state and government assembled in New York in September 2005 failed to agree on a norm-setting definition.

We return to the problems of definition because there must be consensus for norms to be agreed and applied and because there are well-known reasons for the inability of member states to agree on a universal definition in any official UN forum. The most appealing definition is one that isolates terrorism as a tactic and delegitimizes it regardless of the motivation. This definition distinguishes terrorism from criminal violence because it is politically motivated; this puts politics at the heart of any effort to curb and eliminate it. This, in turn, makes it very difficult for the United Nations, a highly political intergovernmental forum, to take the lead.

Policy Gaps: Group Grievances, Intractable Conflicts, Poverty Alleviation, WMDs

The difficulties of defining terrorism is one key to the problems that afflict international efforts to devise common policies to combat and uproot it. Developing policies within the UN system for a topic as contested as terrorism is harder than one imagines, but it is not impossible.

Over the decades, the threat of international terrorism has been addressed internationally, within both the framework of international law and the framework of specific UN resolutions and measures. In the Corfu Channel case in 1949, the International Court of Justice affirmed "every State's obligation not to allow knowingly its territory to be used for acts contrary to the rights of other States."[44] Thirteen global, seven regional, and three related reaties for combating terrorism exist; these can be seen as a substantial corpus of policies.[45] Nevertheless, until the 1970s, terrorism was viewed in UN circles largely as a local phenomenon. As the frequency, violence, and reach of terrorist incidents began to expand, the General Assembly seemed to be as interested in understanding and rationalizing terrorism as in suppressing it, while the Security Council was more concerned with the counterterrorism tactics of Israel and the United States than with the acts of terrorism themselves.[46]

. Many of the traditional support constituencies of the Third UN are instinctively suspicious of potential actions to counter terrorism that are being considered by member states within the debating arenas of the First United Nations. For example, human rights groups want their cause factored in; humanitarian actors and arms control activists are worried about rollbacks to international humanitarian law and disarmament; and many developmentalists want to limit the diversion of resources from development and the "root causes" of terrorism such as poverty and inequality. These concerns were heightened in the immediate aftermath of September 11th.

On 12 September 2001, both the Security Council and the General Assembly adopted resolutions strongly condemning the acts of terrorism of the previous day and urging all states to cooperate to bring the perpetrators, organizers, and sponsors of 9/11 to justice. Resolution 1368 was the first to incorporate acts against terrorism into the right of self-defense. In doing so, the Security Council effectively gave Washington a blank check and sidelined itself from overseeing all subsequent measures taken in Afghanistan. Two weeks later, resolution 1373 imposed significant requirements on member states within their domestic jurisdictions and expanded the council's oversight role in relation to them. "This posed a remarkable dichotomy. The Security Council chooses to exercise no control or oversight on the use of military force in response to terrorism but is vigilant and arguably intrusive when it comes to dealing with terrorism through national mechanisms and controls." Moreover, because neither "self-defense" nor "terrorism" is defined or self-explanatory, the result "compounds the [unlimited] expansiveness of the mandate."[47] The most egregious example of the Security Council's serving propaganda goals came after the Madrid bombings of 2004, when the council strongly condemned the attacks "perpetrated by the terrorist group ETA" in resolution 1530. Many suspected at the time of the attack that Islamist groups had perpetrated the outrage, and this was soon confirmed. However, the

Security Council resolution had less to do in this instance with fighting terrorism than with Washington's desire to help a head of state who was an ally win reelection.

On 13 April 2005, after seven years of negotiations, the General Assembly unanimously adopted the thirteenth UN convention against terrorism, the International Convention for the Suppression of Acts of Nuclear Terrorism. It was opened for signature on 14 September 2005 and entered into force on 7 July 2007, one month after the twenty-second ratification. The convention makes it a crime to possess or demand radioactive material or devices with the aim of causing death or serious injury or substantial damage to property. It calls on states to adopt national laws to make these acts criminal and to institute appropriate penalties for those convicted of such acts. Between them, the thirteen global treaties define, proscribe, and punish such individual categories of terrorism as hijacking, piracy, taking hostages, bombing civilians, procuring nuclear materials, and financing terrorist activities. But these conventions are not the same thing as having a global policy; they do not address the totality of terrorist acts within one comprehensive normative or institutional framework.

In his 2005 report, Annan outlined five pillars of a counterterrorism strategy: dissuade people from resorting to or supporting terrorism; deny terrorists access to funds and materials; deter states from sponsoring terrorism; develop capacity so states can defeat terrorism; and defend human rights.[48] The 2005 *World Summit Outcome* endorsed the Secretary-General's counterterrorism strategy.[49] Four topics should guide future policy formulation efforts by all three United Nations: grievances of groups, intractable conflicts, poverty alleviation, and weapons of mass destruction.

Grievances of Groups

Grievances rooted in collective ethnic and religious injustice generate anger and sometimes armed resistance when the weaker resort to asymmetrical warfare. Often the driving force behind fanatical hatred is individual despair born of collective humiliation. The United States becomes the focus of grievances if its arms and policies are seen to be propping up occupying or brutalizing forces.[50] Of all the so-called root causes, the most proximate in the world's most volatile region is the sense of collective humiliation of the collective Arab identity.[51] As journalist Jessica Stern noted, because of "ignorance and negligence" in the way the

United States dismissed world opinion before the war and managed the aftermath of the invasion of Iraq, "even those Iraqis who saw Americans as liberators during the first days after Saddam Hussein was ousted from power now see America as an ignorant, brutal, occupying power." The U.S. occupation of Baghdad with tanks and soldiers, the capital of the Islamic world during its golden age of civilization, is deeply humiliating. For young Muslims, "it is better to carry arms and defend their religion with pride and dignity than to submit to this humiliation."[52]

Terror is the tactic of choice of those who harbor the sense of having been wronged, are too weak to do anything about it through conventional means, and are motivated to seek vengeance. Terrorism is the use of indiscriminate violence to change politics. Therefore, the defeat of terrorism can never be simply a law enforcement problem but must inject political calculations and new policies into the center of debates over tactics and strategy. A refusal to negotiate with terrorists should not be confused with fear of negotiating. Those who resort to the illegitimate tactic of terrorism can be isolated, but their goals may still be worth supporting, and it may even be necessary to support those goals for the sake of separating the perpetrators from their sympathizers in the wider community. While it required decades and the expenditure of substantial resources and political capital, the British managed to successfully end terrorism in Northern Ireland, as did the Indians in the Punjab.

Intractable Conflicts

Long-running conflicts have spawned generations of radicalized populations in areas as geographically diverse as Palestine, Kashmir, Sri Lanka, and Chechnya. Robert Pape, who has compiled a comprehensive database of every single terrorist attack in the world from 1980 to early 2004, argues that 95 percent of suicide terrorists seek to compel military forces to withdraw from the territory that terrorists view as their homeland under foreign occupation.[53]

Al Qaeda, a vast, decentralized, and clandestine operation spread across Asia, the Middle East, and Africa, has repeated over several years its aim to end the U.S. military presence in the Middle East as well as to end U.S. support for Israel's occupation of Palestinian territories and of coercive regimes in the Muslim world. The U.S.-led response after 9/11 achieved many successes in efforts to strangle Al Qaeda: their bases were destroyed, their finances were disrupted, and their sponsors were isolated from them. Yet from another point of view, Al Qaeda arguably has not lost the war. The Middle East is more violent and less stable, the U.S. military is out of Saudi Arabia, a major new front has been opened in Iraq, and the Iraq war has turned out to be a major source of fresh recruitment to the cause. While the Bush adminstration continued to justify the Iraq war as necessary in efforts to combat terrorism linked to Al Qaeda, a declassified summary of an analysis by the National Intelligence Estimate concluded that the U.S. occupation of Iraq had given Al Qaeda a potent rallying cry, recruiting tool, and training ground and that the organization, safely ensconced in Pakistan, had protected or regenerated key elements of its capability to attack the U.S. homeland.[54] British official and private sources came to broadly similar conclusions.

It would be as futile for Indians to deny that governance in Kashmir has often been repressive as for Americans to deny their past propensity to back authoritarian regimes throughout the world. There is a common willingness to look more fondly on thugs when they are allies. It is hard for many Americans to accept the notion that, as Saudi analyst Mai Yamani has noted, "the anger of young Muslims results primarily from revulsion at their corrupt leaders, and the subservience of these rulers to the United States."[55] Victims—Chechnyans, Kashmiris, Palestinians, Tamils—cannot be made to give up their right to resist, which is difficult to fathom for the states who are challenged.

Providing security from terrorism cannot be done selectively. President George W. Bush declared that the United States would make no distinction between terrorists and those who harbor them. However, the United States and other Security Council members must not make a distinction between "our" terrorists and "theirs," condoning some extremist groups while battling others. How many of today's radical extremists are yesterday's "freedom fighters" trained and financed by the West as *jihadis?* Muslims from all over the world flocked to the Afghan resistance against Soviet occupation, received CIA training in and arms and explosives for guerrilla fighting, became battle hardened, and acquired pride, power, and comradeship in the victorious struggle. After the expulsion of the Soviets, Afghan veterans fanned out to every struggle involving Islamic communities.

The United States certainly is not the only culprit, nor is it unusual in its approach. There are many other examples, historical and contemporary, of "blowback." Indian prime minister Indira Gandhi paid with her life for trying to harness Sikh religious nationalism to her politics of divide and rule in the Punjab; as prime minister, her son and successor, Rajiv Gandhi, was consumed by Tamil terrorism exported from Sri Lanka, outposts of which had been tolerated on Indian soil by his government. Former Pakistani president Pervez Musharraf knows the feeling of becoming the target of the monsters of terrorism that in the past Pakistan may have created or tolerated.

While the United States will always be the most forceful and sometimes may even be the most welcome mediator and peacemaker, usually the United Nations is a more authoritative and more broadly acceptable forum for conflict resolution. Washington therefore has a vested interest in strengthening the principle of UN-centered multilateralism and the UN's administrative, technical, and financial capacity for resolving conflict. This could and should emerge as *the* policy of choice for many governments.

Poverty Alleviation

No serious analyst postulates a simple and direct causal link between poverty and terrorism. But deprivation certainly can be an incubator of terrorism. A quick and simple review of the countries in which the systematic use of terror by state and nonstate groups is commonplace confirms its link with poverty, underdevelopment, and lack of democracy. Terrorist leaders—like those in most walks of life—tend to be affluent and well educated, but they find ready recruits as foot soldiers among poor, illiterate, and marginalized groups. Alienation, despair, and discontent provide fertile grounds to recruit would-be terrorists and maintain a pool of supporters in society at large.

Poverty also detracts from a state's capacity to provide universal education through the public sector; the result is that thousands of children go to private religious institutions and are schooled in the twin cultures of the Koran and the Kalashnikov. It would be hard to imagine Palestine, Pakistan, Afghanistan, Indonesia, and the Philippines as long-term major recruiting and training bases and safe havens for terrorism if they were comfortably well-off middle-class countries. Better multilateral policies, national and international, are required to reflect the relationship between socioeconomic deprivation and terrorism.

Eliminating poverty is an uphill battle, and it is humanity's challenge. The world organization is dedicated to economic development and the goal of poverty reduction in general and the eradication of extreme poverty in particular. Developing countries do more than simply accept such a role for the UN; they demand it. The world had signed on to the Millennium Development Goals (MDGs) a year prior to 9/11. The calls to help combat the scourge of poverty found a more sympathetic and receptive audience afterward. The effort to reach the agreed targets is an inalienable part of the UN's past, present, and future agenda.

Weapons of Mass Destruction

The nightmare scenario for those concerned about national and international security is the acquisition and use of WMDs by nonstate actors who cannot be deterred by the threat of totally destructive retaliation. Worst-case scenarios see terrorists using nuclear or radiological weapons to kill hundreds of thousands of people.[56] In its annual report to the U.S. Congress for 2004, the CIA warned that Al Qaeda is fully capable of building a radiological "dirty" bomb targeting the United States and others and has "crude procedures" for producing chemical weapons using mustard gas, sarin, the nerve agent VX, and cyanide. The CIA warned that the danger of terrorists using chemical, biological, radiological, and nuclear materials "remained high."[57] Similarly, the Aspen Strategy Group concluded that the danger of nuclear terrorism is greater than most people realize and that the U.S. government has not prepared adequately for it.[58]

An attack that combines the sophistication and ruthlessness of 9/11 with the use of nuclear weapons is possible. According to current intelligence, however, no terrorist group currently has the competence to build nuclear weapons, and there is no evidence that any rogue state has transferred such weapons to terrorist organizations. The most realistic concern is that Al Qaeda or a related group could detonate a "dirty bomb" (a conventional explosive wrapped in radioactive material) that could spray radioactive fallout across a major city. While it would cause significantly less death and devastation than a nuclear bomb, it would cause some casualties and radiation sickness and produce mass panic, making it a weapon of mass disruption more than a weapon of mass destruction.

Bioterrorism may be more likely because pathogens and toxins can be made easily and clandestinely in a small area in sufficient quantities to do significant damage. The absence of effective verification measures and an organization that could implement the Biological Weapons Convention are serious shortcomings. By contrast, the state-of-the-art verification provisions of the Chemical Weapons Convention and the existence of the Organization for the Prohibition of Chemical Weapons as the implementing arm of the convention are effective bulwarks against the ability of terrorists to use chemical weapons.[59]

The international community's tolerance for states out of compliance with WMD nonproliferation and disarmament norms and obligations narrowed dramatically after 9/11. Security Council resolution 1540 of April 2004 broke new conceptual ground in directing sovereign states to enact nonproliferation legislation. Affirming WMD proliferation as a threat to international peace and security and expressing concern over the threat of WMD terrorism and of illicit trafficking in WMD materials and delivery systems, resolution 1540 called on all states to enact and enforce laws to prohibit nonstate actors from developing, acquiring, transferring, or using WMDs; to take and enforce effective domestic control, physical protection, accounting, and border control measures to prevent proliferation; and to set up a committee of the whole to oversee implementation of the resolution.

The unprecedented intrusion into national law-making authority can be read as the First UN's toughened determination to take effective action. But it was not without controversy because "the UN Charter makes no provision for the Council to engage in such global law-making, and the imposition of such obligations runs counter to the principle that international law is based on the consent of states."[60] Abdalmahood Abdalhaleem Mohamad, a former member of the UN/Organization of African Unity Expert Group on the Denuclearization of Africa, has noted that "by arrogating to itself wider powers of legislation," the Security Council departed from its Charter-based mandate and that excessive recourse to Chapter VII could signal a preference for coercion over cooperation. Mohamad argues that the Security Council framed the resolution within the global war against terrorism in order to silence dissenting voices and that the council's unrepresentative composition and the veto power of the P-5 undermine its efforts to seek global adherence to its resolutions.[61] Many members of the Third UN criticized the resolution's silence on the role of disarmament in promoting nonproliferation as well as the Security Council's efforts to transform itself into a world legislature.[62] This development has made Security Council reform even more pressing to powerful states not among the P-5.

The criticisms and the extent of their validity notwithstanding, Security Council resolutions 1368, 1373, and 1540 along with the International Convention for Suppression of the Financing of Terrorism (1999) constitute a multilateral policy of sorts that has led to an impressive number of practical steps. They restrict potential terrorists by denying them the financial means for their nefarious activities, freezing their assets, restricting their freedom of movement across borders, and denying them the weapons they seek to commit terrorist acts.

Institutional Gaps:
Making Better Use of Existing Capacities

The global coalition to combat threats to international peace and security, including terrorism, is already in place. We call it the United Nations. If the Security Council is the geopolitical center of gravity, the General Assembly is the normative center of gravity. It is the unique forum of choice for articulating global values and norms and the arena where contested norms can be debated and reconciled. This was its historical role in its efforts to delegitimize colonialism, even though decolonization came about through policy decisions taken in national capitals. The General Assembly has played the dual role of developing a normative framework on terrorism and encouraging cooperative action among states. While the Security Council has concentrated on preventing acts of terrorism through promoting cooperation between security, law enforcement, and border control authorities, the assembly can mold the global response to terrorism through its power of budgetary allocations.[63] In addition, the international civil and maritime organizations are addressing threats to the world's air and shipping traffic, respectively; the IAEA and the OPCW seek to ensure compliance with chemical and nuclear weapons treaties; the World Health Organization is preparing defenses against terrorist attacks using biochemical weapons; and the Terrorism Prevention Branch of the UN Office on Drugs and Crime (UNODC) provides legislative assistance to many countries in connection with ratifying and implementing antiterrorism conventions and Security Council resolutions.

Security Council resolution 1373 imposed uniform legislative and reporting requirements and established the Counter-Terrorism Committee (made up of all fifteen members of the council) to monitor implementation and increase state capacity.[64] A largely untold success story by the First UN and the Second UN since 9/11, the CTC calls on the advice of experts in the fields of legislative drafting; financial, customs, immigration, and extradition law and practice; police and law enforcement; and illegal arms trafficking. Some states simply lack the capacity to implement the domestic requirements imposed by Security Council resolutions, others lack inclination. Both are the very states that attract the interest of terrorist cells. The CTC helps member states build capacity through disseminating best practices; providing technical, financial, regulatory, and legislative expertise; and facilitating cooperation between national, regional, and international organizations. But it has neither the resources nor the capacity to monitor state compliance with obligations imposed by the council. While human rights per se is beyond the CTC's mandate, it has collaborated with the Office of the High Commissioner for Human Rights with respect to guidelines for states on their human rights obligations in the context of counterterrorism.

Another institutional response from the UN system is the Counter-Terrorism Implementation Task Force (CTITF), established by Kofi Annan in 2005 to promote coherence in UN system-wide efforts. The CTITF also extends beyond the UN in its planning and coordination work, for example ensuring liaison with the International Criminal Police Organization (Interpol). Other UN bodies such as the International Civil Aviation Organization, which secures commercial aviation and airports, and the International Maritime Organization, which secures shipping traffic and port facilities, also play a role. Additionally, the UNODC provides countries with technical assistance on counterterrorism legislation. The CTITF has compiled a *Counter-Terrorism Online Handbook* that details its counterterrorism activities and provides information about and access to UN counterterrorism resources.[65]

Compliance Gaps:
Mixing National and International Measures

Both the Security Council and the General Assembly played a role in filling compliance gaps. Security Council resolution 1566 of October 2004 set up a working group, consisting of all council members, to create a global blacklist of terrorist organizations and recommend ways to curb their activities. These included prosecution and extradition, freezing assets, banning travel, and prohibiting arms sales. The International Convention for the Suppression of Acts of Nuclear Terrorism of 2005 is a good illustration of how the General Assembly can play an important role in the global fight against this scourge when the members of the First UN have the political will to do so.

How can we marry the international legitimacy of the UN with the global reach and power of the United States? The struggle against terrorism is one from which Washington can neither stay disengaged nor win on its own, nor is it a war that the UN and its member states can win without full U.S. engagement. It spans the full range of responses—from social and economic to political and security—and engages every level of government. A wise strategy must be multilayered and must address grievances and counteract the causes of individual and group humiliation and indignity. The object is not to destroy every individual terrorist but to neutralize support for terrorists in the communities in which they live and generate the will and capacity of relevant local and national authorities to act against them.

In addition to addressing the so-called root causes, a robust strategy should address the linkages between global terrorism and organized crime. Indeed, the line between the two has become increasingly blurred.[66] Terrorism is a problem to be tackled mainly by law enforcement agencies, in cooperation with military forces. Its magnitude can be brought down to "tolerable" levels, but it can never be totally defeated, just as we cannot have an absolutely crime-free society. And efforts to combat terrorism and crime are part of the new security agenda that emphasizes human as well as national security.[67]

The final line of defense against international terrorism is preventive national measures in countries that are the targets of attacks. These include counterterrorism intelligence and surveillance efforts by law enforcement, national security, and border control personnel as well as by agencies that monitor and regulate financial transactions. There is probably not much scope for UN involvement here, but the political cover of the world organization can make programs of bilateral technical assistance more palatable to many domestic constituencies. In the end, there can be no totally guaranteed security against suicide terrorists who have unlimited audacity, imagination, and inhumanity.[68]

Efforts to build effective defenses against international terrorism should focus first on countries that harbor or host individuals and groups that advocate, finance, arm, and otherwise support international terrorism. The export of terror can be stopped or contained most cost effectively in this way. This requires building capacity in countries that lack institutional resilience in their security sectors to tackle terrorist cells in their midst and mustering political will in other countries that have the capacity but lack the determination to root out cells from their midst. Fragile states with frail institutions are the soft underbelly for global terrorism. Terrorists take advantage of porous borders, weak and corrupt law enforcement forces, and limp judicial systems.

An appropriate mix of carrots and sticks is required. The security capacity of countries fighting to liquidate terrorist cells should of course be strengthened. Postwar (if that is the term) Iraq has demonstrated that recovery, reconstruction, and rebuilding are not U.S. strong suits. Meanwhile, the UN has accumulated substantial experience. Former U.S. assistant secretary of state James Dobbins and a Rand Corporation evaluation team have argued that the world organization's performance in postconflict situations is remarkably good in comparison with that of Washington; they attribute success to seven of eight UN operations versus only four out of eight for the United States.[69]

Security Council resolution 1535 of 2004 reinforced the work of the CTC by creating the CTC Executive Directorate (CTED) to provide the CTC and member states with expert advice on all areas covered by resolution 1373. By mid-2008, the CTED had identified the technical needs of over ninety countries and created a directory of standards, practices, and sources of counterterrorism assistance. Under the Al Qaeda and Taliban sanctions regime, by January 2006 some thirty-four states had frozen over $90 million of assets of individuals and groups whose names appear on the UN's consolidated list. Pursuant to council resolution 1540, reports from almost 130 states and the European Union have been examined to check compliance with the resolution.

In March 2008, CTED executive director Mike Smith reported to the Security Council that the CTED now devotes less attention to checking whether member states have adopted laws and more time evaluating the effectiveness of their border control arrangements, counterterrorism coordination machinery, and law enforcement capabilities. Most countries had criminalized terrorism, and there is a substantial level of international exchange of information and transborder cooperation with a view to disrupting planned acts of terrorism and facilitating the arrest and prosecution of terrorists. Consequently, the focus now is on making sure that countries have the capacity, expertise, and resources to implement effective counterterrorism rather than on ensuring that they understand the gravity of the challenge.[70]

The United Nations itself does not have the capacity to provide the level of legislative and technical antiterrorism assistance member states demand. Rather, the CTC and the CTED act as "switchboards," matching the requests for technical assistance with states and organizations that have the requisite capacity to provide them. In the meantime, the UNODC has helped over 110 countries join and implement the universal instruments for preventing and suppressing international terrorism and has provided technical assistance to almost seventy countries to strengthen their legal regimes against terrorism.

Following the 2005 World Summit, Secretary-General Annan refined his proposals in May 2006.[71] Based on consultations shaped by this report, the General Assembly unanimously adopted the Global Counter-Terrorism Strategy in September 2006 as the common platform to bring together the efforts of the various UN entities into one coherent framework—the first time all 192 member states had agreed on a common approach to fighting terrorism.[72] Nonetheless, an agreed strategy is not synonymous with complaince.

A related task is coaxing or coercing regimes that are tolerant of terrorist cells to confront the menace instead. There must also be bilateral and multilateral regimes for regulating and controlling in-border production and storage and cross-border transfer of terrorism-related materials, skills, and technology. This would be best accomplished with concerted bilateral encouragement and pressure from relevant states *and* the three United Nations.

Conclusion: Steps to Controlling the Global Menace

Defeating international terrorism requires both military and police action against those who put their questionable causes and skewed priorities before the lives of civilians. But it also requires nation-building through repairing and stabilizing war-torn countries, establishing the institutions and structures of government and the rule of law, consolidating civil society, and building markets. The first part can be left to powerful UN member states. Even unilateral action needs a cooperative institutional context, and many related tasks such as sharing intelligence and impeding money laundering would benefit from the kinds of universal measures that only the United Nations can guarantee. The second, less glamorous part underlines the importance of international norms, agreements, cooperation, policies, and institutions; and these in many instances gives the world organization a comparative advantage vis-à-vis other international actors.

The Security Council will remain the key international player in imposing coercive measures in the form of sanctions and military force. While international judicial pursuit has not yet been applied to terrorists, the International Criminal Court could certainly be an asset. While many in the United States and those countries that still have the death penalty might be appalled, successfully bringing before the ICC the likes of Osama bin Laden for crimes against humanity would gain international sympathy for fighting terrorism. An opportunity was missed when the Iraqi Governing Council, with the backing of the United States, chose not to organize an international trial for Saddam Hussein.

The General Assembly's work in developing international conventions on terrorism, while subsequently overshadowed by the work of the Security Council, remains important and may increase as the Secretary-General pursues a comprehensive counterterrorism strategy. The codification of emerging norms can perhaps best take place in a forum that is able to take a comprehensive, politically informed, and longer-term view. The most significant advantage of the assembly is that it is an inclusive forum. It is also the place where decisions about the allocation of organizational resources are made, thus giving it a direct impact on determining the administrative capability of the world organization to deal with terrorism. Obviously, this capacity is greatly affected by the collective political will of the most powerful member states.

As of late 2009, member states were still negotiating a fourteenth international treaty, a draft comprehensive convention on international terrorism that would complement the existing framework of international antiterrorism instruments and build on the key guiding principles already present in existing antiterrorist conventions: the importance of criminalizing terrorist offenses, making them punishable by law and calling for prosecution or extradition of the perpetrators; the need to eliminate legislation that establishes exceptions to the criminalization of perpetrators on political, philosophical, ideological, racial, ethnic, religious, or similar grounds; a strong call for member states to take action to prevent terrorist acts; and emphasis on the need for member states to cooperate, exchange information, and provide each other with the greatest measure of assistance in connection with the prevention, investigation, and prosecution of terrorist acts.

The Secretary-General and the Secretariat also have the ability to take less reactive, more comprehensive approaches. After 9/11, Kofi Annan established a Policy Working Group on the United Nations and Terrorism to examine how the UN should deal with the phenomenon.[73] He also remained poised to deal with specific situations and respond to events through the use of his good offices. These roles could and should be enhanced.

As in other areas, the United Nations is the forum of choice for regime negotiation and norm promotion in countering international terrorism. Indeed, the establishment of a regime through an interlocking collection of treaties and conventions is one of the more significant achievements of the UN system over the past two decades. It lacks enforcement capacity, to be sure, but it can promulgate and promote the normative and legal framework of a counterterrorism regime. It can also be the coordinating forum for counterterrorism efforts by states, regional organizations, and technical agencies such as the IAEA. The UN could be the central coordinator and clearinghouse for information about biological and chemical weapons, for aligning the work of national and functional agencies, and for the global stockpiling and distribution of drugs and vaccines in a global crisis.

Just as important, the world organization with its multitude of offices, funds, programs, and specialized agencies is also the forum of choice for attacking, in the words of the General Assembly, "the conditions conducive to the spread of terrorism including but not limited to prolonged unresolved conflicts, dehumanization of victims of terrorism in all its forms and manifestations, lack of the rule of law and violations of human rights, ethnic, national and religious discrimination, political exclusion, socio-economic marginalization and lack of good governance."[74]

The tragic attacks on New York and Washington killed almost 3,000 civilians in 2001, twice the number of combatants who died in the Japanese attack on Pearl Harbor in 1941. A few days later, Secretary-General Kofi Annan pointed to the advantage of the world organization in efforts to improve global governance against this blight: "Terrorism is a global menace. It calls for a united, global response. To defeat it, all nations must take counsel together, and act in unison. That is why we have the United Nations."[75] We could not have said it better.

PART 2

Development

5

Trade, Aid, and Finance

- Antecedents: The Long Trek toward Equality and Justice
- Knowledge Gaps: Understanding Development
- Normative Gaps: The Shape of Transfers from Rich to Poor
- Policy Gaps: The NIEO Clash and Aid
- Institutional Gaps: From GATT to the WTO
- Compliance Gaps: Words, Deeds, and the MDGs
- Reforming the Architecture of International Financial and Economic Governance
- Human Development and the Five Global Governance Gaps
- Conclusion: Partial Gap Filling

Although the primary mandate of the United Nations is maintaining international peace and security, the search for international security was polarized around the Cold War almost immediately after the organization came into being. In the meantime, decolonization brought into being a vast number of newly independent countries that joined the United Nations as a final seal of their sovereign statehood; by the mid-1960s some 100 new member states had joined the original fifty-one Charter signers, and today's members total 192. The organization's membership did not simply multiply; the newer members also inscribed their own concerns into the UN's agenda.[1] Those located in what was becoming known as the "Third World" were mainly interested in state-building, nation-building, and economic development in order to lift their peoples out of subsistence, poverty, and unemployment. Because the Security Council was nearly paralyzed by the East-West rivalry and the new member states were united in their concerns, economic and social development became the UN's main activity during the Cold War. During this period, economic and social objectives became essential in and of themselves instead of being mainly viewed as a way to ensure international peace and security.

Antecedents: The Long Trek toward Equality and Justice

In *International Organization and Industrial Change: Global Governance since 1850,* Craig Murphy draws on Antonio Gramsci's work on historical blocs to argue that world order in a particular period is not created solely by the actions of states but through the blocs that become dominant. Through the creation of specific organizational forms, structure can accumulate around historically contingent coalitions of powerful social forces and prevailing ideas. These historical blocs are in constant dialectical contention; when one order declines, another springs from its ashes. Regulatory regimes are thus usually created in the wake of crisis and upheaval, if not actual war. There have been three generations of global governance institutions thus far: "public international unions," whose heyday ran from the age of railroads in the middle of the nineteenth century through the first age of mass production at the outset of the twentieth century; the League of Nations and UN systems, which run from approximately World War I to the 1980s; and "third generation" international organizations, which Murphy dates from the creation of Intelsat (the International Telecommunications Satellite Organization) in 1964.

These agencies have penetrated far into the state by championing certain ideas about the regulation of industrial capitalism—evidence of global governance. Indeed, the notion of establishing "peace by pieces" was the foundation for David Mitrany's scholarly work on functional cooperation during the interwar years,[2] a line of reasoning followed by Jean Monnet, chief architect of European integration, and others who began with cooperation in "low politics" in Europe before moving to the "high politics" of security and foreign policy.[3]

As with so much else, the roots of the UN's interest in social and economic issues and its evolving role in global governance lie in the history of the League of Nations. Another reason for the UN Charter's greater focus on social and economic issues compared to the League Covenant was that the latter had been notably more successful in these domains than in security, including during the interwar period when the League and the ILO continued working on economic issues during the Great Depression. Indeed, some League officials moved to Princeton, New Jersey, and continued their research during the war long after the League's security machinery had stopped.

While we repeatedly note that the UN is not a world government, many readers may not fully appreciate the extent to which this understatement reflects the decentralized notions that drove the creation of the UN system from the outset. The physical locations of UN bodies reflect functional fragmentation. A government has a central location and ministries. Logistical problems are always created when a new capital is created—for example, in Brasilia rather than Rio or Abuja rather than Lagos or Berlin rather than Bonn. However, there is no real UN "capital" and there never has been; New York is the UN's political center while Geneva is its main economic and humanitarian center. The centers for other essential UN components are found in Vienna, Nairobi, Rome, Tokyo, Vancouver, London, The Hague, and many other places. Some national governments are also disbursed (Switzerland is one example), but even by that standard the UN system is exceptionally decentralized and fragmented.

Unpacking the complex structure of UN activities linked to global economic governance reveals four main clusters of somewhat autonomous activity: the United Nations proper—that is, the relevant principal organs, regional commissions, and central parts that are not specialized agencies (especially the UNDP and UNICEF) that operate more or less in tandem with the specialized agencies; the specialized agencies themselves; the IMF and the World Bank (which are de jure but not de facto part of the UN system); and more recently the World Trade Organization (which is not actually part of the system).[4] The organizations in each cluster are comprised of their governing bodies (the First UN), secretariats in addition to field offices and activities throughout the world (the Second UN), and accredited NGOs that function as lobbyist or executing partners (the Third UN).

In the preceding chapters, we have followed the work of the Security Council, the General Assembly, the International Court of Justice, and the Secretariat. These four principal organs—another, the Trusteeship Council, effectively went out of business in 1994 when the last trust territory, Palau, achieved independence—are joined by another, namely ECOSOC. It was created in parallel with the transformation of public policy from the minimalist laissez-faire maintenance of law and order to the provision of essential social services. ECOSOC is thus the institutional node of what is called "welfare internationalism."

When the United Nations first turned to issues of economic and social development in the late 1940s, the adjective used was at first "undeveloped," then "under-developed" countries. In fact, as numerous analyses over the years and several UN Intellectual History Project volumes have demonstrated, both were misnomers. These countries had rich and complex histories, cultures, economies, and societies. They were economically poor rather than underdeveloped. Moreover, the field of "development economics" was not as undeveloped or underdeveloped as it appeared at the time. Adam Smith had published his *Inquiry into the Nature and Cause of the Wealth of Nations* almost two centuries earlier,[5] and the nineteenth century was full of pioneering works on the early experience of development and industrialization in Europe. Robert Malthus, David Ricardo, John Stuart Mill, and Karl Marx were among the greats, but there were many others.[6]

The origins of the concepts and discourse of development studies are rooted in the historical encounter between the European and the non-European. Is tradition necessarily an obstacle to progress and development? Is modernization necessarily good? How much coherence is there to such terms as "Third World" or "global South"? The abundance of terms to refer essentially to the same group of countries reflects continuing dissatisfactions with each: "backward," "developing," "undeveloped," "underdeveloped," "less developed," "Third World," "southern," "low income," "traditional."[7] In these days of political correctness, perhaps we should call them "the economically challenged."

In the project's oral history, Brian Urquhart remembered how development first arose in discussions among his colleagues: "That really started in 1948 with Truman's 'Point Four' speech . . . [which was] considered at that time to be an original idea. Truman's idea was that the only way to keep the world reasonably stable was to have a vast development program run by the UN, coordinating its own specialized agencies in what was then called 'underdeveloped countries.' Soon that phrase was considered rude, so they became 'developing countries.'"[8]

Economics as taught in the 1940s, however, was not really about development. Microeconomics was the standard bill of fare, and Keynesian macro-analyses of unemployment was the exciting frontier for theory and policy.[9] Paul Samuelson's *Economics,* the classic textbook of choice, was then in the first of its now eighteen editions. It devoted three sentences to developing countries.[10] In 1947, the UN recruited Hans Singer, a major figure in the terms-of-trade debate, to fill one of the first posts for an economist who would work on the problems of developing countries. He recalled that when he told his mentor, Harvard's distinguished Professor Joseph Schumpeter, this news, Schumpeter said: "But I thought you were an economist!" Nevertheless, Singer was delighted to be in the Secretariat in those days, when it was an intellectual hothouse: "I had the feeling of being at the center of things, very privileged to be there. After all, the UN was the home of mankind. It was then at the center of international organizations, the Bank and the Fund were very much on the periphery in those days."[11]

Article 55 of the UN Charter specified the importance of promoting conditions of economic and social progress and development and the commitment to achieve full employment. Indeed, this call framed the UN's early work. The unusual character of this early work can be seen in three major UN publications: *National and International Measures for Full Employment* (1949); *Measures for the Economic Development of Under-Developed Countries* (1951); and *Measures for International Economic Stability* (1951).[12]

The UN's efforts in the arena of trade, aid, and finance have predominantly taken the form of international contributions to thinking about national development. One of the world organization's main contributions to enhanced global governance consists of goal setting, which typically is the subject of snide remarks and even derision because goals seem so far from being realized.

Nonetheless, they represent a substantial contribution to filling gaps. As a number of UNIHP's volumes have made clear (but most authoritatively in *UN Contributions to Development Thinking and Practice*[13]), substantial progress has been made over the UN's lifetime toward meeting objectives in education, health, nutrition, and population. In all these areas, advances have been registered in every region and in most countries. As the United Nations stresses, encouraging and supporting achievements does not mean ignoring the distance still to travel.

During the 1960s, every branch of the United Nations became involved in collecting, evaluating, and disseminating the data essential for development planning and policy formulation. Long-term planning and forecasting about key issues for economic and social development— such as population growth, food and educational needs, industrial production, and international trade—became key elements of the UN's First Development Decade.

Planning activities during the 1960s and 1970s at the international level in the UN as well as at the country level consisted mainly in forecasting and analyzing how a country or a region could best work its way toward a more desirable scenario. Important studies were undertaken on the major trends in world trade and trends in gross domestic product (GDP) and per capita income.[14]

The 1970s were paradoxical; it was a decade when creative thinking and action mixed with mounting economic difficulties. Creativity was evident in intellectual contributions to such fields as the environment, population policies, gender questions, employment creation, and development strategies—all themes of UN world conferences during that decade.[15] The ways that we talk and think about these issues today would not be the same without the work of the United Nations.

Here we underline the extent to which discussions in and around the UN beginning in the 1970s moved these issues into the mainstream. The decade witnessed significant increases in oil prices in 1973 and 1979. Initially, this stimulated hope in developing countries for a New International Economic Order (NIEO). For a while, this led to lengthy negotiations on how such an order might be achieved, one of the first systemic attempts to change overall global economic governance. Transnational corporations were an important dimension of these negotiations.[16] But stagflation, mounting debt and interest rates, and recession at the onset of the 1980s killed the NIEO and reversed prospects for alternative economic policies.

The so-called lost decade of the 1980s coincided with the untrammelled liberalization aims of the Washington consensus and structural adjustment programs. Two decades of UN dissent from the mainstream followed, some of which was less than effective. This was not an unusual role for the world organization—indeed, one of the central lessons from UNIHP has been that from early on, the United Nations often stood in sharp contrast to the reigning orthodoxy of the financially well-heeled World Bank and IMF.[17] Partly this reflected the different political base of the two institutions; all countries are equally represented at the UN while the Bretton Woods institutions have a voting system weighted to reflect financial contributors. Not surprisingly, the latter have tended to produce analyses and policy recommendations that reflected the interests and perspectives of developed countries while the UN has tended in the opposite direction—analyses, ideas, and recommendations more in tune with those of developing countries that constitute the bulk of member states. This range of alternative views, we maintain, is an essential contribution to the evolution of global economic governance.

In the 1980s, alternative approaches to adjustment became a focus of UN analysis and debate. UNICEF published *Adjustment with a Human Face*,[18] for instance, and the Economic Commission for Africa produced the *African Alternative Framework to Structural Adjustment Programs for Socio-Economic Recovery and Transformation*.[19] Neither institution denied the need for adjustment, but they argued that the World Bank's criteria were too narrow and led to ineffective programs. Moreover, the neglect of health, education, nutrition, and other basic needs had serious human consequences. If child mortality rose as a consequence of adjustment, for instance, there was no second chance. In the late 1980s, the ILO planned a major international conference to debate alternatives to adjustment. The United States threatened once again to leave the ILO if it proceeded, so the ILO organized a smaller and more technical conference.

Although they were initially greeted with skepticism, UN alternatives to adjustment have over the years become increasingly accepted, at least rhetorically. Indeed, by the late 1990s, the World Bank and the IMF had committed to the broader notion of development that member states agreed on at the Millennium Summit in 2000. At that time, the gathered heads of state and government endorsed the elimination of poverty and the promotion of sustainable development as the world organization's highest priority. Creating the foundation for sustainable human security entails empowering individuals, groups, and communities to become engaged constructively and effectively in satisfying their own needs, values, and interests, thereby providing them with a genuine sense of control over their futures. This goal was given an additional boost with a report from an eminent group of persons headed by former UN high commissioner for refugees Sadako Ogata and Nobel laureate in economics Amartya Sen; the focus of the report was "shielding people from acute threats and empowering them to take charge of their own lives."[20]

The 2000 summit's final document reiterated what virtually all countries saw as a milestone, the Millennium Development Goals that formed the foundation for the United Nations Millennium Declaration, which the General Assembly adopted in September 2000 in resolution 55/2.[21] The MDGs are specific goals and associated targets and indicators that guide the UN's development efforts. The eight main goals and eighteen related targets have been commonly accepted throughout the UN system as a framework for guiding development policies and assessing progress toward poverty reduction and sustainable human development. As such, the MDG process represents a larger strategic vision for mobilizing international action. It changed the discourse from inputs to targets, standardized targets among all development agencies, and facilitated engagement of the private sector in poverty alleviation. It has also proven to be a tool for social mobilization and a system of political as much as economic governance benchmarks.[22] Five years later, at the 2005 World Summit, heads of state and governments met in New York to review progress toward achieving the MDGs and to endeavor to agree on reforms to enhance the capacity and effectiveness of the world organization.

Knowledge Gaps: Understanding Development

The dominant theories that circulated in the aftermath of World War II sought to answer six questions, for which we are still trying to find adequate replies. First, what is the state's role in development? Is the state better placed to liberalize and deregulate or to command and control? Is government the problem or the answer? Second, do the initial material and political conditions of a country matter? And what is the significance of divergent initial conditions of national economies? Third, what is the best balance between agricultural growth and industrialization? Fourth, what is the best balance between growth and equity? Fifth, what can outsiders do? Does foreign aid accelerate the development process or does it impede or even stifle it? Sixth and finally, what should be the end goal of development? Should it be "human security,"[23] encompassing all aspects of life, including one's environment and the ability to provide for one's self and family? And does "packaging" development as a security issue help or hurt?

To be sure, there are important shared characteristics in many developing countries, especially the poorer ones: small subsistence agrarian economies dependent on a narrow range of products in international exchanges, often just one or two cash crops such as coffee, cotton, rubber, or sugar; low levels of life expectancy and literacy; and streamlined political and bureaucratic structures. Yet the more striking feature is their diversity. Despite the similarities, the variations among developing countries are just as significant as those among the developed countries.

"Multifinality" refers to the phenomenon whereby countries with similar starting conditions end up at startlingly different destinations. By contrast, the concept of economic development was predicated on the assumption of "equifinality," or the belief that no matter how divergent states are initially, they can be brought to convergence at the end. The key unit of measurement was economic growth, and the key goal was the attainment of a high level of income through sustained growth in gross domestic product. According to the equifinality thesis, heavy industrialization and the rapid extension of technology into the farthest reaches of social life were more likely to generate pressures toward social and institutional homogeneity. Those who were the least engaged with the world's technological cross-currents were the ones best able to preserve distinctive social structures and belief patterns.

The equifinality thesis clearly neglected historical and international realities. For example, some developing countries—especially India and China—had higher population densities and a worsening land-to-person ratio than western countries did during their period of industrialization. Rapidly rising populations in virtually all developing countries absorbed productivity gains. Developing countries also faced a challenging international context: their trade did not constitute the dominant portion of global economic exchanges, and they had to enter world markets in competition with western firms that had a solid market presence already. Moreover, the negative terms of trade for many of their basic commodities over the long run militated against a strategy of export-led growth: the lack of an export-led sector discouraged capital inflows for investment. Although advanced industrialized countries had built up their development over centuries, developing countries had to telescope the time frame for development into decades because of the urgency of problems they faced. But the attempt to force the rate of change generated resentment and created a backlash against development programs.

The concept of aggregate growth, using such measures as GDP, GNP, or national income, dominated policy and scholarly debate through the 1960s, and as indicated earlier, the UN played an essential role in improving national and international statistics. In fact, the world organization's contribution has often been crucial in ensuring that necessary information is available for analyzing problems and making national and international policies. The UN's work in this area often sets the frame within which economic and social progress—or the lack of it—can be assessed, which is certainly a necessary if rather unglamorous part of filling knowledge gaps. Michael Ward, in *Quantifying the World: UN Ideas and Statistics,* has told the story of how ideas about what should be measured have influenced statistical offices the world over and had a major impact on economic perceptions, priorities, and actions. He concludes that "the creation of a universally acknowledged statistical system and of a general framework guiding the collection and compilation of data according to recognized professional standards, both internationally and nationally, has been one of the great and mostly unsung successes of the UN Organization."[24]

Based on the dominant conventional wisdom of the time, development policy was preoccupied with material productivity as an indicator of economic welfare. Walt Rostow's 1960 book *The Stages of Economic Growth* was especially influential. However, the book was not without its flaws. Its worldview was simplistic, even mechanistic. Moreover, it was ideological, as indicated in its subtitle *A Non-Communist Manifesto.*[25] It was ethnocentric: it structured development models using the historically specific experience of western countries, and Rostow claimed that only the United States had reached the final stage of development. Despite these deficiencies, it was seductively persuasive in communicating the idea that every country had an equal chance to achieve the good life, in pointing out a clear path to progress, and in challenging Marxism. The 1960s were full of such glorious phrases as "take-off," "steady growth," "alliance for progress," and "critical minimum effort."

As dissatisfaction grew with the assumptions and prescriptions of growth-through-modernization theory, analysts tried to think of alternative approaches that would better capture the reality of development.[26] The philosophical debate around the competing conceptions of development can be organized around two alternative principles of distributive justice: maximizing growth or minimizing poverty. Growth-oriented development economists argued that distributive inequalities are justified if—and to the extent that—they are necessary to maximize the rate of growth of national income. Some regard distribution as essentially a political question beyond the purview of economists. Others argued that in moral terms, distributive inequalities should be minimized as long as they are consistent with attaining maximum growth. That is, equality is useful to break a deadlock between two alternative development strategies that are indistinguishable from the point of view of maximizing growth. By contrast, the poverty-minimizing principle would sacrifice growth in order to maximize the well-being of the worst-off groups in society.

In sum, according to modernization theory, "development" involves progress on a number of interrelated measures: an improved performance of the factors of production and improved techniques of technical change that cause a rise in real per capita income over a long period of time; the development of state and market institutions; a change in social attitudes and values by producers and consumers; and a decrease in the number and proportion of people living below the poverty line. Moreover, this teleological paradigm assumed that Third World countries would experience the same linear progress toward industrialization as their Western predecessors had if their governments only pursued appropriate policies. Clearly modernization theory was ahistorical and disregarded the international context that confronted developing countries.

These two points of critique underpinned dependency theory, which was rooted in the analyses of Raúl Prebisch and Hans Singer and became a rival paradigm to modernization theory. One of the most significant gaps in knowledge was filled (or dug deeper, depending on one's views) with the Prebisch-Singer thesis on secular decline in the terms of trade. John Toye and Richard Toye, whose volume in the UNIHP series treats this story in great detail, noted that "the net barter terms of trade between primary products and manufactures have been subject to a long-run downward trend."[27] Primary producers suffer as a result of systematically different institutional features of product and factor markets as well as technological progress.

Toye and Toye spell out the continuing significance of the Prebisch-Singer thesis: "It implies that, barring major changes in the structure of the world economy, the gains from trade will continue to be distributed unequally (and, some would add, unfairly) between nations exporting mainly primary products and those exporting mainly manufactures. Further, inequality of per capita income between these two types of countries will be increased by the growth of trade rather than reduced."[28] The thesis was an argument for protecting infant industries and for protective tariffs.

The Prebisch-Singer thesis flew in the face of a long-standing belief among many economists that the terms of trade of manufacturers relative to agriculture would decline, which was a feature of classical economics from Malthus through Keynes and was a basis for early UN thinking. The world organization was perhaps a predictable incubator for the counter idea, which in part justified the economic nationalism of developing countries and was well suited to Cold War confrontations and polemics.

When Hans Singer started with the UN Statistical Office, the terms-of-trade problem was thought to be a short-term issue, but this proved not to be the case. Singer published the results of his research in 1949 as

Relative Prices of Exports and Imports of Under-developed Countries: A Study of Post-War Terms of Trade between Under-developed and Industrialized Countries. The report used data from 1876 to 1948 and showed a long-term decline in the terms of trade.[29] Secular decline meant that "underdeveloped" countries were losing the capacity to absorb foreign financing for development. A more controversial implication was that these countries were subsidizing the rising standard of living in industrialized countries.

At the heart of the Prebisch-Singer thesis is an argument about path dependence, which implies that specific patterns of timing and sequence matter; that starting from similar conditions, a wide range of social outcomes may be possible; that large consequences may result from relatively "small" or contingent events; and that particular courses of action, once introduced, can be virtually impossible to reverse. In explaining long-term decline, Prebisch and Singer each started from a period when trade was primarily marked by imperialism and colonization. While the crises generated by world wars, depression, and decolonization punctuated the business cycle, they failed to stop the overall trend.[30]

The Prebisch-Singer thesis resembles Jared Diamond's argument about the current state of global inequality in *Guns, Germs, and Steel*, although Diamond uses a much larger data set of some 13,000 years of human history.[31] Diamond believes that initial inequalities in the distribution of plants and animals that could be adapted for human use have reverberated through time and that initial conditions set the stage for further developments.

What happened and did not happen as a result of the Prebisch-Singer thesis? Was the gap in knowledge filled? What were the politics of the ways the new data was used? The reaction from North American economists was swift and fierce. Some argued that the terms of trade of primary commodities had not experienced long-term decline and that the data were suspect. An alternative view was that long-term decline had indeed taken place but that the Prebisch-Singer interpretation was wrong; prominent economists Jacob Viner and Gerald Meier made this argument. Viner argued that one could not use terms-of-trade indices as a measure of welfare because it is difficult to measure changes in the quality of manufactured products: a contemporary Cadillac is a different beast from a Model T. Meier argued that even if there had been a long-term decline in the past, "it was wrong to design policy as if it would continue into the future when the opposite case was more likely."[32]

The end of the early controversy was a draw between the thesis and its critics because the data to settle the matter were unavailable. The immediate consequences of the controversy and resulting impasse were that Prebisch became extremely popular within UN circles and replaced Martinez Cabañas, the first executive-secretary of the Economic Commission for Latin America (ECLA). The reaction of the superpowers was also relevant: Washington at first tried to close down ECLA but ended up participating in it when President John F. Kennedy called for a Development Decade and created the Alliance for Progress. Moscow also used the Prebisch-Singer thesis to buttress arguments about the effects of imperialism.

ECLA was placed squarely in the limelight as a result of the debate, which was helpful to it as an institution. It was able to attract notable economists, set up institutes, and get involved in creating regional and subregional economic agreements such as the Andean Pact. As Yves Berthelot notes in the introduction to his edited volume in this series, "ECLA had the greatest impact [of the regional commissions] because of its strong intellectual leadership and the interaction between the secretariat, the academic community, and the region's political elites."[33]

"Development" was not only the concern of the regional commissions; it gradually became *the* priority of the UN as a whole, exemplified by the launching of the First Development Decade in 1961. Indeed, General Assembly resolution 1707 (XVI) of that year asked the Secretary-General to consult with member states about convening a conference to discuss trade and development. The findings of the so-called Haberler report—named after the chair of the panel of experts that produced the report, Gottfried Haberler—constituted an important element behind this request. Commissioned by the GATT, at the time very much the favored economic institution of wealthy countries, the Haberler report revealed that exports from developing countries were failing to grow as rapidly as those from industrialized countries because the latter had erected tariff and nontariff barriers against products of particular importance to developing countries.[34]

The fractious debate ultimately led to the rise in temperatures for the New International Economic Order in 1974, but the arrival of the conservative governments of UK prime minister Margaret Thatcher and U.S. president Ronald Reagan contributed to the demise of the so-called North-South dialogue in 1981 at Cancún, Mexico. Yet the imprint on international relations remains. UNCTAD developed a group system that launched a multilateral dialogue between the North and South about unequal development, which was a concrete expression of the continuing magnetism of the Prebisch-Singer thesis.[35] The thesis is still much disputed, but the impact of the idea and the new interpretation of data, however incomplete, was clear in terms of changing government policy in many developing countries and international economic negotiations.

The UN system's quest to fill in gaps in knowledge continues. In the early 1990s, the UNDP constructed a new measure of development called the human development index (HDI) under the leadership of Pakistan's Mahbub ul Haq. The new measure was a composite index of life expectancy, adult literacy, and purchasing power parities. Measures of real income are reasonably good indicators of people's command over goods and services, but the UNDP acknowledged that gross national product was a flawed measure of well-being and its own composite index gave a snapshot of welfare as well as wealth.

The inability to measure HDI accurately and definitively continues to vex those who try to gauge such matters. Perfecting such measurement techniques, however arduous, is the key to knowledge about the most fundamental of human issues. And the UN's struggle to get it right—or at least better—is ongoing and necessary.

Normative Gaps:
The Shape of Transfers from Rich to Poor

The international norm that is most relevant to redistribution is the objective of transferring some 0.7 percent of GDP from rich to poor countries, a figure that grew out of the First Development Decade. Recent work suggests a lack of normative consensus in the West, although the target has support and success in countries that to some degree have a positive domestic consensus on welfare policy.[36] At the same time, such objectives are disparaged in places where individual charity is supposed to be the basis for responsibility to those who are poorer. The position of the Nordic countries and the Netherlands at the top of the ODA contributors' list in Box 5.1 and the United States at the bottom can be explained by their differeing normative perspectives on welfare policy.

Here we would like to move beyond the aid debate and focus on a still-more-contested norm, namely the need to involve the private sector in the development process. The end of the Cold War ushered in a threefold change: a collapse of Soviet power as a counterweight to U.S. power; a triumph of liberal democracy over totalitarian communism as a political ideology of the state; and the triumph of the market over the command economy as the organizing principle of production. The last had a profound impact on the North-South divide throughout the UN system which, not coincidentally, replaced the Cold War East-West groupings as the defining divide in the United Nations.[37]

For most developing countries at independence, the private sector had neither the money nor the expertise to finance industrial development on the scale and at the pace of their people's ambitions. Their governments decided that the more visible hand of the state would be used to create socialism in the industrial vacuum. The state, not the private sector, would play the decisive role in producing and distributing material goods. There was agreement among heads of newly independent states about the desirability of rapid economic growth under a feasible rate of resource mobilization and about the benefits of diffusing rather than concentrating growth. There was consensus too on the need to improve infrastructure and on the need for industrial expansion and diversification. The framework for processing these goals into policy outputs was often elaborate planning machinery. Typically, three sets of dichotomies underpinned the strategy of economic development: central planning versus market anarchy; socialist versus private ownership of the means of production; and egalitarian versus class-based income distribution.

Today the need for growth to be led by the private sector is an unquestioned verity among economists; the real debates are over how to attract foreign investment by making domestic policy more friendly to businesses and investors and what role domestic subsidies should play in industrialized countries. The Bretton Woods institutions and the UN system agree on the need for growth led by the private sector, as was reflected in the Monterrey conference (Mexico, 2002), where a pact was reached to reward developing countries that followed the road to good governance. The so-called Monterrey consensus is a pertinent example of international development cooperation that pulls together partners from the North and South to move to common ground. Participants at the Monterrey conference agreed that governments of developing countries had an obligation to reform themselves for the purpose of economic efficiency, while those in developed countries had an obligation to provide

BOX 5.1. ODA as 0.7 percent of GDP

Although the UN proclaimed the 1960s as the First Development Decade, disillusionment set in during that decade among publics and governments about the use of concessional development finance as a foreign policy strategy.[1] This was due in part to domestic difficulties and balance-of-payment problems, in part to perceptions of governmental waste and corruption in recipient countries, and in part due to growing skepticism about the effectiveness of aid. What we now call "donor fatigue" was then referred to as "wariness of will." In 1968, the total flow of official aid decreased for the first time.

The World Bank, the major promoter of concessional development finance, formed an international commission in August 1968 to review the performance and results of two decades of development assistance and make recommendations for the future. The chair was former prime minister of Canada Lester B. Pearson, who was best known internationally for his work with the United Nations, in particular for his seminal role in the creation of the first full-fledged UN peacekeeping force in the Middle East in 1956 (for which he was awarded the Nobel Peace Prize). The commission's report, called *Partners in Development* and known popularly as the Pearson report, was published in September 1969.[2] Its twofold conclusion was that the 20-year record showed that economic development had occurred, albeit unevenly, and was thus feasible and that while the overwhelming bulk of the growth was due to the efforts of the developing countries themselves, development assistance had been critical in such areas as savings and imports and in providing an essential risk absorber for industrial and agricultural enterprise. It offered two justifications for aid: the moral reason based on the duty of the fortunate to help the needy and enlightened self-interest in an interdependent world community. Following from this analysis, it offered three recommendations: the volume of total aid should be set at 1 percent of GNP, ODA should be set at 0.7 percent of GNP, and multilateral aid should form an increasing proportion of the total flow of development assistance.

Only a handful of countries, mainly the Nordic countries and the Netherlands, have met the target of 0.7 percent of GDP (the standard measure used now instead of GNP, which was in commonly used in the 1960s). Yet the target has never been formally rescinded as the norm. This is a clear demonstration of the two different meanings of the word "norm" as what actually happens and as what ought to happen: the statistical norm has varied between 0.3 to 0.4 percent of GDP, but the prescriptive norm has remained set at 0.7 percent. Within the context of our definition of global governance, both meanings—actual policies and shared values—are relevant. And the United Nations has been at the forefront of efforts to bring about a convergence between the two.

That effort continues. In September 2000, world leaders signed the Millennium Declaration that set time-bound and measurable goals and targets for development. The MDGs today constitute the core of the global agenda for development. Goal 8 is the creation of a global partnership for development that includes targets for aid, trade, and debt relief. This was followed by the Monterrey consensus in 2002 in which leaders agreed to match commitments with resources and action and reaffirmed the target of ODA as 0.7 percent of GDP. In his omnibus report *In Larger Freedom,* the Secretary-General noted that the global ODA average had fallen to 0.33 percent of GDP in the late 1980s and had decreased even further to 0.25 percent in 2004. While acknowledging the need to increase the quality, transparency, and accountability of ODA, he called on developed countries to increase the flow of ODA and set fresh targets of 0.5 percent by 2009 and 0.7 percent by 2015 using innovative sources of financing for development if necessary.[3] The 0.7 percent target by 2015 was reaffirmed in the World Summit Outcome, although the 0.5 percent target was moved to 2010.[4]

1. For an analysis of this decade and others, see Richard Jolly, Louis Emmerij, Dharam Ghai, and Frédéric Lapeyre, *UN Contributions to Development Thinking and Practice* (Bloomington: Indiana University Press, 2004).

2. Commission on International Development, *Partners in Development* (New York: Praeger, 1969).

3. Kofi A. Annan, *In Larger Freedom: Towards Development, Security and Human Rights for All* (New York: UN, March 2005), 20–22.

4. *2005 World Summit Outcome,* General Assembly resolution A/RES/60/1, 24 October 2005, 5.

meaningful assistance. The consensus represented an attempt to reconcile the need for market reform with the need to redistribute some wealth from the rich North to impoverished countries in the global South.[38]

How do we instill civic virtue in the global marketplace so that the market serves the people instead of people being served up to the market? Companies operating in developing countries and zones of conflict often evade responsibility for the consequences of their operations and point to the fact that they operate legally. Yet the increasing pressure on companies from NGOs and public opinion makes it impossible for the private sector to ignore the harmful effects of their operations.

The UN's Global Compact is an attempt to address these issues. Through the power of collective action, the compact seeks to advance responsible corporate citizenship so that business can be part of the solution to the challenges of globalization. In this way, the private sector—in partnership with other social actors—can help realize the UN vision of a more sustainable and inclusive global economy. The main normative shift, in the words of its intellectual midwife, Harvard University's John Ruggie, was the shift away from the international effort to regulate the private sector to a "learning model" of how to make the most of the private sector's potential contributions.[39] The Global Compact is a voluntary corporate citizenship initiative with two objectives: to catalyze actions in support of UN goals and to mainstream its human rights, labor, and environmental principles in business activities around the world. It is not a regulatory instrument—it does not police, enforce, or measure the behavior or actions of companies. Rather, it relies on public accountability, transparency, and the enlightened self-interest of companies, labor, and civil society to initiate and share substantive action in pursuing the principles upon which the compact is based. Its operational phase was launched at UN headquarters in New York on 26 July 2000.

After years of high-decibel criticism of both the private sector and the global reach of transnational corporations[40] and the continuing confrontations at Group of 8 (G-8) meetings by representatives of civil society, the Global Compact had to overcome the initial epithet of "capitalist blue-wash." John Ruggie, who is currently the Secretary-General's special representative for business and human rights, sees the effort as one of continual learning; he notes that the "the state-based system of global governance has struggled for more than a generation to adjust to the expanding reach and growing influence of transnational corporations."[41] Within the complex and ever-changing world of globalization, doctrinal disputes about whether firms could be "subjects" of international law have given way to specific realities and contributions and investments on the ground. Corporate social responsibility for the 77,000 transnational corporations that existed in 2007 as well as ten times that number of subsidiaries and millions of suppliers is a necessary form of "soft law" that is an important and growing element of global economic governance.[42]

While accountability is clearly lacking, efforts are at least under way at the little-known International Organization for Standardization (IOS) to develop an international standard that provides guidelines for social responsibility. While the IOS defines itself as a nongovernmental organization, its ability to set standards that often become law (either through treaties or national standards) makes it more influential than most NGOs. Its role as a facilitator of essential economic infrastructure is part of a web of wider global economic governance.[43]

Policy Gaps: The NIEO Clash and Aid

Perhaps the biggest policy gap concerns the redistribution of the benefits of growth. The litany of policies that emerged as part of the "dialogue of the deaf" between the North and South in the mid-1970s provides an intriguing case study about policy gaps that remain gigantic to this day. Indeed, as Alain Noel and Jean-Philippe Thérien argue, "global politics is first and foremost a debate between the left and the right. This is so because the left-right cleavage expresses enduring and profound differences about equality."[44]

Perhaps the most controversial in a series of efforts to foster new relationships between the North and the South emerged in the aftermath of the dramatic quadrupling in oil prices in 1973–1974. This led to a major shift in global income from industrial and developing countries that did not produce oil (nicknamed the "NOPEC countries" by Hans Singer) to the Organization of the Petroleum Exporting Countries. The proposals for establishing the New International Economic Order were more like a shopping list than a single idea to level the economic playing field for the global South. Yet the NIEO proposals served to focus debate on a wide range of ideas that developing countries had put forward in a host of UN and non-UN forums since the early 1960s. Whatever the feasibility of such ideas, they encapsulated the passionate call to change international economic relationships, especially the demands that privileged industrialized states enact substantial measures to level the international playing field.

However, "entrenched interest, national hubris, ideological divisions, and mindless militancy all played their part," Mahfuzur Rahman has written about the demise of the NIEO. "The idea of a new international economic order has long ceased to be a matter of serious discussion . . . [but] the story is worth recounting, if only to ponder the limits of international cooperation."[45]

One of the long-standing elements of debate and dispute within the United Nations—as we have seen, beginning long before the NIEO and continuing afterward through the Millennium Summit in 2000 and World

Summit in 2005—has been about the role of official development assistance. Olav Stokke's *The UN and Development*[46] argues that a major date for international development assistance was 4 December 1948, when the General Assembly passed resolution 198 (III), which recommended that member states "give further and urgent consideration to the whole problem of economic development of underdeveloped countries in *all* aspects."[47] It passed another resolution dealing more particularly with the role of technical assistance in promoting economic development, the field the UN most emphasized during the following years.

As was the case so often in those early years, the response with the greatest impact came from Washington. President Harry Truman, in his inaugural address on 20 January 1949, announced a program "for peace and freedom in four major courses of action." In point four he set out "a bold new program for making the benefits of our scientific advances and industrial progress available for the improvement and growth of under-developed areas" with the aim "to help the free peoples of the world, through their own efforts, to produce more food, more clothing, more material for housing, and more mechanical power to lighten their burden."[48] Other countries were invited to pool their technological resources in this undertaking.

Soon afterward, the United Nations established the Expanded Programme for Technical Assistance (EPTA). This international program removed the national flags and the associated strings that were so characteristic of the emerging bilateral aid programs. The objectives and principles set for UN assistance reflected norms that had signal effects beyond multilateral aid relations. The primary objective was to strengthen the economies of underdeveloped countries through "the development of their industries and agriculture with a view to promoting their economic and political independence in the spirit of the Charter of the United Nations."[49] The guidelines stated explicitly that assistance should be provided only at the request of the recipient government and should not infringe on its sovereignty. The assistance was to be administered on the basis of country programs that were to be integrated into national development plans. From the outset, a division of labor emerged between the UN's specialized agencies and other institutions (on the one hand), and the EPTA (on the other).[50]

The UN recognized early on that economic development required not only technical assistance (or "human investment," as it came to be called) but also major additions to capital—that is, physical investment. In the late 1940s and early 1950s, the world body launched an ambitious plan to provide the latter, initially under the name of the Special United Nations Fund for Economic Development (SUNFED)—the "special" was added to avoid the acronym UNFED, which would have been more accurate for an institution that was starved for finances.[51] This fund was supposed to provide soft loans, even grants, to poor countries, especially for infrastructure development. There were endless discussions about whether SUNFED should be established during the 1950s. A majority of countries favored the idea. However, the major western powers preferred a different arrangement that featured capital aid on concessionary terms outside of the United Nations. In the end, a soft window was established in 1961 within the World Bank—where donor countries were at the helm—the International Development Association (IDA). The UN was left with a small kitty for preinvestment activities, and in 1965 this Special Fund merged with the Expanded Programme for Technical Assistance to become the UNDP.

Other UN bodies were created during this time with the goal of redistribution. An important proposal that was supported by the Kennedy administration resulted in the creation of the World Food Programme in 1963. And as explained earlier, the Kennedy proposal for a development decade led to a goal for aid comprised of public and private transfers that would underpin an acceleration of growth in developing countries. Initially, the rate of transfer was calculated at 1 percent of developed country national income to developing countries. In the Second Development Decade, a similar calculation led to the famous 0.7 percent target for ODA.[52]

In the field of aid and technical assistance, the UN has consistently emphasized social development and the eradication of poverty. This became particularly important in the 1980s when structural adjustment became the leading policy, orchestrated by the World Bank and IMF. The UN, which was initially on the defensive in the face of the new orthodoxy of the Washington consensus, eventually came out with important new initiatives and ideas; UNICEF and the ECA were leaders in this effort, as we discovered earlier in this chapter. Other institutional nodes in the UN system that put forward ideas for economic development with a social conscience include the United Nations Research Institute on Social Development (UNRISD) in Geneva and the United Nations University's World Institute for Development Economics Research (WIDER) in

Helsinki. The annual publication of the Human Development Report (HDR) underlines the need for a broader concept of development, a subject to which we return below.

More than half a century since the UN began its development efforts, similar ideas still are being pursued. The eradication of poverty is now the main objective, national poverty reduction strategy papers are now the major instrument, and national ownership and policy coherence based on the priorities of the aid recipients are UNDP norms.[53] The MDGs may be the start of a more imaginative and realistic type of development assistance than the UN has pursued in the past. At the 2005 World Summit, the British government proposed a new financial instrument, the International Finance Facility (IFF), which would raise and channel the additional financing necessary to meet the Millennium Development Goals by 2015 from the richest to the poorest countries. Its essential aim is to bridge the financing gap between pledged resources and the resources required to achieve the MDGs.[54] Kofi Annan embraced this proposal and made the following recommendation in his 2005 report *In Larger Freedom:*

> The international community should in 2005 launch an International Finance Facility to support an immediate front-loading of ODA, underpinned by scaled-up commitments to achieving the 0.7 per cent ODA target no later than 2015. In the longer term, other innovative sources of finance for development should also be considered to supplement the Facility.[55]

The UN's embrace of this proposal was watered down in the *2005 World Summit Outcome,* the UN's publication of the summit's platform, which acknowledged that mobilizing financial resources for development is "central to a global partnership for development" in achieving the MDGs. The document recognized the value of innovative sources of development financing and in that context only noted that "some countries will implement the International Finance Facility."[56]

Even if the United Nations cannot in every instance generate original knowledge or formulate definitive norms, it can still use its power to convene conferences and meetings to convey knowledge and norms to the international public policy community. At the Millennium Summit in September 2000, for example, the General Assembly requested "a rigorous analysis of the advantages, disadvantages and other implications of proposals for developing new and innovative sources of funding, both public and private, for dedication to social development and poverty eradication programmes."[57] In response, the UN Department of Economic and Social Affairs commissioned WIDER to undertake a project on innovative sources of development finance. The director of the project was Oxford professor Anthony B. Atkinson, and the findings were published in 2004.[58] The project critically examined seven new sources of development finance with respect to feasibility, costs (including who pays), benefits, and additionality: global environmental taxes (carbon-use tax); tax on currency flows (the so-called Tobin tax); creation of new Special Drawing Rights; the International Finance Facility; increased private donations for development; a global lottery and a global premium bond; and increased remittances from emigrants.

Institutional Gaps: From GATT to the WTO

Ultimately, the greatest institutional manifestation of the Prebisch-Singer thesis was the call in General Assembly resolution 1785 (XVII) in 1962 for the first UN Conference on Trade and Development. Convened two years later in Geneva, the conference turned into a permanent meeting place where the voice of the South in international trade was magnified.

Indeed, what Alfred Sauvy had first characterized as le tiers monde (the Third World) at the outset of the 1950s became one of the key mechanisms within the UN system, the Group of 77 (G-77), named after the original number of members in a working caucus of developing countries.[59] The numbers grew almost immediately with new members; and although their number now is over 130, the title stuck.[60] The crystallization of developing countries into a single bloc for the purposes of international economic negotiations represented a direct challenge to industrialized countries.[61] In parallel with the Non-Aligned Movement, which initially focused more on security issues, the Third World's "solidarity," or at least its cohesion for the purposes of many international debates, meant that developing countries were in a better position to champion the NIEO and policies that aimed to change the distribution of benefits from growth and trade in the mid-1970s.[62]

While the creation of UNCTAD is a relatively well known example with mainly political ramifications, we examine four other examples of filling institutional gaps. The first also concerns the trade sector—the establishment in 1995 of the World Trade Organization. Unlike UNCTAD, which complemented or competed with GATT, the WTO replaced GATT. The second case concerns the International Telecommunication

Union, originally established as the International Telegraph Union in 1865. UNICEF is a third example of a UN institution that filled a gap; its projects range across the spectrum of development and humanitarian activities (see box 5.2).

The fourth kind of institutional gap-filling would be the UNDP's metamorphosis into a UN coordinator for overall development and an intellectual leader on human development. This concept is sketched in box 5.3.

From GATT to the WTO

At Bretton Woods, it was agreed that world trade should be "free" but also under a measure of regulation in order to forestall future economic catastrophes. While the World Bank and International Monetary Fund were to oversee the international flow of money and make loans to countries for investment or to meet trade deficits, a companion institution was to oversee trade—the International Trade Organization (ITO). However, this third pillar of John Maynard Keynes's proposed postwar economic order was never established.

After extended negotiations in Havana in 1947–1948, plans to create the ITO fell apart. As part of its jousting with the Soviet Union and the socialist bloc, the U.S. Congress refused to ratify the Havana Charter, which would have established the International Trade Organization and would have placed international constraints on the United States. In a foreshadowing of future reactions in Washington to a host of other issues requiring cooperation and foresight, members of Congress saw the ITO as having "anti-American" social objectives that would infringe on national sovereignty.

Meanwhile, parallel negotiations to reduce tariffs had taken place among countries negotiating the ITO. These resulted in the General Agreement on Tariffs and Trade, which came into force under the Protocol of Provisional Application in 1948. Because the U.S. Congress did not ratify the Havana Charter, the provisional agreement became permanent. Given the politics of the time, some observers argue that GATT probably did the job as well as any ITO could have.

GATT and the subsequent renegotiations of most-favored-nation (MFN) status—GATT's central normative pillar—were designed to get outliers to agree to respect the MFN norm in their domestic legislation as a prerequisite for admission into the agreement. GATT proceeded by rounds, which "offer[ed] a package approach to trade negotiations that

BOX 5.2. The International Promotion and Protection of Children's Rights: UNICEF and the Convention on the Rights of the Child

While many individuals have purchased UNICEF's holiday cards, left loose change in foreign currency in envelopes provided by participating airlines, or otherwise supported the institution through voluntary contributions, few people are aware of its work in the trenches to protect children's rights. How has it earned its reputation as one of the UN's most effective institutions in both operations and norms?

Helping the helpless, especially children, is a quintessential value across cultures and time. However, the sorry fate of children who have endured wars and the lack of competence of governments to provide proper health care, education, and protection is testimony to human myopia. Unfair economic practices and parental neglect have also led the defenders of children to advocate for their protection. Within western societies, many of the earliest social work organizations were founded to protect and assist working-class children. A breakthrough at the global level came in 1919 when a young Englishwoman, Eglantyne Jebb, founded the Save the Children Fund after she witnessed the appalling suffering of children during World War I on a relief mission to Macedonia. Along with her sister, Jebb played a key role in drafting and promoting what became in 1924 the Charter of Child Welfare of the League of Nations.[1]

Following World War II and the widespread horrors that affected both adults and children, the United Nations International Children's Fund was created in 1948—largely against the wishes of other specialized agencies, which feared competition. Financed mainly by voluntary contributions from governments (although about a quarter of its annual $1 billion budget comes from private sources), UNICEF's work in health includes promoting breast-feeding, working toward the goal of global immunization for children in six basic vaccines, the ongoing program to eradicate poliomyelitis, providing community water supplies, and participating in the Joint UN Programme on HIV/AIDS (UNAIDS).

Alongside the birth and growth of UNICEF—the world body's foremost operational arm in the promotion and protection of children's well-being—an expanding body of international law protecting the rights of children has developed.[2] Children figure in all the UN's main declarations, treaties, and covenants that constitute the so-called international bill of rights. In addition, such instruments as the 1951 Convention relating to the Status of Refugees and its 1967 Protocol are important since half of refugees (as well as the other main victims of war, internally displaced persons) are children; and specialized agencies such as the ILO have passed a host of conventions related to protecting children. *(continued on following page)*

But of most direct relevance here is the Convention on the Rights of the Child. In 1959, the General Assembly adopted resolution 1386 (XIV), a nonbinding Declaration of the Rights of the Child that recognized that "the child, by reason of his physical and mental immaturity, needs special safeguard and care, including appropriate legal protection." An enormous advance occurred thirty years later, when the assembly unanimously adopted resolution A/44/25, the legally binding Convention on the Rights of the Child.[3]

The convention is a comprehensive international legal statement that affirms that both parents have the primary responsibility for the upbringing and development of their children, but it makes states parties responsible for giving assistance to parents and taking appropriate legislative, administrative, social, and educational measures to ensure respect for children's rights. The convention establishes the right of children to be actors in their own development and to participate in decisions that affect their lives, communities, and societies. The main rights that the convention protects are the rights to life, health care, free and compulsory education, protection from physical and mental harm, and protection from economic exploitation.

The convention entered into force within nine months, on 2 September 1990. What happened to help the convention break all international records for speed in implementing a new convention? A key factor was the brainchild of UNICEF executive director Jim Grant, the World Summit for Children. While skeptics told him he was bound to fail, Grant insisted that such a meeting could be organized and would have major payoffs.[4] Grant was right. When the summit was held at UN headquarters in New York on 29–30 September 1990, representatives from an unprecedented 159 countries met, including seventy-one heads of state or government and forty-five NGOs, to promote the well-being of children.[5] Participants jointly signed the World Declaration on the Survival, Protection and Development of Children and the Plan of Action for Implementing the World Declaration on the Survival, Protection and Development of Children.

The protection of children is, of course, UNICEF's business. Without this institution doing its job, the global governance of children's welfare would be much poorer.

1. See Yves Beigbeder, *New Challenges for UNICEF: Children, Women and Human Rights* (Basingstoke, UK: Palgrave, 2001), 4–7 and 145–176.

2. Karin Arts, "International Law, Criminal Accountability and the Rights of the Child," in *International Criminal Accountability and the Rights of Children*, ed. Karin Arts and Vesselin Popovski (The Hague: Hague Academic Press, 2006), 3–18.

3. On the convention, see James R. Himes, ed., *Implementing the Convention on the Rights of the Child, Resource Mobilization in Low-Income Countries* (The

Hague: Martinus Nijhoff Publishers, 1995); Rachel Hodgin and Peter Hewell, *Implementation Handbook for the Convention on the Rights of the Child* (New York: UNICEF, 1998); and David A. Balton, "The Convention on the Rights of the Child: Prospects for International Enforcement," *Human Rights Quarterly* 12, no. 1 (1990): 120–129.

4. See Richard Jolly, ed., *Jim Grant: UNICEF Visionary* (Florence, Italy: Innocenti, 2001), especially Jolly, "Jim Grant: The Man behind the Vision," 45–65.

5. "World Summit for Children (1990)," available at www.un.org/geninfo/bp/child.html (accessed 7 December 2008). For further details, see Michael G. Schechter, *United Nations Global Conferences* (London: Routledge, 2005), 111–115.

can sometimes be more fruitful than negotiations on a single issue."[63] The successive negotiating rounds were Geneva (1947), Annecy (1949), Torquay (1951), Geneva II (1956), Dillon (1960–1961), Kennedy (1964–67), Tokyo (1973–1979), and Uruguay (1986–1994). By the 1960s, tariffs had been reduced in industrialized countries to less than 4 percent (they had been in the 40 percent range in the 1940s).[64] However, GATT's success in reducing tariffs to such low levels was combined with a series of economic recessions in the 1970s and early 1980s. As a result, industries threatened by foreign competition began to lobby their governments to create other barriers such as quotas, subsidies, and standards that resulted in the same kind of protective impact that tariffs formerly had. Moreover, the perceived negative effects of nontariff barriers on developing countries were even harder to justify.[65] Another factor in GATT's decreasing credibility and effectiveness resulted from the shift in industrialized countries from manufacturing to services, which GATT rules did not cover.

GATT lasted until 1994 and was replaced by the World Trade Organization in 1995. The transformation of the GATT into the WTO may reflect the fact that cooperation for a common good is not as difficult as Mancur Olson's *The Logic of Collective Action* would have us believe.[66] Recent economic analyses have shown that people and governments will not only cooperate but will actually pay to punish freeloaders if institutional incentives are appropriately structured.[67]

Unlike GATT, the WTO has the significant enforcement mechanisms to ensure compliance with international decisions that had been envisioned for the ITO a half-century earlier. The replacement of a weaker institution by another with more muscle is a development in global governance that has happened in few other issue areas. We often have seen new institutions created (for example, UNEP and the UN Development Fund for Women [UNIFEM]) but without enforcement powers and occasionally institutional forms have changed names (for example, the Human Rights Council has replaced the Commission on Human Rights) without changing their essence. The General Agreement still exists within the WTO as the over-arching treaty for trade in goods, as updated during the Uruguay Round, but as Toye and Toye assert, the WTO "goes much beyond it in scope and ambition. The overall aim has broadened, from nondiscrimination and the reduction of trade barriers to the adoption of policies in support of open markets generally." This makes the organization more intrusive on national sovereignty.[68] Moreover, the dispute settlement mechanism has been significantly altered in the transition from GATT to the WTO.[69]

Toye and Toye believe that the WTO deals with trade disputes better than GATT. However, the WTO's more standardized and quasi-judicial approach is biased against the less wealthy in terms of cost, time, uncertainty, and the unequal distribution of and access to technical knowledge and professional expertise. Furthermore, there is a democratic deficit. The proliferation of new states has meant that voting is heavily weighted against developing countries that have had to acquiesce to the rules in place at the time they joined the international system—they had no voice in their negotiation. Finally, while all states are formally equal in the WTO's voting, "There are two main sources of inequality: differential access to information about which agreements will benefit one's country and differential power to influence the outcome of the informal negotiation."[70] As Morten Bøås and Desmond McNeill add, of all the multilateral institutions, "the WTO is the one that is least open to public control and civil society participation. This has made it possible for staff members to isolate themselves from new impulses and competing worldviews and perspectives."[71]

Although the ITO was envisioned as part of the United Nations, the WTO is not part of the UN system (unlike the World Bank and the IMF, which are at least de jure parts). Neither was its predecessor. UNCTAD grew out of dissatisfaction with the "rich man's club of GATT," but real international institutional power remained in GATT and now lies in the WTO. Thus, the UN continues to remain mainly on the sidelines in this crucial area of global governance, and many concerns of developing countries, from establishing preferences for poor countries to removing agricultural subsidies in rich ones, are marginal issues in the WTO.

The International Telecommunication Union

As in many areas of international public policy, the relative absence of bitter controversies means that an issue or institution that provides substantial services that are essential for global governance is largely unnoticed. We have chosen to focus on the ITU to illustrate a technical institution that works, although we could also have chosen the International Postal Union or the International Civil Aviation Organization to make the same point.

In the twenty years after Samuel Morse sent the first telegraph message in 1844, the use of telegraphs spread throughout the world. Prior to the ITU, states had to painstakingly negotiate bilateral treaties to arrange the interconnection of their national networks. The awkward and traditional system rapidly became untenable, and twenty European states negotiated the first International Telegraph Convention in Paris in 1865.[72]

From its beginning, the ITU (known as the International Telegraph Union before 1934 and as the International Telecommunication Union after that date) has been at the forefront of regulating communications. It does so by setting the standards for infrastructure: it standardizes equipment to facilitate international connections, adopts uniform operating instructions and (most recently) Internet protocols, and establishes common international tariff and accounting rules. The ITU has been so technically successful that its work has been practically invisible.

There is a large and growing gap between information technology for haves and have-nots: "vast disparities exist between developed and developing nations in the cost of connecting to the global net backbone."[73] A comparison of Internet users in the United States and Sub-Saharan Africa illustrates the digital divide: in 2000, over 50 percent of the U.S. population used the Internet while only 0.4 percent of Sub-Saharan Africans were Internet users.[74] The divisiveness at the World Summit on the Information Society in Tunis in 2005 demonstrated that confrontation over communications institutions is hardly a thing of the past because of differences in view among member states over control of the Internet.

The ITU engaged in a wholesale reform in the mid-1990s to respond to changes in information technology,[75] but it still is facing a possible political firestorm because of the disparity in both the cultural content of the Internet as well as its regulation. The fact that the ITU exists and has a reliable track record makes possible compromises as part of the global governance of a technology that is increasingly essential for all economic activities. For example, Internet domain names, which are unique identifiers critical for managing Internet traffic, are controlled by ICANN, the Internet Corporation for Assigned Names and Numbers. ICANN is a private, not-for-profit corporation with international participation that is located in the United States. Ultimately, it is under the control of the U.S. government, whose research and development expenditure originally led to the creation of the Internet.[76]

The issue of the transformation of ICANN into a global body remains unresolved, but alternatives to a U.S.-controlled governance structure are being explored and actively negotiated. For example, the Tunis summit created the Internet Governance Forum, which will have representatives from government, business, and civil society.[77] However, other alternatives might be organized around ideas less benign than freedom of expression. China, Iran, and Cuba, for example, seek control through the "firewall" concept of sovereignty by seeking to limit users' access to the Internet to what amounts to an intranet of nationally controlled sites.

Compliance Gaps: Words, Deeds, and the MDGs

The United Nations Millennium Declaration marked an unprecedented international consensus on the human condition and what to do about it.[78] We have already mentioned that member states pledged to attain eight specific Millennium Development Goals and eighteen quantified and time-bound targets by the year 2015; these are outlined in box 5.4.

Seven of the eight MDGs focus on substantive objectives. The eighth deals with creating the capacity to achieve the other seven. Cumulatively, the MDGs can be seen as both mutually reinforcing and intertwined. Eradicating extreme poverty, for example, would most likely drastically reduce infant mortality, improve maternal health, and better ensure environmental sustainability. Similarly, achieving universal primary education, promoting gender equality, empowering women, and combating HIV/ AIDS, malaria, and other diseases would undoubtedly make progress toward eradicating poverty.

The MDGs represent a global consensus on development policies and targets even in the absence of a common understanding of what constitutes development or agreement on the strategies for achieving it. In that

BOX 5.3. UNDP

In January 1966, the UN Development Programme was created with the merger of the Expanded Programme for Technical Assistance and the UN Special Fund. The UN's early development work through these two agencies had helped to create the infrastructure and institutions to transform economies, societies, and polities. Building on the experience of these two predecessors, the UNDP has become the nerve center of the UN's network of development agencies. The UNDP coordinates development work in the UN family at headquarters in New York and the work of its resident representatives in over 150 host countries. The UNDP administrator chairs the UN Development Group in New York, which has thirty-two member funds, programs, agencies, and offices. Resident representatives coordinate the UN system's in-country development work. The organization played a critical role in making development a priority for the UN system and helped create many of the offshoot agencies that it now coordinates.[1]

The UNDP has also been the source of new ideas, information, and thinking about development. The most notable of these is the Human Development Report, published annually since 1990, which provides global statistics on measures of human development. Many nations and regions now publish their own human development reports using the same measures as the HDR. The HDR helped broaden the concept, scope, and objectives of development and shift the focus away from the World Bank's single indicator of per capita income to the broader matrix of people-friendly indicators. The UNDP has helped expand and nurture development discourse by mainstreaming such issues as poverty elimination, access to clean water and sanitation, democratic enfranchisement, gender empowerment, minority protection, political participation, reduction of inequality within and among nations, environmental sustainability, public-private partnerships, and good governance.

Most crucially, the UNDP became the favored development institution of developing countries. It managed to do this by following the "coordinate and cultivate" rather than "command and control" model associated with the World Bank and other development donors and "partners."[2] The UNDP fostered indigenous capacity in states, in public and private organizations, and in individuals, following the formula of "local ownership" long before the concept became fashionable. This explains why the UNDP is the international development organization most trusted by developing countries.

Craig Murphy identifies four areas where the UNDP has been "ahead of the curve":

• Some of the senior founding people behind the UNDP became skeptical of grand development projects such as dams and steel mills as early

continued on following page

as the 1950s. This left them relatively more open to the notion that development should be environmentally sustainable and sensitive to the wishes of the people most affected by "development" projects.

- In the 1970s and 1980s, the UNDP was among the earliest to recognize and emphasize the central role of women in development and was the incubator of the UN Development Fund for Women (UNIFEM).

- In the late 1980s and subsequently in the Human Development Report, the UNDP became a strong skeptic and dissenter from the Washington consensus on liberal economic orthodoxy.

- In the 1990s, the UNDP was among the first to push for broad-ranging administrative reform across the UN system if development goals were going to be attained.[3]

1. Craig N. Murphy, *The United Nations Development Programme: A Better Way?* (New York: Cambridge University Press, 2006), 6.

2. Ibid., 18.

3. Ibid., 15–16.

ments on contested concepts in favor of reaching agreement on shared goals and milestones.

It is worth parsing three key functions. First, the MDGs not only encapsulate and articulate the norm of development as one of the international community's most fundamental and basic values and commitments, they also contain suggested ways of assessing policies. Columbia University's Michael Doyle, a former assistant-secretary-general, describes them as the equivalent of a constitution for the UN's development agencies, funds, and programs, "the platform under which the UN Development Group (UNDG) convenes."[79] As such they constitute a primary normative mandate that validates many operational agendas. Second, they provide an agreed-upon country framework for development planning. The MDGs are the chief template for measuring a country's development progress against agreed benchmarks and for informing policy and strategy dialogues among a variety of development agencies—the UNDP, the World Bank, the IMF, regional banks, and even bilateral donors—and between them and individual countries. Third, they define and validate the terms of relationships between the industrial and developing countries, setting forth reciprocal rights and obligations.

The MDGs are neither radical nor overly ambitious. Proponents view them as the minimum necessary to restore dignity and give practical expression to the call for a world free of fear and want in conditions of sustainability. Yet if trends since 2000 are extrapolated to 2015, much of the world, especially the poorest countries, is unlikely to achieve the goals. This reality is somewhat concealed by the fact that substantial growth in China and India (which together account for a third of the world's population and half of the population of developing countries) means that global statistics indicate progress toward meeting the MDGs.

It is worth looking at what the UN can do and has done to ensure implementation and compliance. Kofi Annan launched the Millennium Development Project in 2002 under the jurisdiction of the UNDP. The project analyzed and proposed the best strategies for meeting and monitoring the MDGs; it engaged in advocacy and resource mobilization efforts; and it reviewed priority policy reforms, identified their means of implementation, and evaluated financing options. Its main analytical work was performed by task forces—comprised of scholars, policymakers, and practitioners with broad geographical and UN agency representation—whose focus areas corresponded closely to the MDG targets. The task forces submitted interim reports in 2003 that were consolidated into an overall report presented to the Secretary-General in 2005 and incorporated into his own synthesis for the summit, *In Larger Freedom: Towards Development, Security and Human Rights for All.*[80] Accompanying these was another breathtakingly ambitious series, *Investing in Development: A Practical Plan to Achieve the Millennium Development Goals,* which was authored by a team headed by Jeffrey Sachs, author of his own utopian blueprint, *The End of Poverty.*[81]

The UN published a midterm report in 2007 that documented significant progress but also documented major shortfalls in efforts to meet the MDGs by 2015.[82] The poverty reduction targets were on track for the world as a whole but not for all regions. There was significant progress in most areas, including literacy, gender equality, child mortality, and health. Yet half the people in developing countries lacked access to basic sanitation, over half a million women continue to die every year of preventable and treatable complications during pregnancy and childbirth, the proportion of underweight children had not been reduced significantly, and the number of people dying of AIDS had increased from 2.2 million in 2001 to 2.9 million in 2006. Although the G-8 had pledged to double aid to

BOX 5.4. Millennium Development Goals and Targets

Goal 1: Eradicate extreme poverty and hunger

Target 1   Halve, between 1990 and 2015, the proportion of people whose income is less than $1 a day

Target 2   Halve, between 1990 and 2015, the proportion of people who suffer from hunger

Goal 2: Achieve universal primary education

Target 3   Ensure that, by 2015, children everywhere, boys and girls alike, will be able to complete a full course of primary schooling

Goal 3: Promote gender equality and empower women

Target 4   Eliminate gender disparity in primary and secondary education, preferably by 2005, and to all levels of education no later than 2015

Goal 4: Reduce child mortality

Target 5   Reduce by two-thirds, between 1990 and 2015, the under-five mortality rate

Goal 5: Improve maternal health

Target 6   Reduce by three-quarters, between 1990 and 2015, the maternal mortality ratio

Goal 6: Combat HIV/AIDS, malaria and other diseases

Target 7   Have halted by 2015 and begun to reverse the spread of HIV/AIDS

Target 8   Have halted by 2015 and begun to reverse the incidence of malaria and other major diseases

Goal 7: Ensure environmental sustainability

Target 9   Integrate the principles of sustainable development into country policies and programs and reverse the loss of environmental resources

Target 10   Halve, by 2015, the proportion of people without sustainable access to safe drinking water and basic sanitation

Target 11   By 2020, to have achieved a significant improvement in the lives of at least 100 million slum dwellers

Goal 8: Develop a global partnership for development

Target 12   Develop further an open, rule-based, predictable, nondiscriminatory trading and financial system (includes a commitment to good governance, development, and poverty reduction—both nationally and internationally)

Target 13   Address the special needs of the Least Developed Countries (includes tariff- and quota-free access for Least Developed Countries' exports; enhanced program of debt relief for heavily indebted poor countries (HIPC) and cancellation of official bilateral debt, and more generous official development assistance for countries committed to poverty reduction)

Target 14   Address the special needs of landlocked countries and small island developing states (through the Program of Action for the Sustainable Development of Small Island Developing States and the outcome of the 22nd General Assembly provisions)

Target 15   Deal comprehensively with the debt problems of developing countries through national and international measures in order to make debt sustainable in the long term

Target 16   In cooperation with developing countries, develop and implement strategies for decent and productive work for youth

Target 17   In cooperation with pharmaceutical companies, provide access to affordable essential drugs in developing countries

Target 18   In cooperation with the private sector, make available the benefits of new technologies, especially information and communications technologies

Source: UN Millennium Project, "Goals, Targets, and Indicators," available at http://www.unmillenniumproject.org/goals/gti.htm#goal1.

Africa at their Gleneagles summit in 2005, total official aid declined by 5.1 percent from 2005 to 2006.

In 2002, the George W. Bush administration announced a new Millennium Challenge Account (MCA) of foreign assistance to the poorest countries, one of the few positive foreign policy innovations of the administration. The MCA is not a multilateral arrangement; it is administered by an independent corporation of the United States, the Millennium Challenge Corporation. Recipient countries must meet certain criteria related to economic effectiveness on such indicators as inflation, fiscal policy, management of natural resources, investments in health and education, and good governance.[83] However, congressional appropriations for the MCA consistently fell short by about half of the administration's budgetary requests. Moreover, in light of restrictive funding criteria, only some of the world's poorest countries are able to qualify. While Rwanda, Cape Verde, and Burkina Faso have qualified for the incentives, far more countries with acute needs have not. In the words of expert Jochen Steinhilber, "MCA funds are in effect reserved for the 'happy few,' that is, for those countries with the least pressing development problems."[84]

Even though the MDGs are a triumph of consensus, they also represent a quintessential UN shortcoming: little can be done to ensure compliance besides embarrassing a country that fails to meet a particular MDG, such as providing education to girls or meeting its aid targets. As we go to press, the latest data regarding the attainment of MDG 8, outside assistance for development, was issued by the United Nations. An interagency task force reported that ODA had decreased by 8.4 percent in 2007, and that was hard on the heels of a 4.7 percent drop in 2006. It also pointed out that commitments to help the least developed countries, and Africa in particular, had lagged substantially.[85]

Thus, the United Nations can provide policy advice and technical assistance, collect and collate data, identify shortfalls as well as progress, and issue appeals and exhortations. But in the end it cannot impose its preferences and policies on sovereign member states. It does not have the power to tax industrial countries and redirect additional aid money to developing countries, nor does it have the power to assume control of national development plans. In other words, by its very nature, the world organization is severely limited and handicapped in ensuring implementation and compliance; all it can do is to report on member states' performance. And that it has done. But the embarrassment factor is not a trivial one in international affairs, and it may even help bring about compliance.

It is worth repeating here that the UN's contribution of such goal-setting exercises as the MDGs is substantial, even though such goals are often questioned by those who see them as empty vessels.[86] The record of achievement is mixed but more positive than many realize. The UNIHP volume *UN Contributions to Development Thinking and Practice* reviewed all UN goals that had a quantified target and a date fixed for their achievement over the period 1950 to 2000.[87] Success with the goal of economic growth in the First Development Decade led to a higher goal of 6 percent a year in the Second Development Decade. This goal was achieved by thirty-five countries, and the average rate of growth for all countries was 5.6 percent, a bit higher than in the 1960s. After 1980 economic performance deteriorated for most countries; the only exceptions were China and (in the 1990s) India. Though the UN continued to set goals for economic growth, such growth averaged only 4 percent in developing countries in the 1980s and 4.7 percent in the 1990s. In both decades, the overall rate of growth was pulled up by the exceptional performance of the two giants, China and India.[88]

The record for the key goals for aspects of human development has been considerably better. In 1980, the goal was set that life expectancy should reach sixty years at a minimum—a goal achieved in 124 of 173 countries. At the same time, the goal for reducing infant mortality by 2000 was set at 120 per 1,000 live births in the poorest countries and fifty in all others. By 2000, after impressive acceleration of immunization programs and other child survival measures, 138 developing countries had attained this goal. Progress in other areas has been considerable. Reductions in malnutrition, iron deficiency anaemia, and vitamin A deficiency advanced over the 1990s. During the 1980s, access was more than doubled by the expansion of water and sanitation facilities by 2000.[89]

The review of progress for all fifty goals reveals that results have been generally positive but mixed—far from full achievement but rarely total failures. Progress on economic growth has slipped badly over the decades; average growth among developing countries was only marginally better in the 1990s than in the 1980s, but in both cases it was below the rates of the 1960s and 1970s. *UN Contributions* makes clear that the most serious failures have been in Sub-Saharan Africa and the least developed countries. But even here, performance in meeting the human goals has often been considerably better than in meeting the targets for economic growth or international aid.

Reforming the Architecture of International Financial and Economic Governance

As noted at the outset, this book was completed in the midst of the global financial and economic turmoil following the subprime mortgage crisis in 2007–2008 and the Wall Street collapse in September–October 2008. The turmoil made apparent the necessity of reforming the current international financial architecture, which has its historical roots in the Great Depression.

The first and most dramatic impact of the 2008 banking and financial crisis on the architecture of governance was to bring the worlds of politics, money, and banking more sharply together. One after another, governments underwrote massive bailouts by buying toxic debts and/or injecting capital into banks in order to stabilize financial markets and provide liquidity to keep credit lines open. The UK's prime minister, Gordon Brown, was the first to provide bailouts for banks; the United States followed shortly thereafter.[90]

A growing recognition that the system to manage the modern world of banking, capital, and finance had to be redesigned accompanied such short-term emergency measures as bailouts. The reality is that corporations, markets, and financial flows are all global, but the regulatory and surveillance systems are national or, in a few cases such as Europe, regional. The Group of 7's (G-7) inability to tackle the global financial crisis led to calls for a new steering group that includes rising economic powers. U.S. treasury secretary Henry Paulson, responding to a question about whether the G-7 should be expanded to include developing powers such as China, India, Russia, Brazil, and Mexico, said, "If you look at the global financial architecture, I don't think it reflects the global economy today. . . . It's a big world, and it's a lot bigger than the G7."[91]

In response to the crisis, Gordon Brown and several other G-7 leaders supported the idea of expanding their group. They called for a major global meeting to redesign the world's financial system and rewrite the rulebook of global capitalism. Writing in the *Washington Post,* Brown argued that while the "old postwar international financial institutions are out of date . . . the same sort of visionary internationalism [that was displayed at Bretton Woods in 1944] is needed to resolve the crises and challenges of a different age." He proposed "cross-border supervision of financial institutions; shared global standards for accounting and regulation; a more responsible approach to executive remuneration that rewards hard work, effort and enterprise but not irresponsible risk-taking . . . the renewal of our international institutions to make them effective early-warning systems for the world economy" and a rejection of "the beggar-thy-neighbor protectionism that has been a feature of past crises."[92] He warned that "we are in the first financial crisis of the new global age. . . . We need to recognize that if risks are globalized, then responsibilities have to be globalized as well."[93]

In other words, under the current deficient system of global governance, "We get the global perils without global benefits."[94] None of the existing political or economic institutions—the IMF, the G-7, or the Group of 20 (G-20)—proved adequate to the task of coordinating a response to a global crisis. It is hard to imagine any major worldwide challenge that can be effectively addressed without involving all three Asian giants (China, India, and Japan). Yet two of the three (India and Japan) are not permanent members of the UN's Security Council, and two of the three (China and India) were not part of the G-7. The IMF has shown more skill at preaching to developing countries than at persuading industrial countries to act together, while the G-20 is more prone to ask for handouts from developed countries than to tackle the domestic governance gaps of its own membership.

For some time it has been clear that any new architecture of global governance must bring together the existing G-8 (G-7 plus Russia) and the major emerging markets of Brazil, China, India, Mexico, South Africa, Saudi Arabia, and Indonesia.[95]

In Pittsburgh in late September, at the third gathering of the G-20 in 2009 (the first had been in Washington in November 2008, convened by the iconic opponent of multilateralism and global governance George W. Bush, and the second in London in April 2009), the group declared that it would become a permanent fixture of the global governance institutional network. The new G-20 encompasses 4.2 billion people (instead of 900 million in the G-8), but another 2.6 billion mainly poor people are left out. And they and their governments—including almost all of Sub-Saharan Africa—are a prerequisite for solving most global problems. Whatever the advantages of consultations about economic and financial matters among the upgraded G-20 that account for 90 percent of the world's GDP, only the United Nations can formulate global norms, set global standards, make global law, and enforce global treaties. The G-192 has advantages that the upgraded G-20, ad hoc coalitions of the willing, and various proposals for a league of democracies do not. The G-20 may well be a better forum for coming to common positions on global problems among the countries that count; but its policy preferences will still need formal endorsement by the United Nations system as the only legitimate global forum and font of international authority.

Human Development and the Five Global Governance Gaps

The concept of human development is by now well established and has been mainstreamed in the scholarly literature and in policy discourse.[96]

The concept's UN lineage is clear and well known. As in so much else, the story involves a group of gifted and dedicated individuals acting within the UN—in this case, the UNDP.[97]

Upon assuming leadership of the UNDP, its new head administrator, William H. Draper, asked a two-part question: What does UNDP believe in? Should it not be advocating what it believes in?[98] The answer to the first question included the virtues of democracy, the desire to improve the lives of the disadvantaged, and a focus on gender, the environment, NGOs, and the role of the private sector. In 1990 all of this was brought under the conceptual umbrella of "human development," which is now officially adopted as the UNDP's overriding priority. Draper recruited Mahbub ul Haq and gave him complete intellectual freedom to write a sort of "state of the human condition" report.

The rest, as they say, is history. Ul Haq published the first Human Development Report in 1990 and the UNDP has published one each year since then. They have become standard reference points for scholars and policymakers alike and have expanded and multiplied with a plethora of regional, national, and even provincial reports that typically engage the leading scholars of the community, thereby ensuring that the process and the product are locally owned. The institutional impact of local engagement is clear from the fact that more than 10,000 people work on HDRs around the world.[99] The 1990 report also introduced the annual human development index. Mark Malloch Brown, one of Draper's successors, noted in 1999 that the HDR created "an extraordinary advocacy tool" whose strength lies in the way that it "benchmarks progress" with a clear set of indicators.[100]

The HDRs have had a major impact in informing and influencing development debates. They helped shape the debate on financial austerity in Latin America in the 1990s to cope with economic crises, the debate on the cultural deficit that accumulated during Augusto Pinochet's military dictatorship in Chile, the debate on democratization in Eastern Europe, and the debate on the HIV/AIDS pandemic in Africa. One of the most notable reports in recent memory was the inaugural Arab Human Development Report,[101] published in 2002, which was sharply critical of the Arab world's internal failings and identified the policy decisions of repressive governments as the proximate cause of the region's stagnation on any number of measures.

For a UN publication, the Arab HDR was refreshingly free of preemptive self-censorship. The independence of the HDR has been jealously protected, which has lent it credibility among various civil society groups who in turn have worked diligently to help refine the methodology and improve data collection. The HDR has become a tool in the hands of citizens to demand accountability from their own governments. It has become a tool in the hands of opposition political parties to demand explanations from the government for regress on indicators and slippage in rank on the global index. It has informed the development discourse and agendas of many governments. At a memorial service for Mahbub ul Haq in 1998, World Bank president James Wolfensohn explicitly acknowledged, "Mahbub—you were right."[102] By now the World Bank rivals the UNDP in the resources and attention devoted to human development, even though the Bank's disbursements dwarf those of the UNDP.

In part the popularity and utility of the HDRs lies in the way the concept of human development filled key knowledge gaps. GDP per capita may be a good proxy variable for economic prosperity, but it is inherently unsatisfactory as a complete measure of development for many reasons. Economic activities that destroy the long-term base and potential of a country and cause significant and demonstrable harm to communities should hardly be included as indicators of "positive growth." Hence, some seriously doubt whether investments that pollute, produce cigarettes or armaments, and result in deforestation or urban paralysis can be considered viable economic efforts. Yet some of the most valuable domains of social life—the attributes that define a meaningful society—do not count in the measurement of GDP because they have no market price. The quality of the air that we breathe, the joy and happiness of children at play, and the pleasure of reading poetry are absent from GDP. The crucial contribution of the HDRs has been to provide the framework and methodology for measuring key proxy indicators of human development, starting with the original unweighted three indicators of life expectancy, literacy, and per capita income using purchasing power parity.

Once the knowledge gap was filled, the next stage, which was achieved in this case with surprising rapidity, was the identification of a normative gap and the establishment of the norm of human development. The acceptance of the norm in turn highlighted policy gaps in terms of neglecting important dimensions of the human condition and social welfare that focused too narrowly on economic growth. Factoring in human development in government policies and donor practices is now commonplace. For example, the 1995 HDR, which focused on women and noted that they contributed more than half of the world's economic output but received less than a quarter of the economic rewards and were singularly underrepresented in the corridors of political power, had a major impact on the Beijing UN World Conference on Women in the same year. It has been the catalyst for regular calculations of the contributions of women to the economic activities of nations (which had not been measured before 1995) and for estimates of the impact of public policies on women.

The institutional gaps have been filled by the dedicated HDR office at UNDP headquarters in New York and the extensive regional and national offices and secretariats staffed by keen advocates of the concept. And HDR reports are the major annual audit on national implementation and compliance gaps. For example, India's former prime minister Indar K. Gujral notes that the head of a state government has to answer to his or her legislature on how many points the country may have slipped in the index, why that may have happened, and what the proposed remedies are that will enable the state to climb up the index again.[103]

Finally, the story of human development is an exemplar of the key role that the creative mixture of the Second UN and the Third UN plays in the development and validation of an idea into a worldwide norm and public policy. Mahbub ul Haq and Amartya Sen were influenced in their thinking on the human condition by economist Barbara Ward, who was arguing as early as the 1950s that the West's physical capacity was outpacing its ethical capacity and that being a human being meant more than producing wealth. Ul Haq and Sen, who were fellow undergraduates and roommates at Cambridge University, had discussions in 1953 about what dimensions were measurable beyond money, such as life expectancy and literacy, that might better capture the completeness of the human condition. They, along with several others, went on to publish seminal work on notions of empowerment, entitlement, and capabilities that fleshed out the inchoate concept of human development and gave it scholarly backbone. This is an example where key senior people in key agencies brought their work into the UN system and from there it spread to the rest of the UN system and to national governments. The UN imprimatur has been vital to the validation of the concept and the norm, its receptivity in almost all countries, and its translation into national development policy.

Human development was the necessary precursor to the concept of human security. The United Nations has also been critical in the development and popularization of this concept.[104] The world body has been instrumental in the shift in security thinking in three ways. First, it has served as an incubator and generator of new ideas on key aspects of human security thinking, most notably through the *Human Development Report 1994* and the UNDP's Human Development Report Office thereafter. Second, a number of UN organs, including the UN High Commissioner for Refugees (UNHCR) under Sadako Ogata's leadership, were used as forums where states and NGOs could debate, articulate, and advocate alternative conceptions of security. The UN was used also as a forum for forming complex coalitions of civil society and state actors on particular issues such as land mines and international criminal justice. Third, parts of the UN system embedded the new concept of human security into their operations and practices, again including the UNHCR but also Secretary-General Kofi Annan, who pushed the envelope of international intervention to protect civilians at risk of mass deaths. In doing so, the UN system was a key legitimizing device for the new concept of human security.

Perhaps a final word on the UN's role in the intellectual history of the development discourse can go to Kofi Annan:

> We have defined what development means, what development should mean for the individual through our *Human Development Reports*. . . . You are dealing with health, you are dealing with clean water, you are dealing with education, and all that. So we have given a functional and meaningful definition to poverty and development which wasn't there before. And I think this is very important for policymakers and for people who want to measure progress.[105]

Conclusion: Partial Gap Filling

This chapter has argued that although the United Nations has not been a central player in filling knowledge gaps in terms of understanding what defines and causes the process of economic development, it is a useful and essential repository of statistics and indicators, particularly in the Department of Economic and Social Affairs. By contrast, the organization *has* been the central player in conceptualizing and giving empirical content to the alternative and complementary notion of human development. It was also a central player in filling the gap in understanding the long-term implications of the terms of trade. In addition to promoting human development, the world organization has filled normative gaps by promoting the norms of equity, equality, and international redistributive justice with respect both to development and trade. It has held fast also to the norm that rich countries should give 0.7 percent of their GDP as ODA to developing countries. And more recently, it has actively promoted the norm of corporate social responsibility through the Global Compact. On the policy front, while different branches of the UN system have actively promoted items such as poverty reduction strategy papers, setting policies about development is essentially a national-level responsibility. But the UN has promoted international policy tools such as levels of financing and the rules that govern disbursement of ODA for development. GATT was the first central governance institution to regulate international trade, followed by the WTO, both of which have been continually criticized by UNCTAD since 1964. And as we see in the next chapter, the UNDP is probably more respected today than the World Bank but does not have anything like the same resources. Finally, the UN system is doubly handicapped with regard to implementation and compliance: developing countries are very sensitive to encroachments on their sovereignty in setting economic policy, and enforcing donor countries to comply with UN development policy agreements is inherently impossible.

As we are writing this passage, the world appears to be experiencing elements of a perfect economic storm. The global housing and financial crisis that began in the United States and is spreading worldwide illustrates, for us at least, the impact of having missed critical opportunities to construct the architecture for better global governance precisely to protect countries and individuals against the evident downsides of globalization.[106] Moreover, these financial difficulties should not hide the ugly reality for many of the increasing and highly variable prices in commodities, including oil. Estimates show increases in the proportion of hungry people, and the skyrocketing increases in food prices in 2008 are likely to be sustained even without higher prices for transport and fertilizers. Such increases are good for farmers and net food producers but are likely to increase problems for the urban poor and others who consume more food than they produce. Again, a stronger fabric of global economic governance—better knowledge, norms, policies, institutions, and compliance mechanisms—would provide a stronger safety net in the future.

As the two preceding chapters on arms control and terrorism found, it is easier for the UN system to identify what needs to be done—on norms, policies, and institutions—than to get them done. There can be no better illustration of this than the MDGs.

6

Sustainable Development

- Antecedents: From Development to Conservation to Sustainability
- Knowledge Gaps: A Clear UN Contribution
- Normative Gaps: Sustainable Development as the Norm
- Policy Gaps: Déjà Vu All Over Again
- Institutional Gaps: UNEP, UNESCO, and the IWC
- Compliance Gaps: Still Searching
- Conclusion: Conference Diplomacy and Global Governance

Former UNEP executive director Mostafa Tolba recalls that the term "sustainable development" emerged in UNEP's governing council in the early 1980s. Previous incarnations were "eco-development," "development without destruction," and "environmentally sound development"—all attempts to tie social development and economic growth to environmental protection.[1] This chapter links the previous chapter on development and the next chapter, which is about environmental protection, by focusing on the UN's engagement with the concept of sustainable development.

Early in 2008 we once again were reminded of the pertinence of this topic when the world was blasted with a major crisis as rapidly rising food prices threatened the social cohesion and political stability of a number of countries. The United Nations formed a task force to confront an old question: were the Malthusians right after all? The Malthusian thesis has always been as popular as it was simple. It states that the world cannot sustain an ever-increasing growth in population and food supply. Its adherents argue that as growing populations create stress on the food supply and generate food scarcity, the population will decline.

The world's sustainability problems demonstrate the contemporary relevance of the Malthusian thesis. In industrial societies, these include overconsumption. The sustainability problems of developing countries include managing economic growth without destroying the resource base, adjusting to pressures of population growth, and sustaining patterns of production in agriculture while striving for rapid industrialization. The most recent manifestations of the problem of sustainability include the challenge of climate change, which cuts across the global North-South divide; a growing scarcity of water and energy; galloping desertification; and loss of nature's life support systems for a variety of species. In brief, how can growth be managed to sustain an acceptable lifestyle while ensuring equity for different peoples within and among countries and across generations?

Antecedents:
From Development to Conservation to Sustainability

At the time of the UN's establishment, the dominant development paradigm was self-sustaining economic growth through industrialization. When, how, and from where did knowledge first arise of problems with this model and of the need to conserve resources? When and how did the norm of conservation arise and become established? How was that converted into public policy around the world, and which institutions were the lead actors in the conversion process? How successful have efforts been to move from policy to action and to correct individual tendencies to deviate from the norm and policy? In particular, of course, where is the United Nations in this narrative?

Since at least 1798, when the Reverend Thomas R. Malthus first wrote his "Essay on the Principle of Population,"[2] people have worried about the "carrying capacity" of the planet. For the first half of the twentieth century, the most evident concerns about the quality of the human environment centered on the concept of "conservation," which refers to preserving natural resources for future use instead of exhausting them indiscriminately.

The conservation movement began in the United States in the first decade of the twentieth century, when U.S. president Theodore Roosevelt made conservation a cornerstone of his presidency. Roosevelt embraced conservation by creating national parks, stopping the sale of public lands, and pushing for the creation of a new cabinet-level department of the interior for the purpose of resource management. A key figure of the conservation movement was Gifford Pinchot, chief of the U.S. Department of Agriculture's forestry division from 1898 to 1910. Pinchot firmly believed that natural resources should be used, albeit carefully, and that nature's methods of control could be vastly improved with methods of scientific management.

In *The Legacy of Conquest: The Unbroken Past of the American West,* Patricia Nelson Limerick recounts two anecdotes that foreshadowed the birth of ecology and environmentalism:

> In 1891, Gifford Pinchot—then a self-confessed "tenderfoot"— first saw the Grand Canyon. He was speechless, but his arbitrarily acquired traveling companion, an office boy named Doran, was not. While Pinchot "strove to grasp the vastness and the beauty of the greatest sight this world has to offer," Doran kept repeating, "My, ain't it pretty?" Pinchot remembered, "I wanted to throw him in." . . . In 1897, Pinchot returned to the Grand Canyon with a more suitable companion, the naturalist John Muir. . . . During this agreeable time together, the only moment of disagreement came when they encountered a tarantula. Pinchot wanted to kill it, but Muir defended the spider, arguing that it had every right to be there. . . . Muir's sentiments echoed the refrain of Doran the office boy.[3]

As Limerick notes, "Extended to its logical conclusion, 'Ain't it pretty?' becomes 'So leave it like it is.'"[4] This static notion of conservation would one day confront the need to balance environmental concerns with the need for continued economic growth.

As late as the early 1960s, Pinchot's views that natural resources should be managed to benefit humans predominated. For instance, *The Earth,* a volume in the popular Life Nature Library, ended with a chapter called "An Uncertain Destiny," which listed the problems of overpopulation, the depletion of mineral resources, the pollution and overconsumption of water, and so on. The conceptual framework was unabashedly that of conservation—that is, human control. For example, the introduction to a photo essay stated: "The past saw a squandering of resources; the present is witnessing a search for new ones."[5] It went on to explore agricultural efficiency, asteroid mining, atomic energy, desalinization, and population and weather control as possible solutions.

Some books and other events have been more influential than others in propagating the norm of protecting the human environment. One of the most influential early books was Rachel Carson's *Silent Spring* (1962), which evoked a world where the increasing use of chemicals and pesticides was killing nature and wildlife to the point where one day we would witness spring without the song of birds. The 1968 Earthrise photo—characterized as "the most influential environmental photo ever taken"—communicated fragility and vulnerability in a way that few words could.[6]

Yet Carson's earlier words were powerful. A zoologist and already a best-selling author of popular science books, she documented the impact of pesticides on flora and fauna. In her first chapter, she described a fictional town where almost every conceivable disaster had occurred. Although each was a real event, they had not actually occurred in the same place. Nevertheless, she swung the intellectual equivalent of a sledgehammer:

> There was a strange stillness. The birds, for example—where had they gone? Many people spoke of them, puzzled and disturbed. The feeding stations in the backyards were deserted. The few birds seen anywhere were moribund; they trembled violently and could not fly. It was a spring without voices. On the mornings that had once throbbed with the dawn chorus of robins, catbirds, doves, jays, wrens, and scores of other bird voices, there was now no sound; only silence lay over the fields and woods and marsh.[7]

Carson was attacked by the pesticide industry, but she altered forever the way that people looked at the earth and their place in it. Other authors used that same sledgehammer, such as Julian Huxley in his 1956 discussion of overpopulation and Barry Commoner in his 1971 work on the exhaustion of nonrenewable energy resources.[8]

By the 1970s, the tide had turned. Secretary-General U Thant's *Man and His Environment* (1969) addressed serious issues of pollution, erosion, and waste and was among the UN's first documents that explicitly called for action at all levels: local, national, and global.[9] Indicative of the change was *Ecology*, another volume in the Life Nature Library series that was published in 1963 but then extensively rewritten and released again in 1970. In this volume, the previously unheralded interrelationships between living organisms and their environment is made explicit and a warning is sounded about the impact of reckless human activity, including wildlife species that had become endangered, overpopulation, and the possibility of climate change through air pollution.[10] For the first time, people began to realize that pollution had global and not just local effects and that global solutions undoubtedly would be necessary.

On 22 April 1970, some 20 million Americans took part in a rally for Earth Day—one of the biggest mass rallies in U.S. history. That same year the federal government set up the Environmental Protection Agency.

As environmental consciousness increased in the industrialized world, developing countries began to realize that successful development would require at least revisiting the patterns and costs of traditional approaches to economic growth. But they also asked, "Why now? Why us? Why do we have to play by different rules than the industrialized North?"

Perhaps the most visible volume on sustainability in analytical and policy circles was the report written by a group of MIT academics and published for the independent Club of Rome in 1972, *The Limits to Growth*.[11] The report made the global scope of environmental problems and the urgent need for global solutions starkly apparent. Indeed, the subtitle of the book offered an ambiguous—partially hopeful, partially fearful—concept: *The Predicament of Mankind*. The volume was a sophisticated modeling exercise that extrapolated trends and reached the conclusion that planetary limits would be met within a hundred years—that in short, past patterns of development were unsustainable. This controversial volume provided the context for Sweden's call for the first UN global gathering on the topic, which was held in Stockholm in 1972. This gathering marked the beginning of the UN's contribution to filling knowledge gaps on sustainability.

Knowledge Gaps: A Clear UN Contribution

When the UN was established in 1945, the twin threats of environmental degradation and exhaustion of resources were not on the international agenda. It was not until the 1960s that influential individuals and groups began to sound the alarm about the finite resources of the planet and the seemingly infinite thirst for consumption that threatened to exhaust the resource base. This changed when the Club of Rome published *The Limits to Growth*. Sales of the book have exceeded 30 million, and it has been published in more than thirty languages; the book is one of the best-selling environmental titles of all time. Its basic thesis was that economic growth could not continue indefinitely because natural resources—in particular oil—were finite. The 1973 oil crisis following the Yom Kippur War seemed to validate the gloomy prognosis and increased public concern about the underlying sustainability problem.

Another milestone in raising awareness of the need for sustainable policies to care for the earth's resources was the Brundtland Commission's *Our Common Future*, published in 1987.[12] This report brought environmental issues to the top of the agenda once more. It contributed the new concept of "sustainable development," or meeting the development needs of the present without destroying the environment and thus compromising the ability of future generations to meet their own needs. The book noted three dimensions of "interlocking crises." First, it argued, the environmental crisis, the development crisis, and the energy crisis were all aspects of the same problem. Second, this crisis knew no national boundaries. And third, the growing inequality between the rich and the poor was driving the crisis. The report stressed the basic needs of the world's poor and the limitations imposed by the early stages of development. While economic and ecological, international and national policymakers and institutions operate independently, the effects of their policies are intertwined, the report noted. It urged institutional reform to reflect this reality and called for a world conference on environment and development.

The Brundtland report was memorable for its opening sentence: "The Earth is one but the world is not."[13] The single sentence captured the cacophony of views and disparities in power among those engaged in the debate about sustainability. This singular UN achievement has framed the dominant approach to development since its publication. The first section of this chapter discusses in considerable detail the extent to which various knowledge gaps about sustainability have been filled through UN deliberations.

The Stockholm Conference

"Sometime during the late 1960s the term environment began to take on its contemporary meaning, complete with its undercurrent of urgent concern, and emerged as a real issue in industrialized countries," writes Maurice Strong, the secretary-general of the UN Conference on the Human Environment and champion of the cause.[14] In 1968, the General Assembly called for such a conference to be convened to discuss the problems of "the human environment" and identify which of them could be solved solely or best through international collaboration.

Although early General Assembly resolutions expressed concerns about conserving natural resources, the contemporary debate is usually dated to a Swedish initiative in 1969 to convene what later became known as the 1972 Stockholm conference, officially the UN Conference on the Human Environment. The Stockholm conference was the first single-issue global conference as well as the first UN conference on the environment. In addition to the delegates from 113 governments that took part in the official conference, NGOs were active in three parallel conferences: the

Environment Forum, the Peoples Forum, and the Dai Dong Independent Conference on the Environment.

Preparatory meetings can be more critical in uncovering problems and helping to find diplomatic solutions than the conference itself. In this case, during preparatory meetings for the Stockholm conference, Strong encountered substantial objections from developing countries to what seemed like accepted wisdom in the West. This "wisdom" was sometimes impelled by polemics—for instance, Paul Ehrlich's book *The Population Bomb* (1968),[15] which observers even at the time characterized as verging on the apocalyptic. Developing countries were uneasy about the Stockholm conference because they saw the not-so-hidden agenda of the "zero quantifiable growth" for which *The Limits to Growth* had called. From the perspective of the South, the North acted as if growth by rich nations was tolerable but then it discouraged the have-nots from aspiring to reach its own level of development.

Strong recalls in his autobiography that Pakistan's Mahbub ul Haq unabashedly pointed out at a preparatory meeting for Stockholm that:

> industrialization had given developed countries disproportionate benefits and huge reservoirs of wealth and at the same time had caused the very environmental problems we were now asking developing countries to join in resolving. The cost of cleaning up the mess, therefore, should be borne by the countries that had caused it in the first place. If they wanted developing countries to go along, they'd have to provide the financial resources to enable them to do so.[16]

Other developing-country leaders were suspicious that environmental standards were being used as a pretext for discriminatory trade practices, given the growing trend in nontariff barriers to market access.

Developed countries were mainly preoccupied with the negative impacts of industrialization, while developing countries perceived this kind of environmentalism as a blatant threat to their own growth aspirations. Developing countries explicitly proclaimed the right to economic and social development and insisted that environmental concerns could not be used to limit their pursuit. At her opening speech in Stockholm, Indian prime minister Indira Gandhi uttered a memorable sound-bite: "Poverty is the greatest polluter."[17]

Bridging this North-South division required a reframing of the argument. As a quintessential compromiser, Strong acted on his hunch that protection of the environment and economic development were different aspects of the same problem. In an attempt to get developing countries on board, in June 1971 Strong gathered what he called his twenty-seven "gurus" for a brainstorming session at a motel in Founex, Switzerland (just outside Geneva), to probe the interconnectedness of the environment and development from a Third World perspective. Those who attended the meeting—which included Enrique Iglesias, Mahbub ul Haq, Gamani Corea, and Ignacy Sachs—emphasized that environmental issues should become an integral part of development strategy.[18]

The debate at Founex produced a report that asserted that pollution sprang from two causes. In the industrial world, it was production and consumption patterns; in the developing world, it was underdevelopment and poverty. They explicitly linked the environment with development and provided a rationale for integrating what states usually pursued as separate strategies. Moreover, the Founex group pointed out that it was in the interest of rich countries to help poorer countries accelerate their growth—there was only one earth.

Only One Earth became the title of a best-selling book that Strong commissioned. He persuaded French scientist René Dubos, British economist Barbara Ward, and dozens of other experts to collaborate with him in writing the book.[19] Strong recalled: "In doing so, I once again ran head-on into the UN bureaucracy and rediscovered how it can sometimes act as a barrier to rather than a facilitator of initiatives."[20] He put his usual business acumen and entrepreneurship to work and raised the money to publish outside the UN; the book promptly made a profit in twelve languages.

Geopolitically, a period of détente was beginning, and both the United States and the Soviet Union agreed that there could and should be East-West cooperation on the environment. Michael G. Schechter explains that disagreements about excluding the East Germans from the Stockholm conference proved to be unresolvable, and most of the Soviet bloc boycotted the conference. Strong minimized the damage by keeping the Soviets informed about developments at the conference.[21] The conclusions of the brainstorming session at Founex as well as the overall framing of the problem in *Only One Earth* were reiterated at Stockholm and in subsequent UN publications.

The conference set a precedent for its engagement of nongovernmental organizations. NGOs were allowed to observe and speak at open plenary and committee sessions—including groups that did not have consultative status with ECOSOC. Furthermore, alternative NGO forums involving around 200 groups were held concurrently, and these influenced both media coverage and (ultimately) the policymaking process.[22] Including nongovernmental and dissenting voices in the United Nations, once an exclusive club of governmental representatives, is of course by now one of the essential components of global governance and an expected part of UN global conferences.

At Stockholm, *"Only One Earth* [became] the theme and the rallying cry," Strong writes. Yet because of the wide disparity in starting positions among countries, the first headline in the NGO newspaper published at Stockholm read "Only 113 Earths," referring to the number of country delegations present.[23] In spite of clashes in views, compromise was eventually reached. The Stockholm Declaration on the Human Environment contained twenty-six principles, an action plan with 109 recommendations, and a resolution on institutional and financial arrangements. What began as a debate among environmentalists who argued for a no-growth strategy, industrialized countries who wanted business as usual, and developing countries who wanted expanded growth evolved into something else. Participants deemed growth necessary if poverty was to be alleviated, but sovereign states acknowledged responsibility for domestic actions that affected other states. And all sides agreed that profound changes in attitudes, values, and behavior toward the ecosphere were necessary for an evolving international agenda that sought to protect the environment while at the same time fostering economic and social development.[24]

The Stockholm conference's impact on thinking, while it had lasting institutional effects, was temporarily diluted by the economic impact of the oil price shocks of the 1970s as well as by the publication of many overwrought and wildly inaccurate predictions of impending doom. These pieces for a time decreased the amount of attention to and legitimacy of the environmental movement.[25]

Poverty elimination was increasingly joined to the growing conservation and environmental movements in other ways within UN circles in the following years. The overexploitation of extractive resources in developing countries to meet the demand for consumer goods in rich countries often had dire consequences for peasants, who were losing their livelihoods and their traditional grazing and habitation rights. Residents of developing countries were being forced to cope with the interlinked pressures of deforestation, expanding acreage under plantation, and urbanization.

The Brundtland Report and the Rio Conference

In 1983, the General Assembly established the World Commission on Environment and Development, which was chaired by Prime Minister Gro Harlem Brundtland of Norway. Its work took place against the backdrop of the Third World debt crisis (Mexico defaulted on its debt in August 1982), self-confidence in the industrialized West, and the rise of neoliberalism with its emphasis on deregulation and liberalization.

As we have seen already, the 1987 Brundtland report changed the language and substance of international discourse by reconciling the two seemingly opposed concepts of economic development and environmental protection.[26] It sided with developing countries in arguing that poverty was harmful to the environmental cause, rejecting arguments to limit growth, and concluding that the key to development was environmentally sustainable growth. It popularized and mainstreamed the concept of sustainable development, defining it as development that "meets the need of the present without compromising the ability of future generations to meet their own needs."[27] Developing countries would need transfers of economic assistance and environmental technologies in order to be able to pursue strategies of sustainable development, the report argued. The UNDP, UNEP, the World Bank, national development agencies, and many NGOs quickly adopted the concept of sustainable development.

Following the Brundtland report, in 1989 the General Assembly called for another environmental conference to be held in Rio de Janeiro on the occasion of the twentieth anniversary of the Stockholm conference. The Rio conference, also known as the Earth Summit, was held in 1992. It took place as the Cold War ended, a development that led to a burgeoning of civil society groups in the former socialist bloc and in many parts of the developing world. This context constituted an important political backdrop for the UN Conference on Environment and Development (UNCED). The conference was also held at a time when evidence was accumulating on unsustainable practices, the fragility of the ecosystem, damage to the environment (for example, the hole in the ozone layer), the depletion of fish stocks, and the loss of biodiversity. More than any other previous conference or meeting, the Earth Summit brought together the dynamic relationship between agricultural practices, industrial processes and products, consumption patterns, and the human environment. It also highlighted the tension between the sovereign prerogative of states to exploit, utilize, and develop resources within their jurisdiction as they saw fit and the global impact of deforestation, stock depletions, desertification, and atmospheric pollution.

It was the largest world conference at the time; 179 countries, including 110 heads of government and state, attended Rio. Some 2,400 NGOs were formally accredited to observe the main gatherings and another 17,000 took part in a parallel NGO forum. The Brundtland report's recommendations framed the conference's substantive agenda; all sides found the report's twin emphasis on growth and sustainability palatable. Nevertheless, developing countries demanded and industrialized countries resisted compensatory financial transfers for "green growth" on the argument that industrialization in the North had caused most of the world's pollution. This divide foreshadowed a disagreement that became far more acute regarding climate change and the Kyoto Protocol.

The Rio Declaration consisted of twenty-seven principles that described the rights and responsibilities of states regarding development and the environment; a 300-page action program to promote sustainable development known as Agenda 21, most of which had been negotiated in preparatory meetings leading up to the conference; and two legally binding conventions, the UN Framework Convention on Climate Change (UNFCCC) and the Convention on Biological Diversity. Finally, the conference set up the UN Commission on Sustainable Development (CSD) to monitor and evaluate progress in meeting the provisions of Agenda 21 and initiated discussions on a desertification treaty.

A significant part of the NGO constituency was disenchanted with the Earth Summit; they believed that growth had been prioritized at the cost of conservation; that the harmful consequences of continuing industrialization, such as increasing inequality and overconsumption, were being ignored to the earth's greater peril; and that a top-down managerial approach was being imposed instead of heeding voices from the field and adopting local solutions.[28]

The Johannesburg World Summit on Sustainable Development

A UN review in 1997 established that most of the Agenda 21 goals were not being met. But world conferences remained in vogue, including "+5" and "+10" anniversary conferences. Even as the high priests of trade and investment-led globalization commanded the attention of policymakers in the decade after Rio, an antiglobalization coalition gathered pace as a social protest movement that was itself globalized in terms of its orientation, networking, methods, operations, and meeting venues. Alleged environmental damage, growing inequality, and social dislocation and marginalization of the weakest and most vulnerable groups drew their greatest ire. The presence of the Secretary-General at the annual World Economic Forum of political and business elites but not at the alternative globalization movement's World Social Forum was an indication of the UN Secretariat's position in this debate.

Ten years after Rio, the UN organized the World Summit on Sustainable Development (WSSD, also known as Rio+10) in Johannesburg to evaluate progress and set targets for implementation. Two international milestones were set en route to Johannesburg: the Millennium Development Goals, which were adopted in 2000, and the Monterrey Conference on Financing for Development, which was held in Mexico in 2002. More than 190 countries attended the Johannesburg conference. In addition to the 10,000 official delegates at the conference, more than 40,000 participants attended the parallel NGO forum, 21,000 of whom were accredited to the UN conference itself. Following earlier precedents, Johannesburg adopted a Declaration on Development and a Plan of Implementation. The Johannesburg action plan was both shorter and rather more concrete than UNCED's Agenda 21 and included measurable targets on water, health, agriculture, and energy. Its emphasis on public-private partnerships, including calls for corporate social responsibility, marked a point of departure from Rio. Yet compared to Rio, the Johannesburg action plan downgraded and understated the importance of environmental protection. Some critics even referred to the summit as "Rio minus 10."[29]

One possible explanation for the disappointing results of Johannesburg is the growing feeling among environmental activists that proponents of development had co-opted the concept of sustainable development in a way that excluded notions of conservation. These activists felt that sustainable development had come to mean in practice "sustainable growth"— that is, continued growth rather than a balance between growth and conservation. To many concerned environmentalists it had become a "buzzword largely devoid of content."[30]

Yet there was one advance worthy of note. As one analyst describes, "At Rio, Northern delegates were primarily going to an environmental conference while Southern ones were attending a development one."[31] By contrast, at Johannesburg ten years later, southern countries had begun to realize that they could not sustain their development if they continued to ignore pressing constraints on resources and environmental limits, while some leading northern countries had subordinated environmental concerns to the need for continued economic growth and market-led development unhampered by governments or international organizations.

Millennium Ecosystem Assessment

In 2001, Secretary-General Kofi Annan formally launched the Millennium Ecosystem Assessment—the largest assessment of the health of the world's ecosystems to date—which was completed in 2005. It involved around 1,350 scientific experts from ninety-five countries under the joint chairmanship of Robert Watson of the World Bank and Hamid Zakri of the UN University. While this was not a UN-led initiative, representatives of UN agencies were among the members of its governing board. UNEP managed its funds. The assessment's dual purpose was to evaluate the consequences of past and likely future changes in the ecosystem for human well-being and establish a scientific basis for enhanced conservation and sustainable usage.

The assessment produced four main findings. First, ecosystems have changed more rapidly and extensively over the last half-century than in any other 50-year period in human history, largely in order to meet growing demands for food, fresh water, timber, fiber, and fuel. Second, the changes to ecosystems have contributed to and underpinned major gains in human well-being and economic development, but only at the cost of substantial degradation that will significantly limit the ability of future generations to obtain comparable benefits from ecosystems. Third, at present rates of use and exploitation, the degradation of ecosystems will worsen dramatically in the next fifty years. And fourth, the challenge of reversing the degradation of ecosystems while meeting increasing demands for their services requires significant changes in practices, policies, and institutions.

The ecosystem approach is relatively new. While this was not the first scientific assessment of the world's ecosystems, most previous ones had been conducted on an issue-by-issue basis in response to specific environmental problems. As a result, there are many different types of assessments of the availability of fresh water, climate change, the ozone layer, and other issues. The problem with this piecemeal approach is that the natural environment is not comprised of discrete components: soils, oceans, rivers, forests, plants, animals, and microorganisms are all part of the same ecosystem. They are interdependent and highly interactive. On a global scale, the same principle applies. In order to assess fully the natural environment and its capacity for supporting human life, scientists must take better account of this connectivity and adopt a more integrated approach to environmental assessment. Within the scientific community, the ecosystem approach refers to this cross-sectoral methodology.

The Millennium Ecosystem Assessment provides a critical study of the status of ecosystems worldwide and the services they provide to human beings who depend on them. It found that two-thirds of the services that ecosystems provide to humankind are in decline. Many of them, such as global fisheries, have been weakened beyond repair. But although these ecosystem services are already in a state of stress, the eradication of hunger and poverty requires significant increases in their supply.

One of the assessment's most important conclusions was that income alone is an inadequate measure of poverty. This was the first study to make a concrete link between the environment and poverty. Living on one dollar a day—or even on five—will make little difference to the poor if there is no fertile soil for growing crops or if the fisheries or forests on which they depend for subsistence are so depleted that they cannot supplement their existence. The dynamics of poverty cannot be delinked from the natural environment in which people live. Their natural environment, more than the feted dollar a day, is in many cases the foundation of their livelihood. For this reason, environmental issues cannot be neatly compartmentalized and dealt with separately. The environment underpins all aspects of development, and environmental concerns must be mainstreamed into finance and planning ministries in order to eradicate extreme poverty and disease.[32]

Normative Gaps: Sustainable Development as the Norm

For many, sustainable development constitutes the most consequential normative shift since 1945. As mentioned, the conceptual origins of the term date from the Founex report of early 1971,[33] which led to the historic compromise at Stockholm that fused the need to protect the human environment *and* the need to accelerate development in the Third World. The first policy statement to connect development to the environment was the World Conservation Strategy of 1980 issued by the International Union for Conservation of Nature with support from the World Wildlife Fund and UNEP. In particular, it stressed sustainability as a way to support human needs.

The UN considerably enhanced the international visibility of such issues when it set up the World Commission on Environment and Development in 1983. The General Assembly suggested that the commission focus on the following issues:

- Long-term environmental strategies for achieving sustainable development to the year 2000 and beyond;
- Ways in which concern for the environment might be translated into greater cooperation among developing countries and between countries at different stages of economic and social development and lead to the achievement of common and mutually supportive objectives which take account of the interrelationships between people, resources, environment, and development; and
- Helping to define shared perceptions of long-term environmental issues and of the appropriate efforts needed to deal successfully with the problems of protecting and enhancing the environment, a long-term agenda for action during the coming decades, and aspirational goals for the world community.[34]

Building on the essential contribution of the Stockholm conference—namely, that for poorer countries, environmental protection could not be pursued at the expense of development because poverty itself undermined the environmental cause—Norwegian prime minister Gro Harlem Brundtland was given the task of squaring the circle between development and environment by Secretary-General Javier Pérez de Cuéllar and UNEP's Mostafa Tolba.[35] The so-called Brundtland Commission popularized the notion of sustainable development, which is now the normative point of departure for virtually all policy documents.

The concept of "sustainable development" was contested from the start and has become only somewhat less so since.[36] For example, how can we know the needs, wants, expectations, and demands of future generations? Will they aspire to match the affluent and extravagant lifestyles and consumption patterns of today's generation or will they accept sacrifices in order to promote a better balance between consumption, conservation, and environmental protection? And what of equity and needs between *current* generations? In the absence of precise and measurable answers to these questions, the Brundtland definition of sustainable development is merely a slogan, not a policy. Yet governments and international organizations have adopted, mainstreamed, validated, legitimized, and reinforced it in their development agendas.

Part of the explanation for the concept's enduring popularity is that it satisfied the calls from the South for recognition of their special developmental needs without sacrificing the North's stated objective of sustained growth with environmental protection.[37] It articulated shared vulnerability and shared responsibility yet was silent on the North's complicity in the environmental crisis. At the same time, it acknowledged the importance of continuing growth in the South for the global economy yet postponed the pressing nature of the need to halt various practices. Thus, ecological integrity was necessarily a secondary and subordinate consideration in the consensus. The ideas in the final text of the Brundtland report were radically different from the beliefs and practices of many indigenous communities who live in harmony with nature. By the time of the Rio conference of 1992 and Agenda 21, sustainable development had elided into sustainable growth; states seemed to abandon even the pretense of a boundary between the two ideas.[38]

The original insight and impulse—that the natural environment will be increasingly stressed if economic growth and consumption patterns are sustained—was forgotten until the global warming crisis brought it back to the center of the debate again in the 2000s. Once again the world finds itself grappling with the conundrum that development policy choices that favor ecological integrity exact some costs on consumption. That is the story of the next chapter.

Policy Gaps: Déjà Vu All Over Again

In order to appreciate the ever-changing policy gaps, it is worth returning to the 1992 Earth Summit, where important steps were taken to fill policy gaps by moving toward defining the content of a global partnership between developing and more industrialized countries based on mutual needs and common interests in order to ensure a healthy future for the planet. Of course, the range of environmental issues had evolved in the twenty years between Stockholm and Rio. In those two decades, consensus had been reached that global problems included the hole in the ozone layer and global warming, threats to the biosphere, and difficulties caused by permanent sovereignty of states over their resources—all this in the framework of sustainable development. However, the North-South divide had not changed significantly: northern countries sought legal obligations to protect the environment from harmful development policies while southern governments continued to see this as a threat to their national sovereignty and a limit to their economic growth.[39]

As Michael Schechter explains, Agenda 21 "set international and national objectives and provided programmatic suggestions on how to fulfill those objectives." With more than 2,500 specific policy recommendations in areas as widely diverse as desertification and poverty eradication, Agenda 21 has led to the more systematic consideration of sustainable development within the UN system. However, as Schechter argues, Agenda 21 "failed to serve as a useful guide to action" for national governments because the goals were not concrete and measurable.[40]

As we saw in the previous chapter, the Millennium Development Goals are the most recent consolidation of attempts to frame and pursue sustainable development policies, especially MDG 7, "Ensure environmental sustainability," and MDG 8, "Develop a global partnership for development." The first target in MDG 7 addresses the failure of Agenda 21: "Integrate the principles of sustainable development into country policies and programs and reverse the loss of environmental resources."[41] The Millennium Development Goals have target dates of 2015, indicating a belief that the goals can be attained if the political will can be mustered. However, the review of these policy goals at the 2005 World Summit indicated that five years had passed without substantial progress. Clearly, political will, enforcement mechanisms, and compliance are lacking.

Institutional Gaps: UNEP, UNESCO, and the IWC

The arena of the environment and sustainability demonstrates a chasm between the size and nature of global problems, on the one hand, and the feebleness of global institutions and the inadequacy of their budgets, on the other hand. The environmental arena seems to be the one where the discrepancy between the knowledge of threats and the adequacy of institutional responses is the greatest. According to some scientists, there is very little time left to take decisive action to reverse global warming.[42] But perhaps we can discover a useful model for international cooperation. Perhaps it is possible to start small and build gradually on small technical successes.

UNEP

One of the most visible and measurable impacts of the Stockholm conference was the creation of national environment ministries and of UNEP and Earthwatch to help ensure follow-up of its 106 recommendations. A "Brussels Group" of industrialized countries tried to restrict the impact of the conference by limiting follow-up measures,[43] but the creation of UNEP, in particular, should be seen as a defeat of that group's strategy. In addition, the conference prompted the establishment of many new national and international agencies and departments for the express purpose of protecting the environment, including at the World Bank.

The General Assembly established UNEP in 1972 as "the lynchpin and environmental conscience of the UN system . . . the hub from which spokes of policy networks extend to deal with a wide array of global environmental threats."[44] On the one hand, UNEP has underperformed because of its modest budget, its low profile within the UN system, and the rise of environmental concerns to the top of the agendas of the heavyweight international organizations like the World Bank. Its small budget reflects its soft political constituency of environment ministers (who themselves have traditionally been among the more lightweight members of national cabinets) and largely northern NGOs because many southern NGOs remain suspicious of UNEP's northern-influenced agenda. On the other hand, it may be said to have fallen victim to its success in persuading influential international organizations to upgrade the importance of the environment in their policy priorities.

Agenda 21 at Rio called upon the General Assembly to create a new functional commission within ECOSOC, the Commission on Sustainable Development. The CSD allows civil society a great amount of participation: specialized agencies, NGOs, and intergovernmental organizations are all involved. In addition, the CSD is the only ECOSOC commission that is chaired by a government minister. While created to act as the primary mechanism within the UN system for coordinating sustainable development, its relationship to UNEP and other institutions was not clearly defined. As environmental studies scholar Elizabeth De Sombre has argued, "Its weaknesses suggest that it was created as a way to avoid, rather than institutionalize action."[45]

Repeated calls for a new UN environmental council or organization that could serve as a high-powered umbrella body to integrate the fragmentary efforts of many entities dispersed across the UN system reflect a basic level of dissatisfaction with the world body's existing institutional architecture. UNEP today is struggling to reconcile an ambitious, critical, and ever-expanding mandate with an inadequate budget, a blurred profile, and a weak political position. This is not so much an institutional void but rather a gap in capabilities in relationship to the size of the problem. While budgets do not tell everything, it is significant that the World Wildlife Fund has a budget that is three times that of UNEP.[46]

UNEP's impact was limited from the start by the decision to base it in Nairobi, Kenya. While this was the first time a developing country had hosted a new global institution, Nairobi was simply too far away physically and politically from the more central and powerful international organizations it was trying to influence.[47] Its location has made fulfilling its functions of helping developing countries set up environmental agencies and legislation, coordinating environmental programs within the UN system, and linking to other interested organizations that much more difficult.

Former assistant-secretary-general John Ruggie's comments in an oral history interview for the UNIHP project highlight this problem:

> Maurice Strong clearly had in mind a model whereby UNEP would basically manage networks from some set of central nodes. Where those locations were didn't matter very much. But in order to do that, in order to have a system of cooperation based on interacting networks, you need to have very clear objectives. And the various actors need to share those objectives. You need to have a sufficient resource base to help build up the constituents of the network. None of those conditions ended up holding for UNEP, and it sort of sank into the morass of Nairobi, where it has been since. And as much as I appreciated the desirability of locating a UN agency in a developing country, I thought that UNEP was the one agency that should not have been. If any agency should have been in a major UN center—Geneva or one of the European capitals—it should have been UNEP. You couldn't then, and cannot now coordinate fast-moving networks from places that lack the communication and other infrastructure, and that are so far removed from the thing they are supposed to be coordinating.[48]

UNESCO

Another specialized agency that reports to ECOSOC is UNESCO, the United Nations Educational, Scientific and Cultural Organization. This may seem like a strange choice for a discussion on sustainability. It is often difficult for an outside observer to understand that some UN organizations that appear at first glance not to belong within a particular issue area often make little known but significant contributions to that field. And the sum of such contributions is crucial for the crazy quilt of contemporary global governance because they all provide foundations for the global superstructure of problem solving. While many would prefer a more centralized and coherent picture, that is not the current or likely near-term future situation. Hence, it is important to understand the partial filling of institutional gaps by unlikely candidates.

UNESCO may also seem to be a strange choice given the political difficulty the agency has experienced, for example, over its ill-advised and ill-fated efforts to establish a New World Information and Communication Order in the 1970s and 1980s. In addition, around 80 percent of its budget is spent at its Paris headquarters rather than for activities in the field. UNESCO is not known for environmentalism per se but for the helpful technical steps it has made possible. Its support has been critical for building capacity in science and education and for protecting sites of cultural importance. It also provides the science for policy on global environment problems and executes UNEP projects within countries. For example, in 2005, World Water Day was celebrated by the world's largest search engine, Google.com, with a special logo on its home page and links to UNESCO reports as a way to promote public awareness of water resources. Another example is UNESCO's Regional Action Program for Central America for natural disaster reduction, which trains professionals in the use of geographic information systems data and remote sensing techniques to generate information regarding such natural phenomena as earthquakes, landslides, and volcanic eruptions for disaster reduction purposes.[49]

Endangered Species:
CITES and the International Whaling Commission

Institutions can also be successful when previous gaps in global governance (in knowledge, norms, and policy) have already been filled, a match exists between the magnitude of a problem and the institution's configuration, and political consensus exists about how to solve a problem. Efforts to interdict the trade in exotic and endangered species has had limited amounts of success. UNEP monitors the 1973 Convention on International Trade in Endangered Species (CITES), but states enforce it unevenly. Some multilateral treaties have been successful in conserving species, including the 1911 treaty on fur seals between Russia, Canada, the United States, and Japan and the 1918 International Migratory Bird Treaty, originally between the United States and Canada, which was subsequently extended to include Mexico. One possible reason for the success of these treaties is the fact that fewer signatories tend to mean more transparency. In addition, the treaties do not pertain to cases where one country is exporting and another is importing animals; instead, they address internally controlled trades.

Responses can of course be incomplete and incoherent in part because national policies are inconsistent and because important players defect. The International Whaling Commission (IWC), created by the International Convention for the Regulation of Whaling, which was signed in 1946, is a case in point. The purposes of the convention were to conserve whale stocks in order to protect the commercial whaling industry and to regulate aboriginal whaling. To that end the IWC was to "provide for the complete protection of certain species; designate specified areas as whale sanctuaries; set limits on the numbers and size of whales which may be taken; prescribe open and closed seasons and areas for whaling; and prohibit the capture of suckling calves and female whales accompanied by calves."[50] When whale stocks continued to decline, the IWC imposed an open-ended moratorium in 1986.

The story does not end there: three states that are primary hunters have continued to allow whaling. But they are not the usual suspects that are rounded up when environmental offenses become the object of public obloquy and activists climb on international soapboxes. Japan and Iceland allow whaling for commercial purposes by exploiting a loophole in the convention that allows whaling for scientific purposes.[51] And Norway, after registering an objection to the ban in 1993, no longer uses even the pretense of "scientific whaling."[52]

These three states are generally at the forefront of global environmental protection and multilateral approaches to other issues—indeed, the Kyoto Convention was signed in Japan, and Iceland and Norway are among the most generous donors of official development assistance for sustainable development. Yet in this case, they insist on hunting practices that are widely viewed as abhorrent. In fact, there have been allegations that Japan has engaged in buying the votes of other signatories to the convention in order to reverse the ban.[53] In any case, the trend at the IWC's annual meetings is such that the ban may be overturned in the near future. Australian environment minister Ian Campbell believes that "there's a serious chance that Iceland, Norway and Japan will have the numbers to defeat our pro-conservation majority."[54]

Compliance Gaps: Still Searching

While we have discussed only a few of the international institutions that constitute essential components of the system of global governance, it is clear that some of them make a difference. At the same time, the reader who is passionate about sustainable development is left with a question in his or her mind, "So what?" Even if knowledge gaps have been filled and norms and policies and institutions are in place, what are the chances for anything other than policies that rely on voluntary compliance? As should be obvious from the tone of the previous discussion, the biggest gap for sustainable development in the current system—as for other issue areas—remains that of compliance mechanisms. And as the IWC case suggests, even when the other gaps are filled, institutions can be stopped by key players.

Many international conferences and commissions repeat the same familiar themes of persisting poverty; widening inequality among and within countries; the need to match actual aid flows to the rhetoric of development assistance; the need for debt relief; the role of science and technology transfers as enablers of development; the threats posed by degradation of arable land, loss of soil fertility, deforestation, overfishing of coastal waters and deep oceans; and the loss of biodiversity. They all provide a comprehensive catalogue of the ills of poverty, hunger, and disease and issue clarion calls to reduce and eventually eliminate these problems. They all affirm that the rich have a special responsibility in alleviating the sufferings of the poor.

Almost all major blue-ribbon commissions and summit conferences are mobilized and convened by the UN system or are convened with the consent, encouragement, and support of the world organization. Their recommendations and prescriptions are addressed to world leaders and decision makers through the UN in an effort to invoke the organization's unique legitimacy and authority. They have also been major platforms and core legitimizing mechanisms for advancing global norms. Yet over time, it must be admitted, such commissions and conferences have also in some respects served to erode the legitimacy of the United Nations and dilute its brand value because of the persisting gaps between rhetoric and commitments and implementation.

The total costs of such conferences as Rio in 1992 and Johannesburg in 2002 would be extremely difficult, if not impossible, to compute. Hundreds of heads of government and state attended with large delegations in tow, as did the more modestly staffed but still sizable numbers of NGO delegations. Add to this to the costs of conference facilities and UN Secretariat resources, not to mention all the preparatory and follow-up work. In the face of all this expense, who could argue that they represent good value for the money?

Moreover, the leaders come to deliver their respective speeches, not to listen to those of others; the talkers dominate the conferences to the exclusion of the doers; and the consensus outcome documents are restatements of lofty rhetoric and grandiose ambitions disconnected from the resources, capacity, and authority to convert them into feasible, achievable, and measurable targets. Given all this, what is the opportunity cost of investing vast resources in actual policies and programs to alleviate poverty, protect the environment, and conserve resources? As one critic comments, "The weary litany of persistent ills, inequities and degradations described in reports from UNCED, other international conferences and commissions, and the actions needed for their eradication or alleviation have been substantially ignored by the world's most affluent and powerful nations."[55]

One reason for this is that most documents end up trying to solve all of the world's ills and make little or no effort to define contested terms, assign priorities, specify realistic time frames, and identify the sources of funding and other resources necessary to implement their programs. In *Sustainable Development at Risk,* Joseph Hulse describes the Johannesburg document as a "record and regurgitation of virtually every recommendation and suggestion proposed by the organizations, agencies and individuals who participated." The net result, Hulse notes, is that "the ambitious magnitude and all-embracing diversity of this document would strain the credibility of the most devoted supporter."[56]

Conclusion:
Conference Diplomacy and Global Governance

One of our central themes is that the UN's unique legitimacy derives from its universal membership. In turn, both universal membership and international legitimacy give the world organization an unmatched power to convene gatherings and mobilize people. That power has been used to organize a large number of global conferences on a diverse range of topics as a way to fill various gaps in global governance, including gaps in knowledge, norms, policies, institutes, and implementation. Moreover, these conferences typically involve all the actors of global governance—states, NGOs, and private sector firms (to a lesser degree)—while highlighting the role of individual leadership—for example, the leadership of Maurice Strong on environmental issues.

In spite of the definite downsides indicated above, here we would like to emphasize that global conferences and multilateral diplomacy around sustainability are a major net UN contribution to improved global governance. The Stockholm and Rio conferences have been important parts of the story in this chapter, but they are part of a more general pattern of such conferences that have touched upon a host of issues in the 1970s and 1990s, ranging from women's rights to human rights, from population to social development. Global conferences were not merely an innovative framework for registering shifts in norms away from unsustainable exploitation toward conservation and protection; they often also led to the creation of new institutions for implementing and monitoring compliance with the new norms. Thus, Stockholm was the midwife to UNEP and Rio to the UNFCCC and the CSD. One author defines environmental governance as "the establishment, reaffirmation or change of institutions to resolve conflicts over environmental resources" and argues that "the choice of governance solutions is a matter of social justice rather than of economic efficiency."[57] Thus, environmental decisions should be concerned with distributive impacts on health and ecology as well as on goods and services.

Stockholm and Rio are part of a long lineage that might well begin with the two Hague conferences around the turn of the last century (1899 and 1907), which anticipated the global conferences that began with the League of Nations and then expanded in numbers, frequency, and scope by the United Nations. They have become a major mode of conducting the business of global governance. The traditional intergovernmental conference is the standard mode for negotiating legal conventions and treaties; examples include the Rome Statute that established the International Criminal Court in 1998 or the UN Conference on the Law of the Sea (1973–1982). The ICC came into force in 2002 and the UN Convention on the Law of the Sea in 1994. Because these were intergovernmental negotiations, the decision-making participants were government officials whose deliberations were serviced by UN staff and nudged along by experts, NGOs, and corporations.

The more interesting practice in recent times has been that most of the actors involved in global governance at international UN conferences take part in years of preparations where the bulk of the agreements are reached before they attend the actual conferences. Where the intergovernmental conferences are the sites for the growth of treaty law, the global conferences have been prime sites for the evolution of norms and "soft law," which over time exert a binding effect in the form of customary international law.

Many of the normative and institutional gaps in global governance have been filled at or after such global conferences. UNEP and the CSD are similar to other institutional creations, including the Office of the High Commissioner for Human Rights (following the human rights conference held in Vienna in 1994), the International Fund for Agricultural Development and the World Food Council (following the UN World Food Conference held in Rome in 1974), and the Institute for Training and Research for the Advancement of Women and the Development Fund for Women (following the first UN World Conference on Women in 1975). In addition, conferences can help pull institutions together, as when the Monterrey conference brought together the Bretton Woods institutions and the UN's development agencies in a common commitment to the MDGs.

As two scholars of the UN note, generally these conferences "have been important for articulating new international norms, expanding international law, creating new structures, setting agendas . . . and promoting linkages among the UN, the specialized agencies, NGOs, and governments."[58] In other words, in our terms, these gatherings and the diplomacy that takes place at them advanced the agenda for global governance. The United Nations has institutionalized the global conference system as a transmission belt that conveys ideas to decision makers and elite opinion makers in response to global problems and concerns. No topic highlights the comparative advantage of the United Nations more than sustainability does.

One explanation for the proliferation of UN global conferences— including follow-up sessions at five- and ten-year intervals—is the expansion in the number of newly independent states that became UN members in successive waves of decolonization. Although they were keenly interested in issues of economic, social, and human development, there was not always a lead actor in the UN system in the form of a specialized agency or other body to address these concerns. However, these nations had the votes in the General Assembly or ECOSOC to convene ad hoc special conferences to deal with these issues. Advances in communications technology facilitated wide media coverage, and the decreasing cost of international travel made it possible for NGOs and poorer governments to participate.

Some of the patterns at these conferences are clear. The UN Secretary-General usually appoints a prominent international personality or a senior UN official to serve as the conference secretary-general. The conference proper is preceded by a series of preparatory committee meetings that bring governments, regional organizations/agencies, and NGOs into the discussion and reach agreement on most of the issues before the conference is even opened. Whereas in the 1970s mainly ministers attended global conferences, the trend since the 1990s has been that heads of government and state attend. Some conferences are meant to establish and uphold standards of behavior (human rights, racial equality, women's rights, arms control). Others are directed at finding operational solutions to practical problems such as access to food and water or addressing the increase in population.

What would a balance sheet for these global gatherings look like? On the positive side of the ledger, we would place the following achievements: they have synthesized existing knowledge; they have changed discourses, priorities, and policies; they have established or endorsed global norms and international standards, principles, and guidelines; they have mobilized governments, NGOs, and global public opinion; they have catalyzed resources, institutions, national institutional infrastructures (e.g., for reporting on human rights, health, and gender equality indicators); and they have legitimized and empowered national ministries and bureaucracies and transnational social movements and networks. These are all aspects of global governance as we defined them, and they would have been far more difficult to accomplish by means other than UN global conferences. At the time of the Stockholm conference in 1972 and the first UN world conference on women in Mexico City in 1975, for instance, most economic and social policymakers saw environmental issues and gender consciousness as peripheral. Today there are very few issues that would not be subjected to both environmental and gender impact assessments in most countries, in UN agencies, and at the World Bank. UN conferences have been crucial agents of changes in norms if not in behavior, policies, and actions. As Noeleen Heyzer has noted, "The environment conference managed to get people from the grassroots to talk about the way the environmental erosion and the ecological crisis affected them. And it definitely changed the whole dialogue."[59]

At the same time, we also have a debit side to our ledger without even calculating their carbon footprint. Most important, such conferences rarely result in legally binding conventions and treaties. Not setting measurable targets and benchmarks leaves conferences with symbolic rather than substantive accomplishments. Setting targets but not monitoring and achieving them undermines the conference as well as the legitimacy of the United Nations as the convening authority. However, "failure" would be too strong and misleading. A conference might be said to have failed if there is no agreed final document, if the final document is a formula to mask substantive disagreement, or if the final document expresses aspirations and endorses principles but does not contain binding and measurable commitments, benchmarks, and targets. Yet none of this would give us a true indication of the global and long-term impact of the conference in raising a new issue, reframing an existing issue, or even focusing more international attention on an issue so that the existing consensus could be shifted and the boundaries of possible action could be expanded.[60]

There are good reasons for these shortcomings of global conferences: they deal with overly broad themes; the lead time for their convening is usually quite short; recommendations are made by the conference as a collective entity, while follow-up action and implementation is left to governments individually; the goals of conference participants are divergent and conflicting; and there are unintended consequences and impacts. UN global conferences have been a frequent target of criticisms from diverse constituencies. While many right-wing critics attack them as efforts to govern globally in ways that would usurp the prerogatives of sovereign states and impose too much "government" on citizens, many social activists have expressed disappointment at how weak and ineffectual they are in imposing any sort of binding targets and enforcement mechanisms. They can be duplicative, repetitive, and overlapping. Shining the torchlight on one issue means that attention and resources are diverted from others. The politics of high-publicity summit diplomacy tends to favor compromise resolutions over effective solutions. They offer palliative relief without trying to address the root causes of the problem. Thus, the commitment to women's emancipation and empowerment since the 1995 Fourth UN World Conference on Women in Beijing has been more rhetorical flourish than policies and actions to challenge the entrenched gendered forms of power relations within and among nations (global patriarchy).[61]

After almost four decades of multilateral encounters, there seem to be three links between growth and environmental action for sustainability. First, groups such as the World Bank argue that growth should be continued in order to generate the income and surplus required to pay for technology and other environmental actions. Second, proponents of the dominant structuralist view within the UN system argue that growth can be continued, perhaps at a slower rate and certainly with changes in the pattern of growth, in a way that will cause less environmental damage and ensure that poverty is reduced in poor countries and that inequality is reduced worldwide. Third, the Malthusian or green extremists argue that growth is not possible without exceeding resource limits.

In effect, sustainable development attempts to navigate among these contending views. We are still confronting a basic contradiction, that of equity between the global North and South. As Shridath ("Sonny") Ramphal, co-chair of the Commission on Global Governance and former head of the Commonwealth Secretariat, put it: "If the rich countries continue to consume at their present rate, then it is not going to be possible for the poor countries to develop to a tolerable level of consumption."[62]

The continuing frictions between the North and the South with regard to who has caused climate change and who is responsible for ameliorating the effects of that change suggest that efforts to combat climate change will have to be integrated into the broader context of sustainable social and economic development.[63] The causes of global warming span most sectors of modern social and economic activity: power production and distribution, heating and air conditioning, industrial processes and agricultural production, and transportation and waste management. This chapter on sustainable development is thus a good precursor to the issue of environmental protection.[64]

7

Saving the Environment:
The Ozone Layer and Climate Change

- Antecedents: Scientific Consensus Emerges
- Knowledge Gaps: Climate Change Rises to the Top of the Agenda
- Normative Gaps: Do No Harm
- Policy Gaps: The Montreal Protocol Revisited
- Institutional Gaps: The IPCC to the Rescue
- Compliance Gaps: Montreal and Kyoto
- Conclusion: The Third and the Second UNs Prod the First

The impetus for sustainable growth and development was driven by the needs of poorer countries. This chapter emphasizes what appear to be unavoidable environmental constraints that loom as real barriers to economic growth as we have known it. We have chosen to stress two pressing issues—the deterioration in the ozone layer and irreversible climate change—that challenge the notion that sustainability is possible in the absence of a dramatic change in global business as usual. The words of two scholars eloquently capture the basic thrust of this chapter and the findings of UNIHP: "The history of global environmental politics is inextricably tied to contests of ideas: battles of worldviews and discourses. We have seen new environmental ideas and language enter into the mainstream discourse as global awareness rises and as environmental conditions deteriorate."[1]

Governments have widely adopted new norms and policies and the appropriate regulatory framework of institutions to accompany them, and the United Nations has played a familiar pivotal role in filling normative, policy, and institutional gaps. In this instance, the world organization also has played an invaluable role in filling knowledge gaps. But, as always, it has played a lesser role in plugging compliance gaps.

Antecedents: Scientific Consensus Emerges

For thousands of years, humans lived in balance with nature. Two huge changes in the way humans relate to the planet greatly altered the balance between human activity, resource conservation, and environmental protection: the shift from nomadic hunting and gathering to settled agriculture and the industrial revolution. These two large changes made a dramatic increase in population possible.

The era of decolonization after World War II produced a number of independent states keen to pursue the lifestyles of the departing western colonial powers. The economic theory of the mid-twentieth century assumed growth, and many economists believed that successful development was a function of adopting the right mix of institutions and policies. After two decades of global economic expansion after 1945, a backlash against mainstream development economics emerged as awareness grew of the strain on the earth's finite resources and of the harm, possibly irreparable, being done to the environment. What began as a minority view in the 1960s is currently widely accepted.

The scientific evidence of the role of greenhouse gases (GHGs) in global warming is indisputable. A greenhouse gas prevents infrared radiation from the sun from bouncing back into space from the Earth's surface, instead trapping it within the atmosphere. If there were no greenhouse gases, the Earth would resemble the planet Mars, cold and lifeless. But with too much of them, the Earth could resemble Venus, hot and poisonous. When the UN's Intergovernmental Panel on Climate Change (IPCC) presented its final report in November 2007, it noted that eleven of the previous twelve years (1995–2006) had been among the dozen warmest years since recording of temperatures began in 1850. Temperatures have risen by an average of 0.74 degrees Celsius over the past 100 years. Average temperatures in the northern hemisphere were higher in the second half of the twentieth century than during any other 50-year period in the previous 500 years (very likely) and perhaps even the last 1,300 years (likely). Consistent with global warming, the sea level has risen at an annual rate of 1.8 mm per year since 1961 and 3.1 mm per year since 1993. The average Arctic sea has shrunk by 2.7 percent per decade, and the summer shrinkage was 7.4 percent per decade. Global GHG emissions due to human activities have grown since preindustrial times, increasing by 70 percent just between 1970 and 2004. The emissions of carbon dioxide (CO_2)—the most important anthropogenic GHG—grew by 80 percent in the same period.

More extreme weather will be one of the consequences of global warming; the number and intensity of heat waves will increase, and rainfall and snowfall will be heavier. But the shifts in global weather patterns will be uneven, not uniform, and they could be sudden and dramatic rather than steady and gradual. The poorest countries and peoples of the world will be the most vulnerable. As the IPCC has explained, adaptive capacity "is intimately connected to social and economic development" and is "unevenly distributed across and within societies."[2]

Because the effects will be nonlocalized—a butterfly fluttering in one country producing a storm in another country—and have long time lags with our great-grandchildren paying the price of the environmental irresponsibility of our generation, it has proven difficult to persuade political leaders to take urgent and costly national action today to prevent harm to other peoples and future generations. A stitch in time may indeed save nine, as the old adage goes, but what is cost effective in the long run clashes with the reality of domestic politics in the short run. Democratically elected governments rarely entertain policies with time horizons that extend beyond the next public opinion poll. They exaggerate immediate expenditures and discount future ones.

Over the last two decades, global climate change has been one of the most disputed scientific concepts of our times. The last few years, however, have witnessed a truly unusual scientific consensus: it has become virtually impossible to ignore record temperatures, storms, and other indicators as well as great agreement among knowledgeable experts (90 percent of them) that climate change is a looming threat that requires urgent action to reverse or at least slow down human-induced environmental damage. Scientists and policymakers disagree about which scientific model accurately describes how fast the world's climate is changing, about how much of that change is attributable to human activity, and about what the effects of that change will be.[3] However, there is increasing consensus in the scientific community, at least and at last, that climate warming *is* happening.

What role has the United Nations played in bringing about consensus about global warming?

Knowledge Gaps:
Climate Change Rises to the Top of the Agenda

How does the world learn about new global problems such as the hole in the ozone layer or the fact that the global climate is gradually warming? And how have we discovered that these problems are linked to skin cancer or are in part responsible for the destruction of precious forests, agricultural crops, and marine life? Who determined that global warming could trigger catastrophes such as hurricanes, heat waves, and other extreme climatic events? Scientists have discovered these environmental problems and their impacts on human life and health. But someone or some institution often commissions studies to fill gaps in existing knowledge and then to disseminate the findings to the wider scientific and policymaking communities and to the interested and informed public.

Since 1945, there has been an enormous change in what we know about the environment and a growing awareness of the earth's carrying capacity. The environment was invisible as a political policy issue until relatively recently; for example, it was totally absent in the minds of the UN's founders. But saving the environment, especially the urgent task of slowing climate change, is currently one of the most pressing issues on the international agenda. As we saw in the previous chapter, the UN conferences devoted to parsing the environment, especially in Stockholm in 1972 and in Rio de Janeiro in 1992, are convenient and essential markers of changes in the knowledge gap. They dramatically illustrate the difference that discussing, confronting, and disseminating ideas can make to the intellectual context in which governments and individuals make decisions.

The depletion of the ozone layer first drew significant attention in the scientific community in 1973 in response to the work of two University of California chemists, Frank S. Rowland and Mario Molina. In 1973, they began studying the impacts of chlorofluorocarbons (CFCs) in the earth's atmosphere. Rowland and Molina concluded that although CFC molecules remained stable in the atmosphere, ultraviolet radiation broke them down in the stratosphere. The scientists postulated that the chlorine atom released by the process would in turn destroy large amounts of ozone in the atmosphere. They built on the work of two other scientists, Paul J. Crutzen and Harold Johnston, who had proven how nitric oxide could cause the breakdown of the ozone layer.[4] The ozone layer helps absorb most of the ultraviolet-B radiation that reaches the earth's surface. Any depletion of the ozone layer by CFCs will therefore increase radiation levels and cause damage to crops, destroy marine phytoplankton, and cause an increase in the incidence of skin cancer. A pathbreaking paper by Rowland and Molina was published in June 1974, and in December 1974 they were asked to testify at a hearing of the U.S. House of Representatives, following which funds were provided for further studies of the problem. In 1976, the U.S. National Academy of Sciences confirmed the ozone depletion hypothesis and continued to study the *problématique* for the next decade.

Six questions have been debated about climate change:

- Is the climate changing and if so, at what rate?
- What are the causes of climate change?
- What are the consequences of the change at present and what are they likely to be in the future?
- Can the causes of climate change be controlled in order to control and stop climate change (adaptation)?
- How can we cope with the consequences of climate change (mitigation)?
- Who pays for controlling and stopping climate change?

The IPCC with its worldwide network of some 3,000 leading scientists has provided the most authoritative answers to the first five questions, which are essentially scientific questions. Its chair, Rajendra K. Pachauri, explains that "every successive [IPCC assessment] report attempts to address existing gaps in knowledge."[5] And the most likely forum for finding an answer to the sixth question, which is essentially a political question, is the United Nations. The world organization has been a central site for the contest of ideas in this issue area.

In 1979, the first World Climate Conference, which was organized by the World Meteorological Organization (WMO), expressed concern that human activities could change the earth's climate and called for global cooperation to study and respond to such change. In 1985, a joint conference of UNEP, the WMO, and the International Council for Science (ICSU) was convened in Villach, Austria, to assess the role of carbon dioxide and other GHGs in climate change. The conference concluded that the growth in GHGs were likely to raise the global mean temperature significantly in the twenty-first century. It further noted that past climate data might not be a reliable guide for long-term projections; that climate change and increases in sea level are closely linked with other major environmental issues; that some warming appears inevitable because of past activities; and that the future rate and amount of warming could be profoundly affected by policies on GHG emissions. UNEP, the WMO, and the ICSU set up the Advisory Group on Greenhouse Gases to ensure periodic assessments of the state of scientific knowledge on climate change and its implications.

In 1987, the tenth congress of the WMO recognized the need for objective, balanced, and internationally coordinated scientific assessment of the understanding of the effects of increasing concentrations of GHGs on the earth's climate and about how these changes may impact socioeconomic patterns. The WMO's secretary-general was asked to establish, in coordination with UNEP's executive director, an ad hoc intergovernmental mechanism to provide scientific assessments of climate change. The two chief executives agreed that efforts should be channeled into two separate streams. One stream would concentrate on assessing available scientific information (that is, fill knowledge gaps) while the second stream would focus on formulating realistic response strategies for national and global action (that is, fill policy gaps).

In 1988, the WMO Executive Council established the IPCC with support from UNEP, and they set up the IPCC secretariat at WMO headquarters in Geneva. The WMO and UNEP suggested that the panel should consider the need for:

- Identification of uncertainties and gaps in our present knowledge with regard to climate changes and its potential impacts, and preparation of a plan of action over the short-term in filling these gaps;
- Identification of information needed to evaluate policy implications of climate change and response strategies;
- Review of current and planned national/international policies related to the greenhouse gas issue; and
- Scientific and environmental assessments of all aspects of the greenhouse gas issue and the transfer of these assessments and other relevant information to governments and intergovernmental organisations to be taken into account in their policies on social and economic development and environmental programmes.[6]

In November 1988, the IPCC held its first plenary session and established three working groups to prepare assessment reports on available scientific information on climate change, the environmental and socioeconomic impacts of climate change, and strategies for responding to climate change. In the meantime, the General Assembly recognized the need to adopt effective measures within a global framework to actually combat climate change. In 1988, it adopted a resolution endorsing the establishment of the IPCC and asked the IPCC for a comprehensive review of and recommendations about the state of knowledge of the science of climate and climatic change; possible response strategies that could delay, limit, or mitigate the impact of adverse climate change; the identification and possible strengthening of relevant existing international legal instruments that have a bearing on climate; and elements that should be included in a possible future international convention on climate.[7]

Responding to this request, the IPCC adopted its first assessment report at the end of August 1990 in Sweden. Working Group I concluded that emissions from human activities are substantially increasing the atmospheric concentrations of GHGs and that this will enhance the greenhouse effect and will result in an additional warming of the earth's surface. But it also pointed out a number of uncertainties in knowledge about climate change, including sources and sinks of GHGs and the role of clouds, oceans, and polar ice sheets. Working Group II summarized the scientific understanding of the impacts of climate change on agriculture and forestry, natural terrestrial ecosystems, hydrology and water resources, human settlements, oceans and coastal zones, and seasonal snow cover, ice, and permafrost. It highlighted important uncertainties about the timing, magnitude, and regional patterns of climate change, but it also noted that impacts could be felt most severely in regions already under stress, mainly in developing countries. Working Group III outlined both shorter-term mitigation and adaptation measures and proposals for more intensive action over the long term and developed possible elements to be included in a framework convention on climate change.

In 1991, the IPCC decided to prepare a second comprehensive assessment that included socioeconomic aspects of climate change as a new subject area. The scope of the reports of Working Groups II and III were adjusted to better meet this requirement. The IPCC's second assessment report was completed in late 1995.[8] While noting continuing areas of scientific uncertainty, it concluded that the balance of evidence suggested a discernible human influence on global climate; that GHG concentrations had continued to increase since about 1750; and that successful adaptation depended upon "technological advances, institutional arrangements, availability of financing and information exchange."[9] The synthesis report also addressed the likely impact of different levels and time scales of stabilization.

In 2001, the IPCC published its third assessment report. Among its con-clusions: emissions of GHGs and aerosols due to human activities had con-tinued to alter the atmosphere in ways that affected the climate; confidence in the ability of models to project future climate change had increased; recent regional climate changes, particularly temperature increases, had already affected many physical and biological systems; natural systems were vulnerable to climate change and some would be irreversibly dam-aged; many human systems were sensitive to climate change and some were vulnerable; those with the least resources had the least capacity to adapt and were the most vulnerable; and further action was required to address remaining gaps in information and understanding. The report con-firmed the second assessment report's findings that earlier actions, includ-ing mitigating emissions, developing technology, and reducing scientific uncertainty, would increase flexibility in stabilizing atmospheric concentra-tions of GHGs.[10]

The IPCC's fourth assessment report was finalized in 2007. Working Group I, focusing on the state of scientific knowledge, concluded that global atmospheric concentrations of carbon dioxide, methane, and nitrous oxide had increased markedly as a result of human activities since 1750 (before the industrial revolution) as determined from ice cores that spanned thousands of years. The global increases in carbon dioxide con-centration were due primarily to the use of fossil fuels and changes in land use, while increases in levels of methane and nitrous oxide were due primarily to agriculture. Empirical data, including increases in global air and ocean temperatures, the widespread melting of snow and ice, and the rising global average sea level, pointed unequivocally to a warming of the climate system.[11]

In slightly more than five years, our understanding of the probability that human activity was the cause of global warming had increased from 66 percent (the statistic in the third assessment report) to 90 percent (the statistic in the fourth assessment report). The knowledge gap had effectively disappeared—in 2007, virtually no one denied the existence of a threat to the planet. Moreover, there was broad agreement that global warming and the rise in sea levels would continue for centuries even if GHG concentra-tions were to be stabilized immediately or relatively soon, owing to the time scales associated with climate processes and feedbacks.[12]

The 2007 synthesis report's detailed scientific findings included the following:

- Carbon dioxide is the most important anthropogenic greenhouse gas. Its global atmospheric concentration had increased from a preindustrial value of about 280 parts per million (ppm) to 379 ppm in 2005, far exceeding the natural range of 180–300 ppm over the last 650,000 years. While the annual growth rate in carbon dioxide concentration was 1.4 ppm per year from 1960–2005, the annual growth rate was 1.9 ppm per year from 1995–2005.

- The global atmospheric concentration of methane increased from a preindustrial value of 715 parts per billion (ppb) to 1,732 ppb in the early 1990s and 1,774 ppb in 2005, far exceeding the natural range of 320–790 ppb of the last 650,000 years. The probability that this was due to anthropogenic activities, predominantly agriculture and the use of fossil fuels, was 90 percent.

- The global atmospheric concentration of nitrous oxide rose from a preindustrial value of about 270 ppb to 319 ppb in 2005.[13]

Working Group II, which focused on how the world could adapt to global warming, examined the current knowledge about the impacts of climate change on the natural and human environment based both on empirical observations (drawing on over 29,000 observational data series from seventy-five studies) at the regional and global levels and on modeling. It concluded that observed evidence "from all continents and most oceans shows that many natural [physical and biological] systems are being affected by regional climate changes, particularly temperature increases."[14] The observed effects included changes in levels of snow, ice, and permafrost; changes in polar ecosystems; increased runoff and earlier spring peak discharge in many glacier and snow-fed rivers; warming of lakes and rivers in many regions; earlier timing of spring events such as leaves unfolding and birds migrating and laying eggs; poleward and upward shifts in ranges in plant and animal species; and changes in the range and timing of migration of fish species.

The working group concluded that adaptation would be necessary to address impacts resulting from warming caused by previous emissions;

that future vulnerability depends not just on climate change but also on the development path chosen; that sustainable development (using the Brundtland Commission definition of development that "meets the needs of the present without compromising the ability of future generations to meet their own needs"[15]) can reduce vulnerability to climate change but that climate change can impede the ability of countries to achieve sustainable development both directly (through increased exposure to adverse impact) and indirectly (through erosion of the capacity to adapt); and that many impacts can be avoided, reduced, or delayed. The overarching two-part conclusion was that the risks associated with climate change could be lowered through adaptation and mitigation measures but that "unmitigated climate change would, in the long term, be likely to exceed the capacity of natural, managed and human systems to adapt."[16]

Working Group III examined the literature on the scientific, technological, environmental, economic, and social aspects of efforts to mitigate climate change since the third assessment report.[17] It concluded that global GHG emissions had grown by 70 percent from 1970 to 2004 and that CO_2 emissions accounted for 77 percent of total anthropogenic GHG emissions in 2004. The largest growth in global GHG in this 35-year period came from the energy supply sector. Although global energy intensity[18] had diminished by one-third since 1970 and emissions of ozone-depleting substances under the jurisdiction of the Montreal Protocol (which are also GHGs) had fallen to about 20 percent of their 1990 level by 2004, the effect of such decreases on global GHG emissions had been overtaken by the rate of global population growth of 69 percent and an increase in global per capita income of 77 percent.

Of greater political import were two conclusions of the fourth assessment. First, under current policies to mitigate climate change, global GHG emissions would continue to grow over the next few decades; it projected that CO_2 emissions from energy use alone would increase from between 40 to 110 percent from 2000 to 2030. Second, "differences in terms of per capita income, per capita emissions, and energy intensity among countries remain significant."[19] Yet additional mitigation efforts that would reduce global GHG emissions in net terms have a substantial potential economic impact; the economic cost of stabilization could bring about up to a 3 percent decrease in global GDP.[20] Potential environment-friendly efforts include educating people about lifestyle and behavior changes; upgrading the energy infrastructure in industrialized countries and making new energy infrastructure investments in developing countries that use energy-efficient technology; making investments in end-use improvements in energy efficiency (which are often more cost effective than increasing energy supplies); exploiting renewable energy sources; using nuclear power if safety, weapons proliferation, and waste disposal constraints can be overcome; improving and making use of mitigation options in transport, bearing in mind the multiple barriers of consumer preferences and lack of policy frameworks; tapping into energy efficiency options for new and existing buildings; changing agricultural practices; changing forest-related mitigation activities; and implementing waste-management practices such as recycling.

The IPCC's synthesis report, which it issued at Valencia in November 2007, marked the culmination of a five-year process of filling the knowledge gap about climate change that involved participants from around the world.[21] It offered the firmest and sternest conclusion and warning of all the IPCC reports. It said that the evidence (the increases in global average air and ocean temperatures, the widespread melting of ice and snow, the increases in global average sea level) for climate change is "unequivocal." It also reported that the probability that these changes have been brought about by the behavior of humanity is 90 percent. It noted that the impacts can be reduced at a reasonable cost (an annual loss of 0.12 percent GDP until 2050), but if the impacts are not addressed over the next seven years, they will be "abrupt or irreversible."[22]

For example, if average global temperature increases by a mere 1.5–2.5°C (relative to the 1980–1989 mean), between one-fifth to one-third of species will face extinction. If the average global temperature increases by more than 3.5°C, 40–70 percent of the assessed species will be at increased risk of extinction, an additional 75–250 million people will face water scarcity, and yields from rain-fed agriculture could be halved, aggravating the problem of food security in Africa in particular. Moreover, even if CO_2 emissions stabilize at present levels, the sea level will rise between 0.4 to 1.4 meters because of continued warming, and this would cause major impacts on coastlines, low-lying islands and areas, and river deltas. In addition, many of the impacts are larger and are occurring earlier than had been projected in the 2001 report. For instance, some changes that had been projected to occur in 2020 or 2030 were already being seen in 2007. Finally, the 2007 report also put much more emphasis on the dynamic or ripple effects of even small degrees of temperature change (1–3°C), particularly in terms of the loss of biodiversity and the extinction of some species.[23]

BOX 7.1. Definitions of Climate Change

According to the IPCC, "Climate change refers to a statistically signifi-cant variation in either the mean state of the climate or in its variability, persisting for an extended period (typically decades or longer). Climate change may be due to natural internal processes or external forces, or to persistent anthropogenic changes in the composition of the atmosphere or in land use." This is notably different from the definition of the 1992 UN Framework Convention on Climate Change which, in Article 1, says that cli-mate change is "a change of climate which is attributed directly or indirectly to human activity that alters the composition of the global atmosphere and which is in addition to natural climate variability observed over comparable time periods."[1] The convention thus makes a distinction between "climate change" that is attributable to human activities that alter the composition of the atmosphere and "climate variability" that is attributable to natural causes—a distinction that leads to a policy bias against adaptation and in favor of mitigation as our response to climate change.[2]

1. Both definitions are reproduced in Rajendra K. Pachauri, "IPCC—Past Achievements and Future Challenges," in WMO and UNEP, *Intergovernmental Panel on Climate Change: 16 Years of Scientific Assessment in Support of the Climate Convention* (Geneva: IPCC Secretariat, December 2004), 4.

2. Roger A. Pielke, "Misdefining 'Climate Change': Consequences for Science and Action," *Environmental Science & Policy* 8, no. 6 (2005): 548–561.

The successive IPCC assessment reports have clearly demonstrated the growing level of expertise harnessed by the world organization. Thanks to the work of the UN panel, what appeared on the international agenda as an interesting hypothesis in the 1980s had garnered clear scientific support by 2007. The 2007 Nobel Peace Prize was awarded jointly to former U.S. vice president Al Gore for his lifetime role in raising American and inter-national awareness about global warming and to the IPCC for advancing the frontiers of scientific knowledge about the climate.

The Nobel Committee praised both recipients "for their efforts to build up and disseminate greater knowledge about man-made climate change, and to lay the foundations for the measures that are needed to counteract such change."[24] The IPCC is now generally acknowledged to be the world's leading authority on climate change and was commended for creating "an ever-broader informed consensus about the connection between human activities and global warming." In responding on behalf of the UN panel,

Chairman Rajendra K. Pachauri recalled how in its early days skeptics vili-
fied the IPCC. Pachauri felt that the Nobel Prize represented the vindica-
tion of science over skepticism and was just recognition of the panel's
meticulous scientific work.[25]

Normative Gaps: Do No Harm

The ethic of environmental protection first found expression in the
norm of "do no harm to the ozone." But in practice this dictum created
tension between industrialized countries (which had released most of the
CFCs that were depleting the ozone) and developing countries (which
aspired to the standard of living and lifestyle of the affluent societies in
the West who had released CFCs over the course of centuries in order
to industrialize). At the Rio conference in 1992, therefore, participants
adopted the cognate norm of a common but differentiated responsibility
to protect and manage the global commons. The principle, which embodies the notion of equity in the allocation of responsibility for causing and
solving problems, has been a staple of climate change discourse in the first
decade of the twenty-first century. As this was developed in some depth
in the last chapter, we do not repeat ourselves here.

However, two critical shortcomings appear obvious from even this
brief summary of the dominant normative context. First, the do-no-
harm norm falls short because substantial harm has already been done.
Some passionately argue that the harm is already irreversible. Even if
scientists are now basically in agreement on global warming, politicians
and social scientists are not. The consensus among natural scientists
confronts a lack of consensus among economists. Sir Nicholas Stern, for
example, in his highly influential 2006 report to the British government,
argued for immediate, aggressive action to counteract climate change
and proposed the investment of 1 percent of global gross domestic
product to mitigate the effects of global warming for future generations.
The report's reliance on a near-zero discount rate to calculate current
costs and future benefits is hardly conventional wisdom among many
of Stern's colleagues.[26]

The *Stern Review* contends that since the threat is urgent and future
generations are involved, then caution about drastic programs to protect
the human environment should be thrown to the winds. The dominant
norm in such a situation is commonly called the "precautionary principle," meaning that if the available information on the harm likely to be

caused is less than certain but the harm would be irreversible if it happened, then it is prudent to err on the side of caution and not take the potentially harm-producing action until such time as we can be sure of avoiding the harm. In thinking about future generations, is there not an obligation—since the potential harm is so high—for action to prevent or minimize the risks even without enough evidence to predict with absolute certainty that such harm will occur?

Second, the do-no-harm norm has been used to argue in favor of a differentiation that is impossible to sustain in either logical or practical terms, namely that developing countries such as China, India, and Brazil are not bound by the same strictures as industrialized countries. China's economy has grown at a rate of some 10 percent for over a decade and has surpassed the United States as the world's biggest total polluter in absolute although obviously not per capita terms; it should be obliged to take seriously the calls in MDG 7 to ensure environmental sustainability.[27] In May 2009, the *Guardian* reported that toward the end of the Bush administration and in the initial months of the Obama administration, emissaries from China and the United States had engaged in a series of secret back-channel negotiations aimed at securing a deal on climate emissions. Although the draft agreement was not signed, the March 2009 memorandum could yet provide the basis for a new deal, including voluntary but verifiable reductions of emissions by China before the Copenhagen meeting in December 2009. The three main elements would be a 20 percent reduction in carbon emissions by 2010 using existing technologies, cooperation on new technology for greater automotive fuel efficiency and carbon capture and storage, and China and the U.S. signing up to a new global climate deal at Copenhagen.[28]

As we have seen, the compelling new norm of protecting the environment did not exist in 1945 and evolved toward a norm of "do no harm." The modified norm now asks individuals, corporations, and governments to alter their behavior to limit damage. It also contains a new precautionary principle: "If in doubt, don't proceed."

Policy Gaps: From Montreal to the Kyoto Protocol

If CFCs contribute to depleting the ozone layer, which in turn causes various harms to flora and fauna as well as to human beings, then the use of CFCs must be curtailed and eliminated. That was the purpose behind and the goal of the Montreal Protocol in which signatories undertook to phase out the production and use of ozone-depleting compounds, including CFCs.

The Montreal Protocol on Substances that Deplete the Ozone Layer, signed in 1987 and in force since 1 January 1989, was a groundbreaking international agreement that first slowed and then reversed the thinning of the ozone layer. Its current 191 signatories, an increase from the twenty-four who signed the protocol at its inception, have phased out more than 95 percent of ozone-depleting substances. As a result, scientists estimate that the earth's protective ozone layer will return to pre-1980 levels by 2075.[29] In recognition of the principle of common but differentiated responsibility of industrialized and developing countries, the protocol allowed developing countries a grace period of ten years and offered them financial incentives. It was the first legally binding international environmental agreement that engaged both industrialized and developing countries, and it should have ushered in an era of global environmental responsibility. Unfortunately, the familiar story of climate change tells us it ain't so.

Noting the findings of the IPCC's first assessment report, the General Assembly decided in 1990 to initiate negotiations on a framework convention on climate change that was to be completed prior to the Rio conference in 1992. The UN Framework Convention on Climate Change was adopted on 9 May 1992, opened for signature in June 1992 at UNCED, and entered into force on 21 March 1994. Under the UNFCCC, thirty-six industrialized countries and transition economies made legally binding commitments to reduce and limit GHG emissions.

The First Conference to the Parties of the Climate Change Convention (COP-1) held in Germany in 1995 led to the adoption of the Berlin Mandate, which was premised on the recognition that the commitments made in the UNFCCC were inadequate and established the development of a protocol or another legal instrument with concrete targets and timetables for the reduction of GHG emissions as a goal.[30] The Berlin Mandate did not call for new obligations for developing countries but it did set the stage for an enhanced commitment from developed countries to confront climate change. Essentially, it laid the groundwork for the adoption of the Kyoto Protocol at the COP-3.

Midway on the road to Kyoto, UNFCCC members adopted the Geneva Ministerial Declaration at the COP-2 in 1996. The declaration embraced the IPCC's conclusions that human behavior influences global climate; that the projected changes in climate will result in significant, often adverse, and in some cases potentially irreversible impacts on many ecological systems and socioeconomic sectors (including food supply and water sources) and on human health; and that significant reductions in net GHG emissions are technically possible and economically feasible by utilizing an array of policy measures that accelerate the development, diffusion, and transfer of technology.[31]

At the COP-3 in 1997, states adopted the Kyoto Protocol, which went into effect in February 2005 with Russia's ratification. Similar to the UNFCCC, its central goal is to stabilize GHG concentrations in the atmosphere to a level that will stop and then reverse harmful global warming. The protocol sets targets for industrialized nations (also known as the "Annex 1" countries, from a list in the first annex to the protocol) to cut their emissions of five different GHGs: carbon dioxide, methane, hydrofluorocarbons, perfluorocarbons, and sulfur hexafluoride. It does not contain targets for developing countries—including such large and fast-growing economies as China and India—or call them to limit or reduce emissions.

In the Delhi Ministerial Declaration on Climate Change and Sustainable Development, senior officials present at the COP-8 (2002) noted the findings of the IPCC's third assessment report "with concern."[32] The case for environmental protection is no longer hampered by a lack of knowledge about a threat or lack of empirical data. Rather, robust action to confront climate change is hindered by the policy gap between two opposing ideologies—neoliberal economics and sustainable development. As we have seen, sustainable development also confronts differences in economic interpretations about how to calculate an appropriate rate of return on investments that counteract the negative externalities of growth. This is a topic about which there is little consensus among economists.[33]

In 2006, Nicholas Stern issued a deadly and sober warning in his report *The Economics of Climate Change*. Without urgent action, global output will decrease by some 20 percent, he said, producing economic devastation and social dislocation on a scale comparable to that of the Great Depression and the two world wars. Some have argued that given the scientific uncertainties built into the climate change models and the high costs of action that may ultimately prove excessive, the prudent policy is to wait, see, and adapt if necessary. Stern reversed the argument: given the same uncertainties and the relatively much lower costs of acting now rather than later, the best policy is immediate action. He argued that delayed action will cost more and deliver fewer benefits.[34]

In 2008, Stern asserted that his analysis was vindicated by the findings of the IPCC's fourth assessment report,[35] which was the most forceful and specific of all its reports for two reasons. First, the panel was greatly buoyed by the announcement of the joint award of the Nobel Peace Prize a month before its meeting in Valencia in 2007. Second, as the IPCC convened, it was conscious that it was about to deliver a document that would help define policy at the UN Climate Change Conference in Bali within a month and would be cited for years to come. The hope was to generate a policy response in Bali "quick enough and big enough," in the words of Princeton University's Michael Oppenheimer, one of the IPCC's scientists.[36] The urgency about setting policy came from the startling conclusion that by 2007 emissions were already at or beyond the most pessimistic forecasts made by the IPCC.

Indeed, because of a lag time in reporting data, some scientists expressed the fear that the IPCC report had understated the scale and rapidity of global warming and its impacts. For example, a 2007 report by the International Energy Agency had noted that the rapid economic growth in China and India had created levels of emissions that were unexpectedly high. If current trends were not halted and reversed, the world could be warmer by 6°C on average by 2030 instead of the 1–4 degrees predicted earlier.[37] The panel deliberately laid out the consequences of different degrees of climate change, the different options, and the consequences and costs of deferring action.

The Kyoto Protocol expires in 2012. Almost all UN member states participated in the Bali conference in December 2007 and began the painstaking work of constructing a successor regime. Bali was the setting for the most recent illustration of the unwillingness of states to face the dramatic consequences of failing to formulate a consensual policy for global warming. Secretary-General Ban Ki-moon exerted leadership and pleaded with delegates to "deliver to the people of the world a successful outcome." The conference's dramatic eleventh hour included tears from the head of the UN Climate Change Secretariat and Papua New Guinea's open challenge to the United States: "If you're not willing to lead, get out of the way."[38]

After the deadline for an agreement had been reached, 187 states (including China and the United States) unexpectedly resumed talks on the global effort to rescue the planet from climate change, which culminated in the so-called Bali roadmap—a two-year negotiation process to guide the establishment of a new treaty by 2009 to replace the Kyoto Protocol in 2012. At the close of the conference, newspaper pieces with such titles as "We've Been Suckered Again by the US: So Far the Bali Deal Is Worse Than Kyoto,"[39] and "Answer to Hot Air Was in Fact a Chilling Blunder"[40] accurately captured the disappointing outcome. While countries agreed to "green" technology transfer, funding for poorer countries, and "deep cuts" in GHG emissions, no clear goals or timetables were set.[41]

Deep concessions were made so that the United States would sign on, yet Washington still had "serious concerns" about the inadequacy of responsibilities assigned to developing countries,[42] and Russia, Canada, and Japan also objected to some of the agreement's key aspects. Meanwhile, the G-77 and some NGOs were disappointed at the lackluster final text. Indeed, the ambassador of Grenada described the outcome as "so watered-down" that "there was no need for 12,000 people to gather . . . in Bali. We could have done that by email."[43]

The basic policy framework for making decisions about the appropriate level of global mitigation is one of risk management guided by the principles of actual and avoided damages caused by climate change, co-benefits, sustainability, equity, and attitudes toward risk. In sum, "Choices about the scale and timing of GHG mitigation involve balancing the economic costs of more rapid emission reductions now against the corresponding medium-term and long-term climate risks of delay."[44] Public policy instruments (setting regulations and standards, instituting taxes and charges, creating financial incentives, integrating climate policies in broader development policies, etc.) are important when they are based on four criteria: environmental effectiveness, cost effectiveness, distributional effects (including equity), and institutional feasibility. If these policies are to succeed, governments must be on board. It is crucial that they be supported through financial contributions, tax credits, standard setting, and market creation.

In 2008, most of the world's peoples and governments decided to mark time in the struggle to fill policy gaps until the U.S. presidential elections were completed and the winning candidate and party were known. Serious negotiations on a post-Kyoto regime are likely to resume in 2009 and hopes are high that the avowedly more multilateral Barack Obama administration will once again exert U.S. leadership. Indeed, his emphasis on climate change during his first address to the General Assembly in September 2009 was well received and interpreted as a good harbinger for the Copenhagen gathering in December.

Institutional Gaps: The IPCC to the Rescue

As should be clear by now, the establishment of the IPCC in 1988 is a UN success story not only in filling a knowledge gap but also in filling an institutional gap that has made critical contributions in numerous ways to ameliorating global governance to protect the environment. Its establishment was made possible because of the previous work that was done to fill gaps by the WMO and UNEP. Open to all members of the UN and the WMO, the IPCC's role is to assess on a comprehensive, objective, and transparent basis information relevant to understanding the risk and potential impacts of human-induced climate change and options for adaptation and mitigation. The IPCC does not carry out research or monitor climate-related data or other relevant parameters. It bases its assessment mainly on peer-reviewed and published scientific or technical literature.

The IPCC has remained the most important source for its scientific, technical, and socioeconomic information and has had a strong impact on the further development of the UNFCCC. The relationship between the UNFCCC and the IPCC has become a model for interaction between scientists and decision makers, even after several failed attempts to establish a similar assessment process for other environmental issues. What are the unique features that have made IPCC so successful? One of the IPCC's most important principles is that it generates reports that are relevant to policies but do not prescribe policy. Other important principles include scientific integrity, objectivity, openness, and transparency. All IPCC reports must go through a rigorous review process, and the adoption and approval process is open to all member governments.

Compliance Gaps: Montreal and Kyoto

The Multilateral Fund for the Implementation of the Montreal Protocol was the first financial mechanism specifically created by an international treaty to counteract the impact of human activity on climate change. It provides funds to assist developing countries in phasing out ozone-depleting substances used, for example, in refrigeration, industrial cleaning, and fumigation.

Although the ozone layer is still thin in some spots, overall the general conclusion seems to be that the Montreal Protocol can be considered an exceptional success because it provided a credible and achievable roadmap for efforts to cut the production and use of over 95 percent of

ozone-depleting substances. The Montreal Protocol thus has been exceptional for its repair and recovery policy. To that extent, the Montreal
and Kyoto protocols are mutually supportive, a point underlined by
Achim Steiner, the executive director of UNEP, which houses the Ozone
Secretariat.[45]

Yet of all the stories of compliance so far, the Kyoto Protocol is the
least satisfactory because of the clash between the goal of universal participation and the practicalities of complying with an agreed text. Not
only was everyone not on board in the first place, but now the rats are
deserting the sinking ship, even as new scientific evidence suggests that
environmental change may be moving faster than previously thought.[46]
Canada, usually a pillar of multilateralism, contemplated leaving the
treaty after the election of Stephen Harper in 2006 (and possibly because
it was unable to reach its first-round targets), and now the entire universal
climate treaty exercise is being questioned.

Kyoto is an example of groping to fill a gaping global governance gap
in compliance. What replaces it may be messier theoretically and more
patchwork in coverage, but it may in fact be more effective in reaching
objectives and securing greater compliance from state parties. Learning
lessons is also part of the journey toward better global governance.

At present, there is really no way to punish countries that fail to
meet their targets—although the WTO levies fines on parties that do not
respect its rules and sometimes they pay. Except by making their next-
round targets more onerous—if in fact there is a next round—the Kyoto
Protocol is toothless. It includes a provision called the Clean Development
Mechanism that awards tradable credits for investments that cut emissions in developing countries. However, the emissions trading schemes
may encourage the export of carbon-intensive industries to nations without energy-saving technology, thus actually creating more pollution.[47]
Developed countries cut their emissions by about 3 percent between 1990
and 2000; however, this was largely the result of the collapse of the Soviet
bloc's economy. It is unlikely that most developed economies will meet
the targets for the end of the decade—especially when one considers that
the United States, the source of about a quarter of all GHG emissions,
has never ratified the protocol.[48]

The success of Montreal and the problems with Kyoto are not hard
to explain. The science behind Montreal was relatively cleaner and more
immediate in explaining both the causes (the relationship between ozone-
depleting substances and the thinning of the ozone layer) and conse-

quences (in particular, skin cancer caused by ozone depletion) of global warming. The number of problem countries and companies involved was quite small: fewer than two dozen firms in fewer than twenty countries were producing CFCs in the mid-1980s. The economic costs were within tolerable limits because substitutes for CFCs that could be produced at affordable costs already existed.

By contrast, the number of countries and firms, the uncertainties and complexities, and the extent of time and costs involved are now considerably greater with regard to global warming. Moreover, the activities that contribute the most to climate change—energy use, agricultural practices, and deforestation—are the core defining elements of modern economies, and doing anything about them will undoubtedly entail substantial costs and political blowback. According to the International Energy Agency, if the world follows current trends and policies, its energy consumption will increase by more than 50 percent from 2005 to 2030; China and India alone will account for 45 percent of the extra growth in demand.[49] While the worldwide economic downturn of 2008–2009 slowed the growth rate, nonetheless a continuation of recent patterns is clearly unsustainable.

The differences in science and economics in turn have changed the key equations in politics, both domestically and internationally. The toll will be heaviest on poor and marginalized citizens and countries. The sacrifices will have to be shared by all, and they are huge and have to be made today by individuals, firms, and governments. At the same time—and this is the obvious catch—while some returns on preventive investments may occur in the shorter and medium term, the major payoffs will be delivered in 50–100 years—when most of today's decision makers will no longer be alive to reap the political benefits, which are typically calculated for the next election cycle. The success story in switching from CFCs to substitutes is therefore an altogether false argument for demonstrating the logic of collective action in solving other major problems of the global commons, including climate change.

According to policy analysts Shardul Agrawala and Steinar Andresen, the U.S. political climate about global climate change has been determined by powerful ideologues, the constitutional separation between the executive and legislative branches of government, and a political culture that favors the market over state regulation.[50] This, they argue, consistently leads the United States to join international negotiations that spin out of its control as other countries fail to take into account U.S. domestic politics. In their postmortem of the failed climate talks at The Hague in November 2000, climate change scholars Michael Grubb and Farhana Yamin go further:

> European—and worldwide—frustration at U.S. energy profligacy blinded [conference delegates] to this harsh reality [that any meaningful reduction in U.S. emissions would be tremendously painful]. Positions were based on the hope that somehow the United States could be forced by international pressure to deliver something that is politically impossible on the timescale remaining, given the nature of the US system.[51]

Since the United States tenaciously holds on to its positions and certainly will not change its political culture or constitutional structure, the EU's environmentally progressive position strikes some American observers as cynical. It is easy to take the high ground when one knows that the deal will not be struck.

All this is not to say that there is no hope for the climate, only that the regime that will develop is likely to look a lot less neat and tidy than a universal treaty. As environmental scholars Sverker C. Jagers and Johannes Stripple note, the insurance industry has been playing an increasing role in the governance necessary for mitigation of and adaptation to climate change.[52] It has established a collaboration between firms through UNEP, and its impact on investment strategies will have profound implications for global climate governance. For example, the force of Hurricane Katrina is beginning to be felt in the rest of the United States as insurers refuse to renew policies for property owners near the sea.[53] The United States has also led the creation of a six-nation pact to limit global warming through the promotion of technology; China, India, Japan, South Korea, and Australia (and their business sectors) are participants.[54] Furthermore, the Regional Greenhouse Gas Initiative, a state-level emissions-capping and -trading program, has the participation of seven (soon to be eight) states in the northeast; other states, Canadian provinces, and the District of Columbia serve as observers.[55] Again, the multiplicity of actors and levels of analysis are an essential lens for understanding how global governance matures.

Conclusion:
The Third and the Second UNs Prod the First

The United Nations thus has been at the center of establishing the global environmental agenda. Milestones for both the previous chapter and this one are listed in box 7.2. The UN has been both a major actor in

BOX 7.2. UN Milestones in Protecting the Environment

- 1972—UN Conference on the Human Environment, Stockholm
- 1972—General Assembly creates UNEP
- 1975—UNEP brokers the Mediterranean Action Plan, the first regional seas agreement
- 1985—Vienna Convention for the Protection of the Ozone Layer
- 1987—Montreal Protocol on Substances that Deplete the Ozone Layer; publication of *Our Common Future*
- 1988—Intergovernmental Panel on Climate Change
- 1989—Basel Convention on the Control of Transboundary Movements of Hazardous Wastes and Their Disposal
- 1991—Global Environment Facility
- 1991—UN Commission on Sustainable Development
- 1992—UN Conference on Environment and Development (Earth Summit), Rio de Janeiro
- 1992—UN Framework Convention on Climate Change
- 1992—Convention on Biological Diversity
- 1995—Global Programme of Action launched to protect marine environment from land-based sources of pollution
- 1997—Nairobi Declaration on the Role and Mandate of the United Nations Environment Programme
- 1997—Kyoto Protocol
- 2000—Malmö Ministerial Declaration of the first Global Ministerial Forum on the Environment, sponsored by UNEP, calls for strengthened international environmental governance
- 2000—United Nations Millennium Declaration includes environmental sustainability as one of eight Millennium Development Goals
- 2001—Stockholm Convention on Persistent Organic Pollutants
- 2002—World Summit on Sustainable Development
- 2005—Millennium Ecosystem Assessment highlights the importance of ecosystems to human well-being and the extent of ecosystem decline
- 2005—World Summit Outcome document highlights the key role of the environment in sustainable development
- 2007—UN Climate Change Conference in Bali
- 2009—UN Climate Change Conference in Copenhagen

its own right in mainstreaming the environment in international policy discourse and a principal forum for all major actors. The lead institutional actors are the IPCC, the UNFCCC, and UNEP.[56] These institutions have also carried the prime responsibility for monitoring compliance.

It is clear that the United Nations has been the lead actor and champion in attempts to fill all the gaps in global governance regarding climate change. As the publication of the fourth assessment report showed, the IPCC is the most authoritative and influential body for collecting, collating, synthesizing, and pronouncing on the current scientific consensus regarding filling the knowledge gaps. Moreover, during its short lifetime after being commissioned by two UN agencies, the panel has become increasingly more confident that global warming is occurring, climate change is real and substantial, and human activity is the principal cause. The UN system has also most aggressively promoted emissions reductions, adaptation, mitigation, and a "common but differentiated responsibility" between developed and developing countries. The policy gaps were addressed in Kyoto and Bali.

The UN, through the IPCC's work, has emerged as an essential actor in assembling and advancing the state of knowledge about the reality, gravity, and urgency of the causes and consequences of climate change. This is almost unique among the major challenges of global governance. It has been the most crucial agent in articulating and globalizing the norm of environmental protection, in particular though the innovative global governance modality of global conferences that incorporated civil society actors and the scientific community, and it has been the principal site for converting the norm into a legislative agenda by serving as a forum for the negotiation of a series of treaties and conventions among member states. In the process, NGOs have also injected voices that are not easily silenced.

But as with many other areas of its work, the organization has not been effective in ensuring compliance with global norms and regimes. Surveillance and enforcement mechanisms are weak, and the collective will to comply is even weaker. In a clash between national and international interests regarding the environment, the logic of collective inaction by the First United Nations has usually triumphed over collective action. The disjuncture between the level at which this problem should be addressed—the globe—and the locus of political and financial decision making—the state—could hardly be more clear. Yet by the end of 2007, at least with respect to climate change, the political pendulum seemed to be shifting toward more effective action through the UN framework to forestall one of the gravest threats to the earth and all its life forms. Only time will tell whether this will prove to be too little too late.

Gaps remain in the state of our knowledge of climate change, and undoubtedly new gaps will continue to appear. In part this is due to different assumptions regarding the use of fossil fuels and GHG emissions, and in part it is due to the limits to our understanding of how clouds, oceans, and aerosols mix and interact. Within this margin of uncertainty, the UN through the IPCC has authoritatively provided the twin scientific conclusion that climate change is occurring and that human activity has caused and continues to contribute to it. Simply put, although weather patterns will continue to fluctuate across regions from day to day and season to season, the shift in the statistical distribution of means, ranges, and extremes will dramatically accelerate. The panel has also provided assessments of the impacts of climate change, the options for policymakers, and the costs of different options.

While the earth's warming is a global phenomenon, its impact will be neither uniform nor equal between countries and socioeconomic groups. The main forum for conducting negotiations and reaching agreements on climate change is the UNFCC. According to Seung-soo Han, special envoy on climate change of the secretary-general, "The Convention . . . and the Kyoto Protocol are the pillars of the international climate change regime that is currently in effect."[57] Adaptation, mitigation, technology transfers, and financial transfers are the four ways to confront climate change. Only the United Nations has the authority to convene and the capacity to mobilize the necessary resources for the enhanced global response that is urgently required. But actual implementation will require tough decisions by sovereign states and collaborative partnerships between states, international organizations, civil society, business, and even individual citizens with respect to changed behavior and lifestyle patterns. Box 7.3 summarizes the actual state of the planet as put forward by the UNDP in its *Human Development Report 2007/2008*, a report that can most usefully be viewed through the lenses of global governance gaps.

The defining feature of global environmental governance—the strengths and achievements as well as the frailties and shortfalls—has been the development of multilateral environmental agreements on the initiative of the UN or under UN auspices.[58] The largely UN-centered system of international environmental governance has generated and disseminated increasing volumes of data and information on environmental

BOX 7.3. The Human Development Report 2007/2008

The 2007/2008 edition of the UNDP's annual Human Development Report focused on climate change as its special theme.[1] With respect to *knowledge gaps,* it warned that the world was approaching a tipping point on climate change that could lock millions of the poorest people in the world's poorest countries in a downward spiral created by malnutrition, water scarcity, and loss of livelihoods. The report argued that the carbon-intensive growth and profligate consumption patterns of the advanced industrialized nations had created the problem and thus they were responsible for finding solutions, especially because they have the financial and technological capabilities to undertake necessary action. The three worst GHG emitters per capita are the United States, Canada, and Australia. If the whole world adopted U.S. and Canadian levels of production, consumption, and waste generation per person, we would need nine planet Earths to sustain them; with Australian levels, seven would do. Yet while the responsibility for causing climate change rests largely with the richest countries, it is poor people who will be the hardest hit by worsening drought, weather volatility and extremes, and rising sea levels. The UNDP calculated that the cost of stabilizing GHG at 450 particles per million could be limited to an average of 1.6 percent of world GDP to 2030. It repeated the *Stern Review*'s warning that just the economic costs of inaction, let alone the social and human costs, will be much more than this.[2]

Climate change could lead to a breakdown in many parts of the world; key features would be increased periods of drought, increasing temperatures, and erratic rainfall. An estimated additional 600 million people could face malnutrition. By 2060, the semi-arid regions of Sub-Saharan Africa could face productivity losses of more than 25 percent. By 2080, almost two billion people more could face water scarcity. Glacial retreat and changed rainfall could produce an ecological crisis in large swathes of northern China and southern Asia. Intensified flooding and storms could displace an additional 330 million people in coastal and low-lying areas (including 70 million in Bangladesh, 22 million in Vietnam, and 6 million in Egypt). Droughts, floods, and storms are already among the most powerful drivers of poverty and inequality because they wipe out assets, lead to malnutrition, and impede literacy as children are withdrawn from school.[3]

Addressing the fundamental *normative gap,* the report called for global warming in the twenty-first century to be limited to less than 2°C above preindustrial levels. The present global level is 0.7°C above preindustrial levels; if current trends persist, the world is set to surpass 4°C by the end of the twenty-first century.

The *policy gaps* can be filled through the twin-track approach of stringent mitigation and strengthened international cooperation on adaptation.

The forthcoming UN negotiations in Bali provide the opportunity to convert this norm into an international convention or treaty. To that extent the *Human Development Report 2007/2008* was a call for international action.

Industrial countries must assume their responsibility for mitigation and take the lead in cutting their 1990 GHG levels by 20 to 30 percent by 2020 and 80 percent by 2050.[4] This can be done through a mix of carbon taxation; more stringent cap-and-trade programs; regulation of energy use for vehicles, buildings, electrical appliances, and so forth; and increased use of renewable energies and carbon capture and storage.

Developing countries have less responsibility for having created the climate change problem and less capacity for both mitigation and adaptation. They therefore need more transition time, financing for low-carbon technology transfer, and assistance with adaptation.[5] Their target should be to reduce emissions by 20 percent of 1990 levels by 2050, starting in 2020, and should be supported by international transfers of finance and low-carbon technology. The report recommends that a climate change mitigation facility be created to provide $25–50 billion annually for low-carbon energy investments in developing countries.[6]

Even with stringent mitigation, warming will continue at least until 2050. Adaptation is necessary to cope with the implications of this and as insurance against the threat of insufficiently stringent mitigation. However, differential capacity between the rich and poor countries carries the risk of a developing "adaptation apartheid."[7] The spending to date on multilateral mechanisms for adaptation total a mere $26 million, and the transaction costs associated with such low levels of financing are high. Additional annual financing for adaptation, for example for climate-proofing infrastructure, will require $86 billion by 2015.[8]

With respect to *institutional gaps,* the IPCC has helped collate and disseminate the scientific consensus on the state of existing knowledge to the public as well as to elite policymakers, it has helped transform our conceptions of the timescale within which the norm of halting and then reversing global warming must move to policy and action, and it has helped alter our conception of the use of science as an aid to policy.[9] The *Human Development Report 2007/2008* draws on the findings of the IPCC.

With respect to *implementation gaps,* the report points out that developed countries have failed to align climate security goals with concrete energy policies and thus far have fallen well short of achieving even the modest Kyoto Protocol goals of around 5 percent reductions of greenhouse gas emissions from 1990 levels. If current trends continue, CO_2 emissions could increase by 50 percent by 2030. As the HDR asserts, sustainability requires an urgent realignment of the global energy system with the earth's ecological system.

(continued on following page)

1. UNDP, *Human Development Report 2007/2008: Fighting Climate Change: Human Solidarity in a Divided World* (New York: Palgrave Macmillan, 2007). Available at http://athdr.undp.org/en/reports/global/hdr2007-2008/ (accessed 7 December 2008).

2. Ibid., 8.

3. Ibid., 9.

4. Ibid., 17.

5. Ibid.

6. Ibid., 18.

7. Desmond Tutu, quoted in ibid., 13.

8. Ibid., 18.

9. Bruce Tonn, "The Intergovernmental Panel on Climate Change: A Global Scale Transformative Initiative," *Futures* 39, no. 5 (2007): 614–618.

trends, improved the systematic monitoring and assessment of the state of global environment, and resulted in numerous legally binding and voluntary instruments that provide norms, principles, procedures, guidelines, and codes of conduct on environmental issues. At the same time, serious gaps and problems persist regarding the continuing deterioration of the environment. There is "an alarming discrepancy between commitments and action and an inadequate level of integration of environmental considerations into mainstream decision making for economic and social development."[59] To put it bluntly, international commitments have failed to shape national environment policies to the same extent as they have shaped other policy areas such as trade.

Although the conservative government of Australia's John Howard signed but refused to ratify the Kyoto Protocol in 1997, his successor, Kevin Rudd, ratified the protocol as one of his first official acts; his Labor Party had made ratification one of the key issues of the 2007 campaign. Once again, this demonstrates that implementation and compliance are the responsibility of the UN's member states, not of the world organization's international civil servants or of civil society.

We have argued throughout that global governance requires many actors and takes place at many levels. The United Nations has acted as the node of interacting clusters of the different drivers of global environmental governance, including states, international organizations, regional organizations, NGOs, corporations, and communities of scientists.[60] The business community will be an increasingly important element in this picture; industry accounts for about 40 percent of the world's GHG emissions.[61] It is crucial that business leaders engage with international environmental governance. Many businesses are vigorously involved in efforts to "green" their industry, reduce environmental footprints, and embrace corporate social responsibility. In 2007, the International Chamber of Commerce issued a statement that "a strong, efficient and effective United Nations in the areas of sustainable economic and social development and environmental management is central to the interests of business."[62]

A recurring refrain in our story is how the authority for addressing the world's most pressing problems remains vested in states.[63] The disconnect between the nature of making decisions about the nature of solving a problem such as climate change could not be more stark.

One can go further and argue that formal engagement with the forums of international policymaking is not a good indicator of domestic policy development or emissions reductions, even for a good international citizen such as Canada, let alone for the United States.[64] For most countries, the context of national jurisdictions and the varying resources available to substate levels of governments for developing and implementing policy are at least as important—if not more so—than international commitments. This is especially the case because an issue such as climate change cuts across so many conventional policy and agency lines. In addition, there is a need to examine both the domestic "push" factors and the international "pull" factors in any explanation of a state's engagement with global commitments and norms.[65]

The next iteration of global climate governance is more likely to depend on the evolution of institutions that start small and build up, and the chance of success is much greater if a future regime is built around the United States because of how much it contributes to the problems and because of the technological prowess it possesses that can help solve them. And China and India, whose economic growth is currently in the double digits and who have enormous populations, also have to participate in solving this problem and not cling to the notion that they have the right to follow the same unsustainable path followed by industrialized countries in an earlier period.

As James Madison wrote in *Federalist #51*:

> If men were angels, no government would be necessary. If angels were to govern men, neither external nor internal controls on government would be necessary. In framing a government which is to

be administered by men over men, the great difficulty lies in this: you must first enable the government to control the governed; and in the next place, oblige it to control itself.[66]

And in fact, the authors of "A Madisonian Approach to Climate Policy" suggest that viable regimes can only be built from the stronger national and regional institutions that have the capacity to enforce emissions trading schemes and that nonbinding goals can be set globally through diplomacy.[67] In essence, for a global climate governance regime to work, it may have to appeal to the base but powerful motivator of greed instead of fear and enact legislation that stems various kinds of pollution by creating markets for buying and selling the right to pollute.

Progression toward better global governance is rarely linear. It moves in fits and starts, it is messy, and it rarely happens on a first attempt. Politics, context, and unanticipated consequences all play a role. All of the examples used in this chapter have gone through (or are still going through) trial-and-error phases. Hopefully, practice will make these efforts somewhat more perfect.

PART 3

Human Rights

8

Generations of Rights

Human rights deal with the proper balance in relations between individuals, society, and the state. Universalizing the norm of human rights was one of the great achievements of the twentieth century. A fundamental tension pervades every facet of the UN's role in promoting this norm and protecting the human rights of people. While human rights are most endangered in conditions of anarchy when there is no functioning state to legislate and defend human rights through law enforcement and judicial machinery, the gravest threats in a substantial number of cases to the human rights of citizens actually are posed by their own states.

The assertion of a human right is a claim on the state for protection from threats emanating from other individuals and groups or from the agents of the state themselves. Because the United Nations is an intergovernmental organization, a voluntary association of, by, and for member states, members share an interest in limiting the jurisdiction of international organizations in scrutinizing the actions of governments vis-à-vis their own citizens. UN human rights declarations and treaties, however, provide a platform from which international civil servants and especially civil society actors can champion norms and lobby for their translation into effective laws and state practices that can be policed by appropriate international agencies. Mexican anthropologist Lourdes Arizpe relays how this works:

> I've seen it in many meetings, where the powerless Indian groups or women's groups have actually taken documents from . . . the United Nations and presented these to the officials from their governments and have forced their governments to be more accountable because there exists this document which has been signed and ratified by a majority of countries in the world, showing that this is the way that governments should behave or corporations should behave or men should behave.[1]

Similarly, UNIFEM's former director, Noeleen Heyzer, who is now executive secretary of the Economic Commission for Asia and the Pacific argues that issues ignored at the national level can be taken to the United Nations, where they gain international legitimacy. Often, the result is that the international spotlight shines on the delinquent national government. In the case of women's rights, Heyzer says that "with these international norms, women pressured for the revisions of national norms and policies based on international standards."[2]

Unless state behavior crosses the very high threshold of mass atrocity crimes, the resort to international military force is ruled out as a mechanism to bring errant state behavior into compliance with international norms and standards. Coercive measures that do not involve the threat or use of force such as sanctions and arms embargoes have evolved as policy instruments that exist on a spectrum between mere resolutions that censure but do little else and military intervention. In addition to our usual template of gaps, this chapter contains a final section that examines gaps related to the policy of using nonforcible sanctions. This policy has relevance for areas of global governance as well as human rights.

Antecedents: The Growth of a "Curious Grapevine"

Many observers from the First, Second, and Third United Nations would argue that human rights is the boldest idea in the Charter.[3] The compelling claim is that all individuals have inalienable human rights. During World War II, the Allies used references to human rights to mobilize support for the war effort. In 1939, Churchill proclaimed that the war was being fought "to establish, on impregnable rocks, the rights of the individual." In January 1941, Roosevelt announced his vision of security based on four freedoms: "freedom of speech and expression, freedom of worship, freedom from want and freedom from fear."[4] Human rights appeared in background documents to the Atlantic Charter of 1941, and they were mentioned formally for the first time in the preamble of the Declaration of the United Nations signed in Washington, D.C., in January 1942.

This initiative emerged from the genuine enthusiasm of the United States for an international order based on rules and law at that time. In a speech at the United Nations just after the adoption of the Universal Declaration of Human Rights in December 1948, Eleanor Roosevelt predicted that "a curious grapevine" would spread the ideas contained in the declaration far and wide, an exceptionally apt characterization for what has actually taken place.[5] International concern with human rights prior to World War II dwelled on the laws of war, outlawing slavery, and protecting minorities. The emergence of fascism strengthened the concern and enlarged its scope. The Universal Declaration of Human Rights is usually considered with the other great historical documents—for example, the French Declaration of the Rights of Man and the American Declaration of Independence—and was the first international affirmation of the rights held in common by all.[6]

Although no "bill of rights" like the one in the U.S. Constitution was agreed at the UN's founding conference in San Francisco, a drafting commission was established almost immediately to define human rights, and the General Assembly adopted the Universal Declaration containing thirty detailed articles in December 1948. Together, the Charter and the Universal Declaration broke new ground and sowed the seeds for many subsequent intrusions into what formerly had been considered the exclusive jurisdiction of states.

The origins of the Universal Declaration in the experiences of European civilization are important, not for the reason that most critics cite but for the opposite reason. It is not simply an expression of European triumphalism and self-confidence but also a guilt-ridden Christendom's renunciation of its ugly recent record; less an assertion of the superiority of European human nature than revulsion at the recent history of European savagery; not an effort to universalize western values but an effort to ban the dark side of western vices such as racial and religious bigotry.[7]

In retrospect, we can see how the Charter's language led to a different approach to the equilibrium between state sovereignty and human rights. The attempt to finesse the obvious tensions between these two ideas did not succeed completely, but the basis for sometimes weighing rights more heavily than sovereignty was established and has made a difference. The basic conflict was built in and has often resulted in substantial intrusions on traditional state prerogatives, including a host of military interventions beginning in the 1990s, a subject to which we return in our concluding chapter.

It is useful to provide some historical perspective because current disagreements about whether development or counter-terrorism trumps civil and political rights echo an earlier clash during the Cold War. The East-West rivalry had serious repercussions because efforts to convert the Universal Declaration of Human Rights into a single covenant that countries could ratify were delayed when ideological debates became intensely polarized. Political and civil rights (of the "first generation" emphasized by the West) became separated from economic, social, and cultural rights (of the "second generation" emphasized by the East). The West challenged the communist bloc because of its failures to respect political and civil rights, and communist countries pointed to the failures of the West to address poverty amid affluence and to ensure basic human needs. ILO director-general Juan Somavía, whose father-in-law (Hernan Santa Cruz) was a drafter of the Universal Declaration, spoke about that chilly time: "The Cold War made the western world forget about human rights, not to give a damn about human rights. . . . If you were supported on the Cold War front, there were no questions asked on the human rights front and the democracy front."[8]

Less emphasized was a more fundamental failure—human rights were separated from development. To a large extent within the UN until the 1980s, human rights were an ideological football that the East and the West kicked back and forth in an international game. Western players wore the colors of political and civil rights, Eastern players those of economic and social rights. Depending on their political affiliations, southern players actively joined one team or the other in the scrum or cheered from the sidelines for whoever seemed to be in the lead. The international game was mainly a shouting match characterized by attacks and denunciations but little attention to the practical problems and issues that were often high on the domestic agendas at the time. Both sides could have benefited by sharing lessons and new approaches. Only as the Cold War was beginning to thaw and groups concerned with the rights of women and children entered the stadium did the game and the playing field change.[9] In looking back, former Secretary-General Kurt Waldheim, whose past included a much-criticized association with Nazi concentration camps during World War II, correctly reflected on the sea change in human rights: "If you see what happens today in this field, we can say that progress was made. . . . Now, no government would dare to make proposals in the political, economic, and social field without referring to human rights."[10]

Beginning as early as the 1980s, a surge of ratifications of human rights conventions occurred along with their increasing implementation and louder and louder outrage over abuses, especially by such NGOs as Amnesty International and Human Rights Watch. About three-quarters have ratified the Covenant on Civil and Political Rights and the Covenant on Economic, Social and Cultural Rights. Over 80 percent of countries have ratified the UN's Convention on the Elimination of All Forms of Racial Discrimination and its Convention on the Elimination of All Forms of Discrimination against Women. According to UNICEF, only two states have not ratified the Convention on the Rights of the Child, Somalia (largely because of its unwillingness to stop recruiting soldiers under eighteen years of age) and the United States (largely because of its unwillingness to renounce capital punishment).

Global conferences have served as an important platform for debates about human rights ideas. An initial review of the progress in the field of human rights since the adoption of the Universal Declaration took place in Teheran in 1968; but the World Conference on Human Rights in Vienna in 1993, forty-five years after the adoption of the declaration, was far more controversial on the issue of universality. The main dispute in Vienna centered on whether human rights were actually universally applicable—as had been agreed in 1948—or were subject to local, religious, and cultural interpretations. Some of the issues discussed in Vienna included female genital mutilation in Sudan, suppression of girls' education in Afghanistan, repression of dissidents in Singapore, or the use of the death penalty in the United States. In spite of the disagreements over whether rights were relative, the 1993 conference reaffirmed that they were indivisible and universal.[11] This occasion also led to the creation of the Office of the High Commissioner for Human Rights, something that had been on the drawing board since 1947, when René Cassin proposed a UN attorney-general. And as we shall see below, the most recent institutional innovation, the Human Rights Council, was created amid controversy in 2006.[12]

In short, since 1945 states have used their sovereignty to create international human rights obligations that in turn have restricted their operational sovereignty. The international law of human rights, which was developed on a global scale at the United Nations, clearly regulates what legal policies states can adopt even within their own territorial jurisdictions. International agreements on human rights norms have been followed at least occasionally by concrete and noteworthy developments that demonstrate the extent to which the global governance of human rights reaches deeply into matters that were once considered the core of national domestic affairs. At the same time, the discrepancy between the rhetoric and reality of human rights remains stark, as anyone would testify in examining the contemporary distress of dissidents in Beijing or Harare or the denizens of Guantánomo.

One final development is worth noting here. The UN Global Compact has proven to be a useful tool for extending the international human rights regime to international business. For all the criticism by civil society organizations, business leaders have voluntarily assumed a new role as duty bearers because of the Global Compact.[13]

Knowledge Gaps: Substantially Filled

The knowledge gap about human rights abuses has narrowed substantially since 1945, stimulated by a host of NGOs from the Third UN and the creation of such Second UN units as the OHCHR. The UN Charter and the Universal Declaration form an arch that supports the entire structure of the UN system. As a career international civil servant and subsequently the head of a nongovernmental human rights group in his native India, Virendra Dayal argued that the basic premises of these two documents are "that you really can't have peace unless the rights of nations great and small are equally respected . . . [and] that you can't have peace within a country or a society unless the rights of all, great or small, are equally respected."[14]

The experience of the League of Nations in the interwar years and World War II convinced many people of the linkages between social and economic issues, human rights, and peace and security. After all, Nazi Germany is inalienably linked not just to the war but also and just as potently to the Holocaust, one of the most ghastly illustrations of the total absence of a basic respect for rights. As indicated earlier, however, there has been too little meeting of the minds between the East and South, which stress social and economic rights (especially the rights of states relative to other states), and the West, which focuses on civil and political rights as absolutes for individuals.

The utility of the two covenants on human rights of 1966 lies in the requirement imposed on signatories to submit periodic reports on the human rights situation in their countries. Therefore, ratifying and bringing the covenants into force connotes more than acceptance of internationally proclaimed standards of human rights. Signatories also agree to construct long-term national infrastructures to protect and promote human rights and to put in place national authorities to collect data to submit to the UN. The UN's empirical data would be difficult for any other body to match.

But the organization is less efficacious in theoretical research on linkages between human rights, on the one hand, and development and peace and security, on the other. These links are typically simply assumed rather than subjected to rigorous analysis. The United Nations is also less than successful in documenting knowledge on human rights abuses, a point to which we return in our discussion of implementation and compliance.

American University law professor Diane Orentlicher asks, "By whose lights does one determine which rights are '*prima facie* universal' and what local variations in interpretation are permissible? . . . *Who decides?*"[15] This is where the United Nations ought to have a comparative advantage. Precisely because it is the meeting ground for the world's different civilizations and cultures, it should be able to compile data on the "unity in diversity" of human rights that are universal at one level of generality yet variable in their interpretation and application across places and over time.

Normative Gaps: Moving toward Consensus?

Human rights that are owed to every person simply by virtue of the fact of that person's humanity are inherently universal. Human rights are held only by human beings, but they are held equally by all; they do not flow from office, rank, or relationship. As Michael Ignatieff explains, "Human rights is the language that systematically embodies" the intuition that the human species is one "and [that] each of the individuals who compose it is entitled to equal moral consideration."[16]

Karel Vasak, a contributor to the drafting of the Universal Declaration of Human Rights, conceptualized "three generations" of rights. "First-generation negative rights" emerged from constitutional traditions that prevented the state from curtailing the civil rights and political liberties of citizens; "second-generation positive rights" reflected the agenda of many newly independent but poor countries to prescribe an activist agenda of

social and economic rights for their citizens;[17] and "third-generation solidarity rights" pertain to collective entities rather than individuals and are
based on notions of solidarity.[18]

The first two generations of rights are embodied in the two covenants of 1966, which affirmed both civil and political rights and economic,
social, and cultural rights without privileging either set. Together with the
Universal Declaration, they are what most observers would say constitutes
the International Bill of Rights. They map out the international human
rights agenda, establish the benchmark for state conduct, inspire provisions
in many national laws and international conventions, and provide a beacon
of hope to many whose rights have been snuffed out by brutal regimes.
Human rights analyst Michael Ignatieff (who is now a Canadian politician)
correctly calls them our "firewalls against barbarism" and "a toolkit against
oppression," a source of power and authority on behalf of victims.[19]

Brian Urquhart put these normative shifts in historical context: "It is
hard now to remember that there was a time when human rights was the
preoccupation of a very limited number of people."[20] A number of shifts in
the norm of human rights have occurred over the years. Institutionalized
racial discrimination, in particular apartheid, has been delegitimized. The
concept of a state's accountability to the rest of the world has replaced the
concept of impunity,[21] to the point that the rights of individuals are sometimes privileged over the rights of states. It is now widely accepted that
we need to work to improve the status of women. Ideas about the dignity
of human beings, protecting minorities and other vulnerable groups, and
outlawing genocide have been revised and developed.

The UN Charter's preamble refers to "faith in fundamental human
rights," "the dignity and worth of the human person," and "the equal
rights of men and women." The norm entrepreneur who did much to
set the UN on this path, Eleanor Roosevelt, knew that the negotiated
text would not be ratified by the U.S. Senate and that a defeat would be
a tremendous setback. Thus, she pressed for a "declaration" rather than
a treaty instrument.[22] The Universal Declaration is now considered customary law across the planet, but it is not binding hard law. This is why
Sarah Zaidi and Roger Normand refer to the human rights story as "the
unfinished revolution."

Normative gaps remain. We need look no further than practices of
female genital mutilation and "honor" killing, which have been roundly
denounced in the West but have just as fervently been defended elsewhere

by some (albeit a declining minority) as examples of practices integral to a culture. Although the prohibition of torture "appears on every short list of truly universal standards,"[23] the debate in U.S. circles on whether it can be justified under some circumstances if it leads to preventing mass terrorist attacks and may therefore be authorized by judges through "torture warrants" mirrors other long-argued positions on cultural relativism.[24] Human beings do not inhabit a universe of uniformly shared moral values. Instead, diverse moral communities cohabit in international society.

Yet relativism is often the first refuge of repressive governments. A posture of moral relativism can be profoundly racist, proclaiming in effect that "the other" is not worthy of the dignity that belongs inalienably to everyone. By contrast, human rights advocacy, as Ignatieff explains, rests on "the moral imagination to feel the pain of others," as if the pain were one's own; treats others as "rights-bearing equals," not "dependents in tutelage"; and can be viewed as "a juridical articulation of duty by those in zones of safety toward those in zones of danger."[25]

Relativism requires an acknowledgment that each culture has its own moral system and that institutional protection of human rights should be grounded in historically textured conditions and local political culture. For every society, murder is always wrong. But few proscribe the act of killing absolutely under all circumstances. At different times, in different societies, war, capital punishment, abortion, or euthanasia may or may not be morally permissible. So the interpretation and application of the moral proscription of murder varies from one time, place, and society to another. All societies require that retribution be proportionate to the wrong done. All prize children as the link between succeeding generations of human civilization; every culture abhors their abuse.

It is possible also that there is some, perhaps even considerable, convergence between local, village-level, and global norms and that norms of behavior at the national level are disconnected from those both below and above them.[26] This is another knowledge gap that needs to be filled.

Policy Gaps: Putting Unique Legitimacy to Use

The diffusion of human rights norms and conventions and the extension and diffusion of international humanitarian law were among the truly great achievements of the last century. The composite United Nations, prodded continually by individuals and nongovernmental organizations, was at the center of that effort. UN leadership on human rights has helped change the public policy discourse in all parts of the world. As a universal organization, the UN provides a unique setting not only for compiling objective information and data and developing and promoting human rights norms and practices but also for advancing legal, monitoring, and operational policies that seek to uphold the universality of human rights while respecting national and cultural diversity.

In his 2002 report, Secretary-General Kofi Annan reminded us that "the promotion and protection of human rights is a bedrock requirement for the realization of the Charter's vision of a just and peaceful world."[27] Annan was the first Secretary-General to routinely emphasize human rights from one of the world's most visible bully pulpits. Activists and NGOs who use the Universal Declaration as the concrete point of reference against which to judge state conduct have greatly helped UN efforts to fill policy gaps. The most recent advances are in humanitarian law; for example the Ottawa Treaty prohibits land mines, thus subordinating military calculations to humanitarian concerns about a weapon that cannot distinguish a soldier from a child.[28] The Rome Statute of the International Criminal Court provides an enforcement mechanism to hold individuals responsible for acts of genocide, war crimes, and egregious violations of human rights. The failure of the United States to sign on to both the Ottawa Treaty and the Rome Statute shows the extent to which the former standard-bearer for human rights has become a prominent delinquent or "outlier."

Institutional Gaps: The Human Rights Council— Running Faster to Stand Still?

In some ways the UN's Commission on Human Rights became a victim of the world body's growing success in promoting human rights and monitoring abuses. As the international community of states scrutinized governments more directly, many regimes decided that the best defense for human rights abuses was to join the commission. It became morally bankrupt and an embarrassment to the UN system. The Secretary-General's High-level Panel on Threats, Challenges and Change recognized the CHR's "eroding credibility and professionalism" and noted that "states have sought membership of the Commission not to strengthen human rights but to protect themselves against criticism or to criticize others."[29] However, the recommendation of the panel was truly counterintuitive: universal membership instead of "only" one-quarter of the UN's member states! This idea deservedly found its way to the dustbin of UN history.

Secretary-General Kofi Annan supported strengthening the OHCHR, but in his main serious dissent from the High-level Panel's recommendations, he proposed that member states "replace the Commission on Human Rights with a smaller standing Human Rights Council."[30] This idea was discussed at the September 2005 World Summit, where participants argued about whether the new "council" might one day become a principal organ (like the Security Council and ECOSOC) that could review the human rights record of all members.

The World Summit was unable to completely scuttle the old commission's operational shortcomings but did "resolve to create a Human Rights Council" as a subsidiary of the General Assembly, which not only would create it but also decide its "mandate, modalities, functions, size, composition, membership, working methods, and procedures."[31] The language proposing that membership be subjected to a two-thirds vote of the General Assembly was eliminated as well as the possibility that it might someday be transformed into a principal organ, thus requiring a formal amendment in the Charter.

Given the bitter disputes over the shape of the new council, it surprised some that the General Assembly came to an agreement at all. At the assembly's sixtieth session (2005–2006), Jan Eliasson, the assembly's able president, managed to push successfully for a vote on the proposed 47-member United Nations Human Rights Council. Members would serve for three years with the assent of a simple majority of the General Assembly. Some were disgruntled because the numbers of the new council had decreased *only* to forty-seven—hardly a big decrease from fifty-three and perhaps still too large to be businesslike—and because membership was subject only to a simple majority vote instead of the more stringent two-thirds requirement the Secretary-General had proposed. However, the fact that membership entailed scrutiny was designed to discourage the worst human rights offenders. The reality that any state sitting on the council would be subject to review during its term was supposed to dampen the interest of abusers who should think twice about candidacy.[32]

Admittedly, the new body has flaws. A majority vote by the General Assembly facilitated the initial election of such abusers as China, Cuba, Russia, Pakistan, Saudi Arabia, and Azerbaijan. Nonetheless, elections replaced selection by regional power brokers. Moreover, candidates put forward voluntary pledges to promote and uphold human rights in support of their candidacies, which spurred an open discussion of the records of candidate states. Some came close to acknowledging international concerns. For example, Pakistan emphasized its commitment to punishing all forms of violence against women, especially "honor" killing. China drew attention to its invitations to UN investigators to study freedom of religion as well as torture and arbitrary detention in China.

Yet the initial elections also suggested that perhaps change was under way. Two vocal critics of human rights measures, Venezuela and Iran, were rejected as members. Whereas in the past despotic regimes could evade scrutiny by joining the commission, inquiry into members' human rights records is the first order of business for the new council. Hence, Zimbabwe, Sudan, Libya, Vietnam, Nepal, Syria, and Egypt did not even run. Neither did the United States. Some speculated that Abu Ghraib and Guantánamo—or at least the unwillingness to have them discussed— might have threatened a U.S. candidacy.

The new HRC has established a calendar and is developing rules and procedures for the universal periodic review (UPR) process to fulfill the requirement that every member state be reviewed once every four years. Such examinations constitute precedents. While reviews are based on information provided by states under review, they also rely on information from UN agencies and NGOs. The overriding aim of the new council should be equity and transparency. Other big issues include who will conduct country investigations, what type of data will be accepted, how rigorous the debate will be, and what type of follow-up mechanisms will be put into place. The jury is still out about whether the UPR will result in more or less transparency and accountability, but some observers are guardedly optimistic.

The Human Rights Council will meet at least three times a year; this makes responding to human rights abuses more of a full-time concern. In addition, special sessions can be called; this also makes the entity a potentially useful body for responding to human rights crises. The World Summit as well as the Security Council and General Assembly have endorsed the need for collective action when states are unwilling or unable to protect their citizens from mass atrocities. The HRC faces an imperative: it must respond quickly to deteriorating human rights situations to forestall possible international military intervention.

The United States cast one of only four negative votes in March 2006 against the creation of the HRC, supposedly because it wanted a tougher and more effective new institution. It prominently registered its discontent with the modest level of change not only by voting against the council but also by not being a candidate for a seat on the new HRC in 2006. U.S. ambassador John Bolton, who had not previously distinguished himself as a great champion of human rights or of the United Nations in general, told a public radio audience that the United States was outraged and "wants a butterfly, not a caterpillar with lipstick on."[33]

Washington's stance toward the HRC changed with the Obama administration. In announcing the U.S. decision to participate in the HRC's May 2009 elections, Secretary of State Hillary Rodham Clinton asserted that the administration believed that "every nation must live by and help shape global rules that ensure people enjoy the right to live freely and participate fully in their societies."[34] The election of the United States to the council is a hopeful step forward in advancing human rights domestically and internationally.

Along with political support, sufficient resources are clearly a determining factor in measuring institutional gaps. During the Cold War, the UN's total regular budget allocation for human rights hovered around 0.5 percent. High Commissioner Mary Robinson (1997–2002) managed to double that allocation, and it continued to increase under her successors, Sergio Vieira de Mello (2002–2003) and Louise Arbour (2003–2008). But it is the extrabudgetary portion that has increased; discretionary funds now dwarf resources from the regular budget. This has the effect of skewing the office's priorities toward the interests of those who pay the bills. The current high commissioner, Navanethem Pillay, inherits an institution that accounts for about 3 percent of the UN's regular budget.[35] While this allocation is insignificant in relationship to the size of the problem, the work of members of the Third United Nations—especially major international NGOs such as Amnesty International and Human Rights Watch—add considerable financial and human resources to the total UN picture.

Compliance Gaps:
Limping toward More Respect and Less Rhetoric

The "juridical, advocacy and enforcement revolutions" in human rights[36] rest on a partnership between intergovernmental and nongovernmental actors with regard to monitoring and compliance. One of the obvious explanations for compliance problems relates to the seemingly inevitable shortcomings of the UN's intergovernmental machinery for human rights, which consists of member states. As mentioned above, the much-maligned Commission on Human Rights figured prominently in the report from the High-level Panel on Threats, Challenges and Change. Viewed from Washington as well as many other capitals, the performance of the UN's human rights machinery was nothing short of scandalous. The primary evidence for the travesty was the fact that in 2005 the commission's fifty-three elected members included Sudan, during the time that it was pursuing slow-motion genocide in Darfur, and Zimbabwe, while it was bulldozing the houses of 700,000 opposition supporters and rounding up journalists and other critics. That China and Cuba played prominent roles and that Libya was a former chair of the CHR added to the litany of embarrassments.

When the General Assembly finally came to a decision about establishing the new Human Rights Council, some critics were relieved. The Commission on Human Rights held its final session in Geneva in March 2006 and was abolished the following June. At that final session, High Commissioner Louise Arbour, following a characteristic UN habit of putting the most positive spin possible on events, noted: "It would, however, be a distortion of fact, and a gross disservice to this institution, if we failed on this occasion to celebrate the achievements of the Commission even as we, in full knowledge of its flaws, welcome the arrival of its successor." She listed those accomplishments as setting standards, establishing the system of special procedures, considering the situations in specific countries, creating a global forum, and nurturing a unique relationship with civil society.[37]

The first members of the council were elected by the General Assembly in May 2006, and it convened in Geneva for the first time in June. Do these glimmers of change signify a new climate for improved compliance with human rights standards? China is already arguing that the HRC should not "politicize" human rights—another way of saying that it should not point fingers at particular governments. If the promising sprouts of the council are not to shrivel, those committed to human rights must actively nurture them. If the Human Rights Council is not to replicate the tiresome horse-trading and meaningless resolutions of its predecessor, the United States and others supporting human rights—the Europeans as well as the democracies of the global South such as India and South Africa—should strive to ensure independence from political influence and to increase the role of nongovernmental watchdogs such as Human Rights Watch and Amnesty International. The first years of the HRC's operations will be a period of transition (it will be evaluated in 2011) but also an opportunity to build an institution with more enforcement teeth than its predecessor.

Whatever the exact outcome of the new council's work, it is clear that substantial compliance gaps will remain. That is the nature of a universal institution whose member states are rarely on the same wave length, perhaps even less so regarding human rights than other issues. Nonetheless, it will be hard to slow down the continued march of human rights, and in this respect the increase in the budget of the OHCHR is significant, although its regular budget allocation is still insufficient to fulfill its mandate. What also is clear is that protecting internationally recognized human rights will remain a fraught concern in the years to come. Human rights will be unavoidably political as long as the UN's main collective body on human rights affairs is made up of states. Even liberal democratic states often sacrifice human rights on the altar of national security and the economics that pay for it. The United Kingdom, for example, was not anxious to use the old CHR to criticize Saudi Arabia, one of its principal arms clients. France and Italy were not eager to use the CHR to criticize China for its human rights violations when there were business deals to be concluded with Beijing. It is difficult to understand how changing the order of the letters in the acronym from CHR to HRC—or even one day transforming it into a principal organ charged with enforcing human rights—will change these double standards based on national strategic calculations. The basic problem thus is not a question of institutional design or finding compliance gimmicks; the basic problem is the persistent elevation of other interests and values over an impartial approach to human rights.

In individual countries and in the Council of Europe, the routine reliable protection of human rights is achieved by the work of independent individuals who do not take instructions from political bodies and who are not obliged to do the bidding of the country issuing a passport or approving an appointment. International compliance gaps remain because UN member states are hardly ready for a similar serious change in world order.[38] Moreover, given continuing international anarchy and state insecurity, even democratic states may have to prioritize defense of the group at the expense of certain individual human rights, at least sometimes.

Sanctions: Adapting Coercive Measures

Coercive economic sanctions were developed as a conceptual and policy bridge between gently rapping knuckles through diplomacy and breaking kneecaps by using military force to ensure compliance with UN demands. Recourse to imposing sanctions—such as isolating an offending state diplomatically, imposing restrictions on international travel, limiting trade and financial transactions, instituting arms embargoes—increased so dramatically in the decade of the 1990s that David Cortright and George Lopez dubbed it "the sanctions decade."[39] Before 1990, the international community had imposed sanctions only twice (against Rhodesia and South Africa), but the Security Council has imposed more than a dozen sanctions since then (against Afghanistan, Angola [on rebel forces], Ethiopia, Eritrea, Haiti, Iran, Iraq, Liberia, Libya, Rwanda, Sierra Leone, Somalia, Sudan, and the former Yugoslavia). The United Nations has played a central role in the imposition and implementation of sanctions because of its international legitimacy.

Sanctions figure in Charter Article 41 in language that implies that they should be used before ratcheting up to the next step, the use of military force. This is the sequence that the Security Council used in Iraq before the Gulf War in 1990–1991 and in Haiti in 1991–1994.

Although once seen as an attractive nonviolent alternative to war, comprehensive sanctions became discredited for their harsh humanitarian consequences for civilian populations. Moreover, there is some evidence that sanctions permit even thuggish leaders to rally citizens around the flag.[40] The negative effects of sanctions and the paucity of intellectual and institutional foundations for the UN's sanctions policy had an adverse affect on the world body's legitimacy in the early 1990s. Interest shifted to incorporating humanitarian exemptions from sanctions and to searching for "smarter" alternatives to comprehensive sanctions that would put pressure on regimes rather than peoples. Smart sanctions have not been proven in practice, even though they are conceptually compelling and are a great improvement from moral, political, and technical points of view.

And the larger question remains: are sanctions a substitute for, a complement to, or a precursor to war? That these are not empty questions was illustrated with the dilemmas that confronted the international community with respect to the humanitarian crisis that began in Darfur in 2003 and continues virtually unabated as we write.

Sanctions have a bad history. They inflict undeniable pain on ordinary citizens while imposing questionable costs on leaders. Indeed, often leaders are enriched and strengthened on the backs of their impoverished and oppressed peoples by the law of perverse consequences. The bulk of the hard data on the impact of sanctions has been compiled by non-UN sources.[41] The one major exception, and it is a highly influential one, is the UNICEF study on the impact of sanctions on Iraqi civilians.

In 1967, Johan Galtung was the first to postulate the naïve theory of sanctions, without empirical support, according to which economic pain in target countries would mysteriously produce political gain for the sanctions-imposing countries.[42] Since then, no body of intellectual work has developed Galtung's theory. Remarkably for a tool of national and international statecraft that is used so often, not a single major study establishes the efficacy of sanctions. Part of the difficulty is definitional and methodological: What constitutes success and how does one establish a conclusive link between sanctions and a successful outcome? And how can one disaggregate the effects of sanctions from other variables? Sanctions have multiple impacts, and outcomes can be traced back to multiple causes. For example, how can we know whether sanctions or air strikes were more effective by Slobodan Milosevic to accept a peace settlement at Dayton in 1995? Although we know that sanctions nudged Libya into releasing its agents to stand trial for the Lockerbie bombing, we do not know whether it was sanctions or the demonstration effect of the Iraq war that led Libya to abandon the pursuit of weapons of mass destruction. By contrast, many persuasive studies point to the limitations of sanctions as diplomatic tools.[43]

The methodological difficulty of assigning weight to sanctions as causes of success was replicated in the methodological difficulties of assigning blame to sanctions for humanitarian suffering. UNICEF's widely cited estimates of half a million child deaths caused by the sanctions against Iraq relied on an extrapolation of trends (see table 8.1). It used several doubtful assumptions, including the assumption that without sanctions Iraq would have maintained the pace of progress it had achieved in reducing infant and under-five mortality rates; that the extra deaths resulted from the failure to maintain the same reduction in mortality rates; and that this number of "excess deaths" could be attributed to sanctions. Each assumption may be challenged separately; the three together are hotly contestable. But what is not deniable is that sanctions did cause the deaths of more innocent Iraqis than the number of soldiers killed during the Gulf War proper.[44] This is why the international community of states lost the appetite for imposing comprehensive open-ended sanctions again. It seems that the tool of comprehensive sanctions has disappeared, at least for the time being, from the Chapter VII toolkit because of the collateral damage it causes.

Many of the problems associated with sanctions can be minimized through imposing smart sanctions that target members of the ruling elite and are limited in their application.[45] Examples include restrictions on overseas travel and financial transactions and a freeze on foreign assets. All UN sanctions since 1994 have been targeted rather than comprehensive, such as financial sanctions against designated individuals and entities (for instance, the Taliban), embargoes on oil and conflict diamonds against the National Union for the Total Independence of Angola (UNITA) in Angola, and the sweeping counterterrorism measures of resolution 1373, which was adopted after 9/11. Humanitarian impact assessments that measure such indicators as public health and population displacement are now standard practice in sanctions policy. Designated humanitarian agencies can be given blanket exemptions from sanctions.

Smart sanctions are held out as a possible way for the UN to mitigate the subversion of humanitarian goals and efforts. Their costs to third-party countries are negligible. They reduce perverse incentives and consequences such as enriching the elite who manipulate the black market while impoverishing the general population. In addition, the removal of aid denies regimes the capacity to control people by controlling the delivery of aid. They also avoid long-term damage to the social, educational, health, and physical infrastructure. Above all, they make clear to the people that the international community does discriminate between the sins of the leaders and the distress of the people. As Andrew Mack and Asif Khan assert, "They are politically easier to initiate and to sustain in the long run and less likely to bring the sanctions instrument into disrepute."[46]

Their track record in ensuring compliance with UN resolutions is highly "uneven."[47] The difficulties associated with imposing, monitoring, and enforcing "smart" sanctions will become known only with more experience. For example, the well-intentioned arms embargoes ran into

TABLE 8.1. Child Mortality Rates in Iraq, 1960–2005

	1960	1970	1980	1990	1995	1998	2005
Deaths under 5 years old per 1,000 live births	171	127	83	50	117	125	105
Deaths at birth per 1,000 live births	117	90	63	40	98	103	102

Source: UNICEF, *Iraq and Maternal Mortality Survey* (New York: UNICEF, 1999), and *State of the World's Children 2007* (New York: UNICEF, 2007), 103.

the problem of a buyer's market. Another problem is that the Security Council's sanctions resolutions need to be translated into national legislation,[48] which requires competence in the technical drafting of relevant laws, competent surveillance and regulatory mechanisms, and regulatory and law enforcement personnel who are free of corruption to monitor and enforce the laws. Violent conflicts increasingly are internal and involve rapacious and criminal behavior in a regional environment of failed or criminalized states and of warring and profiteering factions who exploit a shadow economy.[49] On whom are the sanctions to be imposed? How are they to be enforced? Where is the financial incentive for the armed factions to comply with international demands instead of simply absorbing the extra costs? Where are the border control mechanisms and state institutions for regulating and controlling the flow of goods that are subject to sanctions? When sanctions are imposed, the people at large, who are already victims of war, dispossession, and dislocation, are further victimized by warlords, black marketeers, and armed gangs. The most marked effect of sanctions in such circumstances may be their disruption of relief efforts and activities. This is why, as Kofi Annan pointed out, all UN sanctions "should be effectively implemented and enforced by strengthening State capacity to implement sanctions, establishing well resourced monitoring mechanisms and mitigating humanitarian consequences."[50]

Three states organized conferences to study how the technical elements of sanctions regimes could be strengthened: these are known as the Interlaken (1998–1999), Bonn-Berlin (1999–2000), and Stockholm (2001–2003) processes.[51] The Swiss were behind the first study, which looked at the implications for the financial and banking sectors of sanctions regimes that target financial assets and transactions. The Germans followed with a study of sanctions that focus on arms embargoes and travel restrictions. Then the Swedes focused on implementation-related issues: guidelines for implementing sanctions on arms, financial institutions, commodities (such as conflict diamonds), and travel and guidelines for improving the UN sanctions committees themselves.

Whenever sanctions are imposed, the Security Council creates a sanctions committee. It is a committee of the whole—that is, all fifteen members of the Security Council serve, represented at deputy permanent representative level. The chair of such a committee is usually the permanent representative of a country that is not one of the permanent five (P-5) members of the council and acts in a personal capacity, taking instructions supposedly only from the council itself rather than from his or her capital, as is the case within the Security Council proper. As with most UN bodies, sanctions committees typically do not have enough resources and technically competent personnel. An exception was the committee in charge of monitoring sanctions against UNITA in Angola. Chaired by Canadian ambassador Robert Fowler, with the full backing of his government, the committee produced a revolution in UN affairs by "naming and shaming" sanctions-busting countries and leaders. But some of the findings of the 2000 report of this sanctions committee were disputed, and many of its recommendations were ignored.[52] The committee's tactics and report provoked hostility in some developing countries that were already critical of aid conditionality by donor governments and international financial institutions.[53]

In April 2000, the Security Council established a working group to develop recommendations on improving the effectiveness of UN sanctions. The group, chaired by Bangladeshi ambassador Anwarul Chowdhury, reached broad agreement on many items but failed to agree on a final report. Nevertheless its draft report contained many interesting recommendations. These were divided into three clusters. The group recommended more staff, expertise, and resources to upgrade the Secretariat's capacity to administer sanctions. It also recommended that the UN construct a database of outside experts. It recommended that the standardized language developed by the Interlaken and Bonn-Berlin processes be used to design resolutions, that specific items and designated humanitarian agencies be exempted from sanctions, and that the conditions that would enable sanctions to be lifted be specified. It also recommended that the Security

Council name the actions it would take short of terminating sanctions in order to reward partial compliance. Finally, the working group suggested that the Security Council could urge states with the relevant expertise to provide technical and legal assistance to requesting states and that it analyze third-party effects in sanctions assessment impact reports.[54]

The two issues on which the working group could not reach consensus were whether there should be time limits for terminating sanctions and whether sanctions committees could move to making decisions by majority voting. In a similar vein, efforts to use the Security Council as the enforcement arm of the international community of states in order to uphold global norms are undermined, to some extent, by the lack of transparency and democratic norms in the council's decision-making procedures. Given that sanctions are mandatory for everyone, the closed-door method of making decisions does grate.

Often the threat of sanctions is more effective than the actual imposition of sanctions. Target regimes respond to threats with gestures and offers of concessions and partial compliance, although it is not always clear whether these are delaying tactics or negotiating gambits. By contrast, imposing sanctions produces a hardening of positions, perhaps because moderate political forces that are willing to compromise are discredited by the international community's clear rejection of earlier gestures.[55]

Another recent notable trend is the involvement of members of the Third UN in designing and evaluating sanctions through their presence on expert working groups. Members of this group serve as academic specialists, as members of private sector firms, and as NGO advocates and field workers.[56] In the Kimberley Process Certification Scheme that was designed to halt the trade in conflict diamonds, for example, the enthusiasm and energy of NGO activists combined with the legitimacy of the UN and the technical expertise of De Beers to come up with a standardized and credible system for certificates of origin for the export of legitimate diamonds. This was paired with the threat of exposure (the diamond industry would be devastated if diamonds became associated in the public mind with objects of shame) and forfeiture of contraband conflict diamonds.[57]

Still, major problems remain, as two analysts point out: "While smart sanctions may seem logically compelling and conceptually attractive . . . the operational problems—due to persistent technical inadequacies, legal loopholes, institutional weaknesses, budgetary and staff scarcities, and political constraints—are daunting."[58] Thus, the Security Council sanctions committee concluded that sanctions imposed against Al Qaeda and the former Taliban by resolution 1267 of 1999 had had little impact on the operations of these groups.[59] There is still a pressing need for serious studies of the compliance and transaction costs of targeted, well-thought-out sanctions regimes with built-in monitoring and enforcement mechanisms that are as effective as they are credible. For example, how is it possible to impose secondary sanctions on sanctions-busting countries, on the one hand, and support third-party states that are adversely affected by sanctions, on the other? What criteria and ground rules govern exceptions and exemptions? What impact do time limits and sunset clauses have? We even have questions about the criteria for smart sanctions: Should they be established on the basis of efficacy? If they are not proving efficacious, should they be lifted, should more comprehensive sanctions be imposed, or should they lead to military enforcement? As we saw in chapter 3, the dilemmas about how to enforce compliance with international norms and treaties by striking the right balance between force, diplomacy, and sanctions haunt the international community with particular urgency with regard to combating the threat of and from nuclear weapons.

Conclusion: NGOs as Major Actors in Global Human Rights Governance

States are more eager to endorse human rights in the abstract than they are to create enforcement machinery, and they are more open to weak supervision of policies than they are to effective UN enforcement of rights. Consequently, UN instruments and techniques to implement human rights norms and standards range from encouragement and coaxing to naming and shaming, but usually these instruments lack meaningful punishment, especially since economic sanctions themselves have a checkered history.

While the UN is better qualified than NGOs and other international organizations to set international human rights standards, Amnesty International and Human Rights Watch are better able to investigate human rights abuses at the grassroots level and the International Committee of the Red Cross (ICRC) has a better record of investigating compliance with international humanitarian law.[60] Measuring success is difficult, perhaps even impossible. No government will voluntarily admit having given in to external pressure. In many cases there may well be several influences at work simultaneously on a government. For the UN, Amnesty International,

Human Rights Watch, or the ICRC to claim success in pressuring government could be boastful, only partially true, and possibly counterproductive for access to victims in future cases. The fact that these organizations cannot demonstrate success in every instance does not diminish the worth of ongoing efforts. The three UNs have achieved some significant goals. Because of the pressure they have created, national laws and international instruments have been improved, many political prisoners have been freed, and some victims of abuse have been compensated. And as we shall see in chapter 10, on occasion the international community of states has sought to give meaning to the phrase "never again."

Using multiple levels of analysis is helpful for understanding the contemporary global governance of the human rights regime.[61] Examples could be chosen from virtually any continent and every decade since World War II to illustrate the various roles that civil society organizations and the First and Second UNs play in this issue area. A good contemporary example is Darfur. Cynicism among western governments and media about UN habits increased when African countries reelected the government of Sudan, which is under intense scrutiny for its atrocities in the south and in Darfur in the West, to one of Africa's slots on the UN Commission on Human Rights in 2004. Sichan Siv, the U.S. ambassador to ECOSOC, the body where the election took place, walked out in protest and said that the United States "will not participate in this absurdity."[62] When the General Assembly refused to vote on a resolution denouncing human rights violations in Sudan, U.S. ambassador John Danforth gave vent to his anger and frustration: "One wonders about the utility of the General Assembly on days like this."[63] The draft resolution to denounce Sudan's violations was sponsored by thirty-eight western countries but was opposed by developing countries, including nearly all the Islamic and African countries and China. In effect, African states decided to vote against a western-sponsored resolution condemning an African state, however aberrant its behavior. Yet earlier, junior and senior UN officials in New York and Geneva had provided consistent criticism of abuses committed in Darfur by or with the connivance of the government of Sudan. Another source of criticism was the UN's special representative in Sudan, Jan Pronk, whom the Sudanese government made persona non grata for his blog that was highly critical of Khartoum. Pronk's case illustrates that it is essential to distinguish between UN officials and UN member states when criticizing "the United Nations."

The relationship between human rights and the war on terror also illustrates the utility of examining multiple layers and multiple actors. UN officials, Amnesty International, Human Rights Watch, and the ICRC led the international push after 9/11 to hold the Bush administration accountable to international humanitarian law. UN high commissioner for human rights Mary Robinson claimed that the Bush administration had blocked her from remaining at her post because she had boldly criticized these policies.[64] Theo van Boven, the UN special rapporteur on torture who had once lost his UN position for being outspoken during the Cold War, also sharply criticized U.S. practices in the war on terror.[65] Under American pressure, the UN eliminated the job of its top investigator on human rights in Afghanistan, American scholar Cherif Bassiouni, because of his temerity in repeatedly criticizing the U.S. military for detaining Afghans without trial and for barring human rights monitors from U.S. prisons in the country.[66] The ICRC has played several roles in holding the United States to international standards of human rights governance. After visits to prisoners in Afghanistan, Guantánamo Bay, and Iraq, the ICRC reported (albeit discreetly) to Washington about the nature and scope of the prisoner abuses its delegates had witnessed. In mid-2003, it went public with its concern about how being held in indefinite detention in Guantánamo without charge or trial was affecting the mental health of detainees.[67] And it was the ICRC that insisted that with the transfer of sovereignty from the occupation authorities to an interim Iraqi government in June 2004, Saddam Hussein and many others had either to be released or charged with specific crimes.[68]

Parts of the UN system have made spasmodic efforts to hold the behavior of states to agreed human rights standards. For example, the Office of the UN High Commissioner for Human Rights has published advice on how the war against terrorism can be balanced with human rights standards and norms.[69] However, because of the politics of the relationship between the UN and the United States, these efforts have been largely ineffectual. By contrast, in their annual reports and in several more focused reports, Amnesty International and Human Rights Watch have tried to document continuing abuses in the name of the war on terror and mobilize public opinion against such practices.[70] In a toughly worded report issued in October 2004, Amnesty International argued that the U.S. response to 9/11 "has resulted in its own iconography of torture, cruelty and degradation."[71] Amnesty International praised Kofi Annan's statements emphasizing the absolute prohibition of torture and other cruel, inhuman, or degrading treatment.[72] The group's 2005 report drew attention to rights violations by the governments of Afghanistan, Australia, China, East Timor, Egypt, India, Israel, Malaysia, Nepal, the Philippines, Russia, Singapore, Thailand, and Uzbekistan, among others.[73] In her foreword to the report, Amnesty International secretary-general Irene Khan wrote that "the detention facility at Guantánamo Bay has become the gulag of our times, entrenching the practice of arbitrary and indefinite detention in violation of international law. Trials by military commissions have made a mockery of justice and due process." She added, "When the most powerful country in the world thumbs its nose at the rule of law and human rights, it grants a licence to others to commit abuse with impunity."[74] The gulag "hyperbole is wrong—but that's cold comfort to those of us who believe America should hold itself to a higher standard than 'we're better than the gulag.'"[75]

In its annual survey of the state of human rights in 2004, Human Rights Watch argued that abuses committed by the United States in Guantánamo and Iraq significantly weakened the world's ability to protect human rights. Not only does the United States invite others to mimic its policy by openly defying the law, but it reduces its leverage over others because Washington seems hypocritical when calling upon others to uphold principles that it violates. Human Rights Watch called on the Bush administration to set up a fully independent investigative commission to look into the Abu Ghraib prisoner abuses. At the same time, it criticized China and Russia in particular for contributing to the world's callous disregard of the large-scale deaths in Darfur in order to protect oil contracts and arms sales.[76] When investigations by the U.S. military exonerated U.S. generals who had direct or command responsibility for the prisoner abuses despite the similarity in the pattern of abuses from Guantánamo to Afghanistan and Iraq, Human Rights Watch called on the U.S. attorney general to appoint a special prosecutor and urged Congress to launch a bipartisan and independent investigation into the roles of senior officials, including the president, the defense secretary, and the former CIA director.[77]

So is the human rights glass half-empty or half-full? Contradictions abound: between the international public's expectations of justice and the determination of states to protect their sovereignty, between powerful states who seek geopolitical hegemony and other states who seek the protection of international law, and between rhetoric that promotes human rights norms and the absence of effective protection of rights. Perhaps in this arena of UN work more than any other, global governance is characterized by a dramatic discrepancy between commitments on paper and actual improvements in conditions. Is the West's almost exclusive emphasis on political freedom an accurate reflection of the core values of most people? Has the failure to seek the Universal Declaration's promise of social and economic justice been a fatal shortcoming? And what about the former standard-bearer's "exceptionalism"[78]—the practices of the United States that set it outside the global legal consensus on issues such as the International Criminal Court and its onslaught on international humanitarian law as part of its war on terror?

These painful examples illustrate the long and ongoing struggle to establish a working and workable international system of human rights. Here, as elsewhere, we confront the stark reality that the territorial state remains the most important legal and political entity in the modern world despite the obvious importance of ethnic, religious, and cultural identifications and an increasing number of actors in civil society everywhere. The state constitutes the basic building block of the United Nations, and the members of the First UN ultimately control the UN agenda and action on human rights, although they are pushed and pulled by human rights groups and UN secretariat officials. The global governance of human rights is remarkably different and better in many ways than it was in 1945, but state authorities still control the most important final decisions and traditional national interests still trump individual human rights far too often.

There is a related danger. Human rights seek to protect individuals from oppression by a collectivity, whether the collective be a state, a society, or a religious system. But the responsibility for enacting appropriate national legislation and constructing the requisite bureaucratic, police, and judicial machinery for monitoring and enforcing human rights is vested in the state. Social and religious groups, whether they are in the majority or minority, can capture the political agenda and subvert the process to "protect" group human rights by penalizing individuals who dissent and depart from community-sanctioned views and behavior. And states can band together at the United Nations to proscribe injuries to religious sensibilities at the expense of individual rights to freedom of expression, for example the publishing of cartoons that are offensive to members of religious groups. This is why even as advocates seek desirable advances in the global governance of human rights, they must constantly hold fast to the critical kernel of truth that human rights is about protecting individual beliefs and actions from group-sanctioned morality at the local, national, and global levels.

9

Protecting against Pandemics

- Antecedents: Smallpox as a Model
- Knowledge Gaps: From Ignorance to Ignorance
- Normative Gaps: A Missing Prelude to Action
- Policy Gaps: The Need to Scale Up the Attack
- Institutional Gaps: Necessary but Insufficient Organizations
- Compliance Gaps: Who Is Listening?
- Close Calls: SARS and Avian Flu
- Conclusion: Fitful and Halting Progress

The rapidity with which some diseases can spread to become global pandemics; the emergence of new, deadly, and highly contagious diseases; the absence of border defenses to protect against such diseases; and the greater vulnerability of poor countries and poor people because of virtually nonexistent preventive and negligible therapeutic care are among the down sides of globalization. A deadly cocktail of exotic diseases crosses borders free of passport and visa regulations due to the back-and-forth movement of business travelers, tourists, traders, soldiers, migrants, and refugees; the modes of transport they use; incubation periods that ensure that many who contract diseases develop symptoms only after borders have been crossed; and the ability of some diseases to jump across plant, bird, and animal species.

Over the last decade, the world has witnessed four potential scares: severe acute respiratory syndrome (SARS, 2002–2003), the Ebola virus (2000–2008), avian influenza (bird flu, 2005–2006), and the H1N1 flu (swine flu, 2008–2010). In combination with HIV/AIDS, they pushed to the very top of the international agenda the issue of the global governance of health. The task is huge, ranging from gathering statistics to creating codes of conduct about breast feeding, from finding ways around patent rights so that poor countries can have access to expensive drugs to efforts to halt smoking. In the case of the latter issue, efforts range from WHO lobbying to halt smoking inside UN buildings to the 2008 pledge by U.S. billionaires Michael Bloomberg and Bill Gates to devote $500 million to public education in developing countries about the lethal consequences of smoking.[1]

We have chosen the example of pandemics, more particularly the HIV/AIDS pandemic, because they illustrate Mark Zacher and Tania Keefe's insight that the planet is "united by contagion."[2] While other international efforts have certainly contributed to increasing life expectancy and improving health in many ways, we concentrate on the acute difficulties in dealing with contemporary pandemics because they suggest lessons for global governance in general. These lessons include the need to monitor infectious diseases, the need to implement emergency medical controls during outbreaks, the need for rules that inhibit the spread of diseases across borders, the need for financial and material assistance to facilitate long-term health programs, and the need for international legal reforms that promote improvements in access to health programs.

Almost 40 million people in the world—approximately 1 percent of the world's total adult population—were living with HIV at the end of 2005. In 2005, 2.8 million died of the disease and another 4.1 million were newly infected.[3] Every day in 2007, almost 7,000 people, including around 1,500 children, mostly newborn, were infected with HIV around the world. As many as 6,000 people die of AIDS every day.[4]

The Security Council held a summit meeting on HIV/AIDS in January 2000 with U.S. ambassador Richard Holbrooke as president. Later that year it adopted resolution 1308, which declared the pandemic a threat to international peace and security.[5] AIDS is a human security issue because of the vicious chain of infection, communal devastation, and social-national disintegration.[6] It is a personal security issue because as prevalence rates reach 5–20 percent, gains in health, life expectancy, and infant mortality are wiped out; agricultural production and food supplies decrease; and families and communities start breaking apart. It is an economic security issue because a 10 percent prevalence rate of HIV/AIDS can reduce the growth of national income by one-third, while a 20 percent infection rate will cause GDP to fall by 1 percent per year.[7] It damages communal security by breaking down national and social institutions and decimating the ranks of the educated and mobile, such as civil servants, teachers, health professionals, and police. It damages national security by enfeebling security forces and corroding the pillars of economic growth and institutional resilience that protect nations against external and internal conflict. It is arguably an international security issue because of its potential to exacerbate international security challenges (disintegration of any one state has potential cross-border implications for neighbors through economic dislocation, refugee flows, and communal violence) and its potential to undermine international capacity for conflict resolution, for example with respect to peacekeeping.

HIV/AIDS infection rates are still increasing in many countries, and defeating the pandemic is the world's highest health priority. Sadly, in Sub-Saharan Africa, women make up the majority of victims and face additional risks of poverty, stigmatization, and social ostracism. These are failures not of science but of policy, politics, and governance.

Unlike earlier examples in this book, it is difficult to argue for even a partial success story when it comes to global governance to combat the spread of HIV/AIDS. For this very reason it offers a useful counterpoint to other illustrations. Attempts to fill gaps in order to confront this pandemic have been fitful, hesitant, and, at least to date, largely inadequate and unsatisfactory. But first, we discuss the successful historical example of efforts to fight the disease of smallpox.

Antecedents: Smallpox as a Model

Mark Zacher divides global health collaboration into three historical regime periods. In the first, from the mid-nineteenth to the early twentieth century, states engaged in protracted negotiations that culminated in the adoption of the International Sanitary Convention in 1903. During the second period, which lasted into the 1980s, states largely ignored the International Health Regulations, as the 1903 rules came to be called. The third period, which dates from the 1990s, has seen a proliferation in multilateral health cooperation.[8] Global health governance was weak from the birth of the regulations in 1903 through the 1980s and did not get stronger until the last decade of the twentieth century.

The international community of states can readily call on the experience of a successful campaign to eradicate a major killer disease. The campaign succeeded when the norm of eradication was accepted, the political will to eradicate the disease was mustered, and the necessary financial and organizational resources were fully mobilized. The elimination of smallpox provides us with perhaps the most spectacular illustration of why having a normative consensus and solid knowledge is essential as we endeavor to improve global governance for pandemics and attack other global health challenges in the years ahead.

For more than 3,000 years smallpox was a scourge on humanity, feared for its high fatality rate—often it accounted for 10 percent of all deaths each year—and for the pockmarks that disfigured those who survived.Edward Jenner, an English country doctor, discovered vaccination in 1796,[9] and the spread of vaccination led to a marked decrease in the death toll from smallpox in industrial countries. Yet the disease continued almost unabated in Africa, Asia, and Latin America. In the early 1950s—a century and a half after the introduction of vaccination—an estimated 50 million cases of smallpox occurred in the world each year. In 1967, the figure fell to around 10–15 million because of vaccination;[10] some 2 million people succumbed to the disease that year.[11]

In 1953, the WHO's first director-general, Brock Chisholm, attempted unsuccessfully to persuade the World Health Assembly, the WHO's governing body, to undertake a global program to eradicate smallpox. Five years later, a Soviet delegate persuaded the WHO to accept responsibility for a global program, but only minimal funds were available. The WHO was preoccupied at the time with a major and eventually unsuccessful effort to eradicate malaria, and many were skeptical about the feasibility of smallpox eradication, especially in Africa.

In 1966, the World Health Assembly established an Intensified Smallpox Eradication Program—though WHO officials still had doubts about its potential for success. At that time, the entire staff numbered just over 3,300 persons, and only about 150 professionals were available to oversee smallpox programs in more than fifty countries.[12]

Once started, however, the program advanced rapidly. A strategic plan concentrated on mass vaccination campaigns, using freeze-dried vaccines of quality assessed by special teams. A surveillance system was set up to detect and investigate cases and contain outbreaks. Three principles were critical in these efforts. First, all countries would need to participate, and there would need to be some form of regional and global coordination. Second, programs would need to be flexible and adapt to the specifics of each country. And third, ongoing field and laboratory research would be needed to evaluate progress and solve problems as they arose.

By the early 1970s, smallpox was on the retreat. The Intensified Smallpox Eradication Program's containment strategy consisted of deploying squads wherever a possible case was discovered. The squads would then make a diagnosis, identify and vaccinate all contacts, and swiftly contain the spread of infection. By 1975, the number of countries where the disease could still be found had fallen from thirty to three—India, Bangladesh, and Ethiopia. By the end of the year, the last case of *variola major,* the most serious form of the disease, was reported in Bangladesh.[13]

Attention then turned to Ethiopia, where the last case was reported in August 1976, but not before nomads had carried the disease across the border into Somalia, where an epidemic occurred in mid-1977. In October, the last case of *variola minor* was finally reported in Somalia. Three years later, the WHO declared victory. The total cost of the eleven-year effort had been around $300 million, one-third of which had come from international sources and two-thirds from the affected countries themselves. The total cost was the equivalent at the time of the cost of three fighter-bombers. Because of eradication, the world now saves at least $2 billion each year by avoiding the cost of purchasing smallpox vaccine, the cost of administration (including applying international health regulations), and other costs.[14] This certainly is one clear way to measure the importance of redefining sovereignty to include fighting diseases far afield with as much vigor as diseases closer to home. Most of the savings have been in the budgets of industrialized countries, which have been able to avoid the up-front costs of implementing smallpox health regulations.

Inspired in part by the successful experience with smallpox, the eradication of polio is under way. The vaccines invented by Jonas Salk (1955) and Albert Sabin (1962) made it possible—with adequate resources and international cooperation that has ignored national boundaries—to come close to extinguishing this disease. In 2006, fewer than 2,000 cases were reported worldwide, and only four countries (Nigeria, India, Pakistan, and Afghanistan) were still polio-endemic.[15] Efforts under way by the WHO and UNICEF lead us to believe that we soon may witness the conquest of this disease as well.

Knowledge Gaps: From Ignorance to Ignorance

We return to the story of HIV/AIDS. In a mere twenty-five years, HIV spread rapidly from a few scattered "hot spots" to all parts of the world, killing 25 million people of the 65 million who had been infected.[16] As with most other subjects we look at in this book, the knowledge gaps were of two types: empirical knowledge of the facts of the case—what was the disease, where was it breaking out, what was the rate of new infections, and so forth; and theoretical knowledge that could link cause and effect to outbreak, spread, and cure.

It was not until the 1980s that the scientific and policy community first began to identify a deadly new disease with the potential to become an epidemic. AIDS was first reported by the U.S. Centers for Disease Control and Prevention on 5 June 1981, when it recorded a cluster of *pneumocystis carinii* pneumonia in five homosexual men in Los Angeles. Once the disease was identified, scientists retraced past records to identify the earliest known cases of HIV infection. Their research included a plasma sample taken from an adult male in Kinshasa (in today's Democratic Republic of the Congo) in 1959; tissue samples from a young African American who died in 1969; and tissue samples from a Norwegian sailor who died around 1976.[17]

This early research was carried out outside the UN system. But once the disease was identified and the magnitude and gravity of the potential pandemic was recognized, the UN's political neutrality and global mobilizing and convening capacity made it a natural center for collecting and collating data from around the world, identifying and disseminating best practices for combating the disease, channeling international technical and financial assistance to needy countries, and promoting new norms.

The first cases were detected in the early and mid-1980s in Africa. In one case, 75 percent of prostitutes tested in Rwanda were found to be HIV positive in 1983. Central Africa had already been identified around this time as being a place where AIDS was likely to spread.[18] The World Bank issued its first strategy report on AIDS in 1988, describing the epidemic in Africa as an emergency that required immediate appropriate action because of an environment that was highly conducive to the spread of the disease.[19] In 1991, a World Bank/IMF journal warned that 30 million people could be infected by the disease by 2000 unless action was taken immediately.[20]

In the 1980s, scientists established Africa as the source of the virus. They also identified a virus in monkeys that in some mysterious way had jumped across species to humans. They were still left with some big puzzles. Why in the 1980s but not before? And why the rapid spread of the disease in Africa? One set of answers to the last question focused on the role of "core transmitters" such as prostitutes and their clients, in particular truck drivers and itinerant workers. Public health specialist and molecular biologist Helen Epstein argues that this explanation is simply wrong and that there is very little empirical evidence to support it. Africans overall are no more promiscuous than westerners as measured by number of sexual partners over a lifetime, casual sex encounters, or even sex with prostitutes.[21] Western sexual norms (in both the "is" and "ought" senses of the word) range from casual sexual encounters (one-night stands) to sex only within marriage. But in the West, where a very high percentage of marriages end in divorce and an even higher percentage of partnerships between unmarried people are short-lived, many people practice "serial monogamy," or monogamous relationships with a sequence of partners. What is different in Africa, Epstein argues, is the number of concurrent relationships, or the long-term multiple partnerships of women as well as men. When both men and women are in long-term relationships with several partners concurrently and those relationships take place in different locations, they form a giant web for the rapid transmission of the virus throughout the sexually active population. The result is the tragedy of HIV/AIDS.

The statistics on AIDS as of 2005, broken down by the world's major regions, are summarized in table 9.1. On aggregate numbers as well as proportionately, Sub-Saharan Africa is the worst affected. Encouragingly, in Asia the share of HIV-infected people has been declining in Cambodia, Thailand, and parts of India. However, the rate of infection has been increasing in China, Vietnam, and Indonesia. The Joint United Nations Programme on HIV/AIDS (UNAIDS) suffered a slight erosion of credibility when it significantly revised its figures in November 2007, stating that the global number of people living with HIV had fallen from almost 40 to 33 million.[22] Rejecting criticism that it had been unnecessarily alarmist in its previous estimate in order to gain publicity, the organization attributed the downscaling to better survey methodology. The decrease in the number of new cases from over 3 million in the 1990s to 2.5 million in 2006 and the decrease in annual deaths over the past two years to 2.1 million in 2007 are partly the result of prevention and care and wider access to antiretroviral (ARV) drugs.

Much valuable time was lost in initiating effective preventive remedies because the theoretical question about cause and effect was answered by western scientists through a lens of prejudice and ignorance. These attitudes in turn fed into the prejudice and ignorance of African leaders and elites. Hypotheses were postulated that stated that the promiscuous

TABLE 9.1: Regional Breakdown of HIV/AIDS Statistics, 2007

	PEOPLE LIVING WITH HIV (MILLIONS)	NEW INFECTIONS (THOU-SANDS)	AIDS DEATHS (THOU-SANDS)	ADULT PREVALENCE IN 2005 (PERCENT)
Sub-Saharan Africa	22.5	1,700	1,600	6.1
Asia	4.8	432	302	0.4
Latin America	1.6	100	58	0.5
North America & Europe	2.1	77	33	0.5
Eastern Europe & Central Asia	1.6	150	55	0.8
Middle East & Northern Africa	0.4	35	25	0.2
Caribbean	0.2	17	11	1.6
Oceania	0.1	14	1	0.3
Total	33.2	2,500	2,100	1.0

Sources: UNAIDS and WHO, *07 AIDS Epidemic Update* (Geneva: UNAIDS, December 2007), 38–41, available at http://news.bbc.co.uk/2/shared/bsp/hi/pdfs/20_11_07_hiv .pdf (accessed 23 June 2009). UNAIDS, "Global Facts and Figures 06" (Geneva: UNAIDS, May 2006), 1, available at http://data.unaids.org/pub/GlobalReport/2006/200605-FS_ globalfactsfigures_en.pdf (accessed 18 November 2007). Discrepancies in totals are the result of rounding.

behavior of Africans was the main driver of the spread of HIV/AIDS. The result was a sweeping stigmatization that in turn provoked a widespread attitude of denial. Others accused the white apartheid regime in South Africa, the CIA, and/or western pharmaceutical companies of conspiring against black Africans at the cost of African lives.[23] It would be interesting to know what proportion of Sub-Saharan Africans are believed by western publics to be infected. No region has a monopoly on ignorance. But to the dismay of many African scientists and to the incomprehension of all well-disposed westerners, the president and health minister of South Africa—the most developed country in all of Sub-Saharan Africa—are among the foremost deniers of the reality of HIV/AIDS in their country and continent. And they also propose herbal cures rather than proven drug cocktails.[24]

Normative Gaps: A Missing Prelude to Action

In the early years of scientists' awareness of how HIV-AIDS was transmitted, their attention was focused on male homosexuals and on men who had sex with prostitutes. But these two populations created special challenges for public health workers who wanted to educate the public about how to prevent transmission, let alone create new norms about sexual behavior. First of all, many men who did not identify primarily as homosexual engaged in casual sex with other men and many men who had sex exclusively with other men were not open about their sexuality; targeting only openly homosexual men with new information would not stop the spread of the disease. Second, it was a near-impossible task to identify the population of men that had sex with prostitutes.

Both homosexuality and prostitution were taboo topics in most societies in the 1980s. It was very difficult for public health workers to reach people with education about new norms of sexual behavior for multiple reasons that had to do with the fear of both the disease and of open discussion of sexual practices, the role of religious leaders in shaping norms of sexual behavior, concepts of privacy, misogyny, homophobia, and macho notions of sexuality. The fact that these topics were taboo generated hypotheses that were uncomfortable for many societies. They also generated their own logic of denial and silence based on social stigma, which has made consensus on normative behavior very problematic for HIV/AIDS. With such ignorance on display, normative advance was difficult.

Tragically, efforts to tackle the HIV/AIDS pandemic have been different from earlier international efforts to tackle smallpox and polio. Of course, the absence of an AIDS vaccine makes the case anomalous in some ways, but even so the basic international approach differs from approaches to smallpox and polio because there is as yet no real normative consensus about how to proceed. Instead of seeing common threats and attacking them regardless of the location of illness, the approach is piecemeal and oriented toward narrow national conceptions of interest and approach. Today, in nine countries, all in Sub-Saharan Africa, more than one adult in ten is infected with the HIV virus. In Botswana, 24 percent of adults are infected, in South Africa 18 percent, in Zimbabwe 15 percent, and in Swaziland 26 percent.[25]

The world is gradually becoming more conscious of the magnitude of the problem. "We are at the beginning of a pandemic, not the middle, not the end," the director of the White House Office of National AIDS policy stated in 2000.[26] Alas, even if a vaccine is developed tomorrow, it would be too late for the 35 million people now living with HIV and AIDS and for the many who will follow. At the 1999 five-year review of the International Conference on Population and Development, the United Nations set a goal of cutting the rate of new infections by 25 percent among the population 15 to 24 years old by 2005 in the countries most affected.[27] That objective was not met, but even attaining it would not have stopped the toll from doubling and doubling again. Part of the effort to raise awareness of the nature of the problem and the need for drastic action has come from celebrities; Box 9.1 profiles a few individuals who are certainly a very visible part of contemporary global governance. We emphasize the contributions of the Third United Nations because, as Andrew Cooper puts it, "the future of global governance will not remain the typecast preserve of those who look, speak, and act in orthodox ways."[28]

In January 2000, then U.S. vice-president Al Gore articulated Washington's position to the Security Council, which was addressing Africa's social security ills: "Today, in sight of all the world, we are putting the AIDS crisis at the top of the world's agenda. We must face the threat as we are facing it right here, in one of the great forums of the earth—openly, boldly, with urgency and compassion."[29] But his loss to George W. Bush in the presidential election later that year meant that a great champion of UN norms was not available in the position of head of state to lead the worldwide fight against the deadly and rapidly spreading disease.

Policy Gaps: The Need to Scale Up the Attack

To date, efforts to address the HIV/AIDS pandemic—and the near-misses with SARS, the Ebola virus, and avian flu along with a question mark for the swine flu as we go to press—have been conducted in a different way than the successful efforts to eradicate smallpox and polio. Of course, the clarity of understanding about the virology and epidemiology of smallpox was a precondition for eradicating that disease. Nonetheless, the embrace of cooperation and transnational interests and a normative agenda instead of pursing eradication on a national basis was also essential. The HIV/AIDS story is one of failing to prevent the disaster and minimal international cooperation.

BOX 9.1. Celebrities as Actors in Global Governance

As Paul Collier has noted, the policies and practices of intergovernmental and nongovernmental organizations are influenced by "development biz" and "development buzz."[1] In the field of global health governance, the increasingly influential role of what Andrew F. Cooper terms "celebrity diplomats" is intriguing.[2] Perhaps the first contributor was U.S. actor and comedian Danny Kaye, who worked for UNICEF as an ambassador-at-large for over thirty years. Moving beyond pledging funds to worthwhile charitable causes, former leaders, businessmen, and even rock stars have established their own foundations and research institutes to push the delivery of medical services forward in developing countries and to advocate for the elimination of widespread infectious diseases.

Under the leadership of former U.S. president Bill Clinton, for example, the Clinton Foundation's HIV/AIDS Initiative has not only worked with major pharmaceutical suppliers to lower the price of HIV/AIDS treatment but is also actively involved with the newly established international drug purchase facility UNITAID. In 2007, the two organizations partnered in a $50 million effort to provide access to treatment for 100,000 children in forty countries.[3] The extraordinary dimension of the activity of private foundations is illustrated by the $9 billion in grants the Bill & Melinda Gates Foundation has given to global health governance initiatives from 1998 to 2007.[4]

Rock singer Bob Geldof came to development fame in 1985 when he mobilized fellow musicians for the Live Aid concert to raise money for relief efforts for those affected by the Ethiopian famine and other famines in Africa. The Live Aid concert was watched live by 1.5 million people in over 100 countries and raised some $280 million.

In addition to this kind of publicity, on-the-ground activity, and fundraising, celebrity diplomats have also gained access to major world leaders in order to pressure them to keep and increase their financial commitments to global health challenges. The role of singers Bono and Bob Geldof at the G-8 Summit in Gleneagles, Scotland, in 2005 is particularly exemplary in this regard. The two pressured the world's most powerful leaders to take robust action regarding African debt relief and health governance. Using contrasting methods—Bono had one-on-one meetings with four of the top-tier leaders, while Geldof piloted the Live 8 enterprise—the two advocates pushed G-8 leaders toward a much-publicized commitment to provide $60 billion over the coming years to treat victims of AIDS, tuberculosis, and malaria.

At the same time, celebrities often work in tandem with analysts; Bono works with Columbia University's Jeffrey Sachs.[5] It is hard to disagree with Heribert Dieter and Rajiv Kumar that "the recipes being suggested by Bono and Sachs are breath-takingly one dimensional and akin to the sweeping propositions of the 1960s."[6] Whatever one's views about the substance of the arguments, however, this manifestation of the Third UN is "one more signal that the traditional script of international relations is changing."[7]

We are grateful to Kelly Jackson of the Centre for International Governance Innovation in Waterloo, Canada, for invaluable assistance with the material for Box 9.1.

1. Paul Collier, *The Bottom Billion: Why the Poorest Countries Are Failing and What Can Be Done about It* (Oxford: Oxford University Press, 2007), 4.

2. Andrew F. Cooper, *Celebrity Diplomacy* (Boulder, Colo.: Paradigm Publishers, 2007).

3. "Clinton Foundation Announces Breakthroughs in Pediatric HIV/AIDS Treatment," available at http://www.infectiousdiseasenews.com/article/33575. aspx (accessed 11 August 2009).

4. David McCoy, Gayatri Kembhavi, Jinesh Patel, and Akish Luintel, "The Bill & Melinda Gates Foundation's Grant-Making Programme for Global Health," *The Lancet* 373, no. 9675 (May 2009): 1645–1653.

5. Jeffrey Sachs, *The End of Poverty* (New York: Penguin, 2005). Bono is the author of the foreword to Sachs's book.

6. Heribert Dieter and Rajiv Kumar, "The Downside of Celebrity Diplomacy: The Neglected Complexity of Development," *Global Governance* 14, no. 3 (2008): 259.

7. Andrew F. Cooper, "Beyond One Image Fits All: Bono and the Complexity of Celebrity Governance," *Global Governance* 14, no. 3 (2008): 265.

The response by western governments was sluggish to begin with, but it was reasonably effective once western public health workers fully grasped the urgency and magnitude of the crisis. In contrast, African governments often responded (and some still do respond) with denials, evasions, and conspiracy theories. The response of the UN system has shown a disconnect between the swelling international bureaucracy devoted to AIDS and results obtained in the field. Yet the UN system aggressively promotes the need for a comprehensive response to get ahead of the epidemic; UN officials argue that HIV prevention efforts should be intensified and scaled up and that access to treatment and care should be expanded. According to UNAIDS, scaling up available prevention strategies in 125 low- and middle-income countries would avert 28 million new infections in the period 2005–2015—more than half the projected new infections that would take place using present interventions—and save $24 billion in treatment costs.[30]

The initial U.S. policy response at the time of the Reagan administration in the 1980s, was one of confusion, uncertainty, and buck-passing.[31] But this was not the case for long. Both public health officials and the activist gay community publicized the threat of the frightening new disease. The U.S. Congress funded research into causes, treatment, and preventive strategies while the gay community encouraged safe sex practices as the primary method of reducing infection rates.[32] The net result was that HIV/AIDS did not spread alarmingly and has been kept mostly under control through expensive yet widely available antiretroviral drugs. The U.S. pattern has been more or less replicated in all the industrialized western countries.

This was and still is not the case in Africa, which has been the main theater where this particular tragedy has played out. Because of the refusal of leaders to accept and act on information that has already been detailed above, the disease has cross-infected the heterosexual population in general and is still spreading more widely. In 2007, 22.5 million Sub-Saharan Africans were believed to be HIV-positive; the population was being infected at a rate of 1.7 million each year.[33]

The international AIDS industry often privileges the goal of capturing more funding and meeting donor priorities instead of pursuing effective solutions to problems in the countries and populations in need and at risk. For example, unlike the worldwide industry behind the distribution of condoms as an AIDS prevention policy, there is no multimillion industry and bureaucracy to profit from and thus support a policy of single-partner sexual fidelity and abstinence, which played a role in reducing HIV transmission in Uganda.[34]

The World Bank's HIV/AIDS policy is set out in a handbook that embraces "managing for results" (governance by slogan is an incurable ailment of international organizations).[35] This strategy consists of a continuous six-stage cycle presented in a flow chart: formulate or revise the HIV strategy → analyze the evidence with respect to outcomes and indicators ↔ select the critical interventions, cost them, and identify the resources for funding them → monitor the results → evaluate the changes in the epidemic → feed the evidence into the next strategy. To make progress, there is a need to scale up and sustain HIV prevention, treatment, and follow-up care. To make the programs more effective, there is a need to integrate HIV into national development plans and enter into partnerships at the country and international level.

UNAIDS offers a six-point policy template for dealing with HIV:

- Strengthen prevention services and education targeted especially at high-risk cohorts like young people, HIV-infected pregnant women, drug users, prostitutes, homosexuals, prisoners;
- Improve access to treatment and care;
- Expand and strengthen human resources and systems;
- Make prevention and treatment products (condoms, ARV drugs) more widely available and affordable through appropriate fiscal, monetary, and regulatory instruments;
- Invest in research and development (R&D); and
- Focus on the social impacts of AIDS to counter ignorance, stigma, and discrimination.[36]

Institutional Gaps:
Necessary but Insufficient Organizations

The institutional core of global health governance is the World Health Organization, founded in 1948. Reflecting the universal nature of its mandate and concern, the WHO is one of the UN's largest, most professional, and most respected specialized agencies. Since 1948, it has contributed in essential ways to the dramatic increase in life expectancy and other improvements in overall health.[37] And as we saw earlier, of its many global initiatives, none has been more acclaimed than the successful campaign to eradicate smallpox.

However, the existence of a respected institution does not necessarily mean that protecting the human species from a pandemic will occur— the UN system's key player was largely missing in action for some time in efforts to confront HIV/AIDS. Early in 1986, the World Health Organization still regarded AIDS as an ailment of the promiscuous few. It was U.S. AIDS researcher Jonathan Mann who convinced the WHO's director-general, Halfdan Mahler, that AIDS was not merely another infectious disease. Mann saw AIDS as much more than simply a virus and understood that it flourishes in, and reinforces, conditions of poverty, oppression, urban migration, and social violence.[38] Mahler recruited Mann to head the WHO's Global Programme on AIDS. However, after Mahler's retirement in 1988, the WHO's AIDS program was slashed by the new director-general, Hiroshi Nakajima. Mann resigned in protest and pursued his crusade from Harvard University.[39]

BOX 9.2. The World Health Organization

The World Health Organization is the UN's directing and coordinating authority on international health. Its membership is comprised of 193 countries and two associate members. It has a staff of around 8,000 recruited from 150 countries. Its budget of $3.3 billion (2006–2007) comes from member dues (28 percent) and voluntary contributions (72 percent). Sixty-seven percent of these contributions come from governments. The WHO spends only 25 percent on personnel and activities at its headquarters; it spends 31 percent of its budget in Africa (2006–2007 figures).[1]

The WHO's initial top priorities were malaria, women's and children's health, tuberculosis, venereal disease, nutrition, and environmental sanitation. In 1948 it assumed responsibility for the international classification of diseases (an effort that had begun in the 1850s). The WHO's classification system is now the main international instrument for categorizing diseases and other health problems. It works to support primary health care; conduct mass immunization campaigns; send response teams to contain outbreaks of mass diseases; help governments create civil defense capacity to cope with disasters; provide emergency assistance to people affected by natural disasters; ensure that local health systems are functioning to mitigate against the effects of crises in public health; promulgate international health regulations (norms, in our terminology) that strengthen countries' capacity to prevent, protect against, and control outbreaks of diseases; and promote universal access to life-saving drugs.

Its achievements include thirty years of work to eliminate onchocerciasis (river blindness) from West Africa that has spared 18 million children from the disease; the publication of the first essential medicines list in 1977 (today 156 countries have a national list of essential medicines); the reduction of polio cases by 99 percent since 1988, from 350,000 to 1,956 (in 2006); and, the accomplishment of which its members are most proud, the eradication of smallpox between 1967 and 1979—the only example to date of the complete eradication of a major infectious disease.[2]

1. WHO, *Working for Health: An Introduction to the World Health Organization* (Geneva: WHO, 2007), 20–21.

2. Ibid., 4–5.

By 1990, the sense of urgency about AIDS in industrialized countries had begun to wane. New drugs and other preventive measures meant that AIDS was no longer seen as the same threat to the West as it had been earlier, and myopia meant that concerns stopped at the border. At the same time, it is hard to overlook the incompetence of health ministries in many developing countries whose leaders denied the problem's existence and refused to cooperate even in gathering data.

The WHO was laggard in developing its promising start. Moreover, the WHO's health promotion, regulatory, and surveillance mandate sometimes pits it, not surprisingly, against the powerful pharmaceutical industry, the archenemy of so many activists.[40] For these and other reasons, the WHO was slow to take its proper place in the fight against AIDS, in contrast to the leadership it demonstrated in previous campaigns against disease. In its 1998 and 1999 world health reports, the WHO, headed by Gro Harlem Brundtland, emphasized the risks from tobacco and tuberculosis rather than the risks from AIDS.[41] The 1999 report did not mention that HIV / AIDS surpassed all other causes of death in Africa, for example. In a secretariat that employed more than 2,000 staff, only a handful of WHO professionals were working on AIDS in the late 1990s.

Finally, by the middle of the 1990s, donor governments began to push for the creation of a joint UN-AIDS program, and ECOSOC responded by setting up the Joint United Nations Programme on HIV and AIDS in January 1996. UNAIDS, which is headquartered in Geneva, now plays the lead role in advocating for accelerated, comprehensive, and coordinated global action to combat the HIV epidemic. Its UN co-sponsors in addition to the WHO are the UNHCR, UNICEF, the World Food Programme, the UNDP, the UN Population Fund, the UNODC, the ILO, UNESCO, and the World Bank. Its work is guided by a Programme Coordinating Board, which has twenty-two government and five NGO representatives (including associations of people living with HIV), plus representatives from the co-sponsors. Its funding comes from voluntary contributions from governments, foundations, corporations, and individuals. However, the participating organizations have cut back sharply on the resources and personnel that they themselves devoted to AIDS.

The role of UNAIDS is to lead, coordinate, strengthen, and support worldwide action. This includes taking action to decelerate and prevent HIV transmission, provide treatment and care to those infected with HIV, reduce the vulnerability of communities and individuals to the disease, and alleviate the impact of HIV. It has a five-part mandate: provide advocacy and leadership for effective action; provide technical support and strategic information to combat the epidemic worldwide; track, monitor, and evaluate the epidemic and responses to it; form strategic partnerships and civil society engagements globally and in the field (including with faith-based organizations, people living with AIDS, philanthropies, and the private sector); and mobilize resources to support an effective response.[42]

Compliance Gaps: Who Is Listening?

In the twenty-first century in particular, much progress has been made in responding to the threat of HIV/AIDS. In many more countries than before, access to HIV treatment, care, and prevention is improving. These services include HIV counseling and testing, prevention education for young people, provision of condoms to the sexually active, and so on. For example, five times as many people had access to ARV treatment in 2005 as in 2001.[43] Research on preventive vaccines and microbicides has also increased, although pharmaceutical patents still constitute an obstacle to affordable medicines in developing countries.

UNAIDS also provides estimates of the resources needed versus the resources that have actually been mobilized. Worldwide, only 20 percent of people living with HIV are receiving ARV therapy and a lower proportion of at-risk people have access to basic prevention services. The amount available for AIDS funding in 2007 was $10 billion, or six times the amount in 2001 ($1.6 billion).[44] Yet this must be seen against an estimated $18 billion that was needed. Governments need to train more medical and paramedical staff; ensure that adequate supplies of necessary drugs are stocked, easily available, and affordable; enact legal and penal reform to improve access of medical and social workers to members of high-risk groups such as prostitutes, drug addicts, prisoners, and homosexuals; invest in educational and informational campaigns and programs to help reduce and eliminate the social stigma and discrimination associated with HIV infection; and provide and encourage the use of counseling and testing services by qualified staff.

The World Bank describes itself as "the largest long-term investor in prevention and mitigation of HIV/AIDS in developing countries."[45] Yet from 1988 to 1999 its total expenditure on all AIDS projects in Africa was a meager $15 million.[46] The paltry size of such sums suggests that there is little political will to fight the pandemic let alone mobilize support to enforce health measures to halt its spread.

The Second UN, in this case the UN Secretary-General and the WHO director-general and their staffs, worked with a large number of influential NGOs—including Africa Action and Oxfam—in a moderately successful campaign to convince the multinational drug firms to reduce their ARV drug prices in developing countries. The initiative was especially important in Africa, where the efforts included persuading patent-holders to desist from legal action against generic drug manufacturers in Brazil and India. Companies who pursued such legal action quickly found themselves in the midst of a public relations disaster that an industry already suffering from negative world public opinion could ill afford.[47]

It would be desirable to have a means to ensure that ARV drugs are available at low cost and to insist that they be distributed in countries in need. The kind of national regime that exists in all normally functioning countries clearly is absent at the global level as well as in many poor countries. The pandemic continues while the means to prevent its worst effects exist but are not available to those in need.

Close Calls: SARS and Avian Flu

We have emphasized HIV/AIDS because of the number of human beings threatened, but other infectious diseases pose challenges for contemporary global health governance. The first severe and easily transmissible disease of the new millennium was SARS, the acronym for severe acute respiratory syndrome. The WHO coordinated the international investigation with the assistance of the Global Outbreak Alert and Response Network and worked closely with health authorities in affected countries to provide epidemiological, clinical, and logistical support as required.

SARS is believed to have originated from somewhere in southern China around November 2002, crossed over to Hong Kong in February 2003, and then spread to Vietnam, Singapore, Mongolia, the Philippines, Canada, and Germany.[48] Public health officials first recognized SARS at the end of February 2003. By the end of July 2003, more than 8,000 possible SARS cases and almost 800 deaths had been reported.[49] Economies were disrupted and schools, hospitals, and in some cases even borders were closed; the daily lives of millions of people were affected. Throughout Asia and the Pacific, international travel and hotel occupancies fell sharply.

WHO headquarters in Geneva issued a global alert on 12 March 2003, warning of the outbreak of unexplained cases of atypical pneumonia. A few days later, the WHO disseminated information about the disease's symptoms to health authorities, airlines, and travelers and a travel advisory for people exhibiting the symptoms. The WHO activated its Global Alert and Response Network, bringing together eleven laboratories in ten countries in a collaborative effort that before long identified the cause of the disease as a new virus, the SARS Corona virus or SARS CoV, which had not previously been detected in humans and animals.[50]

While the total number of countries affected was twenty-six, over 95 percent of the outbreaks were in the western Pacific. Accordingly, the WHO's Western Pacific Regional Office in Manila took lead responsibility for dealing with the pandemic by containing and controlling the outbreaks, supporting the health care infrastructure in affected countries, helping the vulnerable countries prepare for the virus that was leaping to their shores, and collecting and providing the latest information to health officials in the region and around the world.[51] Headquarters contacted WHO staff in the affected areas as well as professionals in the fields of epidemiology, infection control, laboratory diagnosis, and public information. The WHO sent infection control equipment—the ubiquitous masks and gowns that quickly became the public face of the epidemic—to affected and vulnerable countries. A regional laboratory network was established under WHO auspices to carry out testing for countries with limited laboratory facilities. Local public health officials worked with WHO specialists to put in place enhanced surveillance and early detection systems and procedures, and close communication was established and maintained with the media in order to raise public consciousness.

Despite the fact that SARS was a brand-new and rapidly communicable virus, the daily toll fell quite quickly, and on 5 July 2003, Taiwan was the last area to be removed from the SARS sheet.[52] In other words, as with the tsunami example in our introductory chapter, an integral part of the UN system, the WHO, was the lead actor in filling knowledge gaps—by collecting and collating data and acting as a clearinghouse for information. The WHO promulgated the norms for safe international travel to guard against the disease and informed and helped governments institute preventive and curative measures (filling policy gaps) in order to contain and eliminate the threat. The UN system is a trusted agent for these tasks because of its universality and the resulting legitimacy, the expertise it has accumulated over decades of experience, the combination of its scientific objectivity and its political neutrality, its presence in the field in so many countries around the world, and its unmatched convening authority and mobilizing capacity across all levels and sectors of global governance.

A similar analysis can be made for the role the UN is playing during the threat of a pandemic that avian flu poses in the first decade of the twenty-first century.[53] As with the tsunami and with SARS, the UN system is coordinating the emergency response system for the global commons. The WHO is coordinating the global response to human cases of the avian flu caused by the H5N1 virus and is monitoring the corresponding threat of a pandemic. Influenza pandemics can infect almost all countries around the world extremely quickly. Under modern conditions of travel, transport, and communications, a virus is virtually unstoppable because coughing spreads the virus among people, who then carry it across national borders. Because infected people can spread the virus before they show any signs of the symptoms, the risk of spread is magnified by the international travel of asymptomatic carriers. The exceptionally severe 1918 pandemic killed more than 40 million people. The best- and worst-case estimates of an avian flu pandemic range from 2 million with a mild form of the disease to up to 25–30 percent of the total population of the countries most severely affected with a virulent strain. The surge in demand for emergency health and hospital treatment would overwhelm health services.

For a pandemic to start, three conditions must be met: the emergence of a new influenza virus subtype, the infection of humans, and the easy and sustained spread of the virus among humans. Avian flu, a contagious disease of animals caused by viruses that are normally restricted to birds and sometimes pigs, satisfies the first two but not the third condition. Its chief causative agent, the H5N1 virus, is highly pathogenic and is one of the few influenza viruses to have crossed the species barrier from birds and animals to humans. It has proven to be especially tenacious. The most common means of cross-species infection is direct contact with infected poultry or with surfaces and objects contaminated by the feces of infected poultry.

Just as Asia and the Pacific was beginning to control the SARS outbreak, the region was bashed by avian flu in mid-2003, resulting in the loss and culling of an estimated 250 million birds (mainly chickens) across several Southeast Asian countries. The countries affected, in chronological order from 2003 to the end of 2005, were South Korea, Vietnam, Japan, Thailand, Cambodia, Laos, Indonesia, China, Malaysia, Russia, Kazakhstan, Mongolia, Turkey, and Romania. It subsequently spread to South Asia, the Middle East, Europe, and Africa. In the period 2003–2007, 322 humans are known to have been infected, of whom 195 died. The WHO has led the main international campaign against the threat of avian flu. Its recommended integrated strategy includes actions to strengthen national preparedness, improving early warning systems, delaying the spread of the disease internationally, and accelerating vaccine development.[54]

At the same time, that the WHO is part of the UN system was obvious by the blanket refusal of the organization to permit Taiwan's involvement in any of its activities because of China's objection. This lapse in universalism is as lamentable as it is predictably politically correct. It is also dangerous in the context of weakest links that work against the global public good, which "can only be provided with the active participation of *every* country."[55]

Conclusion: Fitful and Halting Progress

As with just about every UN effort, performance and results of efforts to attack pandemics fall short of promise and needs. Yet once more, as with other global challenges encountered in previous chapters, it is difficult to pin the blame solely on the Second UN. Rather, inadequate international responses reflect the disconnect between the transnational scope of such problems and the state-centric locus of policy and authority and mobilization capacity. Given this reality, UN officials and their allies in the Third UN can do little but draw attention to the failures and shortfalls; action has to come from member states. Speaking in Beijing at a global forum on health research for developing countries in October 2007, Margaret Chan, the WHO director-general, said that the world was unlikely to meet the Millennium Development Goals on health. At the midpoint "in the countdown to 2015," she observed, "of all the goals, those directly related to health care are the least likely to be met."[56]

Member states' failures and policies of denial point to the need for a systematized international response from within the framework of global rather than purely national governance. The various gaps described above for dealing with HIV/AIDS suggest that we are quite far removed from being in a position to protect people from pandemics.

For instance, China's initial policy of denial about the SARS outbreak made clear the importance of relying on other sources in addition to government reports. From November 2002 to February 2003, Beijing concealed the outbreak of the disease, denied that it had spread to areas beyond the initial outbreak, refused the WHO access to affected areas, and delayed preventive measures until April 2003.[57] In 2003, the WHO also came into conflict with Canada, where federal and provincial (Ontario) officials rejected the WHO's travel advisory against visiting Toronto.[58]

In May 2003, the World Health Assembly empowered the WHO to receive and take into account reports from unofficial sources.[59] The decision effectively made civil society groups actors in global health governance in terms of monitoring states' compliance with global health norms and best practices. In addition, the WHO has learned from its experience with the SARS outbreak; when the avian flu crisis struck in 2005–2006, the WHO quickly set up an early alert and rapid response center. The Secretary-General himself expressed a willingness to use his broad discretionary authority under Charter Article 99 to refer to the Security Council any "overwhelming outbreak of infectious diseases" as a threat to international peace and security.[60]

Before closing this discussion on global health governance, we permit ourselves a parenthetical remark. An internationalized human conscience should find it intolerable that while life expectancy in the rich countries is eighty years and rising, in parts of Sub-Saharan Africa it is half that and falling. Poverty contributes to epidemics of infection and curtails access to health professionals and medicines. More than half a million women die every year during pregnancy and childbirth; 99 percent of these women are in developing countries. Failing health in turn exacerbates family poverty and retards national development, thereby fueling a vicious cycle that destroys the lives and livelihoods of millions around the world every year. The requisite policy responses would include adequate and fully funded ARV therapies, speedy resolution of deadlocks in negotiations about intellectual property rights to provide affordable medicines to poor people in the poorest countries, the creation of globally interlinked national disease surveillance systems, and improved access to public health care.

10

The Responsibility to Protect

- Antecedents: Roots and Origins of the R2P Idea
- The 1990s: A Gathering Perfect Storm
- Actors: Norm Entrepreneurs, Champions, and Brokers
- From ICISS to the World Summit: Filling the Policy Gap
- R2P as Normative Advancement
- International Criminal Pursuit and Justice: Filling the Institutional Gap
- Tasks Ahead: Helping to Fill the Compliance Gap
- Conclusion: A Model for Enhancing Global Governance?

The most basic human right is to life itself—indeed, what could be more fundamental to a working system of global governance, however defined and however rudimentary? As Pope Benedict XVI put it in his address to the General Assembly in April 2008, "Recognition of the unity of the human family, and attention to the innate dignity of every man and woman, today find renewed emphasis in the principle of the responsibility to protect. . . . This principle has to invoke the idea of the person as image of the Creator."[1] Other religious and secular leaders would agree, but establishing a universal standard to protect life under the most extreme threats represents an enormous challenge for the international system. Outsiders who want to protect or assist affected populations confront the harsh reality of the UN's most sacrosanct principle of nonintervention, as enshrined in Article 2 (7) of the Charter.

Yet no idea has moved faster in the international normative arena than the responsibility to protect, or R2P, as it is now commonly called. The term was introduced in the 2001 report of the International Commission on Intervention and State Sovereignty.[2] Over time, domestic and international jurisdictions have blurred, as is illustrated by the willingness—

sometimes authorized by the United Nations, sometimes by regional organizations—to shelve sacrosanct sovereignty and use military force for human protection purposes in the 1990s. When Secretary-General Kofi Annan issued his "challenge of humanitarian intervention" in September 1999, he provoked such a furious backlash from so many countries that some wondered about his future in the UN. Yet a mere six years later, the norm was endorsed by the world leaders gathered at the 2005 World Summit. Annan called this one of his "most precious" achievements.[3]

In this final chapter, not the least because it represents a joint and very personal memoir for both authors—Ramesh Thakur was an ICISS commissioner and Thomas G. Weiss was its research director—we depart somewhat from the gaps template we have used in the rest of the book. Instead, we present the journey of R2P from an idea to a global norm in need of implementation. Rather than rehashing conclusions from earlier chapters, this final one provides us with, we believe, a more original and intriguing conclusion. The United Nations is a vital part of the story of contemporary global governance, and as we gaze toward the future, the astonishingly rapid journey of R2P from an idea to the center of international normative, policy, and institutional arenas provides us with a powerful and persuasive way to analyze the comparative advantage of contemporary international organizations.

We begin by outlining the origins of the idea. Second, we briefly describe the factors that made the 1990s the decade of humanitarian crises and action. Next, we describe the main actors in the story—the norm entrepreneurs, champions, and brokers, followed by an account of the process by which the ICISS arrived at its landmark report on R2P. This is followed by a description of the sustained engagement with the R2P agenda from 2001, when the ICISS report was published, to its adoption at the 2005 World Summit. We end with a sketch of the tasks and challenges that lie ahead to move R2P from a norm to a template for policy and especially for vigorous enforcement action.[4]

Antecedents: Roots and Origins of the R2P Idea

Possibly the most dramatic normative development of our time—comparable to the Nuremberg trials and the Convention on Genocide in the immediate post–World War II period—relates to the use of military force to protect human beings. No longer is it necessary to finesse the so-called tensions between sovereignty and human rights in the Charter.

They can now be confronted, and they increasingly are, not only by analysts but also by diplomats and soldiers. Sovereignty no longer implies the license to kill.

At the same time, the idea of sovereignty as responsibility is not all that new or fresh. Rather, it has a long evolutionary pedigree. "The principle of 'responsibility to protect' was considered by the ancient *ius gentium* as the foundation of every action taken by those in government with regard to the governed," Pope Benedict XVI told UN diplomats. While the responsibility to protect "has only recently been defined . . . it was always present implicitly at the origins of the United Nations, and is now increasingly characteristic of its activity."[5]

Rising from the ashes of World War II, when the Allies were determined to prevent a repeat of Adolf Hitler's abominations, the United Nations for most of its existence has focused far more on external aggression than on internal mass killings. Yet Nazi Germany was guilty of both. Unlike aggression against other countries, the systematic and large-scale extermination of Jews was a new horror. In the twenty-first century, the world organization is at long last elevating the doctrine of preventing mass atrocities to the same level of collective responsibility as preventing and repelling armed aggression against states.

Going to war was an acknowledged attribute of state sovereignty and war itself was an accepted institution of the Westphalian system that was characterized by distinctive rules, etiquette, and norms and stable patterns of practices that governed armed conflicts.[6] In that quasi-Hobbesian world that was barely removed from the state of nature, the main protection against aggression was countervailing power, which increased both the cost of victory and the risk of failure. Since 1945, the UN has spawned a corpus of law to stigmatize aggression and create a robust norm against it. The United Nations exists to check the predatory instincts of the powerful. Now there are significant restrictions on the authority of states to use force either domestically or internationally.

A second challenge to the Westphalian order came with the adoption of new standards of conduct for states in order to protect and advance international human rights, one of the great achievements of the twentieth century. The Charter contains an inherent tension between the intervention-proscribing principle of state sovereignty and the intervention-prescribing principle of human rights. Individuals became subjects of international law as bearers of duties and holders of rights under a growing corpus of human rights and international humanitarian law treaties and conventions: the Universal Declaration of Human Rights and the two covenants, the Geneva Conventions and Additional Protocols, and the two conventions prohibiting torture and genocide.[7]

The Genocide Convention has its roots in World War II. In his youth, Raphael Lemkin petitioned the League of Nations to outlaw "acts of barbarism and vandalism"; as a Jew in occupied Poland he fought in the underground resistance. In late 1944, he published one of the most fateful works of political thought of the last century: *Axis Rule in Occupied Europe: Laws of Occupation, Analysis of Government, Proposals for Redress.*[8] On the occasion of the centennial of his birth, Kofi Annan recalled that Lemkin had coined the new word "genocide" to describe an old crime in 1943, two years before the world became familiar with Auschwitz, Belsen, and Dachau.[9] He also "almost single-handedly drafted an international multilateral treaty declaring genocide an international crime, and then turned to the United Nations in its earliest days and implored member states to adopt it."[10]

Launched by an individual, the Convention on the Prevention and Punishment of the Crime of Genocide was adopted by the General Assembly on 9 December 1948, one day before the Universal Declaration of Human Rights. Lemkin was discovered weeping in a UN corridor at the news and described the convention as an epitaph for his mother, who had been among many members of his family killed in the Holocaust.[11] The convention is a milestone in defining genocide as a crime against humanity and thus a matter of universal criminal jurisdiction.

Earlier in this volume we discussed the UN's activities related to peace operations, but it is worth quickly repeating a couple of points here. Traditional warfare is the use of force by rival armies of enemy states that are fighting over a clash of interests: us against them. Collective security rests on the use of force by the international community of states to defeat or punish an aggressor: all against one. Traditional peacekeeping inserts neutral and lightly armed third-party soldiers as a physical buffer between enemy combatants who have agreed to a cease-fire. Peace enforcement refers to the use of force by better armed—but still neutral—international soldiers against spoilers.

However, the responsibility to protect is a more sophisticated and politically far more broadly acceptable reformulation of the more familiar concept of humanitarian intervention. It differs from all the above types of operations in that it refers to the use of military force by outsiders in order to protect victims of mass atrocities. R2P redefines sovereignty as responsibility and locates the responsibility in the first instance with the state. But it also argues that if the state is unwilling or unable to honor the responsibility or itself perpetrates atrocities against its people, then the responsibility to protect the victims of atrocity crimes shifts upward to the international community of states, acting ideally through the Security Council.

The 2001 ICISS report consolidated a number of disparate trends and borrowed language first developed by former special representative on internally displaced persons Francis M. Deng and Brookings Institute scholar Roberta Cohen to address the problem of internally displaced persons (IDPs).[12] Instead of creating a new norm, the ICISS registered and dramatized a norm shift that was already under way and found language to make it more palatable to naysayers.

The importance of sovereignty as the key organizing principle for contemporary world order needed and received strong affirmation in the ICISS report. The authors of the report took pains to emphasize that a cohesive and peaceful international system is more likely to be achieved through the cooperation of effective and legitimate states, confident of their place in the world, than in an environment of fragile, collapsed, fragmenting, or generally chaotic states. Sovereignty provides order, stability, and predictability in international relations and is not merely a cover for abuse.

As such, sovereignty implies a dual responsibility: an external responsibility to respect the sovereignty of other states and an internal responsibility to respect the dignity and basic rights of all the people within a state: citizens, immigrants, and visitors alike. Reconceptualizing sovereignty as responsibility has a threefold significance. First, it implies that the state authorities are responsible for the functions of protecting the safety and lives of citizens and the promotion of their welfare. Second, it suggests that national political authorities are responsible to the citizens internally and to the international community of states through the United Nations. And third, it means that state agents are responsible for their actions; that is to say, they are accountable for their acts of commission and omission.

This is a less radical departure from established precept and practice than it appears. The authority of the state is nowhere regarded as absolute. Internally, constitutional power-sharing arrangements constrain and regulate it. Power is shared between different levels of governmental authorities, from the local through the provincial to the national. And it is distributed among different sectors of authorities, such as the legislature, the executive, the judiciary, and bureaucracy.

A pertinent example is India,[13] a powerful democracy that expresses strong opposition to "humanitarian intervention." The Indian constitution guarantees the rights of individuals to dignity; it empowers the judiciary to monitor the state to make sure it does not violate fundamental rights. That is, the state is responsible and can be held accountable for acts of commission that violate citizens' rights.

At the same time, several of India's independence leaders believed that liberty is an empty abstraction to the hungry; freedom is meaningful only with economic security. In the light of India's poverty, economic rights (for example, the right to an adequate means of livelihood) could not realistically be enshrined as a basic right enforceable in the courts, but they were enshrined as ideals. The constitution accordingly incorporated economic rights as directive principles, describing them as "fundamental in the governance of the country and it shall be the duty of the state to apply these principles in making laws." Some of these resemble socioeconomic rights except that they cannot be enforced through the courts. When critics and political opponents criticize the government for failing to honor the directive principles, in essence they are arguing that the state should be held responsible for acts of omission.

Internationally, too, sovereignty is understood as embracing responsibility, not only in human rights covenants but also in UN practice and state practice. The UN Charter is an example of an international obligation that is voluntarily accepted by member states. In granting membership to the United Nations, the members welcome the signatory state as a responsible new member of the community of nations. At the same time, when the state signs the Charter, it accepts the responsibilities of membership flowing from that signature. There is no transfer or dilution of the *status* of state sovereignty. But there is a necessary change in the *exercise* of sovereignty—from sovereignty as control to sovereignty as responsibility in both internal functions and external duties.

Framing the "responsibility to protect" does more than make the concept of state sovereignty cross-ideological. Both liberal humanitarians and right-to-life conservatives can embrace it. The normative advances of the concept of the responsibility to protect can in no small measure be traced to early efforts by the Brookings Project on Internal Displacement to give concrete meaning to the mandate of the representative of the secretary-general for internally displaced persons, a position held at the time by Francis Deng.[14] Although the ICISS never formally acknowledged the parentage of the idea, Lloyd Axworthy—who as Canadian foreign minister launched the commission—has written: "The first time I heard the notion of 'responsibility to protect' was when Deng visited me in Ottawa and argued for a clear commitment by the international community to deal with the IDP issue."[15]

In his work on behalf of IDPs, Deng introduced the concept of "sovereignty as responsibility" into the literature and debates on internal displacement. He, William Zartman, and other scholars developed the concept in their work on governance in Africa in the 1990s.[16] Deng's eventual colleague and project co-director at the Brookings Institution, Roberta Cohen, also emphasized the national dimensions of protection. "Sovereignty," she wrote in 1991, "carries with it a responsibility on the part of governments to protect their citizens."[17] Deng explained its origins in work begun in the late 1980s to see how the end of the Cold War changed the way that African governments perceived conflict and conflict resolution. It was a way of squaring the circle, reconciling the seeming clash of the principles of state sovereignty and nonintervention, on the one hand, with the need to halt the worst kinds of abuse of human rights, on the other hand, and even to intervene militarily in the most egregious of cases.

This conceptualization of "sovereignty as responsibility" to address the phenomenon of internal displacement then gained momentum with Annan's articulation of "two sovereignties" in the late 1990s and the formulation of the responsibility to protect in 2001. As a result, the characteristics of a sovereign—territory, authority, population, independence—that were spelled out in the 1934 Montevideo Convention on the Rights and Duties of States have been complemented by another characteristic: a modicum of respect for human rights. State sovereignty is less sacrosanct today than it was in 1945. When a state is manifestly incapable or unwilling to protect populations within their borders from mass atrocities and peaceful means fail, the resort of the international community of states to international judicial pursuit, sanctions, and even outside military force remains a possibility. The threshold for nonconsensual intervention is high—it requires more than substantial human rights abuses and must reach to genocide, war crimes, crimes against humanity, or ethnic cleansing—but the fact that it remains a policy option represents significant new middle ground in international relations.

While a number of the world's most abusive governments would disagree, nonetheless a normative consensus is emerging in international society about a state's responsibilities and accountabilities both to domestic and international constituencies. Abusers that are major powers (e.g., China and Russia) or rich in resources (e.g., Saudia Arabia) are of course able to exercise their sovereignty with little fear of forceful outside intervention, but it is becoming increasingly difficult for states to claim the prerogatives of sovereignty unless they meet internationally agreed responsibilities, which include protecting the human rights of and providing life-sustaining assistance to all those within its jurisdiction. Failure to meet obligations legitimizes high levels of criticism and intrusions and—when the politics are right—even outside intervention by the United Nations and the community of responsible states—or a coalition of states—against a member of their club that misbehaves egregiously.

The 1990s: A Gathering Perfect Storm

As we saw in some detail in chapter 3, the chief threats to international security since the 1990s have come from violent eruptions of crises within states, including civil wars, while the goals of promoting human rights and democratic governance, protecting civilian victims of humanitarian atrocities, and punishing governmental perpetrators of mass crimes have become more important. Noncombatant fatalities, including those who die from conflict-related starvation and disease, now vastly outnumber troops killed directly in warfare, by a ratio of up to 9 to 1. In practice, the "maintenance of international peace and security," for which primary responsibility is vested in the Security Council, translates today into the protection of civilians. Given the changing nature and victims of armed conflict, the need for clarity, consistency, and reliability in the use of armed force for civilian protection lies at the heart of the UN's credibility.

In a number of cases in the 1990s, the Security Council endorsed the use of force with the primary goal of humanitarian protection: on behalf of Iraqi Kurds after the Gulf War, the proclamation of UN safe areas in Bosnia, the delivery of humanitarian relief in Somalia, the restoration of the democratically elected government of Haiti, and the deployment of a multinational force in Kosovo after the 1999 war.[18]

The proliferation of so-called new wars and complex humanitarian emergencies after the end of the Cold War[19] and the inappropriateness of the classical tenets of UN peacekeeping for dealing with such emergencies[20] highlighted the inherent tension between the neutrality and impartiality of traditional peacekeeping and the partiality of peace enforcement. The Brahimi report confronted the dilemma squarely and concluded that political neutrality has often degenerated into military timidity and the abdication of the duty to protect civilians. Impartiality should not translate into complicity with evil. The report concluded that while it should strive to remain impartial, the UN should soften its principle of neutrality between belligerents in favor of "adherence to the principles of the Charter and to the objectives of [the] mandate."[21]

There is yet another key background factor behind the rise of R2P, namely the softening of sovereignty in so many of its empirical dimensions. It has become commonplace to note that under the impact of globalization, political, social, economic, environmental, and technological influences cross borders without passports. The total range of transborder flows and activities has increased, while the proportion of flows that are subject to control and regulation by governments has diminished. National frontiers are becoming less relevant in determining the flow of ideas, information, goods, services, capital, labor, and technology. The speed of modern communications makes borders increasingly permeable, while the volume of cross-border flows threatens to overwhelm the capacity of states to manage them.

The erosion of the once-sacrosanct principle of national sovereignty is rooted in the reality of global interdependence: no nation is an island unto itself any longer. Moreover, the proliferation of states has led to the creation and recognition of many states that are weak, fragile, disrupted, collapsed, or failed. For example, East Timor has become a de facto protectorate of Australia, and the security (internal and external) and economic viability of Kosovo is ultimately underwritten by Europe. Meanwhile, Somalia continues to hobble along as a state without any of the traditional attributes of statehood, eighteen years, fifteen unity governments, and some $8 billion of investments later in "postconflict" peacebuilding.

The cumulative effect of these changes poses significant conceptual, policy, and operational challenges to the notion and exercise of state sovereignty. The ICISS responded to a series of military-civilian interactions in humanitarian crises.[22] It also directly confronted the divergent reactions—or rather, the nonreactions—of the members of the Security Council to Rwanda and Kosovo. In 1994, intervention was too little and too late to halt or even slow the murder of what may have been as many as 800,000 people in the Great Lakes region of Africa. In 1999, the formidable North Atlantic Treaty Organization finessed the council and waged war for the first time in Kosovo. But many observers saw the 78-day bombing effort as being too much, too late, too little (because it ruled out the use of ground troops), and too counterproductive, perhaps creating as much human suffering among IDPs and refugees as it relieved.[23]

In both cases, the Security Council failed to act expeditiously and authorize the use of deadly force to protect vulnerable populations. In both cases, many—but not all—human rights advocates and humanitarian agencies supported the military protection of civilians whose lives were threatened, thereby exposing the glaring normative gap for collective action more clearly than in the past.

If the UN was going to be relevant, it had to engineer a basis for international involvement in the ugly civil wars that produced such conscience-shocking suffering. The earlier debate about whether humanitarian disasters qualified as "threats to international peace and security" became moot because so many humanitarian crises had been the object of Security Council action for precisely these reasons.

Our review of the work of the ICISS is anything but disengaged; we believe that the lack of reaction to the situation in Rwanda represents a far more serious threat to international order and justice than the Security Council's paralysis regarding Kosovo. The most thorough survey to date of victims in war zones suggests that there is too little rather than too much humanitarian intervention. Fully two-thirds of civilians under siege who were interviewed in twelve war-torn societies by the International Committee of the Red Cross want more intervention; only 10 percent want none.[24] While this survey was done a decade ago, the conclusions undoubtedly remain unchanged. A 2005 study of the operational contexts of humanitarian agencies finds that recipients "are more concerned about *what* is provided than about *who* provides it."[25]

Actors: Norm Entrepreneurs, Champions, and Brokers

Norms are not converted into laws and regimes by some mysterious process. They require identifiable agents. The crucial actors that promoted and shepherded R2P through the maze of UN politics can be broken down into norm entrepreneurs, champions, and brokers.

As a norm entrepreneur, the Secretary-General is a unique international actor with distinctive characteristics and bases of authority and influence. But he also has limitations.[26] In a March 2004 speech on the occasion of the tenth anniversary of the Rwanda genocide, Nobel laureate Kofi Annan openly and honestly regretted that he had not done more.[27] His moral pleas for intervention in contexts of mass atrocities were also driven by his experience of being in charge of the UN Department of Peacekeeping Operations at the time of the Srebrenica massacre in 1995. We too admit our own moral and intellectual indignation at the failure of the international community of states to robustly respond to genocide and ethnic cleansing: how many more times is it permissible to say "never again"?

Annan boldly asserted in 1998 that "state frontiers . . . should no longer be seen as a watertight protection for war criminals or mass murderers."[28] He argued that human rights concerns transcended claims of sovereignty, a theme that he put forward more delicately a year later at the Millennium Summit.[29] The reaction was loud, bitter, and predictable, especially from China, Russia, and much of the Third World. "Intervention"—for whatever reasons, even humanitarian—remains taboo.[30] The chorus of complaints in the General Assembly after Annan's remarks at the Millennium Summit were remarkably similar to negative reactions in the Commission on Human Rights about many aspects of Deng's mandate as the Secretary-General's representative that touched on issues considered to be the domestic affairs of states. Diplomats at UN headquarters are often unaware of the subtleties in opinion in developing countries around the world.[31]

It helped that Annan, the only UN insider to have held the organization's top job, had an unmatched grasp of the organization's politics. He mined the expertise of outside experts to present the issue of intervention to member states, as he explained in his oral history interview:

> There are certain issues that are better done outside and there are certain issues that can only be done inside. . . . But take a look at the intervention issue. I couldn't have done it inside. It would have been very divisive. And the member states were very uncomfortable because, as an organization, sovereignty is our bedrock and bible— here is someone coming with ideas which are almost challenging

it. So I had to sow the seed and let them digest it but take the study outside and then bring in the results for them to look at it. I find that when you are dealing with issues where the member states are divided and have very strong views, and very strong regional views, if you do the work inside the discussions become so acrimonious that however good a document is, sometimes you have problems. . . . But if you bring it from outside . . . they accept it.[32]

Within the First United Nations, the *norm champion* of R2P from start to finish was Canada, a country that is strongly committed to multilateralism and has a history of close engagement with the United Nations, political credibility in both North and South, and a proud tradition of successful global initiatives. Foreign minister Lloyd Axworthy initiated the establishment of the commission in response to Annan's challenge in the fall of 1999. He was still the minister when the commission was assembled but retired from politics not long after. The commission's work continued under his successors, John Manley and Bill Graham. When Jean Chrétien was succeeded by Paul Martin as prime minister, there was again no break in the continuity. Several other like-minded countries such as Norway and Switzerland and major foundations such as the Macarthur Foundation and other actors such as the ICRC worked closely with the ICISS to support the idea.

The *norm broker* was the International Commission on Intervention and State Sovereignty, and we do not disguise some pride in having made our own professional contributions to this enterprise. Its mandate was to build a broader understanding of the tension between intervention and state sovereignty and to find common ground for military intervention to support humanitarian objectives. The fact that humanitarian imperatives and principles of sovereignty are reconciled through R2P has important conceptual and enormous political consequences.

From ICISS to the World Summit: Filling the Policy Gap

The notion of sovereignty as responsibility has moved from the fringes to the mainstream of international relations in the past decade. This change is largely attributable to the increased range of actors that have engaged with the issue, especially at the UN. The Canadian government's initiative in September 2000 followed Secretary-General Annan's poignant rhetorical question: "If humanitarian intervention is, indeed, an unacceptable assault on sovereignty, how should we respond to a Rwanda, to a Srebrenica—to gross and systematic violations of human rights that offend every precept of our common humanity?"[33] Given the supposedly wide disparity of views across the North-South divide—industrialized countries are more enthusiastic in principle, developing countries are more wary about providing a rationale for outside intervention—the ICISS was co-chaired by persons from each camp (Gareth Evans and Mohamed Sahnoun), and its ten other commissioners were also evenly divided. But sovereignty as responsibility is not really a North-versus-South issue other than at a superficial level, even though that is how, like so many other international issues, it is usually parsed. The ICISS's extensive outreach and consultations illustrates how differences across and within regions —Africa, Asia, and Latin America—and between governments and civil society actors within countries are varied and subtle.

In ten consultations in both the Northern and Southern Hemispheres, ICISS sought the views of governments, scholars, intergovernmental and nongovernmental humanitarian actors, and journalists.[34] The range of views cannot be summarized except to say that what was most notable, in historical perspective, is that nowhere did anyone argue that intervention to sustain humanitarian objectives is never justifiable.[35] After the genocide in Rwanda, very few policymakers, pundits, or practitioners exclude protective intervention as a last resort.

The final report of ICISS was published with exceptionally bad timing in December 2001, very shortly after the terrorist attacks of 9/11. Understandably, the world's attention was riveted on the consequences of and responses to that horrific event. The invasion of Iraq and the ouster of Saddam Hussein by a U.S.-led coalition acting without UN authorization had a doubly damaging effect. First, as tensions mounted in late 2002 and early 2003, few had the time to focus on R2P. Second, as the WMD justification for the war fell apart and claims of close links between Saddam's regime and Al Qaeda also proved spurious, the coalition of the willing—Australia, Britain, and the United States as the three main belligerent states—began retroactively to use the language of humanitarian intervention and R2P as the main plank of justification for their actions in Iraq. Richard Haass, who was the director of the policy planning unit in the U.S. State Department at the time, spoke of sovereignty as responsibility and argued that when states fail to discharge their responsibility to fight terrorism, "America will act—ideally with partners, but alone if necessary—to hold them accountable."[36] If this view is limited to self-defense against cross-border terrorism, it would be fine. But if the statement is extended to military intervention for human protection purposes, it posed and continues to pose serious problems because many countries in the global South interpret unilateral action as more likely to hide other motivations than to reflect genuine humanitarian ones.

Some of the ICISS commissioners argued strenuously in the public debate that Iraq would not have met the R2P test for intervention.[37] Co-chair Gareth Evans[38] and the two of us[39] spoke and wrote extensively in the years following the December 2001 report's publication to multiple audiences: policymakers (intergovernmental and government officials), scholars, and members of civil society—that is, to all three United Nations. The Canadian government organized an extensive series of consultations with governments, regional organizations, and civil society forums, typically using the two co-chairs as well as the two of us and other ICISS members within their regions to help promote the report. As the message of the responsibility to protect resonated, many civil society organizations began advocacy and dissemination work on their own as well. And of course, Kofi Annan remained fully engaged.

The Secretary-General's High-level Panel on Threats, Challenges and Change, which included ICISS co-chair Gareth Evans, reaffirmed the importance of the change in terminology from the deeply divisive "humanitarian intervention" to "the responsibility to protect." It explicitly endorsed the ICISS argument that "the issue is not the 'right to intervene' of any State, but the 'responsibility to protect' of *every* State."[40] It proposed five criteria of legitimacy: seriousness of threat, proper purpose, last resort, proportional means, and balance of consequences.[41] In a significant breakthrough for the growing acceptance of the new norm, China's official paper on UN reforms, published in June 2005, noted that "each state shoulders the primary responsibility to protect its own population. . . . When a massive humanitarian crisis occurs, it is the legitimate concern of the international community to ease and defuse the crisis." It went on to list the conditions and safeguards, including Security Council authorization, which form the core of the responsibility to protect.[42] In the United States, the Gingrich-Mitchell task force endorsed the responsibility to protect, including the calls for the Security Council and General Assembly to affirm the norm.[43]

In his own report before the World Summit, Annan explicitly referred to ICISS and R2P as well as to the High-level Panel, endorsed the legitimacy criteria, and urged the Security Council to adopt a resolution "setting out these principles and expressing its intention to be guided by them" when authorizing the use of force. This would "add transparency to its deliberations and make its decisions more likely to be respected, by both Governments and world public opinion."[44]

In the event, the responsibility to protect was one of the few substantive items to survive the negotiations at the World Summit in New York in September 2005. Some of the harshest supportive critics see the emphasis on the state and the requirement for Security Council authorization for the use of force for humanitarian purposes as constituting "R2P lite," and others see the language in the World Summit outcome document as being wordier and woollier than the ICISS version.[45] We do not disagree, but nonetheless the document represents a modest step forward in a long process. It is a solid foundation that all three UNs can and should build upon. Like the subtitle of this book, R2P is "an unfinished journey."

The concept was given its own sub-section title.[46] The document makes clear the need for international intervention when states fail to shield their citizens from (or more likely actively sponsor) mass atrocity crimes. The language contains a clear, unambiguous acceptance by all UN members of individual state responsibility to protect populations from genocide, war crimes, ethnic cleansing, and crimes against humanity. Member states further declared that they "are prepared to take collective action, in timely and decisive manner, through the Security Council . . . and in cooperation with relevant regional organizations as appropriate, should peaceful means be inadequate and national authorities are manifestly failing to protect their populations." Leaders stressed "the need for the General Assembly to continue consideration of the responsibility to protect populations from genocide, war crimes, ethnic cleansing, and crimes against humanity."[47] Leaders at the world summit dropped the legitimacy criteria that would simultaneously make the Security Council more responsive to outbreaks of humanitarian atrocities and make it more difficult for individual states or ad hoc "coalitions of the willing" to appropriate the language of humanitarianism for geopolitical and unilateral interventions.[48]

R2P as Normative Advancement

Although we have organized this chapter differently from the rest of the book, in terms of the various gaps, the most significant achievement of R2P is that it has filled a crucial normative gap. The clearest way to gauge the impact of this emerging norm is to situate the rapid evolution of attitudes and awareness. The political brouhaha over humanitarian intervention provided the basis for compromise in the work by ICISS, whose final report opens with the following words:

> State sovereignty implies responsibility, and the primary responsibility for the protection of its people lies with the state itself. Where a population is suffering serious harm, as a result of internal war, insurgency, repression or state failure, and the state in question is unwilling or unable to halt or avert it, the principle of nonintervention yields to the international responsibility to protect.[49]

These developments are not, of course, without critics among states as well as analysts. A host of the usual suspects in the Third World (e.g., Algeria, Malaysia, Egypt, India, Cuba, Sudan, and Venezuela) along with China and Russia are often, but not always, among the loudest critics. India, Algeria, and Russia together account for what may be 1.5 million IDPs and are clearly uneasy with any publicity about the plight of those people.[50] They are joined by critics ranging from those who fear it will become an instrument of abuse by the most powerful to others who worry that R2P will give the powerful an excuse to avoid international action. For example, Mohammed Ayoob sees it as conjuring up "images of colonial domination under the guise of nineteenth-century 'standard of civilization' doctrine";[51] David Rieff questions whether "it has actually kept a single jackboot out of a single human face";[52] and Alex Bellamy argues that the language itself has been "abused by states keen to avoid assuming any responsibility for saving some of the world's most vulnerable people."[53] And of course Washington drags its feet because it refuses to have its military committed by others. Moreover, skepticism emanates from practitioners such as Paula Banarjee, who judges that sovereignty as responsibility "is of little importance as the government defines both sovereignty and responsibility . . . [and] often sovereignty means powerlessness of marginal groups and responsibility is only to the so-called majority."[54]

We are more sanguine about the potential consequences of having filled this normative gap as well as about the necessity for outside intervention and its beneficial impact. While some judge that the sun seems to have set for the moment and the UN's political atmosphere in New York is as toxic as it was in the 1970s during the debates over the NIEO, we see the current context as the prelude to a new dawn. In fact, the UN General Assembly debate in late July 2009 represented the latest significant step in R2P's normative trajectory. A close reading of remarks by ninety-two countries and two observers who addressed the plenary showed scarce support for undermining R2P or backpedaling on the 2005 World Summit agreement—only Venezuela directly questioned it. Of especial relevance were remarks from major regional powers that had previously been reticent or even hostile, including Brazil, Nigeria, India, Indonesia, South Africa, and Japan. Some African speakers remarked that R2P attempted to strike a balance between noninterference and what the African Union called non-indifference. R2P-supportive statements by East Timor and Rwanda were especially poignant. The general sentiment was to stick closely to the 2005 consensus on the meaning and content of R2P while working to close the gap between what was said then and the ability to act collectively now. The R2P agenda item ended without any resolution but then in mid-September the General Assembly passed resolution 63/308 that agreed to "continue its consideration."[55]

The sea change in mainstream normative views since the beginning of the 1990s contrasts even more sharply with the experience of the 1970s.[56] At that time, the notion of using outside military force when a sovereign state acted irresponsibly toward its citizens simply was too far from the mainstream of acceptable international relations. International order was firmly grounded in the inviolability of sovereignty, and therefore states were more attuned to their own unique political interests than to humanitarian imperatives. Three interventions with very substantial humanitarian payoffs were not even partially framed or justified by the interveners in such terms. India's invasion of East Pakistan in 1971, and Tanzania's invasion of Uganda and Vietnam's invasion of Cambodia later in the decade were unilateral efforts geared to regime change, and they all were explicitly justified as self-defense. In retrospect, all three are frequently cited as evidence of the right to humanitarian intervention. The Security Council, however, did not approve any of them—and it actually condemned Vietnam's action.

Clearly the international normative climate is dramatically different; today it follows the lines recommended first by Deng and Cohen, later by the Secretary-General, and finally by the more visible ICISS. On some occasions, the fundamental rights of civilians assume relatively more weight than the prerogatives of states to act with impunity and hide behind the facade of sovereignty. Of course, UN authorization of military intervention is not an option against major powers, as international tolerance for Russian and Chinese atrocities in Chechnya and Xinjiang aptly demonstrates. However, the good should not be an enemy of the best. Some action, even if inconsistent, is better than none.

The relationship between sovereignty and intervention is thus increasingly viewed as complementary rather than contradictory. Sovereignty is conceived as a conditional right dependent upon respect for a minimum standard of human rights and upon each state's honoring its obligation to protect its citizens. If states are manifestly unwilling or unable to do so, the international community of states should bear the responsibility to protect them.

The sea change also reflected the Security Council's framing of issues, for instance its emphasis on vulnerable groups—including resolution 1261 (1999), which condemns the targeting of children; resolution 1265 (1999), which calls for the protection of civilians in armed conflict; resolution 1325 (2000), which specifically addresses the impact of war on women; and resolution 1400 (2002), which extends the UN mission in Sierra Leone mainly on the basis of IDPs. The Security Council held its first open debate on the protection of civilians in armed conflict in February 1999.[57] The Secretary-General also presented six reports on the subject.[58] A crucial normative shift was buried in these resolutions and reports: the world organization was now interested not just in the rights that human beings hold but in protecting their very life as civilians. Resolution 1674 (2006) specifically mentions R2P in the context of the protection of civilians. Former *New York Times* columnist Anthony Lewis was on target when he characterizes the ICISS's framing of issues as "the international state of mind."[59]

None of this normative development took place in a vacuum. By redefining sovereignty as responsibility, the ICISS report addressed the demand side of intervention, especially the example of Rwanda. It would have been more difficult for the commission to redefine sovereignty had the egregious lack of action by the international community of states not led to hundreds of thousands of deaths. ICISS is part of the expansion of actors so central to global governance—the Third United Nations, which directly influences the other two components of the world organization—states and the secretariat.

The terrain on which the conceptual and policy contest over humanitarian intervention has been fought is essentially normative. Norm displacement has taken place from the entrenched norm of nonintervention to the new norm of the responsibility to protect. The United Nations lies at the center of this contest both metaphorically and literally. The Charter, more than any other document, encapsulates and articulates the agreed consensus on the prevailing norms that give structure and meaning to the foundations of world order. And the "international community"—which is increasingly seen as encompassing far more than peace-loving states but including international civil servants and civil society as well—comes together physically primarily within the UN's hallowed halls. It is not surprising, therefore, that the organization should be the epicenter of the interplay between changing norms and shifting state practice.

International Criminal Pursuit and Justice: Filling the Institutional Gap

Discussion and analyses of the protection of civilians and the prosecution of perpetrators have hitherto proceeded along separate lines. In fact they are two sides of the same coin.[60] The interrelated twin tasks are to protect the victims and punish the perpetrators. Both require substantial derogations of sovereignty, the first with respect to the norm of nonintervention and the second with respect to sovereign impunity up to the level of heads of government and state. At the same time, both require sensitive judgment calls: the use of external military force to protect civilians inside sovereign jurisdiction should first satisfy legitimacy criteria rooted largely in just war theory, while the prosecution of alleged atrocity criminals should be balanced against the consequences for the prospects and process of peace, the need for postconflict reconciliation, and the fragility of international as well as domestic institutions.

We have witnessed what amounts to revolutionary advances in the criminalization of domestic and international violence by armed groups and their individual leaders.[61] The law of the Charter governs *when* force may be used; international humanitarian law governs *how* force may be used. While the International Court of Justice deals with justice among states, the increasing attention and sensitivity to human rights abuses and atrocities raise questions of individual criminal accountability in a world of sovereign states. The international community of states has responded by drafting and adopting international legal instruments that ban it.[62]

Earlier we outlined the crucial importance of international legal developments, mentioning specifically the Geneva Conventions of 1949 and Additional Protocols of 1977 but most importantly the 1948 Convention on the Prevention and Punishment of the Crime of Genocide. Yet Kofi Annan has pointed out that "article VI of the Convention, which binds the Parties to try persons charged with genocide before a national or international tribunal, has for all practical purposes remained a dead letter."[63] Recent developments give hope: the crime of genocide was included in the statutes of the International Criminal Tribunals for Rwanda[64] and the former Yugoslavia,[65] and the International Criminal Court.[66]

The war crime trials in Nuremberg and Tokyo were instances of victors' justice. Yet by historical standards, both tribunals were remarkable for giving defeated leaders the opportunity to defend their actions in a court of law instead of being dispatched for summary execution. The ad hoc tribunals of the 1990s are important milestones in efforts to fill institutional gaps. While they have helped to bring hope and justice to some victims, combat the impunity of some perpetrators, and greatly enrich the jurisprudence of international criminal and humanitarian law, they have been expensive and time consuming and contributed little to sustainable national capacities for justice administration. The 128-article Statute of the ICC was adopted at the conclusion of the UN Diplomatic Conference on the Establishment of the International Criminal Court in Rome in July 1998. Its adoption marked the culmination of a decade-long process initiated by the General Assembly in 1989 when it requested the International Law Commission to study the subject of the establishment of an ICC.

The ICC's permanence, institutionalized identity, and universal jurisdiction are specifically designed to escape the tyranny of episodic and politically motivated investigations and selective justice. Gary Bass describes the "drift to universalism,"[67] which includes the tribunals related to World War II, Yugoslavia, and Rwanda as well as actions such as the detention of Pinochet in Britain. This gradual evolution needs to be replaced with institutionalized international criminal justice. Permanence also helps create precedents to build on. In July 2008, ICC chief prosecutor Luís Moreno Ocampo requested that the ICC charge Sudan's president Omar Hassan al-Bashir with genocide, crimes against humanity, and war crimes. In March 2009, the ICC issued arrest warrants on the first two charges; it rejected the genocide charge. Criticism of Ocampo's theatrical nature as well as the ICC's focus on Africa may or may not be justified,[68] but this potentially is a transformative event for the ICC and for the intractable Darfur war. In the meantime, though, the Obama administration got caught up in a bitter dispute within the United States about whether or not to prosecute Bush-era lawyers who had authorized torture—or "enhanced interrogation techniques" in the repackaging of the attorneys—as part of the misguided war on terror. Should there be no public accountability for possible crimes of torture authorized by senior U.S. officials in domestic and international forums, there will be a doubly deleterious consequence. Would-be torturers will know that they can escape the consequences. And the embryonic institutions of international criminal justice such as the ICC will be compromised, perhaps fatally, as examples of judicial colonialism where only Africans and the defeated can be prosecuted.

The exposure in real time of a serving president follows earlier precedents. In 1999 the United Nations International Criminal Tribunal for the former Yugoslavia indicted Slobodan Milosevic, then Serbian president, on war crimes charges for atrocities carried out by Serbian forces in Kosovo. And in 2003 Charles Taylor, president of Liberia, was indicted on war crimes charges by the Special Court for Sierra Leone.

The landscape of international criminal justice thus has changed dramatically in an astonishingly short period of time.[69] In 1990, tyrants could have been reasonably confident of the guarantee of sovereign impunity for their atrocities. Today, although there is no guarantee of prosecution and accountability, not a single brutish ruler can be totally confident of escaping international justice. The certainty of impunity is gone, as the international criminal pursuit of three serving presidents—Milosevic, Taylor, and al-Bashir—along with Radovan Karadzic, the self-styled head of Serb Republic, aptly demonstrates. The United Nations has been at the center of this great normative, policy, and now institutional advance.

Tasks Ahead: Helping to Fill the Compliance Gap

R2P is a call to action on prevention, intervention, and postconflict reconstruction, not the opening lines of a Socratic dialogue by diplomats. There is always a danger with radical advances that commitments at grand summits will suffer many a slip after the champagne flutes are stored. R2P is not just a slogan, and failure to act will make a mockery of its noble sentiments. The implementation and compliance gap, in short, is especially distasteful when mass murder and ethnic cleansing are the result of sitting on the sidelines. Or, as Princeton University's Gary Bass puts it in his masterful history of nineteenth-century efforts to halt mass atrocities, "We are all atrocitarians now—but so far only in words, and not yet in deeds."[70]

The *World Summit Outcome* notwithstanding, we mentioned the oftentimes poisonous atmosphere in New York because some national diplomats insist that the heads of state and government rejected R2P in 2005.[71] The first danger thus is that of rollback: a shamefaced edging back from the agreed norm of 2005, a form of backsliding and buyer's remorse. Members of civil society need to continue their advocacy and activism, and concerned governments need to remain steadfast and hold the feet of all governments to the fire of individual and collective responsibility to protect at-risk populations. When Gareth Evans gave a lecture in August 2007 in Colombo about R2P and what it meant for Sri Lanka, he unleashed a storm of hostile responses; some claimed that the "so-called" R2P norm "is nothing but a license for the white man to intervene in the affairs of dark sovereign countries, whenever the white man thinks it fit to do so."[72] His 2007 visit to the island armed with R2P was compared to the coming of Christopher Columbus in 1492 armed with the Bible and Vasco da Gama in 1498 armed with the sword.[73] One newspaper said that "crackpot ideas" such as R2P had been "dismissed in academic and political circles as the latest 'neo-imperialist' tactic of the big powers to intervene in the affairs of small nations."[74]

Many regimes that fear the searchlight of international attention being shone on their misdeeds will try to chip away at the norm until only a facade remains. The advocates of R2P cannot allow these regimes to succeed. Better that the serially abusive regimes live with the fear of international intervention than that their people fear death and being visited by disappearance squads. Of course, such regimes could alleviate such fear by working, by themselves or in concert with international friends, to improve their human rights records.

A second, opposite danger of rollback lies with the aggressive humanitarian warriors who gave "humanitarian intervention" such a bad name in the first place. The ex post facto humanitarian justifications for the invasion of Iraq constitute the best example of why the authors and promoters of R2P fear "friends" as much as opponents.[75] The histories of developing countries and the collective memories of their people are full of examples of trauma and suffering rooted in the belief of western colonial powers in the white man's burden. The weight of that historical baggage is simply too heavy to sustain the continued use of the language of humanitarian intervention.

That some analysts cling to that language is puzzling and problematic. It is puzzling because the ICISS report explicitly and forcefully spoke about the shortcomings of this terminology and the merits of a deliberate shift to the conceptual vocabulary of R2P. Many commentators simply ignore that argument, as if it had not been made. If they disagree with the report, they should confront the issue and explain why. The problem arises from the politics of the discourse. The ICISS report offered and the High-level Panel's and Secretary-General Kofi Annan's reports preferred the R2P formulation as less confrontational and less polarizing; these pro-moters of the concept felt that it was more likely than other concepts to lead to a consensus across the bitter North-South divide. "Humanitarian intervention" approaches the topic from the perspective of western interveners and isolates and privileges "intervention." The responsibility to protect is victim-centered and emphasizes prevention before and rebuilding after intervention.

History proves that sovereignty and the norm of nonintervention notwithstanding, regional and global powers have repeatedly intervened in the affairs of weaker states.[76] After the end of the Cold War, the Security Council experienced a spurt of enforcement activity in the context of civil wars to provide international relief and assistance to victims of large-scale atrocities from perpetrator or failing states.[77] From Liberia and the Balkans to Somalia, Kosovo, and East Timor, the council explicitly recognized conscience-shocking humanitarian catastrophes as threats to international peace and security that required and justified forcible responses. When the Security Council was unable to act because it lacked enforcement capacity, it subcontracted the military operation to UN-authorized coalitions. And if it proved unwilling to act, sometimes groups of countries forged coalitions of the willing to act even without Security Council authorization.

R2P offers developing countries better protection through agreed and negotiated-in-advance rules and roadmaps for when outside intervention is justified and how it may be done under UN authority rather than unilaterally. It will thus lead to the "Gulliverization" of the use of force by major global and regional powers, tying them down with numerous threads of global norms and rules. Without R2P, these powers have relatively more freedom, not less, to do what they want. R2P is rooted in human solidarity, not in the exceptionalism of the virtuous West against the evil rest of the world.

A third danger, again from overenthusiastic supporters, is misuse of the concept in non-R2P contexts. A group of retired NATO generals, including ICISS commissioner Klaus Naumann, for example, used it to justify the first use of nuclear weapons to prevent nuclear proliferation.[78] Others have used the label to refer to action to halt the spread of HIV/ AIDS or to protect indigenous populations from climate change. In August 2008, Russia even dressed its defense of geopolitical interests in the Caucasus in the language of R2P.

An admittedly tougher case arose in May 2008 in the context of the deadly Cyclone Nargis in Burma. Contradicting official sources, independent observers estimated that the death toll could surpass 100,000. (The actual total was about 146,000.) As many as 1.5 million people were displaced, homeless, and in desperate need of immediate humanitarian relief. Infuriatingly, the generals running—ruining is more accurate—the country refused to open their borders to supplies of aid piling up around Burma. Bizarrely but predictably, they attached higher priority to going ahead with a sham referendum calculated to give their rule a veneer of legitimacy.[79] Against this backdrop, French foreign minister Bernard Kouchner publicly suggested that the Security Council should invoke R2P.

At first glance, the responsibility to protect would seem a strange principle to cite in order to deliver aid to the Burmese. Its provenance is protecting at-risk populations from mass atrocity crimes. Broadening it to cover contingencies such as nuclear proliferation, environmental vandalism, HIV/AIDS, and natural disasters may have the perverse effects of weakening support for R2P when we face the next Rwanda.

Yet, the ICISS's original report indeed identified "overwhelming natural or environmental catastrophes, where the state concerned is either unwilling or unable to cope, or call for assistance, and significant loss of life is occurring or threatened" as among the conscience-shocking situations that would justify international intervention.[80] This was not included in the 2005 World Summit decision, but "crimes against humanity" were included and, as defined in the 1998 ICC statute, would provide at least some of the necessary legal cover to force aside the recalcitrant and negligent generals and give help directly to afflicted people.

Although the legal case for using crimes against humanity as justification for intervention in Burma was plausible, the politics against such action were more compelling. Unless the western powers were willing and able to launch another war in the jungles of Southeast Asia, it was better not to invoke this language at all. This is why John Holmes, the UN's under-secretary-general for humanitarian affairs and former British ambassador to France, described Kouchner's call as unnecessarily confrontational. The

British cabinet minister for international development, Douglas Alexander, rejected it as "incendiary."[81] Britain's UN ambassador, John Sawers, said R2P did not apply to natural disasters.[82]

Invoking the coercive language of R2P would have riled the generals, who time and time again have proven themselves to be beyond shame, and undoubtedly they would have dug in their heels even more firmly. It would have risked antagonizing the Southeast Asian countries, whose political support was vital to communicating with the generals and persuading them to open up. It would have risked alienating China, India, and Japan, the three big Asian powers whose backing was essential for delivering any meaningful relief in Burma.[83]

Faced with growing opposition at all these levels, would the western powers, which were already overstretched militarily in Afghanistan and Iraq and increasingly despised around the world for their belligerence as their default mode of engagement with regimes that do not kowtow to them, be prepared to use military force? If not, would they not damage their own political credibility and that of R2P by invoking it ineffectually? Those who pride themselves on their intellectual toughness are often limp in following through the logic of their calls to arms.

The urgent task was to provide humanitarian relief and reconstruction; military intervention would not have helped and might have imperiled the delivery of such assistance. It would have also set off another war when the goal should be to end those already being fought and stop the threat of new ones erupting. And it would have jeopardized the chances of creating international consensus and generating the political will to take military action when mass killings break out again in some corner of the world, as will assuredly happen.

In the end, R2P was not officially invoked, but it is not necessary for the Security Council to actually put forth a resolution to have an impact. It is plausible, but not verifiable at this juncture, that the "bad cop" Kouchner made it possible for the "good cops" of the Association of Southeast Asian Nations, the Second UN, and other humanitarians to be more effective than they might otherwise have been. In any event, the worst predictions for the aftermath of Cyclone Nargis proved to be overblown. On this occasion, at least, it was probably preferable not to go to the mat and reintroduce the North-South polarization over "humanitarian intervention" that ICISS worked so hard to overcome with the R2P formula.

A related danger is seeking remedy in R2P when better or more appropriate tools and instruments are available for dealing with the crisis at hand. A good example of this occurred in 2009 when Israel launched a massive offensive in Hamas-ruled Gaza, putatively in response to rocket attacks from Gaza against civilian targets in Israel. There were issues of international and UN Charter law involved, including the well-established rights to self-defense against armed attack and to resist foreign occupation, the validity of these justifications for the resort to violence by Israel and Palestinians, and the limits to the exercise of these rights. There were also issues of international humanitarian law: regardless of whether the use of force itself is lawful or not, the conduct of hostilities is still governed by the Geneva Conventions with respect to proportionality, necessity, and distinction between combatants and civilians. There were charges, including by responsible UN officials and special rapporteurs, of the possible commission of war crimes. In the midst of this flurry of actions and possible international measures, the invocation of R2P did not seem to be pressing or relevant. At the same time, the debate over Gaza also raised the further question of the responsibility of occupying powers to protect all peoples living under their occupation, be they Palestinians or Iraqis or Afghans.

Yet another difficult case arose in April–May 2009, when the Sri Lanka defense forces finally ended the 25-year insurgency by the Liberation Tigers of Tamil Eelam with a decisive military victory. The Tigers have been among the most ruthless terrorist organizations and were designated as such by more than thirty countries in 2009. They pioneered the use of women suicide bombers, including the one who assassinated former Indian prime minister Rajiv Gandhi on Indian soil in 1991, and they invented the explosive suicide belt. They killed many civilians, including Tamils; recruited child soldiers; and often raised funds from the Tamil diaspora community through extortion. The 25-year civil war had left more than 70,000 dead in the country. There was some basis for the government's claim therefore that postconflict recovery and progress was not possible until the Tigers had been defeated. The government also argued that the way to avoid civilian carnage was for the Tigers to surrender or permit civilians—who were forcibly being kept hostage as human shields—to leave. Yet none of this, even if true (and, as always, much of this was contentious and furiously contested) obscured the humanitarian tragedy of large-scale civilian deaths and shelling of civilian targets such as schools and hospitals in the shrinking area still held by the Tigers as government troops closed in. To what extent did R2P apply to the Tigers, the government of Sri Lanka, and the international community of states, particularly the responsibility to evacuate the civilians caught in the cross-fire by land, sea, and air?

In January 2009, UN Secretary-General Ban Ki-moon published his report on implementing R2P.[84] Its point of departure is not the original 2001 ICISS report but the relevant clauses from the 2005 *World Summit Outcome* document. It clarifies and elaborates some things, for example the fact that simply because force is the last resort does not mean we have to go through a sequential or graduated set of responses before responding robustly to an urgent crisis.[85] But in practice, as Washington and London discovered in 2003, it will be exceedingly difficult to get UN agreement on the use of force other than as the last resort, after all other options have been tried, have been exhausted, and have failed. The report does not add much to the substance of what ICISS said in 2001, but it does flesh out in greater and clearer detail many of the ideas of the earlier report. It notes explicitly that all peoples inside a state's territorial jurisdiction, not just citizens, must be protected by a state.[86] Following numerous other reports, it reiterates the requirement for early warning capacity—without explaining how the politics of the UN community will be overcome to achieve this.

The report is effective in repackaging R2P in the language of three pillars: the state's own responsibility to protect all peoples on its territory, international assistance to help build a state's capacity to deliver on its responsibility, and the international responsibility to protect. If the metaphor helps garner more widespread support, all praise to Ban and his team. Still, the report goes over the top in elaborating on the metaphor by insisting that the "edifice" of R2P will tilt, totter, and collapse unless all three pillars are of equal height and strength.[87] The most important element, or the weightiest pillar, has to be a state's own responsibility. And the most critical is the willingness and capability of the international community of states to respond to fresh outbreaks of mass atrocities.

Mercifully, and contrary to what many feared, the report does not retreat from the necessity for outside military action. But it does dilute what was the central defining feature of R2P. The commission was called into existence to deal with the problem of brutal leaders killing large numbers of their own people. It built on the landmark Brahimi report of 2000,[88] which noted that the UN cannot be neutral between perpetrators and victims of large-scale violence. We are all happy to help the good guys build state capacity. The challenge is what to do with the bad guys, those intent on doing grave harm who use sovereignty as a license to kill with impunity.

R2P's added value is that it crystallized an emerging new norm of using international force to prevent and halt mass killings by reconceptualizing sovereignty as responsibility. It aims to convert a shocked international conscience into timely and decisive collective action. This requires urgent clarification both with respect to when it should kick in as an international responsibility and when not, who makes these decisions, and on what basis. Do R2P operations require their own distinctive guidelines on the use of force? How and where can we institute systematic risk assessments and early warning indicators to alert us to developing R2P-type crises? How do we build the international capacity and will to protect at-risk populations when state authorities are complicit either through incapacity or (more culpably) direct complicity?

On these key issues, and despite the General Assembly debate and resolution at the end of its 63rd session, we are no further ahead today than in 2005; we seem to be recreating the consensus of that moment instead of implementing the agreed collective responsibility. The UN's use of force against a state's consent will always be controversial and contested. That is no reason to hand over control of the pace, direction, and substance of the agenda of our shared, solemn responsibility to those who are skeptical about R2P. As Jennifer Welsh tells us, "While the Secretary-General's focus on assistance and capacity-building has been a prudent strategy for gaining buy-in from reluctant members of international society, he may have paid too much deference to the opponents of R2P."[89] The original report of ICISS could be said to be the root of this problem, for it failed to make a clear enough distinction between state incapacity, on the one hand, and state complicity through unwillingness or perpetration, on the other hand. The distinction is fine in principle but enormously consequential for policy.

As the Burmese, South Ossetian, and Gaza conundrums show, to date our responses have typically been ad hoc and reactive rather than consolidated, comprehensive, and systematic. We need a paradigm shift from a culture of reaction to one of prevention and rebuilding. Millions lost their lives during the Holocaust and in Cambodia, Rwanda, Srebrenica, and Darfur. After each event, we said "never again," then looked back each next time with varying degrees of incomprehension, horror, anger, and shame, asking ourselves how we could possibly have let it all happen again.

External military intervention to protect civilians inside sovereign borders without the consent of the state concerned differs from traditional warfare, collective security, and peacekeeping. Protecting victims from mass atrocities requires different guidelines and rules of engagement, as well as different relationships between civil authorities and humanitarian actors. As Victoria K. Holt and Tobias C. Berkman argue, such differences need to be identified, articulated, and incorporated into training manuals and courses for military officers.[90] For example, recalling the tragedy of Rwanda, how does a UN peace operation sent to supervise a peace agreement and process recast its task on the fly to prevent an unfolding genocide?

Operationalizing R2P in terms of protection will mean adopting a bottom-up approach that brings together the humanitarian actors on the ground in conflict zones.[91] Each context requires its own specific actions against threats to the people at risk there. The UN can provide the normative mandate at the global level for the protection of such individuals and the forces necessary for intervention if need be. Action to prevent and rebuild has to be undertaken by UN agencies acting collaboratively with local civil society actors, NGOs, and representatives of the International Federation of Red Cross and Red Crescent Societies. They can be brought together in a distinct cluster to assess needs and priorities for each vulnerable group requiring protection and identifying, in advance, the custom-tailored responses that will promote prevention and rebuilding.

At the same time, opponents have a point in cautioning about the moral hazard that would result from overenthusiastic recourse to international intervention. It can create perverse incentives for rebels and dissidents to provoke state retaliation to armed challenges. Kofi Annan recognized this just one year after his "challenge of humanitarian intervention." In his Millennium report, he conceded that his call for a debate on the challenge of humanitarian intervention had led to fears that the concept "might encourage secessionist movements deliberately to provoke governments into committing gross violations of human rights in order to trigger external interventions that would aid their cause."[92] This too requires further research about a topic that is fundamentally a new knowledge gap.

So too does the question of whether groups who constitute a minority in one country and are targeted for killings or ethnic cleansing based on their group identity are owed any responsibility by their kin state: China vis-à-vis overseas Chinese, say in Indonesia, or India vis-à-vis ethnic Indians in Fiji or Tamil Hindus in Sri Lanka, or Russia vis-à-vis Russians in the Baltic states, or Albania vis-à-vis Albanians around the Balkans, or the West vis-à-vis the whites in Zimbabwe. Thus, the Centre for International Governance Innovation has entered into a partnership with the UN University on a new project that draws on historical and contemporary examples and will explore how to apply R2P to the protection of national minorities. Interethnic conflict and genocide have demonstrated the dangers of failing to protect people targeted by their fellow citizens. But unilateral intervention by a kin state can lead to conflict within and between states. This presents a dilemma: while the world cannot stand by when minority rights are being trampled, the protection of national minorities should not be used as an excuse to violate state sovereignty. Therefore, how can R2P be applied to the protection of persons belonging to national minorities? Whose responsibility is it to protect such persons?

Yet another item on the research agenda is examining past cases of iconic examples of horrific atrocities and genocidal killings in twentieth-century history, including the Holocaust, Bangladesh, Cambodia, Rwanda, and the Balkans. The goal would be to identify when and how R2P could have been invoked to legitimize international intervention and prevent or halt the atrocities. The advantage of such research is that these are all cases on which today there is agreement about the shameful failures of outsiders to take effective action in time. The research should help build a database of R2P-type situations as a guide to future deliberations, evidence-based analyses, and robust action.

The Third UN continues its advocacy regarding this issue. For example, a subunit within the World Federalist Movement's office in New York has been engaged in support of R2P for several years. Recognizing that the global endorsement of the norm in 2005 was but the prelude to translating it into timely action to prevent crises and stop atrocities, the Global Centre for the Responsibility to Protect, based at The CUNY Graduate Center's Ralph Bunche Institute, was launched in February 2008.[93] The Global Centre works with all three UNs to make the R2P doctrine a reality. Secretary-General Ban Ki-moon has welcomed its establishment as "an effective advocate in the struggle to prevent the world's most heinous mass crimes."[94] Supported by friendly governments, foundations, and private donors, the Global Centre will generate research, conduct high-level advocacy, and facilitate the activities of those working to advance the R2P agenda.

Conclusion: A Model for Enhancing Global Governance?

The R2P norm has become accepted with a surprising rapidity. When postelection violence broke out in Kenya in early 2008, for example, Francis Deng urged the authorities to meet their responsibility to protect the civilian population[95] and Archbishop Emeritus Desmond Tutu interpreted the African and global reaction to the Kenyan violence as "action on a fundamental principle—the Responsibility to Protect."[96] The interim government does not provide a definitive solution, but at least the very worst was averted in January 2008. While some estimates put the total death toll above 1,000 and the number of internally displaced persons needing assistance at 300,000,[97] it does not take much imagination to recall the vastly larger horror in neighboring Rwanda a decade and a half earlier.

Unlike humanitarian intervention, R2P seeks to place less emphasis on reaction (that is, coercion under Chapter VII) and more on less intrusive policy measures, what some have called "upstream R2P."[98] The importance of development efforts and preventive measures was demonstrated in the reactions to forestall Kenya's postelection violence from becoming even more horrific. Both former Secretary-General Kofi Annan, who was the chief mediator, and Secretary-General Ban Ki-moon have described the collective efforts in early 2008 as an effective application of the logic of R2P prevention.[99]

If we return to the definition of global governance that we offered in the introduction, R2P is about the changing conceptions of the appropriate relations between citizens and states in an interdependent and globalizing world: the norms, laws, and practices that constitute those relations and the variety of civil society, governmental, and intergovernmental actors engaged in efforts to redefine and reconstitute those norms, laws, and practices. Most of these efforts posit the United Nations as the central reference point. ICISS itself was careful to embed R2P within the context of evolving Security Council practices and customary international law. Based on state practice, council precedents, established and emerging norms, and evolving customary international law, the International Commission on Intervention and State Sovereignty held that the proscription against intervention is not absolute. The foundations of the international responsibility to protect lie in obligations inherent in the concept of sovereignty; the responsibility of the Security Council, under Article 24 of the Charter, to maintain international peace and security; specific legal obligations under human rights and human protection declarations, covenants, and treaties, international humanitarian law, and national law; and the developing practices of states, regional organizations, and the council itself.

The United Nations has played a key role in different ways and phases of the process, from the initial articulation of the notion by an individual UN official to a Secretary-General's open challenge to member states to replace the clearly broken consensus on the use of force in order to stop atrocities inside sovereign borders, the creation of an international commission in response to that challenge, the UN policy community's response to that commission's recommendations, and the endorsement of the norm by a summit of world leaders.

In short, R2P has a decided three-UN flavor. It is a good illustration—we hesitate to use the term "model"—of how the three United Nations worked productively and in tandem. It was framed by the Third UN in the form of the International Commission on Intervention and State Sovereignty (an independent commission that was sponsored and spearheaded by Canada) and the work of Francis Deng and Roberta Cohen, both quintessential outside-insiders. Its roots are to be found also in statements from the bully pulpit by the head of the Second UN, former Secretary-General Kofi Annan. The norm gives pride of place to the Security Council if the international community of states is to honor its international responsibility to protect. And a new international consensus based on this norm can only come about in the various forums, especially the General Assembly, of the First UN. Moreover, its intellectual antecedents are to be found in the broader concept of human security, which also was popularized and legitimized by all three United Nations. As Juan Somavía—currently the head of the ILO after having held positions in the Chilean government and NGOs—observes, "The moment the UN begins discussing an issue and it becomes part of programs and institutional debate," which is what happened with human security, "it legitimizes something that otherwise could be perceived as marginal in society."[100]

R2P is an idea, and we should not forget that ideas matter, for good and for ill. Political theorist Daniel Philpott's study of revolutions in sovereignty demonstrates that they have been driven primarily by the power of ideas; and it may just be that we are in the midst of a new revolution in which state sovereignty is more contingent on upholding the values of human rights.[101] Gareth Evans encourages us in his book on the subject: "And for all the difficulties of acceptance and application that lie ahead, there are—I have come optimistically, but firmly, to believe—not many ideas that have the potential to matter more for good, not only in theory but in practice, than that of the responsibility to protect."[102]

The birth and continued evolution of the responsibility to protect—the mobilizer of last resort of the world's conscience in order to avert, prevent, and stop mass killings—is thus a clear illustration of the claim made by the United Nations Intellectual History Project that the world organization has provided an essential space in which powerful normative and policy agendas have been articulated. In an era of cynicism and negativism, the R2P story provides a modest element of hope that improved global governance is a worthwhile and ongoing United Nations journey, one that readers and the authors are far from finishing.

NOTES

Series Editors' Foreword

1. Richard Jolly, Louis Emmerij, and Thomas G. Weiss, *UN Ideas That Changed the World* (Bloomington: Indiana University Press, 2009).

2. Craig N. Murphy, *The UN Development Programme: A Better Way?* (Cambridge: Cambridge University Press, 2006); D. John Shaw, *UN World Food Programme and the Development of Food Aid* (New York: Palgrave, 2001); Maggie Black, *The Children and the Nations* (New York: UNICEF, 1986); and Maggie Black, *Children First: The Story of UNICEF* (Oxford: Oxford University Press, 1996).

3. Thomas G. Weiss, Tatiana Carayannis, Louis Emmerij, and Richard Jolly, *UN Voices: The Struggle for Development and Social Justice* (Bloomington: Indiana University Press, 2005).

4. Louis Emmerij, Richard Jolly, and Thomas G. Weiss, *Ahead of the Curve? UN Ideas and Global Challenges* (Bloomington: Indiana University Press, 2001), xi.

Introduction

1. See David C. Ellis, "On the Possibility of 'International Community,'" *International Studies Review* 11, no. 1 (2009): 1–26.

2. Rorden Wilkinson, "Global Governance: A Preliminary Interrogation," in *Global Governance: Critical Perspectives,* ed. Rorden Wilkinson and Steve Hughes (London: Routledge, 2002), 6.

3. Robert Gilpin, *Global Political Economy* (Princeton, N.J.: Princeton University Press, 2001), 388–389.

4. Randall D. Germain, "Global Financial Governance and the Problem of Inclusion," *Global Governance* 7, no. 4 (2001): 421.

5. See Ramesh Thakur, Andrew F. Cooper, and John English, eds., *International Commissions and the Power of Ideas* (Tokyo: UN University Press, 2005).

6. Louis W. Pauly, "What New Architecture? International Financial Institutions and Global Economic Order," *Global Governance* 7, no. 4 (2001): 482.

7. High-level Panel on Threats, Challenges and Change, *A More Secure World: Our Shared Responsibility* (New York: UN, 2004); Millennium Development Project, *Investing in Development: A Practical Plan to Achieve the Millennium Development Goals* (New York: UNDP, 2005); and Kofi A. Annan, *In Larger Freedom: Towards Development, Security and Human Rights for All* (New York: UN, 2005).

8. "Collective" is an adjective that means "group-based." This modifier may imply universal or global participation (for example, the UN as a collective security organization), but it may imply a narrower scope of participation (for example, NATO is a collective defense organization). See Stephen F. Szabo and Douglas T. Stuart, eds., *Discord and Collaboration in a New Europe: Essays in Honor of Arnold Wolfers* (Lanham, Md.: University Press of America, 1994).

9. See Ernst-Otto Czempiel, "Governance and Democratization," in *Governance without Government: Order and Change in World Politics,* ed. James N. Rosenau and Ernst-Otto Czempiel (Cambridge: Cambridge University Press, 1992), 250–271. Also see Leon Gordenker and Thomas G. Weiss, "Pluralizing Global Governance: Analytical Approaches and Dimensions," in *NGOs, the UN, and Global Governance,* ed. Leon Gordenker and Thomas G. Weiss (Boulder, Colo.: Lynne Rienner, 1996), 17–47.

10. Inis L. Claude, Jr., *Swords into Plowshares: The Problems and Prospects of International Organization* (New York: Random House, 1956); and Inis L. Claude, Jr., "Peace and Security: Prospective Roles for the Two United Nations," *Global Governance* 2, no. 3 (1996): 289–298.

11. This notion was first spelled out in Thomas G. Weiss, Tatiana Carayannis, and Richard Jolly, "The 'Third' United Nations," *Global Governance* 15, no. 1 (2009): 123–142. It also figures prominently in the summary volume by Richard Jolly, Louis Emmerij, and Thomas G. Weiss, *UN Ideas That Changed the World* (Bloomington: Indiana University Press, 2009).

12. For an account of the special positions of NGOs relative to states and international organizations, see Volker Heins, *Nongovernmental Organizations in International Society: Struggles over Recognition* (New York: Palgrave Macmillan, 2008).

13. See Andrew S. Thompson and James W. St. G. Walker, eds., *Critical Mass: The Emergence of Global Civil Society* (Waterloo: Wilfrid Laurier University Press, 2008).

14. John Gerard Ruggie, *Protect, Respect and Remedy: A Framework for Business and Human Rights: Report of the Special Representative of the Secretary-General on the Issue of Human Rights and Transnational Corporations and Other Business Enterprises* (New York: UN, 2008), 3.

15. Thomas S. Kuhn, *The Structure of Scientific Revolutions,* 2nd ed. (Chicago: University of Chicago Press, 1970), 42.

16. For an argument on how shaming is an effective instrument that underpins the efficacy of the European human rights regime, see Andrew Moravcsik, "Explaining International Human Rights Regimes: Liberal Theory and Western Europe," *European Journal of International Relations* 1, no. 2 (1995): 157–189. For a slightly different interpretation of the domestic impact of norms embedded in the European human rights regime, see Jeffrey T. Checkel, "International Norms and Domestic Politics: Bridging the Rationalist-Constructivist Divide," *European Journal of International Relations* 3, no. 4 (1997): 473–495. See also his "Norms, Institutions, and National Identity in Contemporary Europe," *International Studies Quarterly* 43, no. 1 (1999): 83–114.

17. See Simon Chesterman, *Secretary or General? The UN Secretary-General in World Politics* (Cambridge: Cambridge University Press, 2007).

18. Martha Finnemore and Kathryn Sikkink, "International Norm Dynamics and Political Change," *International Organization* 52, no. 4 (1998): 887–917.

19. See Ramesh Thakur and William Maley, "The Ottawa Convention on Landmines: A Landmark Humanitarian Treaty in Arms Control?" *Global Governance* 5, no. 3 (1999): 273–302. See also Don Hubert, *The Landmine Ban: A Case Study in Humanitarian Advocacy,* occasional paper #42 (Providence, R.I.: Thomas J. Watson Institute for International Studies, 2000); and Richard Price "Reversing the Gun Sights: Transnational Civil Society Targets Land Mines," *International Organization* 52, no. 3 (1998): 613–644.

20. The arguments in this section about the UN and international policymaking first appeared in Ramesh Thakur and Thomas G. Weiss, "United Nations 'Policy': An

Argument with Three Illustrations," *International Studies Perspectives* 10, no. 2 (2009): 18–35.

21. Graham Evans and Jeffrey Newnham, *The Penguin Dictionary of International Relations* (London: Penguin Books), 179.

22. See Ramesh Thakur, *The United Nations, Peace and Security: From Collective Security to the Responsibility to Protect* (Cambridge: Cambridge University Press, 2006), 320–342.

23. Christopher Hill, "Foreign Policy," in *The Oxford Companion to the Politics of the World,* ed. Joel Krieger, 2nd ed. (Oxford: Oxford University Press, 2001), 290.

24. Lorenzo Morris, "Public Policy," in *The Oxford Companion to the Politics of the World,* ed. Joel Krieger, 2nd ed. (Oxford: Oxford University Press, 2001), 703.

25. The General Assembly held apartheid to be "a crime against the conscience and dignity of mankind" in "Declaration on Apartheid and Its Destructive Consequences in Southern Africa," General Assembly resolution S-16/1, 14 December 1989.

26. Paul Cammack, "The Mother of All Governments: The World Bank's Matrix for Global Governance," in *Global Governance: Critical Perspectives,* ed. Rorden Wilkinson and Steve Hughes (London: Routledge, 2002), 36–54.

27. Inge Kaul, "Governing Global Public Goods in a Multi-Actor World: The Role of the United Nations," in *New Millennium, New Perspectives: The United Nations, Security, and Governance,* ed. Ramesh Thakur and Edward Newman (Tokyo: UN University Press, 2000), 296–315. See also Inge Kaul, Isabelle Grunberg, and Marc A. Stern, eds., *Global Public Goods: International Cooperation in the 21st Century* (New York: Oxford University Press, 1999).

28. Kaul, "Governing Global Public Goods," 298.

29. David Mitrany, *The Progress of International Government* (New Haven, Conn.: Yale University Press, 1933); and David Mitrany, *A Working Peace System* (Chicago: University of Chicago Press, 1966).

30. E. Dougherty and Robert L. Pfaltzgraff, Jr., *Contending Theories of International Relations: A Comprehensive Survey,* 4th ed. (New York: Longman, 1997), 422.

31. Peter M. Haas, "Introduction: Epistemic Communities and International Policy Coordination," *International Organization* 46, no. 1 (1992): 1–36; and Peter M. Haas, Robert O. Keohane, and Marc A. Levy, eds., *Institutions for the Earth: Sources of Effective International Environmental Protection* (Cambridge, Mass.: MIT Press, 1992).

32. Peter A. Hall, ed., *The Political Power of Economic Ideas: Keynesianism across Nations* (Princeton, N.J.: Princeton University Press, 1989).

33. Ernst B. Haas, *When Knowledge Is Power: Three Models of Change in International Organizations* (Los Angeles: University of California Press, 1994). See also Peter M. Haas and Ernst B. Haas, "Learning to Learn: Improving International Governance," *Global Governance* 1, no. 3 (1995): 255–284.

34. Margaret E. Keck and Kathryn Sikkink, *Activists beyond Borders: Advocacy Networks in International Politics* (Ithaca, N.Y.: Cornell University Press, 1998).

35. Kuhn, *Structure of Scientific Revolutions.*

36. Hans Singer, "An Historical Perspective," in *The UN and the Bretton Woods Institutions: New Challenges for the Twenty-First Century,* ed. Mahbub ul Haq, Richard Jolly, Paul Streeten, and Khadija Haq (London: Macmillan, 1995), 19.

37. See Ramesh Thakur and Peter Malcontent, eds., *From Sovereign Impunity to International Accountability: The Search for Justice in a World of States* (Tokyo: UN University Press, 2004); and Edel Hughes, William A. Schabas, and Ramesh Thakur,

eds., *Atrocities and International Accountability: Beyond Transitional Justice* (Tokyo: UN University Press, 2007).

38. However, state governments within the United States, particularly in the northeast, have banded together and agreed to align their standards with those of the Kyoto Protocol. See Mark Clayton, "One Region's Bid to Slow Global Warming," *The Christian Science Monitor,* 22 December 2005.

39. David Brancaccio, interview with forensic anthropologist Clea Koff on *NOW with Bill Moyers,* 9 July 2004, PBS, transcript available at http://www.pbs.org/now/transcript/transcript328_full.html (accessed 9 July 2009).

40. Kofi A. Annan, *We the Peoples: The Role of the United Nations in the 21st Century* (New York: UN, 2000), 57–58.

41. "Donations Become Mundane but Life-Saving Tsunami Aid," *USA Today,* 9 April 2005, available at http://www.usatoday.com/news/world/2005-04-09-tsunami_x.htm (accessed 1 July 2009); Paul Keilthy, "Expert Talk: Has Tsunami Compassion Killed Other Aid?" Alertnet, 24 January 2005, available at http://www.alertnet.org/thefacts/reliefresources/110657947835.htm (accessed 1 July 2009).

42. Emma Batha, "Tsunami Response Was World's Best—UN," Reuters, 19 December 2005, available at http://www.alertnet.org/thefacts/reliefresources/113777913049.htm (accessed 5 July 2009).

43. UN News Center, "Highlights of Briefing by UN Emergency Relief Coordination on Tsunami Disaster and Other Humanitarian Appeals—Geneva," 11 January 2009, available at http://www.un.org/apps/news/infocus/iraq/infocusnews.asp?NewsID=849&sID=9 (accessed 3 July 2009).

44. See ReliefWeb, "South Asia: Earthquake and Tsunami—Dec. 2004," available at http://www.reliefweb.int/rw/dbc.nsf/doc108?OpenForm&emid=TS-2004-000147-LKA&rc=3 (accessed 5 July 2009).

45. OCHA, "Indonesia, Sri Lanka, Maldives, Thailand and Seychelles: Earthquake and Tsunami," OCHA Situation Report No. 38, ReliefWeb, 29 April 2005, available at http://www.undp.org/cpr/disred/documents/tsunami/ocha/sitrep38.pdf (accessed 3 July 2009).

46. The Steering Committee for the Tsunami Global Lessons Learned Project (TGLLP), *The Tsunami Legacy: Innovation, Breakthroughs and Change* (TGLLP, 2009), available at http://www.undp.org/asia/the-tsunami-legacy.pdf (accessed 4 July 2009).

1. Tracing the Origins of an Idea and the UN's Contribution

1. Parts of this argument also appear in Ramesh Thakur and Thomas G. Weiss, "Global Governance, Five Gaps," in *The Global Community: Yearbook of International Law and Jurisprudence 2008,* vol. 1, ed. Giuliana Ziccardi Capaldo (New York: Oxford University Press, 2009), 77–98.

2. UNDP, *Human Development Report 1999* (New York: Oxford University Press, 1999), 8.

3. James Rosenau and Ernst-Otto Czempiel, eds., *Governance without Government: Order and Change in World Politics* (Cambridge: Cambridge University Press, 1992).

4. Commission on Global Governance, *Our Global Neighbourhood* (Oxford: Oxford University Press, 1995).

5. See Edward Newman, Ramesh Thakur, and John Tirman, eds., *Multilateralism under Challenge? Power, International Order, and Structural Change* (Tokyo: UN University Press, 2006).

6. Anne-Marie Slaughter, *A New World Order* (Princeton, N.J.: Princeton University Press, 2004).

7. Alan Cowell and Dexter Filkins, "British Authorities Say Plot to Blow Up Airliners Was Foiled," *New York Times,* 10 August 2006.

8. For another view, see James A. Yunker, *Rethinking World Government: A New Approach* (Lanham, Md.: University Press of America, 2005). See also Robert Latham, "Politics in a Floating World: Toward a Critique of Global Governance," in *Approaches to Global Governance Theory,* ed. Martin Hewson and Timothy J. Sinclair (Albany: State University of New York Press, 1999), 23–54.

9. See Craig N. Murphy, *International Organization and Industrial Change: Global Governance since 1850* (Cambridge: Polity Press, 1994), 1.

10. Harold K. Jacobson, *Networks of Interdependence: International Organizations and the Global Political System,* 2nd ed. (New York: Alfred A. Knopf, 1984), 84.

11. Quoted in J. Martin Rochester, *Between Promise and Peril: The Politics of International Law* (Washington, D.C.: CQ Press, 2006), 27.

12. Edward Hallett Carr, *The Twenty Years' Crisis, 1919–1939* (New York: Harper Torchbooks, 1964), 108.

13. See, for example, Ramesh Thakur, *The United Nations, Peace and Security: From Collective Security to the Responsibility to Protect* (Cambridge: Cambridge University Press, 2006); and Thomas G. Weiss, *What's Wrong with the UN and How to Fix It* (Cambridge: Polity Press, 2009), 215–233; and Thomas G. Weiss, "What Happened to the Idea of World Government?" *International Studies Quarterly* 53, no. 2 (2009): 253–271.

14. UNDP, *Human Development Report 1999,* 8.

15. Hedley Bull, *The Anarchical Society: A Study of Order in World Politics* (New York: Columbia University Press, 1977).

16. Martha Craven Nussbaum, *Frontiers of Justice: Disability, Nationality, Species Membership* (Cambridge, Mass: The Belknap Press, 2006); and David Held and Anthony G. McGrew, *Globalization/Anti-Globalization: Beyond the Great Divide* (Cambridge: Polity Press, 2007). See also Antonio Franceschet, *The Ethics of Global Governance* (Boulder, Colo.: Lynn Rienner, 2009).

17. Murphy, *International Organization and Industrial Change,* 9.

18. Oran Young, *International Governance: Protecting the Environment in a Stateless Society* (Ithaca, N.Y.: Cornell University Press, 1994), 30.

19. Ernst-Otto Czempiel, "Governance and Democratization," in *Governance without Government: Order and Change in World Politics,* ed. James Rosenau and Ernst-Otto Czempiel (Cambridge: Cambridge University Press, 1992), 250.

20. For example, see David Held and Anthony McGrew, with David Goldblatt and Jonathan Perraton, *Global Transformations: Politics, Economics, and Culture* (Stanford, Calif.: Stanford University Press, 1999).

21. Moisés Naim, *Illicit: How Smugglers, Traffickers, and Copycats Are Hijacking the Global Economy* (New York: Anchor, 2006); Misha Glenny, *McMafia: A Journey through the Global Criminal Underworld* (New York: Alfred A. Knopf, 2008); and Douglas Farah and Stephen Braun, *Merchant of Death: Money, Guns, Planes, and the Man Who Makes Them Possible* (Hoboken, N.J.: Wiley, 2008).

22. Amit Bhaduri and Deepak Nayyar, *The Intelligent Person's Guide to Liberalization* (New Delhi: Penguin, 1996), 67.

23. See, for example, Paul Hirst Grahame Thompson, *Globalization in Question: The International Economy and the Possibilities of Governance* (Cambridge: Polity Press, 1996).

24. Deepak Nayyar, "Globalisation, History and Development: A Tale of Two Centuries," *Cambridge Journal of Economics* 30, no. 1 (2006): 153–154.

25. Ibid., 137–159 and especially 153–156.

26. World Commission on the Social Dimension of Globalization, *A Fair Globalization: Creating Opportunities for All* (Geneva: ILO, 2004), xi.

27. Deepak Nayyar was a member of the ILO commission and the leader of a UN University project published as Deepak Nayyar, ed., *Governing Globalization: Issues and Orientations* (Oxford: Oxford University Press, 2002).

28. Craig N. Murphy, "Global Governance: Poorly Done and Poorly Understood," *International Affairs* 76, no. 4 (2000): 789.

29. Murphy, *International Organization and Industrial Change,* 47–48. Murphy identifies thirty-three world organizations that existed in 1914–1915 that were charged with the responsibility for fostering industry, five for managing potential social conflict, four for strengthening states and the state system, and nine for strengthening society in such areas as human rights, relief, welfare, health, and education.

30. Inis L. Claude, Jr., *Swords into Plowshares: The Problems and Progress of International Organizations,* 4th ed. (New York: Random House, 1971), 24.

31. Ibid., 34.

32. Ibid.

33. See, for example, David Kennedy, "Challenging Expert Rule: The Politics of Global Governance," *Sydney Law Review* 27, no. 1 (2005), available at www.austlii.edu.au/au/journals/SydLRev/2005/1.html#fn1; and Martin Hewson and Timothy J. Sinclair, "The Emergence of Global Governance Theory," in *Approaches to Global Governance Theory,* ed. Martin Hewson and Timothy J. Sinclair (Albany: State University of New York Press, 1999), 3–22.

34. Rorden Wilkinson, "Global Governance: A Preliminary Interrogation," in *Global Governance: Critical Perspectives,* ed. Rorden Wilkinson and Steve Hughes (London: Routledge, 2002), 2.

35. Jan Aart Scholte, "From Government to Governance: Transition to a New Diplomacy," in *Global Governance and Diplomacy: Worlds Apart,* ed. Andrew F. Cooper, Brian Hocking, and William Maley (Basingstoke, UK: Palgrave Macmillan, 2008), 49–55.

36. High-level Panel on Threats, Challenges and Change, *A More Secure World: Our Shared Responsibility* (New York: UN, 2004); and Kofi A. Annan, *In Larger Freedom: Towards Development, Security and Human Rights for All* (New York: UN, 2005).

37. Raymond Aron, *Peace and War: A Theory of International Relations,* translated from the French by Richard Howard and Annette Baker Fox (New York: Frederick A. Praeger, 1967), 5; emphasis in original.

38. Quoted in Thomas G. Weiss, Tatiana Carayannis, Louis Emmerij, and Richard Jolly, *UN Voices: The Struggle for Development and Social Justice* (Bloomington: Indiana University Press, 2005), 409–410.

39. This is treated in some depth in ibid., 371–405.

40. Friedrich V. Kratochwil, *Rules, Norms, and Decisions: On the Conditions of Practical and Legal Reasoning in International Relations and Domestic Affairs* (Cambridge: Cambridge University Press, 1989), 10–11.

41. See Ramesh Thakur, "The Problem at the UN Is Not National Quotas," *International Herald Tribune,* 12 March 2005.

42. See Weiss, Carayannis, Emmerij, and Jolly, *UN Voices,* 315–405; and Michael Schechter, *Global Conferences* (London: Routledge, 2005).

43. *We the Peoples: Civil Society, the UN and Global Governance,* Report of the Panel of Eminent Persons on UN-Civil Society Relationships, General Assembly document A/58/817, 11 June 2004, 23. (This is the Cardoso report.)

44. Ibid., 13.

45. Ibid., 12.

46. Ibid., 29.

47. See also David Cortright, *A Peaceful Superpower: The Movement against War in Iraq* (Goshen, Ind.: Fourth Freedom Forum, 2004).

48. John Gerard Ruggie, "International Regimes, Transactions, and Change: Embedded Liberalism in the Post-War Economic Order," *International Organization* 36, no. 2 (1982): 196.

49. Robert O. Keohane, "A Functional Theory of Regimes," in *International Politics: Enduring Concepts and Contemporary Issues,* ed. Robert J. Art and Robert Jervis, 5th ed. (New York: Longman, 2000), 135.

50. Judith Goldstein and Robert O. Keohane, "Ideas and Foreign Policy: An Analytical Framework," in *Ideas and Foreign Policy: Beliefs, Institutions, and Political Change,* ed. Judith Goldstein and Robert O. Keohane (Ithaca, N.Y.: Cornell University Press, 1993), 1–30.

51. Quoted in Weiss, Carayannis, Emmerij, and Jolly, *UN Voices,* 420.

52. Ibid., 420–421.

53. Ibid., 423.

54. Quoted in Gardiner Harris and Lawrence K. Altman, "Managing a Flu Threat With Seasoned Urgency," *New York Times,* 10 May 2009.

55. See Chiyuki Aoi, Cedric de Coning, and Ramesh Thakur, eds., *Unintended Consequences of Peacekeeping Operations* (Tokyo: UN University Press, 2007).

56. See Ramesh Thakur and Edward Newman, eds., *New Millennium, New Perspectives: The United Nations, Security, and Governance* (Tokyo: UN University Press, 2000); and Hans van Ginkel and Ramesh Thakur, eds., *Embracing the Millennium: Perspectives and Challenges for the United Nations and the International Community* (Tokyo: UN University, 2001).

57. Kofi Annan, "Problems without Passports," *Foreign Policy* 132 (September–October 2002): 30–31.

58. See Ramesh Thakur, "Human Rights: Amnesty International and the United Nations," in *The Politics of Global Governance: International Organizations in an Interdependent World,* ed. Paul F. Diehl (Boulder, Colo.: Lynne Rienner, 1997), 247–268.

2. The Use of Force

1. See Human Security Centre, *Human Security Report 2005: War and Peace in the 21st Century* (New York: Oxford University Press, 2005). See also Human Security Report Project, *Human Security Brief 2007* (Vancouver, B.C.: Simon Fraser University, 2008); and World Bank and Human Security Report Project, *Miniatlas of Human Security* (Brighton, UK: Myriad Editions, 2008).

2. John Lewis Gaddis, *The Long Peace: Inquiries into the History of the Cold War* (Oxford: Oxford University Press, 1989).

3. Human Security Center, *Human Security Report 2005,* 1–2.

4. The Kellogg-Briand Pact is available at http://www.yale.edu/lawweb/avalon/imt/kbpact.htm (accessed 9 July 2009).

5. Raymond Aron, *Peace & War: A Theory of International Relations* (New York: Doubleday, 1968), 710–711.

6. Abraham Lincoln, "Second Inaugural Address," 4 March 1865, available at http://www.bartleby.com/124/pres32.html (accessed 9 July 2009).

7. The figures are from Tony Judt, "What Have We Learned, If Anything?" *New York Review of Books*, 1 May 2008, available at http://www.nybooks.com/articles/21311 (accessed 9 July 2009).

8. Robert J. Rummel, *Death by Government* (New Brunswick, N.J.: Transaction Publishers, 1994), 1–28.

9. See Hugo Slim, *Killing Civilians: Method, Madness, and Morality in War* (New York: Columbia University Press, 2008).

10. Judt, "What Have We Learned?"

11. Ibid.

12. See Human Rights Watch, *Fatal Strikes: Israel's Indiscriminate Attacks against Civilians in Lebanon* (New York: Human Rights Watch, 2006); Amnesty International, "Lebanon: Deliberate Destruction or 'Collateral Damage'? Israeli Attacks against Civilian Infrastructure," Amnesty International Report MDE 02/018/2006, 23 August 2006, available online at www.amnesty.org/en/library/info/MDE18/007/2006.

13. Les Roberts, Riyadh Lafta, Richard Garfield, Jamal Khudhairi, and Gilbert Burnham, "Mortality Before and After the 2003 Invasion of Iraq: Cluster Sample Survey," *Lancet* 364, no. 9445 (30 October 2004): 1555–1638. The team was from Johns Hopkins University's Bloomberg School of Public Health with assistance from doctors at Al-Mustansiriya University Medical School in Baghdad.

14. Benjamin Coghlan, Richard J. Brennan, Pascal Ngoy, David Dofara, Brad Otto, Mark Clements, and Tony Stewart, "Mortality in the Democratic Republic of Congo: A Nationwide Survey," *The Lancet* 367, no. 9504 (7–13 January 2006): 44–51.

15. See James E. Dougherty and Robert L. Pfaltzgraff, *Contending Theories of International Relations: A Comprehensive Survey*, 5th ed. (New York: Longman, 2001).

16. Geoffrey Blainey, *The Causes of War*, 3rd ed. (New York: Free Press, 1988); and Richard K. Betts, *Conflict after the Cold War: Arguments on the Causes of War and Peace*, 3rd ed. (New York: Pearson, 2008).

17. Kalevi Holsti, *Armed Conflicts and International Order, 1648–1989* (Cambridge: Cambridge University Press, 1991). See also Katharina P. Coleman, *International Organizations and Peace Enforcement* (Cambridge: Cambridge University Press, 2007).

18. Michael W. Doyle, *Ways of War and Peace: Realism, Liberalism, and Socialism* (New York: W. W. Norton, 1997).

19. A good snapshot of contemporary research on issues of war and peace can be seen in any issue of the *Journal of Conflict Resolution*.

20. See Mats R. Berdal and David M. Malone, eds., *Greed and Grievance: Economic Agendas in Civil Wars* (Boulder, Colo.: Lynne Rienner, 2000); Karen Ballentine and Jake Sherman, eds., *The Political Economy of Armed Conflict: Beyond Greed and Grievance* (Boulder, Colo.: Lynne Rienner, 2003); and Michael Pugh and Neil Cooper, *War Economies in a Regional Context: The Challenge of Transformation* (Boulder, Colo.: Lynne Rienner, 2004). Another seminal book on the subject is Paul Collier, *Breaking the Conflict Trap: Civil War and Development Policy* (New York: Oxford University Press, 2003).

21. See Center for International Cooperation, *Annual Review of Global Peace Operations 2008* (Boulder: Colo.: Lynne Rienner, 2008). See also Alex J. Bellamy, Paul Williams, and Stuart Griffin, *Understanding Peacekeeping* (Cambridge: Polity Press,

2004); Alex J. Bellamy and Paul Williams, eds., *Peace Operations and Global Order* (London: Taylor and Francis, 2005); Lise Morjé Howard, *UN Peacekeeping in Civil Wars* (Cambridge: Cambridge University Press, 2007); Beatrice Pouligny, *Peace Operations Seen from Below* (Bloomfield, Conn.: Kumarian Press, 2006); Eli Stamnes, ed., *Peace Support Operations* (New York: Routledge, 2008); and Thierry Tardy, ed., *Peace Operations after 11 September 2001* (London: Frank Cass, 2004).

22. Human Security Center, *Human Security Report 2005*.

23. See Ramesh Thakur, *War in Our Time: Reflections on Iraq, Terrorism and Weapons of Mass Destruction* (Tokyo: UN University Press, 2007).

24. For an early historical overview, see Alan James, *Peacekeeping in International Politics* (London: Macmillan, 1990). See also an authoritative and succinct update in Paul Diehl, *Peace Operations* (Cambridge: Polity Press, 2008). See also Bertrand G. Ramcharan, *Preventive Diplomacy at the UN* (Bloomington: Indiana University Press, 2008).

25. Lester B. Pearson, "Force for U.N.," *Foreign Affairs* 35, no. 3 (1957): 401.

26. *Report of the Secretary-General on Basic Points for the Presence and Functioning in Egypt of the United Nations Emergency Force*, General Assembly document A/3289, 4 November 1956.

27. Ibid.

28. For the use of force in UN operations, see Trevor Findlay, *The Use of Force in UN Peace Operations* (Oxford: Oxford University Press, 2002).

29. Up-to-date figures can always be found at www.un.org/Depts/dpko/dpko. See also Center for International Cooperation, *Annual Review of Global Peace Operations 2008*.

30. Michael C. Doyle and Nicolas Sambanis, *Making War and Building Peace: The United Nations since the 1990s* (Princeton, N.J.: Princeton University Press, 2006).

31. Panel on United Nations Peace Operations, *Report of the Panel on United Nations Peace Operations* (New York: UN, 2000). This report is commonly known as the Brahimi report. For an early assessment, see David M. Malone and Ramesh Thakur, "UN Peacekeeping: Lessons Learned?" *Global Governance* 7, no. 1 (2001): 11–17. See also Kathleen M. Jennings and Anua T. Kaspersen, "Introduction: Integration Revisited," *International Peacekeeping* 15, no. 4 (2008): 443–609.

32. Panel on United Nations Peacekeeping Operations, *Report of the Panel*, viii.

33. Ibid., para. 51.

34. Ironically, in 2004, as the UN special envoy for Iraq, Brahimi was criticized for exceeding his brief when he made the rather obvious point that the Palestinian conflict cast a complicating shadow over efforts to stabilize the security situation in Iraq.

35. Roméo Dallaire, *Shake Hands with the Devil: The Failure of Humanity in Rwanda* (New York: Random House, 2003), 56.

36. UN, *United Nations Peacekeeping: Meeting New Challenges* (New York: UN Department of Public Information, 2006), available at http://www.un.org/Depts/dpko/dpko/faq/q&a.pdf (accessed 9 July 2009).

37. Alexandra Olson, "UN Peacekeeping Split to 2 Departments," Associated Press, 29 June 2007, available at http://www.blnz.com/news/2007/06/30/UN_peacekeeping_split_departments_ents.html (accessed 12 July 2009).

38. See Robert Jenkins, *Peace-Building: From Concept to Commission* (London: Routledge, forthcoming).

39. High-level Panel on Threats, Challenges and Change, *A More Secure World: Our Shared Responsibility* (New York: UN, 2004), 16.

40. Panel on United Nations Peace Operations, *Report of the Panel,* para. 68.

41. International Commission on Intervention and State Sovereignty, *The Responsibility to Protect* (Ottawa: International Development Research Centre, 2001), 21–22.

42. Canadian Peacebuilding Coordinating Committee, *Towards a Rapid Reaction Capability for the UN* (Ottawa: Government of Canada, 1992).

43. Pearson, "Force for U.N."

44. Alan J. Kuperman, *The Limits of Humanitarian Intervention: Genocide in Rwanda* (Washington, D.C.: Brookings Institution Press, 2001).

45. Stephanie Nebehay, "UN Plans Rapid Reaction Aid Force," Reuters, 18 March 2005, available at http://www.globalpolicy.org/security/peacekpg/reform/2005/0318announce.htm.

46. Robert C. Johansen, ed., *A United Nations Emergency Peace Service to Prevent Genocide and Crimes against Humanity* (New York: Global Action to Prevent War, Nuclear Age Peace Foundation, and World Federalist Movement, 2006), available at http://www.globalactionpw.org/wp/wp-content/uploads/uneps_publication.pdf (accessed 9 July 2009).

47. See Arnold Wolfers, *Discord and Collaboration: Essays on International Politics* (Baltimore, Md.: Johns Hopkins University Press, 1962), 167–204.

48. Brian Urquhart, "Peacekeeping: A View from the Operational Center," in *Peacekeeping: Appraisals and Proposals,* ed. Henry Wiseman (New York: Pergamon, 1983), 165.

49. Panel on United Nations Peace Operations, *Report of the Panel,* para. 50.

50. The language and the argument of the Brahimi report is borrowed from a speech by Kofi Annan to the Council on Foreign Relations in New York in 1999; see Ian Johnstone, "The Role of the UN Secretary-General: The Power of Persuasion Based on Law," *Global Governance* 9, no. 4 (2003): 444.

51. See Ruth Wedgwood, "The Multinational Action in Iraq and International Law" for the argument that the war was both legal and legitimate, in *The Iraq Crisis and World Order I: Structural and Normative Challenges,* ed. Ramesh Thakur and W. P. S. Sidhu (Tokyo: UN University Press, 2006), 413–425. See also Charlotte Ku, "Legitimacy as an Assessment of Existing Legal Standards: The Case of the 2003 Iraq War," in ibid., 397–412; and David Kreiger, "The War in Iraq as Illegal and Illegitimate," in ibid., 381–396.

52. Kofi Annan, *Facing the humanitarian challenge: towards a culture of prevention* (New York: UN Department of Public Information, 1999), para. 23.

53. Commission on Global Governance, *Our Global Neighbourhood* (Oxford: Oxford University Press, 1995), 90.

54. Gerald B. Helman and Stephen R. Ratner, "Saving Failed States," *Foreign Policy* 89 (Winter 1992–1993): 3–20.

55. See Martin Meredith, *The State of Africa: A History of Fifty Years of Independence* (London: Free Press, 2005).

56. See, for example, Gérard Prunier, *The Rwanda Crisis: A History of a Genocide* (New York: Columbia University Press, 1995).

57. Thomas G. Weiss, *Military-Civilian Interactions: Humanitarian Crises and the Responsibility to Protect,* 2nd ed. (Lanham, Md.: Rowman & Littlefield, 2005), 97.

58. Jared Diamond, *Collapse: How Societies Choose to Fail or Succeed* (New York: Viking, 2005).

59. Peter Uvin, *Aid and Violence: The Role of Development Assistance in the Rwandan Genocide* (West Hartford, Conn.: Kumarian, 1998); see also Weiss, *Military-Civilian Interactions,* 98.

60. Weiss, *Military-Civilian Interactions.*

61. Data compiled by the International Rescue Committee. See "Mortality in the Democratic Republic of the Congo: An Ongoing Crisis," available at http://www.theirc.org/resources/2007/2006-7_congomortalitysurvey.pdf (10 July 2009).

62. Andrew F. Cooper and John English, "International Commissions and the Mind of Global Governance," in *International Commissions and the Power of Ideas,* ed. Ramesh Thakur, Andrew F. Cooper, and John English (Tokyo: UN University Press, 2005), 23.

63. Carnegie Commission on Preventing Deadly Conflict, *Preventing Deadly Conflict* (New York: Carnegie Commission on Preventing Deadly Conflict, 1997). See also David A. Hamburg, *Preventing Genocide: Practical Steps toward Early Detection and Effective Action* (Boulder, Colo.: Paradigm Publishers, 2008); Chester A. Crocker, Fen Osler Hampson, and Pamela Aall, *Leashing the Dogs of War: Conflict Management in a Divided World* (Washington, D.C.: U.S. Institute of Peace Press, 2007); Fen Osler Hampson and David Malone, eds., *From Reaction to Conflict Prevention: Opportunities for the UN System in the New Millennium* (Boulder, Colo.: Lynne Rienner, 2002); and Chandra Lekha Sriram and Karin Wermester, eds., *From Promise to Practice: Strengthening UN Capacities for the Prevention of Violent Conflict* (Boulder, Colo.: Lynne Rienner, 2003).

64. In addition to International Commission on Intervention and State Sovereignty, *The Responsibility to Protect* (Ottawa: International Development Research Centre, 2001), available at http://www.iciss.ca/pdf/Commission-Report.pdf (accessed 10 July 2009), see also Thomas G. Weiss and Don Hubert, *The Responsibility to Protect: Research, Bibliography, and Background* (Ottawa: International Development Research Centre, 2001). An updated bibliography and both volumes are available at http://web.gc.cuny.edu/RalphBuncheInstitute/ICISS/index.htm.

65. See Ramesh Thakur, Andrew F. Cooper, and John English, eds., *International Commissions and the Power of Ideas* (Tokyo: UN University Press, 2005).

66. Thomas G. Weiss, Tatiana Carayannis, Louis Emmerij, and Richard Jolly, *UN Voices: The Struggle for Development and Social Justice* (Bloomington: Indiana University Press, 2005), 382.

67. David A. Hamburg, *Preventing Genocide: Practical Steps toward Early Detection and Effective Action* (Boulder, Colo.: Paradigm Publishers, 2008).

68. Other members were Virendra Dayal, Alexander L. George, Flora MacDonald, Donald F. McHenry, Olara A. Otunnu, David Owen, Roald Z. Sagdeev, John D. Steinbruner, Brian Urquhart, John C. Whitehead, and Sahabzada Yaqub-Khan.

69. Carnegie Commission on Preventing Deadly Conflict, *Preventing Deadly Conflict,* xviii–xix.

70. Ibid., xxxv.

71. These publications are listed in ibid., 180–181.

72. Thomas G. Weiss, "The UN's Prevention Pipe-Dream," *Berkeley Journal of International Law* 14, no. 2 (1996): 423–437; and Stephen John Stedman, "Alchemy for a New World Order: Overselling 'Preventive Diplomacy,'" *Foreign Affairs* 74, no. 3 (1995): 14–20.

73. In addition to Evans, the representatives from the North included Lee Hamilton, Michael Ignatieff, Klaus Naumann, Cornelio Sommaruga, and Gisèle Côté-

Harper. In addition to Sahnoun, the representatives from the South included Ramesh Thakur, Cyril Ramaphosa, Fidel Ramos, and Eduardo Stein. Russia's Vladimir Lukin completed the group.

74. International Commission on Intervention and State Sovereignty, *The Responsibility to Protect*, 19–27.

75. Ibid., 27.

76. Annan, *Facing the humanitarian challenge*, General Assembly document A/54/1, September 1999, para. 23.

77. High-level Panel on Threats, Challenges and Change, *A More Secure World*, 15–16.

78. Kofi A. Annan, *In Larger Freedom: Towards Development, Security and Human Rights for All* (New York: UN, 2005), 33.

79. *2005 World Summit Outcome*, General Assembly resolution A/RES/60/1, 24 October 2005, para. 71.

80. This section of the chapter draws upon Ramesh Thakur and Luk Van Langenhove, "Enhancing Global Governance through Regional Integration," *Global Governance* 12, no. 3 (2006): 233–240.

81. "Statement by the President of the Security Council," Security Council document S/PRST/2004/27, 20 July 2004.

82. High-level Panel on Threats, Challenges and Change, *A More Secure World*, 85–87.

83. Annan, *In Larger Freedom*, 27.

84. "UN Stresses Key Role of Regional Groups in Peacebuilding," *UN Daily News*, DH/4443, 26 July 2005, 7, available at http://www.un.org/news/dh/pdf/english/2005/26072005.pdf (accessed 10 July 2009).

85. *2005 World Summit Outcome*, paras. 93 and 170.

86. *A Regional-Global Security Partnership: Challenges and Opportunities: Report of the Secretary-General* (New York: UN, 2006).

87. Hedley Bull, *The Anarchical Society: A Study of Order and Disorder in International Society* (New York: Columbia University Press, 1977).

88. See Vesselin Popovski, Gregory M. Reichberg, and Nicholas Turner, eds., *Religion and the Norms of War* (Tokyo: UN University Press, 2009).

89. Thomas Meaney and Harris Mylonas, "Georgia a Policy Debacle for US," *The Age* (Melbourne), 13 August 2008; Juan Cole, "Putin's War Enablers: Bush and Cheney," *Salon.com*, 14 August 2008, available at www.salon.com/opinion/feature/2008/08/14/bush_putin/html; Mark Almond, "Plucky Little Georgia? No, the Cold War Reading Won't Wash," *The Guardian*, 9 August 2008; and Simon Jenkins, "Bush Rebuking Russia? Putin Must Be Splitting His Sides," *The Guardian*, 13 August 2008.

90. Michael J. Glennon, "Platonism, Adaptivism, and Illusion in UN Reform," *Chicago Journal of International Law* 6, no. 2 (2006): 613–641.

91. Ibid., 619.

92. Johansen, ed., *A United Nations Emergency Peace Service*.

3. Arms Control and Disarmament

1. George P. Shultz, William J. Perry, Henry A. Kissinger, and Sam Nunn, "A World Free of Nuclear Weapons," *The Wall Street Journal*, 4 January 2007; and George P. Shultz, William J. Perry, Henry A. Kissinger, and Sam Nunn, "Toward a Nuclear-Free World," *The Wall Street Journal*, 15 January 2008.

2. Ivo Daalder and Jan Lodal, "The Logic of Zero: Toward a World without Nuclear Weapons," *Foreign Affairs* 87, no. 6 (2008): 81.

3. See Center for Strategic and International Studies, *Toward a Grand Strategy for an Uncertain World: Renewing Transatlantic Partnership* (Washington, D.C.: Center for Strategic and International Studies, 2008), 94.

4. For a review of the range of issues, see Jane Boulden, Ramesh Thakur, and Thomas G. Weiss, eds., *The United Nations and Nuclear Orders* (Tokyo: UN University Press, 2009).

5. High-level Panel on Threats, Challenges and Change, *A More Secure World: Our Shared Responsibility* (New York: UN, 2004), 40.

6. ICRC, "Introduction, Final Act of the International Peace Conference, The Hague, 29 July 1899," available at http://www.icrc.org/ihl.nsf/INTRO/145?Open Document (accessed 9 December 2008).

7. For a discussion of antinuclear activism, see, for example, Sam Marullo and David S. Meyer, "Antiwar and Peace Movements," in *The Blackwell Companion to Social Movements,* ed. David A. Snow, Sarah A. Soule, and Hanspeter Kriesi (Oxford: Blackwell Publishing, 2007), 641–665.

8. "Arms Control Chronology," *U.S. Foreign Policy Agenda* 2, no. 3 (1997): 24.

9. Joseph Cirincione, *Bomb Scare: The History and Future of Nuclear Weapons* (New York: Columbia University Press, 2008).

10. The text of the NPT can be found at http://www.un.org/events/npt2005/ npttreaty.html.

11. William M. Arkin, "The Sky-Is-Still-Falling Profession," *Bulletin of the Atomic Scientists* 50, no. 2 (1994): 64. For a useful review of the literature on proliferation, see William C. Potter and Gaukhar Mukhatzhanova, "Divining Nuclear Intentions: A Review Essay," *International Security* 33, no. 1 (2008): 139–169. See also Ramesh Thakur, "The Last Bang Before a Total Ban: French Nuclear Testing in the Pacific," *International Journal* 51, no. 3 (1996): 466–86.

12. Mvemba Phezo Dizolele, Rachel Stohl, and Mgmt. Design, "The Toll of Small Arms," *New York Times,* 4 September 2006. The *Small Arms Survey* is published by the Graduate Institute for International Studies in Geneva.

13. See Jacques E. C. Hymans, *The Psychology of Nuclear Proliferation: Identity, Emotions, and Foreign Policy* (New York: Cambridge University Press, 2006); Etel Solingen, *Nuclear Logics: Alternative Paths in East Asia and the Middle East* (Princeton, N.J.: Princeton University Press, 2007); Richard Rhodes, *Arsenals of Folly: The Making of the Nuclear Arms Race* (New York: Alfred A. Knopf, 2007); Michael A. Levi and Michael E. O'Hanlon, *The Future of Arms Control* (Washington, D.C.: Brookings Institution Press, 2005); Kurt M. Campbell, Robert J. Einhorn, and Mitchell B. Reiss, eds., *The Nuclear Tipping Point: Why States Reconsider Their Nuclear Choices* (Washington, D.C.: Brookings Institution Press, 2004); and Alexander T. J. Lennon, ed., *Contemporary Nuclear Debates: Missile Defenses, Arms Control, and Arms Races in the Twenty-First Century* (Boston: MIT Press, 2002).

14. Quoted in Nuclear Age Peace Foundation, "Albert Einstein: Man of Imagination," available at www.wagingpeace.org/menu/action/urgent-actions/ einstein/index.htm.

15. Kofi Annan, *Assistance in Mine Action: Report of the Secretary-General* (New York: UN, 2001).

16. Conference of the Committee on Disarmament, *Comprehensive Study of the Question of Nuclear-Weapon-Free Zones in All of Its Aspects* (New York: UN, 1976); and

Study on the Question of Nuclear-Weapon-Free Zones. The latter report was never finalized and officially may not exist. (A copy of the draft was given to Ramesh Thakur.) But it forms an annex to a letter of 9 February 1985 from the chairman of the Group of Experts, Klaus Törnudd of Finland, to the Secretary-General of the United Nations. Cited in Jan Prawitz, "Negotiating Nuclear-Weapon-Free Zone," in *Containing the Atom: International Negotiations on Nuclear Security and Safety,* ed. Rudolf Avenhaus, Victor Kremenyuk, and Gunnar Sjöstedt (Lanham, Md.: Lexington Books, 2002), 124n18.

17. Kofi Annan, *United Nations Study on Disarmament and Non-Proliferation Education: Report of the Secretary-General* (New York: UN, 2002).

18. Charles Perrow, *Normal Accidents: Living with High-Risk Technologies* (New York: Basic Books, 1984), 326.

19. Richard Price and Nina Tannenwald, "Norms and Deterrence: The Nuclear and Chemical Weapons Taboos," in *The Culture of National Security: Norms and Identity in World Politics,* ed. Peter J. Katzenstein (New York: Columbia University Press, 1996), 114–152. Price and Tannenwald attribute the fact that the United States has not used nuclear weapons since 1945 to its essentially democratic government and its self-conception as a moral actor in world affairs (139–141), yet they fail to see that this does not explain the equally compelling example of non-use by the Soviet Union.

20. Department of Foreign Affairs and Trade, *Report of the Canberra Commission on the Elimination of Nuclear Weapons Canberra* (Canberra: DFAT, 1996), 18–22.

21. As an editorial in the *Japan Times* put it, "Nuclear stockpiles must be reduced and then eliminated. . . . As the cycle of action and reaction in South Asia has proven, nuclear stockpiles feed on themselves." See "South Asia's Nuclear Chain Reaction," *Japan Times,* 30 May 1998.

22. Japan Institute of International Affairs and Hiroshima Peace Institute, *Facing Nuclear Dangers: An Action Plan for the 21st Century: The Report of the Tokyo Forum for Nuclear Non-Proliferation and Disarmament,* 25 July 1999, available at http://www.mofa .go.jp/policy/un/disarmament/forum/tokyo9907/report-1.html (accessed 15 July 2009).

23. Weapons of Mass Destruction Secretariat, *Weapons of Terror: Freeing the World of Nuclear, Biological and Chemical Arms* (Stockholm: Weapons of Mass Destruction Secretariat, 2006).

24. Jayantha Dhanapala and Ramesh Thakur, "Let's Get Together against Terrorism," *International Herald Tribune,* 4 June 2002.

25. For additional information, see the Web site of the International Commission on Nuclear Non-proliferation and Disarmament at www.icnnd.org.

26. Keith A. Hansen, *The Comprehensive Nuclear Test Ban Treaty: An Insider's Perspective* (Stanford, Calif.: Stanford University Press, 2006). For useful background to the debate on the comprehensive test ban, see Thomas Schmalberger, *In Pursuit of a Nuclear Test Ban Treaty* (New York: UN, 1991).

27. For more about states as depositories, see "United Nations Treaty Collection: Treaty Reference Guide," available at http://untreaty.un.org/ENGLISH/guide.pdf (accessed 14 July 2009).

28. In 2005, a total of 908 facilities were subject to the IAEA routine safeguards inspections in 152 countries that had safeguards agreements with the agency. Moreover, sixty-five NPT states had ratified the IAEA Model Additional Protocol. UN, *2005 Review Conference of the Parties to the Treaty on the Non-Proliferation of Nuclear Weapons, 2–27 May 2005, New York* (New York: UN Department for Disarmament Affairs, April 2005), 3, available at http://www.un.org/events/npt2005/presskit.pdf (accessed 9 July 2009).

29. Savita Pande, *India and the Nuclear Test Ban* (New Delhi: Institute for Defence Studies and Analyses, 1996), 25. See also Šumit Ganguly, *Conflict Unending: India-Pakistan Tensions since 1947* (New York: Columbia University Press, 2001).

30.It was India in the Conference on Disarmament that vetoed the transmittal of the text of the negotiated CTBT to the General Assembly in 1996 and with the advent of the Bush administration, it was the United States that emphatically insisted that the CTBT was no longer in its interest. The United States explained its vote against the CTBT in the First Committee of the General Assembly: "The U.S. delegation has again voted 'no' on draft resolution L.52 because, as we have made clear before, the United States does not support the Comprehensive Nuclear Test-Ban Treaty and will not become a party to that treaty. The United States also intends, however, to maintain its moratorium on nuclear testing, in effect since 1992, and urges all states to maintain existing moratoria on nuclear testing." "Comprehensive Nuclear-Test-Ban Treaty: Draft Resolution," General Assembly document A/C.1/58/L.52, 15 October 2003.

31. Conference of the Committee on Disarmament, *Comprehensive Study of the Question of Nuclear-Weapon-Free Zones*.

32. Jozef Goldblat, "The Sea-Bed Treaty," *Ocean Yearbook* 1 (1978): 388–389.

33. For details on all of these proposals, see Ramesh Thakur, ed., *Nuclear Weapons-Free Zones* (London: Macmillan, 1998).

34. In addition, New Zealand and Mongolia have national nuclear-weapon-free status through legislation adopted in 1987 and 2000, respectively; Mongolia formally reported this status to the UN as well.

35. Julius O. Ihonvbere, "Africa—The Treaty of Pelindaba," in *Nuclear Weapons-Free Zones*, ed. Ramesh Thakur (London: Macmillan, 1998), 119.

36. Celso Amorim, Ahmed Aboul Gheit, Dermot Ahern, Luis Ernesto Derbez Bautista, Phil Goff, Nkosazana Dlamini Zuma, and Laila Freivalds, "What Does Not Exist Cannot Proliferate," *International Herald Tribune*, 2 May 2005.

37. Kofi A. Annan, *In Larger Freedom: Towards Development, Security and Human Rights for All* (New York: UN, 2005), 37–38. See also Mohamed ElBaradei, "Seven Steps to Raise World Security," *Financial Times*, 2 February 2005.

38. William M. Reilly, "Analysis: The U.N.'s Document," United Press International, 14 September 2005, available at http://about.upi.com/products/upi_scitech/UPI-20050914-052229-8545R (accessed 15 September 2005).

39. "Statement to the Conference on Disarmament in Geneva," *UN News Centre*, available at http://www.un.org/apps/news/infocus/sgspeeches/statments_full.asp?statID=174 (accessed 26 January 2008).

40. For analyses of the BWC, see Brad Roberts, ed., *Biological Weapons: Weapons of the Future?* (Washington, D.C.: Center for Strategic and International Studies, 1993).

41. OPCW, "The Chemical Weapons Ban: Facts and Figures," available at http://www.opcw.org/publications/facts-and-figures/ (accessed 16 July 2009).

42. International Action Network on Small Arms, "Small Arms Are Weapons of Mass Destruction," available at http://www.iansa.org/media/wmd.htm (accessed 9 December 2008).

43. This casualty estimate is drawn from the International Campaign to Ban Landmines Web site, available at http://www.icbl.org/problem/what (accessed 9 December 2008).

44. Jessica Tuchman Mathews, "Weapons of Mass Destruction and the United Nations," *Global Governance* 10, no. 3 (2004): 265.

45. We are grateful to Randy Rydell for his interpretation of this situation.

46. Annan, *In Larger Freedom,* 37.

47. Adela Maria Bolet, Charles K. Ebinger, Joseph Pilat, and Robert Pendley, *Atoms for Peace after Thirty Years* (Washington, D.C.: Center for Strategic and International Studies, 1984), vi. For President Eisenhower's speech, see "Atoms for Peace," speech before the General Assembly of the United Nations, New York, 8 December 1953, available at http://www.iaea.org/About/history_speech.html (accessed 22 June 2009). For an overview, see "Civilian Control of Atomic Energy, 1945–1946," available at http://www.mbe.doe.gov/me70/manhattan/civilian_control.htm.

48. David Fischer, *History of the International Atomic Energy Agency: The First Forty Years* (Vienna: IAEA, 1997), 453.

49. Mathews, "Weapons of Mass Destruction and the United Nations," 265.

50. Jean E. Krasno and James S. Sutterlin, *The United Nations and Iraq: Defanging the Viper* (Westport, Conn.: Praeger, 2003). See also Richard Butler, *The Greatest Threat: Iraq, Weapons of Mass Destruction, and the Crisis of Global Security* (New York: Public Affairs, 2000); and Derek Boothby, *The United Nations and Disarmament* (New Haven, Conn.: Academic Council on the UN System, 2002).

51. IAEA, "Latest Iran Safeguards Report Circulated to IAEA Board," 22 February 2008, available at www.iaea.org/NewsCenter/News/2008/iranreport0208.html.

52. For a defense of the organization, see Fischer, *History of the International Atomic Energy Agency* (Vienna: IAEA, 1997).

53. See Richard Dean Burns, ed., *Encyclopedia of Arms Control and Disarmament* (New York: Charles Scribner's Sons, 1993).

54. This section draws on Ramesh Thakur and Ere Haru, eds., *The Chemical Weapons Convention: Implementation, Challenges and Opportunities* (Tokyo: UN University Press, 2006).

55. OPCW, "The Chemical Weapons Ban: Facts and Figures."

56. For a thorough history, see Randy Rydell, "The Secretary-General and the Secretariat," in *The United Nations and Nuclear Orders,* ed. Jane Boulden, Ramesh Thakur, and Thomas G. Weiss (Tokyo: UN University Press, 2009), 73–107.

57. Security Council document S/PV.3046, 31 January 1992.

58. "World: Middle East UNSCOM 'Infiltrated by Spies,'" BBC, 23 March 1999, available at http://news.bbc.co.uk/1/hi/world/middle_east/301168.stm (accessed 14 July 2009).

59. See Ramesh Thakur, "The South Asian Nuclear Challenge," in *Alternative Nuclear Futures: The Role of Nuclear Weapons in the Post–Cold War World,* ed. John Baylis and Robert O'Neill (Oxford: Oxford University Press, 2000), 101–124.

60. High-level Panel on Threats, Challenges and Change, *A More Secure World,* 45.

61. Annan, *In Larger Freedom,* 38.

62. We are grateful to Margaret Joan Anstee, who proposed the categorization of the UN's roles in the context of the United Nations Intellectual History Project.

63. George Perkovich, Jessica Tuchman Mathews, Joseph Cirincione, Rose Gottemoeller, and Jon Wolfsthal, *Universal Compliance: A Strategy for Universal Compliance* (Washington, D.C.: Carnegie Endowment for International Peace, 2005).

64. A Second Special Session of the General Assembly devoted to disarmament was held in 1982; a third was held in 1988.

65. Julian Borger, "Mohamed ElBaradei Warns of New Nuclear Age," *The Guardian,* 14 May 2009.

66. For details on the treaty, see Marco Roscini, "Something Old, Something New: The 2006 Semipalatinsk Treaty on a Nuclear Weapon-Free Zone in Central Asia," *Chinese Journal of International Law* 7, no. 3 (2008): 593–624.

4. Terrorism

1. The case of terrorism in this chapter as well as of sustainability and pandemics in chapters 6 and 9, respectively, also appears in Ramesh Thakur and Thomas G. Weiss, "United Nations 'Policy': An Argument with Three Illustrations," *International Studies Perspectives* 10, no. 2 (2009): 18–35.

2. *Report of the Working Group on the United Nations and Terrorism,* General Assembly document A/57/273, 6 August 2002, Annex 4, para. 11.

3. See, for example, Alex Peter Schmid, A. J. Jongman, Michael Stohl, and Irving Louis Horowitz, *Political Terrorism: A New Guide to Actors, Authors, Concepts, Data Bases, Theories, and Literature* (New Brunswick, N.J.: Transaction Publishers, 2005).

4. See Strobe Talbott and Nayan Chanda, eds., *An Age of Terror: America and the World after September 11* (New York: Basic Books, 2002): and Paul Wilkinson, *Terrorism versus Democracy: The Liberal State Response* (London: Frank Cass, 2000).

5. For an overview, see the essays in Jane Boulden and Thomas G. Weiss, eds., *Terrorism and the UN: Before and after September 11* (Bloomington: Indiana University Press, 2004). See also David Cortright and George A. Lopez, eds. *Uniting against Terror: Cooperative Nonmilitary Responses to the Global* (Boston: MIT Press, 2007); P. J. van Krieken, *Terrorism and the International Legal Order* (The Hague: TMC Asser Press, 2002); and David Cortright, George A. Lopez, Alistair Miller, and Linda Gerbe, *An Action Agenda for Enhancing the United Nations Program on Counter-Terrorism* (Goshen, Ind.: Fourth Freedom Forum, 2004).

6. Quoted in Edward C. Luck, "Another Reluctant Belligerent: The United Nations and the War on Terrorism," in *The United Nations and Global Security,* ed. Richard M. Price and Mark W. Zacher (New York: Palgrave Macmillan, 2004), 97.

7. This historical overview draws on Thomas G. Weiss, David P. Forsythe, Roger A. Coate, and Kelly-Kate Pease, *The United Nations and Changing World Politics,* 5th ed. (Boulder, Colo.: Westview, 2007), 95–134.

8. The thirteen international legal instruments are: Convention on Offences and Certain Other Acts Committed On Board Aircraft (Aircraft Convention; 1963); Convention for the Suppression of Unlawful Seizure of Aircraft (Unlawful Seizure Convention; 1970); Convention for the Suppression of Unlawful Acts against the Safety of Civil Aviation (Civil Aviation Convention; 1971); Convention on the Prevention and Punishment of Crimes Against Internationally Protected Persons (Diplomatic Agents Convention; 1973); International Convention against the Taking of Hostages (Hostages Convention; 1979); 1980 Convention on the Physical Protection of Nuclear Material (Nuclear Materials Convention); Protocol for the Suppression of Unlawful Acts of Violence at Airports Serving International Civil Aviation, supplementary to the Convention for the Suppression of Unlawful Acts against the Safety of Civil Aviation (Airport Protocol); Convention for the Suppression of Unlawful Acts against the Safety of Maritime Navigation (Maritime Convention; 1988); Protocol for the Suppression of Unlawful Acts Against the Safety of Fixed Platforms Located on the Continental Shelf (Fixed Platform Protocol; 1988); Convention on the Marking of Plastic Explosives for the Purpose of Detection (Plastic Explosives Convention; 1991);

International Convention for the Suppression of Terrorist Bombings (Terrorist Bombing Convention; 1997); International Convention for the Suppression of the Financing of Terrorism (Terrorist Financing Convention; 1999); and International Convention for the Suppression of Acts of Nuclear Terrorism (Nuclear Terrorism Convention; 2005).

9. See Adam Roberts, "Terrorism and International Order," in *Terrorism and International Order*, ed. Lawrence Freedman, Christopher Hill, Adam Roberts, R. J. Vincent, Paul Wilkinson, and Philip Windsor (London: Routledge and Kegan Paul/Royal Institute of International Affairs, 1986), 9–10; and M. J. Peterson, "Using the General Assembly," in *Terrorism and the UN: Before and after September 11,* ed. Jane Boulden and Thomas G. Weiss (Bloomington: Indiana University Press, 2004), 173–197.

10. See Malvina Halberstam, "The Evolution of the United Nations Position on Terrorism: From Exempting National Liberation Movements to Criminalizing Terrorism Wherever and by Whomever Committed," *Columbia Journal of Transnational Law* 41, no. 3 (2003): 573–584.

11. Russians similarly remind those who criticize their actions in Chechnya of what the terrorists did in Beslan, and Indians point to Sikh terrorist outrages to explain and justify state terror against Sikhs in the 1980s.

12. See Emma Nicole Kennedy da Silva, "Responding to International Terrorism: The Contribution of the United Nations" (Ph.D. thesis, University of Queensland, 2008).

13. Chantal de Jonge Oudraat, "The Role of the Security Council," in *Terrorism and the UN: Before and after September 11,* ed. Jane Boulden and Thomas G. Weiss (Bloomington: Indiana University Press, 2004), 151–158, quote at 158.

14. High-level Panel on Threats, Challenges and Change, *A More Secure World: Our Shared Responsibility* (New York: UN, 2004), 52. For discussions of the reform, see "The Report of the High-level Panel on Threats, Challenges and Change," *Security Dialogue* 36, no. 3 (2005): 361–394; and Paul Heinbecker and Patricia Goff, eds., *Irrelevant or Indispensable? The United Nations in the 21st Century* (Waterloo, Ontario: Wilfred Laurier University Press, 2005).

15. Kofi A. Annan, *In Larger Freedom: Towards Development, Security and Human Rights for All* (New York: UN, 2005), 35.

16. *2005 World Summit Outcome,* General Assembly resolution A/RES/60/1, 24 October 2005, para. 81.

17. Peter Romaniuk, *Multilateral Counter-terrorism: The global politics of cooperation and contestation* (London: Routledge, forthcoming).

18. For a review of the literature, see Jane Boulden and Thomas G. Weiss, "Whither Terrorism and the United Nations?" in *Terrorism and the UN: Before and after September 11,* ed. Jane Boulden and Thomas G. Weiss (Bloomington: Indiana University Press, 2004), 5–10.

19. Annan, *In Larger Freedom,* 6.

20. See S. Neil MacFarlane, "Charter Values and the Response to Terrorism," in *Terrorism and the UN: Before and after September 11,* ed. Jane Boulden and Thomas G. Weiss (Bloomington: Indiana University Press, 2004), 27–52.

21. The classic statement of the thesis remains Samuel P. Huntington, *The Clash of Civilizations and the Remaking of World Order* (New York: Simon and Schuster, 1998).

22. For a poignant cry from a Muslim woman over the hijacking of her faith by extremists responsible for the massacre of schoolchildren in Beslan, Russia, see Nassrine Azimi, "Beslan Massacre: The Anguish of a Faithful Muslim," *International Herald Tribune,* 8 September 2004.

23. See Ramesh Thakur, "Ayodhya and the Politics of India's Secularism: A Double-Standards Discourse," *Asian Survey* 33, no. 7 (1993): 645–664.

24. Human Security Report Project, *Human Security Brief 2007* (Vancouver, Canada: Simon Fraser University, 2008), 8–21.

25. "Those who make peaceful revolutions impossible make violent revolutions inevitable"; Mai Yamani, "Saudi Arabia Pushing Sand against Tide," *Japan Times,* 29 May 2005.

26. Thus a headline after the May 2005 uprising in Uzbekistan: Jeremy Page, "Uzbek Corruption and Poverty Help Islamist Message to Spread," *Daily Yomiuri* (reprinted from *The Times,* London), 29 May 2005.

27. Annan, *In Larger Freedom,* 36.

28. Office of the High Commissioner for Human Rights, *Digest of Jurisprudence of the UN and Regional Organizations on the Protection of Human Rights while Countering Terrorism* (Geneva: OHCHR, 2003).

29. Annan, *In Larger Freedom,* 52–53. For a study of the UN's role, see Edward Newman and Roland Rich, eds., *The UN Role in Promoting Democracy: Between Ideals and Reality* (Tokyo: UN University Press, 2004).

30. Kofi Annan, *Report of the Secretary-General on the Work of the Organization* (New York: UN, 2004), para. 77.

31. Michael Ignatieff, *The Lesser Evil: Political Ethics in an Age of Terror* (Princeton, N.J.: Princeton University Press, 2004).

32. Nasra Hassan, "Al-Qaeda's Understudy," *Atlantic Monthly,* June 2004, 44.

33. See Mark Danner, "US Torture: Voices from the Black Sites," *The New York Review of Books,* 9 April 2009, 69–77, available at http://www.nybooks.com/articles/22530 (accessed 14 July 2009).

34. See Sidney Blumenthal, "This Is the New Gulag," *The Guardian,* 6 May 2004.

35. Hannah Arendt, *Eichmann in Jerusalem: A Report on the Banality of Evil* (New York: Viking Press, 1963).

36. Eugene Robinson, "Torture Whitewash," *Washington Post,* 3 May 2005.

37. Christopher C. Joyner, "The United Nations and Terrorism: Rethinking Legal Tension between National Security, Human Rights, and Civil Liberties," *International Studies Perspectives* 5, no. 3 (2004): 241–242.

38. High-level Panel on Threats, Challenges and Change, *A More Secure World,* 52.

39. Ibid., 51.

40. Ibid.

41. Tom Farer, "The UN Reports: Addressing the Gnarled Issues of Our Time," *International Spectator,* February 2005, 12.

42. Annan, *In Larger Freedom,* paras. 84, 88, 91.

43. *2005 World Summit Outcome,* paras. 34–35.

44. Milan Sahović and William W. Bishop, "The Authority of the State: Its Range with Respect to Persons and Places," in *Manual of Public International Law,* ed. Max Sørensen (London: Macmillan, 1968), 316. In 1949, the United Kingdom sued Albania for damage sustained to British ships from mine explosions off Albania's coast. The ICJ ordered Albania to pay compensation. For further details of the case, see UN, *Digest of International Cases on the Law of the Sea* (New York: UN, 2007), 32–37.

45. V. S. Mani, "ISAF in Afghanistan: A Study in Recuperation after a 'Humanitarian Surgery,'" paper presented at a UN University and Chuo University

workshop entitled UN and Japan: Political and Legal Analyses of UN Peace Activities, Hakone, 9–11 March 2005.

46. Luck, "Another Reluctant Belligerent," 98.

47. Boulden and Weiss, "Whither Terrorism and the United Nations?" 11–12.

48. Annan, *In Larger Freedom,* para. 88.

49. *2005 World Summit Outcome,* paras. 81–83.

50. To cite just one example: "Planner of Attacks Was Motivated by U.S. Support for Israel," *Japan Times,* 24 July 2004.

51. See Jessica Stern, *Terror in the Name of God: Why Religious Militants Kill* (St. Paul, Minn.: Ecco, 2003).

52. Jessica Stern, "Terrorism's New Mecca," *Globe and Mail* (Toronto), 28 November 2003.

53. Robert Pape, *Dying to Win: The Strategic Logic of Suicide Terrorism* (New York: Random House, 2005).

54. National Intelligence Estimate, *The Terrorist Threat to the US Homeland* (Washington, D.C.: U.S. Government Printing Office, 2007).

55. Mai Yamani, "Alienated Muslims Build Internet Shrine," *Australian Financial Review,* 30 June 2004.

56. See Robin Frost, "Nuclear Terrorism Post-9/11: Assessing the Risks," *Global Society: Journal of Interdisciplinary International Relations* 18, no. 4 (2004): 397–422.

57. The unclassified portions of the report can be found at *CIA Report on Rogue Nations' Efforts to Acquire WMD* (November 2004), available at http://www.jewishvirtual library.org/jsource/Threats_to_Israel/ciarep1.html (accessed 22 June 2009). VX is the nerve gas $C_{11}H_{26}NO_2PS$. It is a chemical weapon.

58. Nicholas D. Kristof, "An American Hiroshima Is All Too Likely," *International Herald Tribune,* 12 August 2004.

59. See Ramesh Thakur and Eru Haru, eds., *The Chemical Weapons Convention: Implementation Challenges and Opportunities* (Tokyo: UN University Press, 2006).

60. John Burroughs, "The WMD Commission One Year On: Impact and Assessment," *Disarmament Diplomacy* 85 (Summer 2007): 32.

61. Abdalnahmood Abdalhaleem Mohamad, "Security Council and Non-Proliferation," *Hindu,* 28 May 2004.

62. Jim Wurst, "NGOs Criticize Nonproliferation Draft for Ignoring Disarmament," *UN Wire,* 1 April 2004.

63. See Petersen, "Using the General Assembly."

64. Information on the CTC is available at www.un.org/Docs/sc/committees/1373.

65. *UN Counter-Terrorism Online Handbook,* available at http://www.un.org/terrorism/cthandbook/index.html (accessed 25 June 2009).

66. Frank Madsen, *Transnational Organized Crime* (London: Routledge, 2009).

67. See S. Neil MacFarlane and Yuen Foong Khong, *Human Security and the UN: A Critical History* (Bloomington: Indiana University Press, 2006).

68. For some recent books on the phenomenon of suicide bombing, see Joyce M. Davis, *Martyrs: Innocence, Vengeance and Despair in the Middle East* (London: Palgrave Macmillan, 2003); Aharon Farkash, *The Shahids: Islam and Suicide Attacks* (Piscataway, N.J.: Transaction, 2004); Christoph Reuter, *My Life Is a Weapon: A Modern History of Suicide Bombing* (Princeton, N.J.: Princeton University Press, 2004); and Barbara Victor, *Army of Roses: Inside the World of Palestinian Suicide Bombers* (New York: Rodale Books, 2003).

69. James Dobbins, Seth G. Jones, Keith Crane, Andrew Rathmell, Brett Steele, Richard Teltschik, and Anga Timilsina, *The UN's Role in Nation-Building: From the Congo to Iraq* (New York: Rand Corporation, 2005), xxxvii.

70. "Progress Being Made in Global Fight against Terrorism, UN Official Says," UN News Centre, 19 March 2008.

71. Kofi A. Annan, *Uniting against Terrorism: Recommendations for a Global Counter-Terrorism Strategy: Report of the Secretary-General* (New York: UN, 2006).

72. For the text of "The United Nations Global Counter-Terrorism Strategy,"General Assembly resolution 60/288, 20 September 2006, see www.un.org/terrorism/strategy-counter-terrorism.shtml.

73. *Report of the Policy Working Group on the United Nations and Terrorism,* General Assembly document A/57/273-S/2002/875, 6 August 2002.

74. "The United Nations Global Counter-Terrorism Strategy," General Assembly resolution 60/288, 20 September 2006, 3. See also "Making a Difference,"on the UN Action to Counter Terrorism Web site, available at http://www.un.org/terrorism/makingadifference.shtml (accessed 28 April 2008). For almost exactly the same quote from Ban Ki-moon, see "Address to the International Conference on Terrorism: Dimensions, Threats and Counter-Measures," 15 November 2007, available at http://www.un.org/apps/news/infocus/sgspeeches/search_full.asp?statID=149 (accessed 10 July 2009).

75. "True Faith Is Respectful, Compassionate, Devoid of Hatred, Says Secretary-General at Temple Emanuel in New York," UN Press Release, SG/SM/7962/Rev.1, 18 September 2001.

5. Trade, Aid, and Finance

1. This change was already evident at the time to Harold Jacobson. See Jacobson, "The Changing United Nations," in *Foreign Policies in the Sixties: The Issues and the Instruments,* ed. Roger Hilsman and Robert C. Good (Baltimore, Md.: Johns Hopkins University Press, 1965), 67–89.

2. David Mitrany, *The Progress of International Government* (New Haven, Conn.: Yale University Press, 1933); and *The Road to Security,* Peace Aims pamphlet 29 (London: National Peace Council, 1945) and *A Working Peace System,* Peace Aims pamphlet 40 (London: National Peace Council, 1946). For a discussion of functionalism, see A. J. R. Groom and Paul Taylor, *Functionalism: Theory and Practice in International Relations* (London: University of London Press, 1975).

3. The academic literature on functionalism is substantial, but the best early view is Ernst B. Haas, *Beyond the Nation-State: Functionalism and International Organization* (Palo Alto, Calif.: Stanford University Press, 1964).

4. For overviews of the IMF, the WTO, and the World Bank, see James Raymond Vreeland, *The International Monetary Fund: Politics of Conditional Lending* (London: Routledge, 2007); Bernard M. Hoekmman and Petros C. Mavroidis, *The World Trade Organization* (London: Routledge, 2007); and Katherine Marshall, *The World Bank* (London: Routledge, 2008).

5. Adam Smith, *An Inquiry into the Nature and Causes of the Wealth of Nations* (1776; Oxford: Clarendon Press, 1969).

6. See Richard Jolly, Louis Emmerij, Dharam Ghai, and Frédéric Lapeyre, *UN Contributions to Development Theory and Practice* (Bloomington: Indiana University Press, 2004), 16–45.

7. See Ramesh Thakur, *The Government and Politics of India* (London: Macmillan, 1995), 289–308, from which parts of the present chapter are adapted.

8. Thomas G. Weiss, Tatiana Carayannis, Louis Emmerij, and Richard Jolly, *UN Voices: The Struggle for Development and Social Justice* (Bloomington: Indiana University Press, 2005), 187. The discussion in this chapter draws on chapter 5.

9. For a discussion, see Peter A. Hall, ed., *The Political Power of Economic Ideas: Keynesianism across Nations* (Princeton, N.J.: Princeton University Press, 1989).

10. Paul Samuelson, *Economics* (New York: McGraw-Hill, 1948). This point was made by Devesh Kapur, John P. Lewis, and Richard Webb in *The World Bank: Its First Half Century*, vol. 1, *History* (Washington, D.C.: Brookings Institution Press, 1997), 67.

11. Weiss, Carayannis, Emmerij, and Jolly, *UN Voices*, 187.

12. UN, *Measures for Full Employment* (New York: UN, 1949); UN, *Measures for the Economic Development of Under-Developed Countries* (New York: UN, 1951); and UN, *Measures for International Economic Stability* (New York: UN, 1951). For an overview, see Louis Emmerij, Richard Jolly, and Thomas G. Weiss, *Ahead of the Curve? UN Ideas and Global Challenges* (Bloomington: Indiana University Press, 2001), 26–42.

13. See "Building the Human Foundations," in Jolly, Emmerij, Ghai, and Lapeyre, *UN Contributions*, 186–219, which provides a qualitative and quantitative summary of these achievements.

14. UN, *World Economic Survey*, Part I, *Trade and Development: Trends, Needs and Policies* (New York: UN, 1963).

15. See UN, *The World Conferences: Developing Priorities for the 21st Century* (New York: UN, 1997), 35–36; Michael Schechter, ed., *United Nations-Sponsored World Conferences: Focus on Impact and Follow-Up* (Tokyo: UN University Press, 2001); Jacques Fomerand, "UN Conferences: Media Events or Genuine Diplomacy," *Global Governance* 2, no. 3 (1996): 361–375; and Michael Schechter, *UN Global Conferences* (London: Routledge, 2005).

16. Tagi Sagafi-nejad in collaboration with John Dunning, *The UN and Transnational Corporations: From Code of Conduct to Global Compact* (Bloomington: Indiana University Press, 2008).

17. See Richard Jolly, Louis Emmerij, and Thomas G. Weiss, *The Power of UN Ideas: Lessons from the First 60 Years* (New York: UNIHP, 2005), 44–46.

18. Andrea Cornia, Richard Jolly, and Frances Stewart, eds., *Adjustment with a Human Face*, vol. 1, *Protecting the Vulnerable and Promoting Growth* (Oxford: Clarendon Press, 1987); and Andrea Cornia, Richard Jolly, and Frances Stewart, eds., *Adjustment with a Human Face*, vol. 2, *Country Case Studies* (Oxford: Clarendon Press, 1988).

19. ECA, *African Alternative Framework to Structural Adjustment Programs for Socio-Economic Recovery and Transformation* (Addis Ababa: ECA, 1989).

20. Commission on Human Security, *Human Security Now* (New York: Commission on Human Security, 2003), iv.

21. For an overview of the importance of the MDGs, see Sakiko Fukada-Parr, "Millennium Development Goals: Why They Matter," *Global Governance* 10, no. 4 (2004): 395–402. See also Sakiko Fukada-Parr, *Millennium Development Goals: For a People Centered Deveopment Agenda?* (London: Routledge, forthcoming).

22. We are grateful to John Gerard Ruggie, one of the architects of the MDGs, for highlighting these aspects of the MDGs in an e-mail to the authors dated 11 October 2008.

23. See S. Neil MacFarlane and Yuen Foong Khong, *Human Security and the UN: A Critical History* (Bloomington: Indiana University Press, 2006).

24. Michael Ward, *Quantifying the World: UN Ideas and Statistics* (Bloomington: Indiana University Press, 2004), 2.

25. W. W. Rostow, *The Stages of Economic Growth: A Non-Communist Manifesto* (Cambridge: Cambridge University Press, 1960).

26. For a sample of such approaches, see Hollis Chenery, Montek Ahluwalia, Clive Bell, John Duloy, and Richard Jolly, eds., *Redistribution with Growth* (Oxford: Oxford University Press, 1974); Morris D. Morris, *Measuring the Condition of the World's Poor: The Physical Quality of Life Index* (New York: Pergamon Press, 1979); and Paul Streeten, *First Things First: Meeting Basic Human Needs in Developing Countries* (New York: Oxford University Press, 1981).

27. John Toye and Richard Toye, *The UN and Global Political Economy: Trade, Finance, and Development* (Bloomington: Indiana University Press, 2004), 111.

28. Ibid.

29. UN, *Relative Prices of Exports and Imports of Under-developed Countries: A Study of Post-War Terms of Trade between Under-developed and Industrialized Countries* (New York: UN, 1949).

30. Paul Pierson, "Increasing Returns, Path Dependence, and the Study of Politics," *American Political Science Review* 94, no. 2 (2000): 251–267. He explains path dependence through the Polya urn process, in which the element of chance is combined with a decision rule that links current probabilities to the outcomes of preceding (and partly random) sequences: "Imagine a very large urn containing two balls, one black, one red. Remove one ball, and then return it to the urn, accompanied by an additional ball of the same color. Repeat this process until the urn fills up" (253).

31. Jared Diamond, *Guns, Germs, and Steel* (New York: Norton, 1997).

32. Quoted in Toye and Toye, *The UN and Global Political Economy,* 133.

33. Yves Berthelot, "Unity and Diversity in Development: The Regional Commissions' Experience," in *Unity and Diversity in Development Ideas: Perspectives from the UN Regional Commissions,* ed. Yves Berthelot (Bloomington: Indiana University Press, 2004), 37.

34. GATT, *Trends in International Trade: A Report by a Panel of Experts* (Geneva: GATT, 1958).

35. See Thomas G. Weiss, "Moving Beyond North-South Theater," *Third World Quarterly* 30, no. 2 (2009): 271–284.

36. David Halloran Lumsdaine, *Moral Vision in International Politics: The Foreign Aid Regime, 1949–1989* (Princeton, N.J.: Princeton University Press, 1993). See also Alain Noel and Jean-Philippe Thérien, *Left and Right in Global Politics* (Cambridge: Cambridge University Press, 2008); Jean-Philippe Thérien and Alain Noel, "Political Parties and Foreign Aid," *American Political Science Review* 94, no. 1 (2000): 151–162; and Paul Collier, *The Bottom Billion: The Poorest Countries Are Failing and What Can Be Done About It* (Oxford: Oxford University Press, 2007).

37. See Ramesh Thakur, *Towards a Less Imperfect State of the World: The Gulf between North and South,* Dialogue on Globalization Briefing Paper 4 (Berlin: Friedrich Ebert Stiftung, 2008).

38. See Thomas G. Weiss, David P. Forsythe, Roger A. Coate, and Kelly-Kate Pease, *The United Nations and Changing World Politics,* 5th ed. (Boulder, Colo.: Westview, 2007), 295–296.

39. John Gerard Ruggie, "Global_governance.net: The Global Compact as Learning Network," *Global Governance* 7, no. 4 (2001): 371–378.

40. For a discussion of this atmosphere, see Sagafi-nejad in collaboration with Dunning, *The UN and Transnational Corporations*, 41–54.

41. John Gerard Ruggie, "Business and Human Rights: The Evolving International Agenda," *American Journal of International Law* 101 (October 2007): 819. See also John Gerard Ruggie, *Promotion and Protection of All Human Rights, Civil, Political, Economic, Social and Cultural Rights, Including the Right to Development,* General Assembly document A/HRC/8/5, 7 April 2008.

42. Ruggie, "Business and Human Rights: The Evolving International Agenda," 819.

43. See Craig N. Murphy and JoAnne Yates, *International Organization for Standardization* (London: Routledge, 2009).

44. Noel and Thérien, *Left and Right in Global Politics,* 3.

45. Mahfuzur Rahman, *World Economic Issues at the United Nations: Half a Century of Debate* (Dordrecht: Kluwer, 2002), 145.

46. See Olav Stokke, *The UN and Development: From Aid to Cooperation* (Bloomington: Indiana University Press, 2009). See also Digambar Bhouraskar, *United Nations Development Aid: A Study in History and Politics* (New Delhi: Academic Foundation, 2007).

47. "Economic Development of Under-developed Countries," General Assembly resolution 198(III), 4 December 1948.

48. Harry S. Truman, inaugural address, 20 January 1949, in *Public Papers of the Presidents, Harry S. Truman, 1949: Containing the Public Messages, Speeches, and Statements of the President, January 1 to December 31, 1949* (Washington, D.C.: Government Printing Office, 1964), 114–115.

49. "Economic Development of Under-developed Countries," ECOSOC resolution 222 (IX), 14 and 15 August 1949. This resolution established the EPTA.

50. Jolly, Emmerij, Ghai, and Lapeyre, *UN Contributions,* 70–83; Stokke, *The UN and Development,* 43–82.

51. As was also the case with the "UN Safe Area" in Srebrenica in 1995. For more about SUNFED, see Stokke, *The UN and Development,* 83–114; Jolly, Emmerij, Ghai, and Lapeyre, *UN Contributions,* 73–83.

52. Stokke, *The UN and Development,* 10.

53. As the IMF Web site states, Poverty Reduction Strategy Papers "describe a country's macroeconomic, structural and social policies over a three year or longer horizon to promote broad-based growth and reduce poverty, as well as associated external financing needs and major sources of financing." See IMF, "Poverty Reduction Strategy Papers (PRSP)," available at http://www.imf.org/external/NP/prsp/prsp.asp (accessed 28 June 2009).

54. HM Treasury and the Department for International Development, *International Finance Facility* (London: HM Treasury, 2003), available at http://www.uneca.org/debtforum/iff.pdf (accessed 28 June 2009).

55. Kofi A. Annan, *In Larger Freedom: Towards Development, Security and Human Rights for All* (New York: UN, 2005), 21.

56. *2005 World Summit Outcome,* General Assembly resolution A/RES/60/1, 24 October 2005, 5.

57. A. B. Atkinson, *New Sources of Development Finance: Funding the Millennium Development Goals,* Policy Brief No. 10 (Helsinki: UNU-WIDER, 2004), v.

58. Ibid.

59. Georges Balandier and Alfred Sauvy, *Le "Tiers-Monde," Sous Développement et Développement* (Paris: Presse Universitaire de France, 1961).

60. For information about the G-77, see "About the Group of 77," available at http://www.g77.org/doc/ (accessed 6 July 2009).

61. See Joseph S. Nye, "UNCTAD: Poor Nations' Pressure Group," in *The Anatomy of Influence—Decision Making in International Organization,* ed. Robert W. Cox and Harold K. Jacobson (New Haven, Conn.: Yale University Press, 1973), 334–370.

62. For details, see especially Toye and Toye, *The UN and Global Political Economy;* and Ian Taylor and Karen Smith, *United Nations Conference on Trade and Development (UNCTAD)* (London: Routledge, 2007). For older inquiries, see also Michael Zammit Cutajar, ed., *UNCTAD and the South-North Dialogue: The First Twenty Years* (London: Pergamon, 1985); Robert L. Rothstein, *Global Bargaining: UNCTAD and the Quest for a New International Economic Order* (Princeton, N.J.: Princeton University Press, 1979); Branislov Gosovic, *UNCTAD: Compromise and Conflict* (Leiden: Sijthoff, 1972); Diego Cordovez, *UNCTAD and Development Diplomacy: From Conference to Strategy* (London: Journal of World Trade Law, 1970); Kamal Hagras, *United Nations Conference on Trade and Development: A Case Study in UN Diplomacy* (New York: Praeger, 1965); and Thomas G. Weiss, *Multilateral Development Diplomacy in UNCTAD: The Lessons of Group Negotiations, 1964–84* (London: Macmillan, 1986).

63. WTO Information and Media Relations Division, *Understanding the WTO,* 4th ed. (Geneva: WTO, 2008), available at http://www.wto .org/english/thewto_e/whatis_e/tif_e/understanding_e.pdf (accessed 20 June 2009).

64. Robert Gilpin, *Global Political Economy: Understanding the International Economic Order* (Princeton, N.J.: Princeton University Press, 2001), 232.

65. WTO Information and Media Relations Division, *Understanding the WTO,* 18–19.

66. Mancur Olson, *The Logic of Collective Action: Public Goods and the Theory of Groups,* 2nd ed. (Cambridge, Mass.: Harvard University Press, 1971).

67. For example, see Özgür Gürerk, Bernd Irlenbusch, and Bettina Rockenbach, "The Competitive Advantage of Sanctioning Institutions," *Science* 312, no. 5770 (2006): 108–111.

68. Toye and Toye, *The UN and Global Political Economy,* 287.

69. Gilpin, *Global Political Economy,* 229–230.

70. Toye and Toye, *The UN and Global Political Economy,* 292.

71. Morten Bøås and Desmond McNeill, *Multilateral Institutions: A Critical Introduction* (London: Pluto Press, 2003), 41.

72. George Arthur Codding, *The International Telecommunication Union: An Experiment in International Cooperation* (Leiden: E. J. Brill, 1952).

73. Jo Twist, "Essential Test for UN Net Summit," *BBC News World Service,* 19 November 2005, available at news.bbc.co.uk/2/hi/technology/4451950.stm (accessed 23 January 2006).

74. UNDP, *Human Development Report 2001: Making New Technologies Work for Human Development* (New York: Oxford University Press, 2001), 40.

75. See T. Irmer, "Shaping Future Telecommunications: The Challenge of Global Standardization," *Communications Magazine* 32, no. 1 (1994): 20–28.

76. A thorough treatment of the origins of and current controversies about the Internet is found in John Matthiason, *Internet Governance: The New Frontier of Global Institutions* (London: Routledge, 2009). See also Derrick Cogburn, "The US Role in Running the Net," *BBC News World Service,* 14 November 2005, available at news.bbc .co.uk/go/pr/fr/-/1/hi/technology/4435352.stm (accessed 23 January 2006); and

Lawrence G. Roberts, "Internet Chronology 1960–2001," available at www.packet.cc/internet.html (accessed 12 March 2006).

77. Michael Geist, "Analysis: Net Control Debate Rumbles On," *BBC News,* 17 November 2005, available at news.bbc.co.uk/go/pr/fr/-/1/hi/technology/4446242.stm (accessed 23 January 2006).

78. "United Nations Millennium Declaration," General Assembly resolution A/RES/55/2, 8 September 2000.

79. Weiss, Carayannis, Emmerij, and Jolly, *UN Voices,* 418.

80. UN Millennium Project, *Investing in Development: A Practical Plan to Achieve the Millennium Development Goals* (New York: UNDP, 2005); and Annan, *In Larger Freedom.*

81. Millennium Project, *Investing in Development;* and Jeffrey Sachs, *The End of Poverty: Economic Possibilities for Our Time* (New York: Penguin Books, 2005).

82. UN, *The Millennium Development Goals Report* (New York: UN, 2007).

83. See the Millennium Challenge Web site at http://www.mcc.gov (accessed 5 August 2009).

84. Quoted in Jochen Steinhilber, "Millennium Challenge Account: Goals and Strategies of US Development Policy," Friedrich Ebert Stiftung Briefing Paper, March 2004, available at http://library.fes.de/pdf-files/iez/02007.pdf (accessed 12 July 2009).

85. MDG Gap Task Force, *Delivering on the Global Partnership for Addressing the Millennium Development Goals* (New York: UN, 2008), vii–viii.

86. This argument is made succinctly in Jolly, Emmerij, and Weiss, *The Power of UN Ideas,* 18–20.

87. Jolly, Emmerij, Ghai, and Lapeyre, *UN Contributions,* 247–275. The fifty or so goals cover a wide range of virtually all activities related to the UN system's efforts at global economic governance, including faster economic growth, higher life expectancy, lower child and maternal mortality, better health, broader access to safe water and sanitation, greater access to education, less hunger and malnutrition, moves toward sustainable development, and financial support for these efforts.

88. Jolly, Emmerij, Ghai, and Lapeyre, *UN Contributions,* 268.

89. Ibid., 269–270.

90. "Banking Crisis Timeline," *The Guardian,* 30 October 2008, available at http://www.guardian.co.uk/business/2008/oct/08/creditcrunch.marketturmoil (accessed 5 July 2009).

91. Emily Kaiser, "World Looks for New Leaders as Crisis Outgrows G7," Reuters, 12 October 2008, available at http://uk.reuters.com/article/idUKTRE49B3KX20081012 (accessed 13 July 2009).

92. Gordon Brown, "Out of the Ashes," *Washington Post,* 17 October 2008.

93. Doug Saunders, "The Man Who Saved the World Banking System," *Globe and Mail* (Toronto), 15 October 2008.

94. Gerald F. Seib, "We Get the Global Perils without Global Benefits," *Wall Street Journal,* 13 October 2008.

95. See Andrew F. Cooper, John English, and Ramesh Thakur, eds., *Reforming from the Top: A Leaders' 20 Summit* (Tokyo: UN University Press, 2005); and Peter C. Heap, *Globalization and Summit Reform: An Experiment in International Governance* (Heidelberg: Springer, 2008).

96. See Sakiko Fukada-Parr and A. K. Shiva Kumar, eds., *Readings in Human Development* (Oxford: Oxford University Press, 2003).

97. The UN University had a vice-rector for human and social development, Kinhide Mushakoji, from 1975 to 1980.

98. The story is told in Murphy, *The United Nations Development Programme,* 238–262; and Richard Ponzio, "The Advent of the *Human Development Report,*" in *Pioneering the Human Development Revolution: An Intellectual Biography of Mahbub ul Haq,* ed. Khadija Haq and Richard Ponzio (Oxford: Oxford University Press, 2008), 88–111.

99. Murphy, *The United Nations Development Programme,* 259.

100. Quoted in ibid., 242.

101. UNDP, *Arab Human Development Report 2002* (New York: UNDP, 2002).

102. Murphy, *The United Nations Development Programme,* 246.

103. Quoted in ibid., 256.

104. MacFarlane and Khong, *Human Security and the UN,* 9–10 and 16–18.

105. Weiss, Carayannis, Emmerij, and Jolly, *UN Voices,* 410.

106. See Geoffrey R. D. Underhill and Xiaoke Zhang, *International Financial Governance under Stress: Global Structures versus National Imperatives* (Cambridge University Press, 2003); Ralph C. Bryant, *Turbulent Waters: Cross-Border Finance and International Governance* (Washington, D.C.: Brookings Institution Press, 2003); Karl Kaiser, John J. Kirton, and Joseph P. Daniels, *Shaping a New International Financial System: Challenges of Governance in a Globalizing World* (Burlington, Vt.: Ashgate, 2000); and Meghnad Desai and Yahia Said, *Global Governance and Financial Crises* (London: Routledge, 2004).

6. Sustainable Development

1. Thomas G. Weiss, Tatiana Carayannis, Louis Emmerij, and Richard Jolly, *UN Voices: The Struggle for Development and Social Justice* (Bloomington: Indiana University Press, 2005), 222.

2. Thomas R. Malthus, *An Essay on the Principle of Population* (London: Printed for J. Johnson in St. Paul's Churchyard, 1798).

3. Patricia Nelson Limerick, *The Legacy of Conquest: The Unbroken Past of the American West* (New York: W.W. Norton & Co., 1987), 293–294.

4. Ibid., 301.

5. Robert Sullivan, ed., *100 Photographs That Changed the World* (New York: Time, 2003); "Earthrise 1968," available at http://www.digitaljournalist.org/issue0309/lm11.html (accessed 4 August 2009). For further elaboration on the photo's significance, see Juliette Jowit, "How Astronauts Went to the Moon and Ended Up Discovering the Earth," *The Guardian,* 20 December 2008, available at http://www.guardian.co.uk/science/2008/dec/20/space-exploration-usa-earth-moon (accessed 4 August 2009).

6. Arthur Beiser and the editors of TIME-LIFE Books, *The Earth* (New York: Time Inc., 1963), 167.

7. Rachel Carson, *Silent Spring* (Greenwich, Conn.: Crest Books-Fawcett Publications, 1964), 14.

8. Julian Huxley, "World Population," *Scientific American* (March 1956): 68–69; Barry Commoner, *The Closing Circle: Nature, Man & Technology* (New York: Alfred A. Knopf, 1971).

9. U Thant, *Man and His Environment: Report of the Secretary-General* (New York: UN, May 1969).

10. Peter Farb and the editors of TIME-LIFE Books, *Ecology* (New York: Time Inc., 1970).

11. Donella H. Meadows, Jørgen Randers, and Dennis Meadows, *The Limits to Growth: A Report to the Club of Rome's Project on the Predicament of Mankind* (London: Pan, 1972). The Club of Rome, a global think tank, was founded in 1968 by Italian industrialist Aurelio Peccei and Scottish scientist Alexander King.

12. Gro Harlem Brundtland, *Our Common Future: Report of the World Commission on Environment and Development* (Oxford: Oxford University Press, 1987).

13. Ibid., 27.

14. Maurice Strong, *Where on Earth Are We Going?* (Toronto: Alred A. Knopf, 2000), 115.

15. Paul Ehrlich, *The Population Bomb* (New York: Ballantine, 1968).

16. Strong, *Where on Earth Are We Going?* 123.

17. Quoted in Maurice Strong, "Policy Lessons Learned in a Thirty Years' Perspective," in Ministry of the Environment, *Stockholm Thirty Years On* (Stockholm: Ministry of the Environment, 2003), 16.

18. See *Development and Environment: Report and Working Papers of a Panel of Experts Convened by the Secretary-General of the UN Conference on the Human Environment* (New York: UN, 1972).

19. René Dubos and Barbara Ward, *Only One Earth: The Care and Maintenance of a Small Planet* (New York: WW Norton & Co., 1972).

20. Strong, *Where on Earth Are We Going?* 126.

21. Michael G. Schechter, *United Nations Global Conferences* (London: Routledge, 2005), 34.

22. Ibid., 30–31.

23. Strong, *Where on Earth Are We Going?* 126 and 129.

24. Strong, *Where on Earth Are We Going?*; Schechter, *United Nations Global Conferences,* 19–40.

25. Ehrlich, *The Population Bomb;* Gordon Rattray Taylor, *The Doomsday Book: Can the World Survive?* (Greenwich, Conn.: Fawcett Publications, 1971).

26. See Heather A. Smith, "The World Commission on Environment and Development: Ideas and Institutions Intersect," in *International Commissions and the Power of Ideas,* ed. Ramesh Thakur, Andrew F. Cooper, and John English (Tokyo: UN University Press, 2005), 76–98.

27. Brundtland, *Our Common Future,* 8.

28. Jennifer Clapp and Peter Dauvergne, *Paths to a Green World: The Political Economy of the Global Environment* (Cambridge, Mass.: MIT Press, 2005), 64–67. For the contributions of the June 1997 Special Session of the General Assembly to Review and Appraise the Implementation of Agenda 21 (also known as Earth Summit+5), see "Programme for the Further Implementation of Agenda 21," General Assembly resolution 2-19/2, 19 September 1997.

29. Karen A. Mingst and Margaret P. Karns, *The United Nations in the 21st Century,* 3rd ed. (Boulder, Colo.: Westview, 2006), 219.

30. Elizabeth R. De Sombre, *Global Environmental Institutions* (London: Routledge, 2006), 28–30; Paul Wapner, "World Summit on Sustainable Development: Toward a Post-Jo'burg Environmentalism," *Global Environmental Politics* 3, no. 1 (2003): 4.

31. Wapner, "World Summit on Sustainable Development, 5.

32. Millennium Ecosystem Assessment, *Ecosystems and Human Well-Being: Synthesis* (Washington, D.C.: Island Press, 2005), 12–13, 49–63.

33. Strong, *Where on Earth Are We Going?* 125.

34. "Process of Preparation of the Environmental Perspective to the Year 2000 and Beyond," UN General Assembly resolution 38/161, 19 December 1983, available at www.un.org/documents/ga/res/38/a38r161.htm (accessed 10 December 2008).

35. Gro Harlem Brundtland, *Madame Prime Minister: A Life in Power and Politics* (New York: Farrar, Straus and Giroux, 2002), 192.

36. One of the most trenchant critics of the concept of sustainable development is Wolfgang Sachs, *Planet Dialectics: Explorations in Environment and Development* (London: Zed Books, 1999).

37. Organisation for Economic Co-operation and Development, *Institutionalising Sustainable Development: Implementing National Sustainable Development Strategies* (Paris: OECD, 2007); Georgina Ayre and Rosalie Callway, *Governance for Sustainable Development: A Foundation for the Future* (London: Earthscan, 2005); and Alan Boyle and David Freestone, *International Law and Sustainable Development: Past Achievements and Future Challenges* (Oxford: Oxford University Press, 2001).

38. Clapp and Dauvergne, *Paths to a Green World*, 64–67.

39. Schechter, *United Nations Global Conferences*, 119.

40. Ibid., 121, 157.

41. Jeffrey D. Sachs, *The End of Poverty: Economic Possibilities for Our Time* (New York: Penguin, 2005), 212.

42. York University scientists have warned that global warming could trigger a "mass extinction" event within the next century. See Peter J. Mayhew, Gareth B. Jenkins, Timothy G. Benton, "A Long-Term Association between Global Temperature and Bio-Diversity, Origination, and Extinction in the Fossil Record," *Proceedings of the Royal Society B* 275, no. 1630 (23 October 2007): 47–53. See also Tim Flannery, *The Weather Makers: The History and Future Impact of Climate Change* (Melbourne: Text Publishing, 2005).

43. Schechter, *United Nations Global Conferences*, 33.

44. Peter M. Haas, "Turning up the Heat on Global Environmental Governance," *The Forum* 5, no. 2 (2007): 1. On environmental governance more generally, see W. Bradnee Chambers and Jessica F. Green, eds., *Reforming Environmental Governance* (Tokyo: UN University Press, 2005).

45. De Sombre, *Global Environmental Institutions*, 35.

46. Clapp and Dauvergne, *Paths to a Green World*, 73, 78.

47. Strong, *Where on Earth Are We Going?* 136.

48. Transcript of oral history interview with John Ruggie, in *The Complete Oral History Transcripts from UN Voices*, CD-ROM (New York: UNIHP, 2007), 15.

49. "Capacity Building for Natural Disaster Reduction (CBNDR) Regional Action Program for Central America (RAPCA), Use of Geographic Information Systems For the Assessment of Hazards, Vulnerability and Risks in Central America," available at http://www.itc.nl/external/unesco-rapca/english/start.html (accessed 7 July 2009).

50. IWC, "IWC Information," available at http://www.iwcoffice.org/commission/iwcmain.htm (accessed 7 July 2009).

51. The Humane Society of the United States, "International Whaling Commission," available at www.hsus.org/about_us/humane_society_international_hsi/international_policy/treaties/international_whaling_commission/ (accessed 23 February 2006).

52. Campaign Whale, "No Way Norway!" available at http://www.campaign-whale.org/campaigns.php?act=full&article=No%20Way%20Norway! (accessed 5 August 2009).

53. Jonathan Stein, "Enemies of the Ocean," *Mother Jones* (March/April 2006), available at www.motherjones.com/news/feature/2006/03/enemies_of_the_ocean .html (accessed 23 February 2006).

54. Toko Sekiguchi, "Why Japan's Whale Hunt Continues," *Time,* 20 November 2007, available at http://www.time.com/time/world/article/0,8599,1686486,00.html (accessed 7 July 2009).

55. Joseph H. Hulse, *Sustainable Development at Risk: Ignoring the Past* (Ottawa: Foundation Books/International Development Research Centre, 2007), 15.

56. Ibid., 16.

57. Jouni Paavola, "Institutions and Environmental Governance: A Reconceptualization," *Ecological Economics* 63, no. 1 (2006): 94, 101.

58. Mingst and Karns, *The United Nations in the 21st Century,* 42.

59. Weiss, Carayannis, Emmerij, and Jolly, *UN Voices,* 408.

60. See Peter Willetts, "The Pattern of Conferences," in *Global Issues in the United Nations' Framework,* ed. Paul Taylor and A. J. R. Groom (New York: St. Martin's Press, 1989), 46.

61. See in particular, Hilary Charlesworth, "Women as Sherpas: Are Global Summits Useful for Women?" *Feminist Studies* 22 (Fall 1996): 537–547.

62. Weiss, Carayannis, Emmerij, and Jolly, *UN Voices,* 425.

63. See Freidrich Soltau, "Climate Change and Sustainable Development: Understanding the Linkages," *Natural Resources Forum* 30, no. 4 (2006): 253–255.

64. See Adil Najam, Atiq A. Rahman, Saleemul Huq, and Youba Sokona, "Integrating Sustainable Development into the Fourth Assessment Report of the Intergovernmental Panel on Climate Change," *Climate Policy* 3S1 (2003): S9–S17.

7. Saving the Environment

1. Jennifer Clapp and Peter Dauvergne, *Paths to a Green World: The Political Economy of the Global Environment* (Cambridge, Mass.: MIT Press, 2005), 45.

2. IPCC, *Summary for Policymakers of the Synthesis Report of the IPCC Fourth Assessment Report of the IPCC* (Geneva: IPCC, 2007), 1, 4, 14.

3. For a skeptic's guide, see Nigel Lawson, *An Appeal to Reason: A Cool Look at Global Warming* (London: Duckworth Overlook, 2008). George Musser listed the reasons that skeptics cite on SciAm Observations (Scientific American's blog): "Warming may not actually be occurring; the present warming could be a natural uptick; CO2 emissions cannot explain the warming; climate models are unconvincing; warming is a good thing, so we shouldn't try to stop it; Kyoto is useless, or worse; people who argue that human activity causes global warming can't be trusted." See George Musser, "Are You a Global Warming Skeptic? Part III," 24 April 2006, available at http://blog.sciam.com/index.php?title=are_you_a_global_warming_skeptic_part_ ii_1&more=1&c=1&tb=1&pb= (accessed 1 June 2006).

4. Rowland, Molina, and Crutzen were awarded the Nobel Prize for Chemistry in 1995.

5. Rajendra K. Pachauri, "IPCC—Past Achievements and Future Challenges," in WMO and UNEP, *Intergovernmental Panel on Climate Change: 16 Years of Scientific Assessment in Support of the Climate Convention* (Geneva: IPCC Secretariat, 2004), 1. Available at http://www.ipcc.ch/pdf/10th-anniversary/anniversary-brochure.pdf (accessed 4 May 2008).

6. IPCC, "16 Years of Scientific Assessment in Support of the Climate Convention," December 2004, available at http://www.ipcc.ch/pdf/10th-anniversary/anniversary-brochure.pdf (accessed 5 August 2009).

7. Ibid.

8. IPCC, *Climate Change 1995: A Report of the Intergovernmental Panel on Climate Change* (Geneva: IPCC, 1995).

9. Ibid., 21.

10. Robert T. Watson and the Core Writing Team, eds., *Climate Changes 2001: Synthesis Report* (Cambridge: Cambridge University Press, 2001).

11. The Core Writing Team, Rajendra K. Pachauri, and Andy Reisinger, eds., *Climate Change 2007: Synthesis Report* (Geneva: IPCC, 2007).

12. IPCC, *Summary for Policymakers: A Report of Working Group I of the IPCC* (Geneva: IPCC, 2007), 10, 16.

13. Ibid., 2–3.

14. IPCC, *Summary for Policymakers: Contribution of Working Group II to the Fourth Assessment Report of the IPCC* (Geneva: IPCC, 2007), 8.

15. World Commission on Environment and Development, *Our Common Future* (New York: Oxford University Press, 1987), 43.

16. Ibid., 20.

17. IPCC, *Summary for Policymakers: Contribution of Working Group III to the Fourth Assessment Report of the IPCC* (Geneva: IPCC, 2007).

18. *Carbon intensity* is the total volume of carbon dioxide divided by the total primary energy supply; *energy intensity* is the total primary energy supply divided by GDP; and *emission intensity* is CO_2 divided by GDP. Ibid., 5.

19. IPCC, *Summary for Policymakers: Contribution of Working Group III to the Fourth Assessment Report of the IPCC*, 3–4.

20. Ibid., 9, 11–14.

21. IPCC, *Summary for Policymakers of the Synthesis Report of the Fourth Assessment Report of the IPCC* (Geneva: IPCC, 2007).

22. Ibid., 53.

23. Ibid., 50.

24. Nobel Foundation, The Nobel Prize 2007, available at http://nobelprize.org/nobel_prizes/peace/laureates/2007 (accessed 5 August 2009).

25. Walter Gibbs and Sarah Lyall, "Gore and U.N. Panel Win Peace Prize for Climate Work," *New York Times,* 13 October 2007; Howard Schneider, Debbi Wilgoren, and William Branigan, "Gore, U.N. Body Win Nobel Peace Prize," *Washington Post,* 13 October 2007.

26. Nicholas Stern, *The Economics of Climate Change: The Stern Review* (Cambridge: Cambridge University Press, 2006), available at http://www.hm-treasury.gov.uk/stern_review_report.htm (accessed 9 July 2009). See also Nicholas Stern, *The Global Deal: Climate Change and the Creation of a New Era of Progress and Prosperity* (London: Bodley Head, 2009).

27. It could be argued that the United States and other industrialized countries have in effect outsourced their pollution to China because so many of China's factories now produce foreign investment–based goods for sale in western markets.

28. Suzanne Goldenberg, "China and US Held Secret Talks on Climate Change Deal," *The Guardian,* 18 May 2009, available at http://www.guardian.co.uk/world/2009/may/18/secret-us-china-emissions-talks/print (accessed 19 May 2009).

29. As of September 2007, the nonsignatories were Andorra, East Timor, Iraq, San Marino, and Vatican City. Current information can be obtained from the Web site of UNEP's Ozone Secretariat: ozone.unep.org.

30. Sebastian Oberthür and Hermann E. Ott, *The Kyoto Protocol: International Climate Policy in the 21st Century* (Berlin: Springer, 1999), 46.

31. The Geneva Ministerial Declaration, Annex to the *Report of the Conference of the Parties on its Second Session, held at Geneva from 8 to 19 July 1996*, UN Framework Convention on Climate Change document FCCC/CP/1996/15/Add.1, 29 October 1996, 71–72.

32. *Report of the Conference to the Parties on its Eighth Session, held at New Delhi from 23 October to 1 November 2002*, UN Framework Convention on Climate Change document FCCC/CP/2002/7/Add.1, 28 March 2003, 3.

33. See, for example, Freeman Dyson, "The Question of Global Warming," *New York Review of Books*, 12 June 2008, 43–45.

34. Stern, *The Economics of Climate Change*.

35. David Adam, "I Underestimated the Threat, Says Stern," *The Guardian*, 18 April 2008.

36. Elisabeth Rosenthal, "U.N. Report Describes Risks of Inaction on Climate Change," *New York Times*, 17 November 2007, A1.

37. Both are quoted in Rosenthal, "U.N. Report Describes Risks of Inaction on Climate Change."

38. Juliette Jowit, Caroline Davies, and David Adam, "Late-Night Drama Pushes US into Climate Deal," *The Observer* (London), 16 December 2007.

39. George Monbiot, "We've Been Suckered Again by the US: So Far the Bali Deal Is Worse than Kyoto," *Guardian Unlimited*, 17 December 2007.

40. Ben Cubby, "Answer to Hot Air Was in Fact a Chilling Blunder," *The Sydney Morning Herald*, 18 December 2007.

41. John Vidal, "US Pours Cold Water on Bali Optimism," *Guardian Unlimited*, 17 December 2007.

42. Ibid.

43. Jowit, Davies, and Adam, "Late-Night Drama Pushes US into Climate Deal."

44. IPCC, *Summary for Policymakers: Contribution of Working Group III to the Fourth Assessment Report of the IPCC*, 18.

45. "The Montreal Protocol and Kyoto Protocol Mutually Supportive Say Top UN Officials," UNEP Press Release, 17 September 2007, available at http://unfccc.int/files/press/news_room/press_releases_and_advisories/application/pdf/070917_hcfc_press-rel.pdf (accessed 15 June 2009). Steiner is also the former head of the International Union for Conservation of Nature—another example of lateral mobility between the Second and Third UNs.

46. Liz Minchin, "UN Climate Chief Criticizes Downer," *Age* (Melbourne), 30 August 2007.

47. Richard Black, "Trade Can 'Export' CO2 Emissions," *BBC News World Service*, 19 December 2005, available at http://news.bbc.co.uk/2/hi/science/nature/4542104.stm (accessed 11 June 2006).

48. "Q & A: The Kyoto Protocol," *BBC News World Service*, 16 February 2005, available at http://news.bbc.co.uk/1/hi/sci/tech/4269921.stm.

49. International Energy Agency, *World Energy Outlook 2007* (Paris: IEA, 2007).

50. Shardul Agrawala and Steinar Andresen, "Indispensability and Indefensibility? The United States in the Climate Treaty Negotiations," *Global Governance* 5, no. 4 (1999): 457.

51. Michael Grubb and Farhana Yamin, "Climate Collapse at The Hague: What Happened, Why, and Where Do We Go from Here?" *International Affairs* 77, no. 2 (2001): 261–276.

52. Sverker C. Jagers and Johannes Stripple, "Climate Governance beyond the State," *Global Governance* 9, no. 3 (2003): 385.

53. Julia C. Mead, "Allstate Won't Renew Some Home Policies," *New York Times,* 12 February 2006.

54. "Kyoto Opponents Hold Climate Talks," *AlJazeera.net,* 11 January 2006, available at http://english.aljazeera.net/archive/2006/01/200849154048329968.html (accessed 23 May 2006).

55. Regional Greenhouse Gas Initiative, "About RGGI," available at www.rggi.org/about.

56. See Peter Newell, *Governing Climate Change* (London: Routledge, forthcoming).

57. Seung-soo Han, "The Global Challenge of Climate Change," *Global Asia* 2, no. 3 (2007): 11.

58. Mukul Sanwal, "Evolution of Global Environmental Governance and the United Nations," *Global Environmental Politics* 7, no. 3 (2007): 1–13.

59. Nils Meyer-Ohlendorf, "Would a United Nations Environment Organization Help to Achieve the Millennium Development Goals?" *Review of European Community & International Environmental Law* 15, no. 1 (2006): 26.

60. See David A. Sonnenfeld and Arthur P. J. Mol, "Globalization and the Transformation of Environmental Governance," *American Behavioral Scientist* 45, no. 9 (2002): 1318–1339.

61. Vlasis Oikonomou, Martin Patel, and Ernst Worrell, "Climate Policy: Bucket or Drainer?" *Energy Policy* 34 (2006): 3656.

62. Quoted in Maria Ivanova, David Gordon, and Jennifer Roy, "Towards Institutional Symbiosis: Business and the United Nations in Environmental Governance," *Review of European Community & International Environmental Law* 16, no. 2 (2007): 123.

63. For a discussion of the range of international efforts, see Elizabeth R. DeSombre, *Global Environmental Institutions* (London: Routledge, 2006); Peter M. Haas, Robert O. Keohane, and Marc A. Levy, eds., *Institutions for the Earth: Sources of Effective International Environmental Protection* (Cambridge, Mass.: MIT Press, 1993); Regina S. Axelrod, David Leonard Downie, and Norman J. Vig, eds., *The Global Environment: Institutions, Law and Policy* (Washington, D.C.: CQ Press, 2005); Frank Biermann and Steven Bauer, eds., *A World Environment Organization* (Aldershot, UK: Ashgate, 2005); W. Bradnee Chambers and Jessica F. Green, eds., *Reforming International Environmental Governance: From Institutional Limits to Innovative Reforms* (Tokyo: UN University Press, 2005.); Pamela S. Chasek, David L. Downie, and Janet Welsh Brown, *Global Environmental Politics,* 4th ed. (Boulder, Colo.: Westview Press, 2006.); and Pamela S. Chasek, *Earth Negotiations: Analyzing Thirty Years of Environmental Diplomacy* (Tokyo: UN University Press, 2001).

64. See Barry G. Rabe, "Beyond Kyoto: Climate Change Policy in Multilevel Governance Systems," *Governance: An International Journal of Policy, Administration,*

and Institutions 20, no. 3 (2007): 423–444; Alter Christer Christiansen, "Convergence or Divergence? Status and Prospects for US Climate Strategy," *Climate Policy* 3 (2003): 343–358; and Henrik Selin and Stacy D. VanDeveer, "Political Science and Prediction: What's Next for U.S. Climate Change Policy?" *Review of Policy Research* 24, no. 1 (2007): 1–27.

65. See Guri Bang, Camilla Bretteville Froyn, Jon Hovi, and Fredric C. Menz, "The United States and International Climate Cooperation: International 'Pull' versus Domestic 'Push,'" *Energy Policy* 35, no. 2 (2007): 1282–1291.

66. Federalist No. 51, 8 February 1788, available at http://www.foundingfathers. info/federalistpapers/fed51.htm (accessed 15 June 2009).

67. David G. Victor, Joshua C. House, and Sarah Joy, "A Madisonian Approach to Climate Policy," *Science* 309, no. 5742 (2005): 1820–1821.

8. Generations of Rights

1. Thomas G. Weiss, Tatiana Carayannis, Louis Emmerij, and Richard Jolly, *UN Voices: The Struggle for Development and Social Justice* (Bloomington: Indiana University Press, 2005), 413.

2. Ibid., 415.

3. See, for example, Roger Normand and Sarah Zaidi, *Human Rights at the UN: The Political History of Universal Justice* (Bloomington: Indiana University Press, 2008); Bertrand G. Ramcharan, *Contemporary Human Rights Ideas* (London: Routledge, 2008); Julie Mertus, *The United Nations and Human Rights,* 2nd ed. (London: Routledge, 2009); Philip Alston and Frederic Megret, eds., *The United Nations and Human Rights: A Critical Appraisal,* 2nd ed. (Oxford: Oxford University Press, 2005); David P. Forsythe, *Human Rights in International Relations* (Cambridge: Cambridge University Press, 2006); and Michael Haas, *International Human Rights* (New York: Routledge, 2008).

4. Quoted in Normand and Zaidi, *Human Rights and the UN,* 83, 88.

5. Quoted in William Korey, *NGOs and the Universal Declaration of Human Rights: "A Curious Grapevine"* (New York: St. Martin's Press, 1998), 9.

6. See Johannes Morsink, *The Universal Declaration of Human Rights: Origins, Drafting and Intent* (Philadelphia: University of Pennsylvania Press, 1999).

7. Jack Donnelly, "Human Rights and Asian Values: A Defense of Western Universalism," in *The East Asian Challenge for Human Rights,* ed. Joanne R. Bauer and Daniel A. Bell (Cambridge: Cambridge University Press, 1999), 68. See also W. J. Talbott, *Which Rights Should Be Universal?* (Oxford: Oxford University Press, 2005).

8. Weiss, Carayannis, Emmerij, and Jolly, *UN Voices,* 153.

9. For a snapshot of the changes in the field of human rights, see UNDP, *Human Development Report 2000* (New York: Oxford University Press, 2000). For historical examinations of human rights, see Jack Donnelly, *International Human Rights* (Boulder, Colo.: Westview, 1993); Tim Dunne and Nicholas J. Wheeler, eds., *Human Rights in Global Politics* (Cambridge: Cambridge University Press, 1999); David P. Forsythe, *The Internationalization of Human Rights* (Lexington, Mass.: D. C. Heath, 1991); and Forsythe, *Human Rights in International Relations.*

10. Weiss, Carayannis, Emmerij, and Jolly, *UN Voices,* 154.

11. "The Vienna Declaration and Programme of Action," General Assembly document A/CONF.157/23, 12 July 1993.

12. Bertrand G. Ramcharan, *The UN High Commissioner for Human Rights: The Challenges of International Protection* (Leiden: Martinus Nijhoff, 2002). For a discussion of

efforts outside headquarters to protect human rights, see Bertrand G. Ramcharan, ed., *Human Rights Protection in the Field* (Leiden: Martinus Nijhoff, 2006).

13. John Gerard Ruggie highlighted this role of the Global Compact in an e-mail to the authors dated 11 October 2008.

14. Weiss, Carayannis, Emmerij, and Jolly, *UN Voices,* 150.

15. Diane F. Orentlicher, "Relativism and Religion," in Michael Ignatieff, *Human Rights as Politics and Idolatry,* ed. and intro. Amy Gutmann (Princeton, N.J.: Princeton University Press, 2001), 144; emphasis in original.

16. Ignatieff, *Human Rights as Politics and Idolatry,* 3–4.

17. Isfahan Merali and Valerie Oosterveld, eds., *Giving Meaning to Economic, Social, and Cultural Rights* (Philadelphia: University of Pennsylvania Press, 2001); Sandra Fredman, *Human Rights Transformed: Positive Rights and Positive Duties* (Oxford: Oxford University Press, 2008).

18. For a discussion, see Thomas G. Weiss, David P. Forsythe, Roger A. Coate, and Kelly-Kate Pease, *The United Nations and Changing World Politics,* 5th ed. (Boulder, Colo.: Westview, 2007), 137–238.

19. Ignatieff, *Human Rights as Politics and Idolatry,* 5, 57–58.

20. Weiss, Carayannis, Emmerij, and Jolly, *UN Voices,* 158.

21. See Ramesh Thakur and Peter Malcontent, eds., *From Sovereign Impunity to International Accountability: The Search for Justice in a World of States* (Tokyo: UN University Press, 2004); and Edel Hughes, William A. Schabas, and Ramesh Thakur, eds., *Atrocities and International Accountability: Beyond Transitional Justice* (Tokyo: UN University Press, 2007).

22. Weiss, Carayannis, Emmerij, and Jolly, *UN Voices,* 149–150.

23. Orentlicher, "Relativism and Religion," 150.

24. Such debates also took place outside the United States. For example, in Australia a law professor at Deakin University has argued the case for torture, saying that if torture can produce information that will save innocent lives, then "it is verging on moral indecency to prefer the interests of the wrongdoer." See Mirko Bagaric, "A Case for Torture," *Age* (Melbourne), 17 May 2005.

25. Ignatieff, *Human Rights as Politics and Idolatry,* 163.

26. We acknowledge this insight from Olara Otunnu, at the time the special representative of the secretary-general for children in armed conflict.

27. *Strengthening of the United Nations: An Agenda for Further Change: Report of the Secretary-General* (New York: UN, 2002), para. 45.

28. See Ramesh Thakur and William Maley, "The Ottawa Convention on Landmines: A Landmark Humanitarian Treaty in Arms Control?" *Global Governance* 5, no. 3 (1999): 273–302.

29. High-level Panel on Threats, Challenges and Change, *A More Secure World: Our Shared Responsibility* (New York: UN, 2004), paras. 283 and 285.

30. Kofi A. Annan, *In Larger Freedom: Towards Development, Security and Human Rights for All* (New York: UN, 2005), para. 183.

31. *2005 World Summit Outcome,* General Assembly resolution A/RES/60/1, 24 October 2005, paras. 157 and 160.

32. Bertrand G. Ramcharan, "Norms and Machinery," in *The Oxford Handbook on the United Nations,* ed. Thomas G. Weiss and Sam Daws (Oxford: Oxford University Press, 2007), 439–462. See also Julie A. Mertus, *The United Nations and Human Rights: A Guide for New Era,* 2nd ed. (London: Routledge, 2009).

33. "Bad Counsel; UN Human-Rights Rows," *Economist*, 4 April 2007, 5–7

34. Colum Lynch, "U.S. to Join U.N. Human Rights Council, Reversing Bush Policy," *Washington Post*, 31 March 2009, available at http://www.washingtonpost.com/wp-dyn/content/article/2009/03/31/AR2009033102782.html (accessed 29 June 2009).

35. OHCHR, "Funding and Budget," available at http://www.ohchr.org/EN/AboutUs/Pages/FundingBudget.aspx (accessed 29 June 2009).

36. Ignatieff, *Human Rights as Politics and Idolatry*, 17.

37. Louise Arbour, "Statement by High Commissioner for Human Rights to Last Meeting of Commission on Human Rights," UN press release, 27 March 2006, 3–6, available at http://www.unhchr.ch/huricane/huricane.nsf/view01/5A23A835EEF0F7F5C125713E00541659?opendocument (accessed 15 June 2009).

38. One of the few works to deal with partial learning and incomplete change in international organizations is Ernst B. Haas, *When Knowledge Is Power* (Berkeley: University of California Press, 1990).

39. See David Cortright and George A. Lopez, *The Sanctions Decade: Assessing UN Strategies in the 1990s* (Boulder, Colo.: Lynne Rienner, 2000).

40. See Thomas G. Weiss, David Cortright, George A. Lopez, and Larry Minear, eds., *Political Gain and Civilian Pain: Humanitarian Impacts of Economic Sanctions* (Lanham, Md.: Rowman & Littlefield, 1997); and Tim Niblock, *Pariah States and Sanctions in the Middle East: Iraq, Libya, Sudan* (Boulder, Colo.: Lynne Rienner, 2001).

41. Gary C. Hufbauer, Jeffrey J. Schott, and Kimberly Ann Elliott, *Economic Sanctions Reconsidered: History and Current Policy*, 2nd ed. (Washington, D.C.: Institute for International Economics, 1990). See also Lisa L. Martin, *Coercive Cooperation: Explaining Multilateral Economic Sanctions* (Princeton, N.J.: Princeton University Press, 1992).

42. Johan Galtung, "On the Effects of International Economic Sanctions: With Examples from the Case of Rhodesia," *World Politics* 19, no. 3 (1967): 378–416.

43. See, for example, David Cortright and George A. Lopez with Linda Gerber, *Sanctions and the Search for Security: Challenges to UN Action* (Boulder, Colo.: Lynne Rienner, 2002); Cortright and Lopez, *The Sanctions Decade*; and Weiss, Cortright, Lopez, and Minear, eds., *Political Gain and Civilian Pain*.

44. The more scientifically reliable studies include Albert A. Ascherio, Mary C. Smith, Robert Chase, Tim Cote, Godelieave Dehaes, Eric Hoskins, Jilali Laaouej, Megan Passey, Saleh Qaderi, Saher Shuqaidef, and Sarah Zaidi, "Effect of the Gulf War on Infant and Child Mortality in Iraq," *New England Journal of Medicine* 327, no. 13 (1992): 931–936; Richard Garfield, *Morbidity and Mortality among Iraqi Children from 1990 to 1998: Assessing the Impact of Economic Sanctions*, Occasional Paper Series 16:OP:3 (Goshen, Ind.: Joan B. Kroc Institute for International Peace Studies of the University of Notre Dame and the Fourth Freedom Forum, 1999); and Mohamed M. Ali and Iqbal H. Shah, "Sanctions and Childhood Mortality in Iraq," *Lancet* 355 (May 2000): 1837–1857.

45. See Cortright and Lopez with Gerber, *Sanctions and the Search for Security*; David Cortright and George A. Lopez, eds., *Smart Sanctions: Targeting Economic Statecraft* (Lanham, Md.: Rowman & Littlefield, 2002); Daniel W. Drezner, *The Sanctions Paradox: Economic Statecraft and International Relations* (Cambridge: Cambridge University Press, 1999); and *Report of the Panel of Experts on Violations of Security Council Sanctions against UNITA (Fowler Report)* (New York: UN, March 2000).

46. Andrew Mack and Asif Khan, "UN Sanctions: A Glass Half Full?" in *The United Nations and Global Security*, ed. Richard M. Price and Mark W. Zacher (New York: Palgrave Macmillan, 2004), 119.

47. Kofi A. Annan, *We the Peoples: The Role of the United Nations in the 21st Century* (New York: UN, 2000), 49.

48. See Vera Gowlland-Debbas, ed., with the assistance of Djacoba Liva Tehindrazanarivelo, *National Implementation of United Nations Sanctions: A Comparative Study* (Leiden: Martinus Nijhoff, 2004).

49. See Carolyn Nordstrom, *A Different Kind of War Story* (Philadelphia: University of Pennsylvania Press, 1997).

50. Annan, *In Larger Freedom,* 39–40.

51. The three studies are The Swiss Confederation in cooperation with the UN Secretariat and the Watson Institute for International Studies Brown University, *Targeted Financial Sanctions: A Manual for Design and Implementation: Contributions from the Interlaken Process* (Providence, R.I.: Thomas J. Watson Institute for International Studies, 2001); Bonn International Center for Conversion in Cooperation with the Auswärtiges Amt (German Foreign Office) and the UN Secretariat, *Design and Implementation of Arms Embargoes and Travel and Aviation Related Sanctions: Results of the "Bonn-Berlin Process"* (Bonn: BICC, 2001); Peter Wallensteen, Carina Staibano, and Mikael Eriksson, eds., *Making Targeted Sanctions Effective: Guidelines for the Implementation of UN Policy Options* (Uppsala: Uppsala University, 2003). See also Michael Brzoska, ed., *Design and Implementation of Arms Embargoes and Travel and Aviation Related Sanctions—Results of the "Bonn-Berlin Process"* (Bonn: Bonn International Centre for Conversion, 2001).

52. Michael Brzoska, "From Dumb to Smart? Recent Reforms on UN Sanctions," *Global Governance* 9, no. 4 (2003): 524.

53. "UNITA 'Allies' in the Firing Line," *BBC News,* 15 March 2000, available at http://news.bbc.co.uk/2/hi/africa/678273.stm (accessed 7 July 2009).

54. Informal Working Group of the Security Council on General Issues of Sanctions, "Chairman's Proposed Outcome," Non-paper/Rev 10, 26 September 2002, available at http://www.un.org/Docs/sc/committees/sanctions/Prop_out10.pdf (accessed 7 July 2009).

55. See Cortright and Lopez, *Sanctions and the Search for Security,* 13–15.

56. See Susan Burgerman, *Moral Victories: How Activists Provoke Multilateral Action* (Ithaca, N.Y.: Cornell University Press, 2001).

57. Ian Smillie, "Whose Security? Innovation and Responsibility, Perception and Reality," in *A Decade of Human Security: Global Governance and New Multilateralisms,* ed. Sandra J. MacLean, David R. Black, and Timothy M. Shaw (Aldershot, UK: Ashgate, 2006), 23–26.

58. Arne Tostensen and Beate Ball, "Are Smart Sanctions Feasible?" *World Politics* 54, no. 2 (2002): 402. See also Brzoska's review essay, "From Dumb to Smart?."

59. *First Report of the Analytical Support and Sanctions Monitoring Team Appointed Pursuant to Resolution 1526 (2004) Concerning Al-Qaida and the Taliban and Associated Individuals and Entities,* Security Council document S/2004/679, 25 August 2004.

60. See Ramesh Thakur, *The United Nations, Peace and Security: From Collective Security to the Responsibility to Protect* (Cambridge: Cambridge University Press, 2006), 93–112.

61. See the essays in Thomas Risse, Stephen C. Ropp, and Kathryn Sikkink, eds., *The Power of Human Rights: International Norms and Domestic Change* (Cambridge: Cambridge University Press, 1999); Henry Steiner and Philip Alston, eds., *International Human Rights in Context: Law, Politics, Morals,* 2nd ed. (Oxford: Oxford University Press, 2000); and Jean-Marc Coicaud, Michael W. Doyle, and Anne-Marie Gardner, eds., *The*

Globalization of Human Rights: The United Nations System in the Twenty-First Century (Tokyo: UN University Press, 2003). See also Christian Tomuschat, *Human Rights: Between Idealism and Realism* (New York: Oxford University Press, 2003).

62. "Sudan Keeps Seat on U.N. Rights Commission; U.S. Walks Out," *UN Wire*, 5 May 2004.

63. "US Castigates UN Assembly on Sudan Human Rights," Reuters, 25 November 2004.

64. Brian Knowlton, "UN Rights Chief Cites U.S. Role in Departure," *International Herald Tribune*, 1 August 2002.

65. John H. Cushman, "U.N. Condemns Harsh Methods in Campaign against Terror," *New York Times*, 28 October 2004.

66. For the story, see Douglass Cassel, "The U.S. and the UN: See No Evil," *Chicago Tribune*, 29 May 2005.

67. The ICRC balances discretion and publicity by first making representations about violations of international humanitarian law discreetly to the authorities concerned, giving them reasonable time to make the necessary changes, and reserving the right to go public if adequate changes are not forthcoming and if public comment is likely to help the prisoners. See David P. Forsythe, *The Humanitarians: The International Committee of the Red Cross* (Cambridge: Cambridge University Press, 2005).

68. Jonathan Steele, "Red Cross Ultimatum to US on Saddam," *The Guardian*, 14 June 2004; Edward Wong, "Saddam's Status Raises Legal Complications," *International Herald Tribune*, 16 June 2004.

69. OHCHR, *Digest of Jurisprudence of the UN and Regional Organizations on the Protection of Human Rights While Countering Terrorism* (Geneva: OHCHR, July 2003).

70. *Amnesty International Report 2004* (London: Amnesty International, 2004); Human Rights Watch, *World Report 2005* (New York: Human Rights Watch, 2005). See also Human Rights Watch, "The Legal Prohibition against Torture," 1 June 2004, available at http://www.hrw.org/legacy/press/2001/11/TortureQandA.htm (accessed 15 June 2009); Human Rights Watch, "Guantánamo: Detainee Accounts," *Background Briefing*, 26 October 2004; and Human Rights Watch, "U.S.: Did President Bush Order Torture?" 20 December 2004, available at http://www.hrw.org/en/news/2004/12/20/us-did-president-bush-order-torture (accessed 15 June 2009).

71. Amnesty International, "Guantánamo—An Icon of Lawlessness," 6 January 2005, available at http://www.amnesty.org/en/library/asset/AMR51/002/2005/en/e5bd5c3b-d538-11dd-8a23-d58a49c0d652/amr510022005en.pdf (accessed 15 June 2009).

72. Amnesty International, "USA: Human Dignity Denied. Torture and Accountability in the 'War on Terror,'" available at http://www.amnesty.org/en/library/asset/AMR51/146/2004/en/d76be740-d56c-11dd-bb24-1fb85fe8fa05/amr511462004en.html (accessed 15 June 2009).

73. Amnesty International, *Amnesty International Report 2005: The State of the World's Human Rights* (London: Amnesty International, 2005).

74. Irene Khan, "Foreword," in *Amnesty International Report 2005: The State of the World's Human Rights* (London: Amnesty International, 2005), available at http://www.amnesty.org/en/library/asset/POL10/001/2005/en/608ee669-d53a-11dd-8a23-d58a49c0d652/pol100012005en.pdf (accessed 15 June 2009). Although effective, Khan's sound bite may also be deeply flawed in equating two phenomena that are simply not comparable in their scale and historical significance. See Pavel Litvinov, "Far from a Soviet 'Gulag,'" *Japan Times* (reprint of a *Washington Post* article), 24 June 2005. Litvinov is a dissident and human rights activist in the former Soviet Union. The idea of moral

equivalency between an imperfect democracy and Stalin's totalitarian dictatorship trivialized the Soviet gulags and in doing so allowed the Bush administration to deflect attention away from U.S. abuses and toward Amnesty International's hyperbole.

75. Cathy Young, "Guantánamo Is Not the Gulag," *International Herald Tribune,* 10 June 2005.

76. Human Rights Watch, *World Report 2005.*

77. "Rights Groups Reject Iraq Prison Findings," *Japan Times,* 25 April 2005.

78. See Julie Mertus, *Bait and Switch: Human Rights and U.S. Foreign Policy* (London: Routledge, 2004).

9. Protecting against Pandemics

1. Donald G. McNeil, Jr., "Pledging $500 Million, Bloomberg and Gates Take Aim at Smoking," *New York Times,* 24 July 2008, available at http://query.nytimes.com/gst/fullpage.html?res=9D02E7D8153CF937A15754C0A96E9C8B63 (accessed 4 August 2009).

2. Mark W. Zacher and Tania J. Keefe, *The Politics of Global Health Governance: United by Contagion* (New York: Palgrave Macmillan, 2008).

3. Statistics drawn from UNAIDS, *Report on the Global AIDS Epidemic 2006* (Geneva: UNAIDS, May 2006). "Global Facts and Figures 06," downloaded on 18 November 2007 from http://data.unaids.org/pub/GlobalReport/2006/200605-FS_globalfactsfigures_en.pdf.

4. UNAIDS/WHO, "2007 AIDS Epidemic Update," December 2007, available at http://data.unaids.org/pub/EPISlides/2007/2007_epiupdate_en.pdf (accessed 4 August 2009).

5. On the securitization of public health, see James Orbinski, "Global Health, Social Movements, and Governance," and David P. Fidler, "A Pathology of Public Health Securitism: Approaching Pandemics as Security Threats," both in *Governing Global Health: Challenge, Response, Innovation,* ed. Andrew F. Cooper, John J. Kirton, and Ted Schrecker (Aldershot, UK: Ashgate, 2007), 20–40 and 41–64, respectively.

6. International Crisis Group, "HIV/AIDS as a Security Issue," Issues Report No. 1, 19 June 2001, available at http://www.crisisgroup.org/home/index.cfm?l=1&id=1831 (accessed 4 August 2009).

7. International Crisis Group, *HIV/AIDS as a Security Issue,* Issue Report No. 1 (Brussels: International Crisis Group, 2001).

8. Mark W. Zacher, "The Transformation in Global Health Collaboration since the 1990s," in *Governing Global Health: Challenge, Response, Innovation,* ed. Andrew F. Cooper, John J. Kirton, and Ted Schrecker (Aldershot, UK: Ashgate, 2007), 15–27.

9. As with all history, this story is not uncontested. Immunization was apparently known in the seventeenth century in what is now known as Burkina Faso. Cotton Mather had a slave from that region, and Jenner apparently used Mather's writing as one source. See Sheldon Watts, "Small Pox in the New World and in the Old: From Holocaust to Eradication, 1518 to 1977," in Watts, *Epidemics and History: Disease, Power and Imperialism* (New Haven, Conn.: Yale University Press, 1999), 84–121.

10. WHO, "Smallpox," n.d., available at http://www.who.int/mediacentre/factsheets/smallpox/en/ (accessed 31 July 2008).

11. Frank Fenner, ed., *Smallpox and Its Eradication,* History of International Public Health No. 6 (Geneva: WHO, 1988); and Maggie Black, *The Children and the Nations: The Story of UNICEF* (New York: UNICEF, 1986).

12. Frank Fenner, Donald A. Henderson, Isao Arita, Zdenek Jezek, and Ivan D. Ladnyi, *Smallpox and Its Eradication* (Geneva: WHO, 1988).

13. Ibid.

14. Ibid.

15. The Global Polio Eradication Initiative, "The History," available at http://www.polioeradication.org/history.asp (accessed 30 June 2009).

16. UNAIDS/WHO, *2006 Report on the Global AIDS Epidemic* (Geneva: UNAIDS and WHO, 2006), 4.

17. Adesoji A. Oni, "Education: An Antidote for the Spread of HIV/AIDS," *Journal of the Association of Nurses in AIDS Care* 16, no. 2 (2005): 40–48.

18. Bekki J. Johnson and Robert S. Pond, *AIDS In Africa: A Review of Medical, Public Health, Social Science and Popular Literature* (Aachen: Campaign Against Hunger and Disease In the World, 1988).

19. World Bank, "Acquired Immunodeficiency Syndrome (AIDS): The Bank's Agenda for Action in Africa," Technical Paper, World Bank, Africa Technical Department, 24 October 1988, cited in William Easterly, "How, and How Not, to Stop AIDS in Africa," *New York Review of Books* 54, no. 13 (2007): 24.

20. Jill Armstrong, "Socioeconomic Implications of AIDS in Developing Countries," *Finance and Development* 28, no. 4 (1991): 14–17.

21. Helen Epstein, *The Invisible Cure: Africa, the West, and the Fight against AIDS* (New York: Farrar, Strauss and Giroux, 2007).

22. "UN HIV Estimates Reduced to 33m," *BBC News,* 20 November 2007, available at http://news.bbc.co.uk/2/hi/health/7103163.stm (accessed 10 December 2008).

23. During the 2007 U.S. presidential primary campaign, Senator Barack Obama's longtime pastor, Rev. Jeremiah Wright, spoke out about his belief in the theory that the U.S. government had deliberately infected African Americans with the HIV-AIDS virus. Obama quickly repudiated such comments.

24. Katherine Butler, "A President in Denial, a Ravaged Nation Denied Hope," *The Independent* (London), 10 August 2007, available at http://www.independent.co.uk/news/world/africa/a-president-in-denial-a-ravaged-nation-denied-hope-460967.html (accessed 5 August 2009).

25. UNAIDS, "A Global View of HIV Infection," available at http://data.unaids.org/pub/GlobalReport/2008/GR08_2007_HIVPrevWallMap_GR08_en.jpg (accessed 18 June 2008). See also UNAIDS, *2008 Report on the Global AIDS Epidemic* (Geneva: UNAIDS, 2008).

26. Quoted in Barton Gellman, "Death Watch: The Global Response to AIDS in Africa," *The Washington Post,* 5 July 2000, available at http://www.washingtonpost.com/wp-dyn/content/article/2006/06/09/AR2006060901326.html (accessed 10 December 2008).

27. UN Population Fund, "Key Actions for the Further Implementation of the Programme of Action of the IPCD—IPCD+5," available at http://www.unfpa.org/icpd/icpd5-key actions.cfm (accessed 18 June 2008).

28. Andrew F. Cooper, "Beyond One Image Fits All: Bono and the Complexity of Celebrity Governance," *Global Governance* 14, no. 3 (2008): 271.

29. Quoted in Gellman, "Death Watch."

30. UNAIDS, "Global Facts and Figures 06," available at http://data.unaids.org/pub/GlobalReport/2006/200605-FS_globalfactsfigures_en.pdf (accessed 18 November 2007).

31. See Randy Shilts, *And the Band Played On: Politics, People and the AIDS Epidemic* (New York: St. Martin's Griffin Press, 2007).

32. PBS, "Global Health: America's Response. AIDS Policy Timeline," 4 November 2005, available at http://www.pbs.org/now/science/aidstimeline.html (accessed 19 June 2009).

33. UNAIDS and WHO, *AIDS Epidemic Update: December 2007* (Geneva: UNAIDS and WHO, 2007).

34. While Uganda's single-partner policy was effective at first, it is no longer as effective, according to the international AIDS charity AVERT, which cites 2006 data from the Uganda Ministry of Health:

> Unfortunately, the early emphasis on avoiding casual sex appears to have lost its impact in recent years. A 2006 study by the Ugandan Ministry of Health found an apparent increase in multiple partnering. The proportion of sexually active Ugandans who reported having had two or more sexual partners in the previous 12 months increased from 2 to 4 percent between 2000–01 and 2004–05 among women, and from 25 to 29 percent among men.

AVERT, "The History of AIDS in Uganda," available at http://www.avert.org/aidsuganda.htm (accessed 4 August 2009). See also Helen Epstein, *The Invisible Cure: Why We Are Losing the Fight Against AIDS in Africa* (New York: Picador, 2008), 176.

35. Global HIV/AIDS Monitoring and Evaluation Team, *The Global HIV/AIDS Program: A Handbook* (Washington, D.C.: World Bank, 2007). The publication is generously sprinkled with the standard jargon of international bureaucracy such as strategies, policies, action plans, and monitoring and evaluation plans.

36. UNAIDS, *2006 Report on the Global AIDS Epidemic: Executive Summary* (Geneva: UNAIDS, 2006), available at http://data.unaids.org/pub/GlobalReport/2006/2006_GR-ExecutiveSummary_en.pdf (accessed 4 August 2009).

37. See Gian Luca Burci and Claude-Henri Vignes, *World Health Organization* (The Hague: Kluwer International, 2004); Kelley Lee, *The World Health Organization* (London: Routledge, 2009); and David Fidler, *International Law and Infectious Diseases* (Oxford: Oxford University Press, 1999).

38. See "Jonathan Mann, AIDS Pioneer, Is Dead," *New York Times,* 4 September 1998, available at http://www.nytimes.com/1998/09/04/us/jonathan-mann-aids-pioneer-is-dead-at-51.html (accessed 4 August 2009).

39. See Leon Gordenker, Roger A. Coate, Christer Jönsson, and Peter Söderholm, *International Cooperation in Response to AIDS* (London: Pinter, 1995); and Franklyn Lisk, *Global Institutions and the HIV/AIDS Epidemic: Responding to an International Crisis* (London: Routledge, 2009).

40. For example, campaigns to eradicate smoking and curtail substitutes for breast milk run up against rich and influential industry interests, a conflict that is usually camouflaged in the philosophical language of government regulation versus private enterprise. See Tagi Sagafi-nejad in collaboration with John H. Dunning, *The UN and Transnational Corporations: From Code of Conduct to Global Compact* (Bloomington: Indiana University Press, 2008), 181–187.

41. WHO, *World Health Report 1998* (Geneva: WHO, 1998); and World Health Organization, *World Health Report 1999* (Geneva: WHO, 1999).

42. UNAIDS, "UNAIDS Secretariat," available at http://www.unaids.org/en/AboutUNAIDS/Secretariat/default.asp (accessed 9 July 2009).

43. UNAIDS, "Global Facts and Figures 06."

44. UNAIDS, *2008 Report on the Global AIDS Epidemic* (Geneva: UNAIDS, 2008), 179.

45. Quoted in Easterly, "How, and How Not, to Stop AIDS in Africa," 24. In June 2009, the World Bank's HIV/AIDS site had not been updated since October 2003 and was still giving figures from that date! See World Bank, "Public Health at a Glance: HIV/AIDS, available at http://web.worldbank.org/WBSITE/EXTERNAL/TOPICS/EXTHEALTHNUTRITIONANDPOPULATION/EXTPHAAG/0,,contentMDK:20550808~menuPK:64229755~pagePK:64229817~piPK:64229743~theSitePK:672263,00.html (accessed 16 June 2009).

46. Ibid.

47. Amy Nunn, *The Politics and History of AIDS Treatment in Brazil* (New York: Springer, 2008), 120–123.

48. WHO, "The WHO Response to the Challenges of SARS in the Western Pacific Region," available at http://www.wpro.who.int/sars/ (accessed 9 July 2009).

49. Ibid.

50. Rhoda Margesson and Tiaji Salaam, "Severe Acute Respiratory Syndrome (SARS): The International Response," CRS Report for Congress, 8 September 2003, available at https://www.policyarchive.org/bitstream/handle/10207/1833/RL32072_20030908.pdf?sequence=1 (accessed 20 June 2009); K. Stöhr, "A Multicentre Collaboration to Investigate the Cause of Severe Acute Respiratory Syndrome," *The Lancet* 361, no. 9370 (2003): 1730–1733.

51. See Souk Kai Chew, "SARS—How WHO's Western Pacific Regional Office Responded to the Threat of a Global Health Crisis," *Bulletin of the World Health Organization* 85, no. 4 (April 2007), available at http://www.scielosp.org/scielo.php?pid=S0042-96862007000400021&script=sci_arttext (accessed 27 April 2009).

52. WHO, "Update 96—Taiwan, China: SARS Transmission Interrupted in Last Outbreak Area," 5 July 2003, available at Update 96—Taiwan, China: SARS Transmission Interrupted in Last Outbreak Area (accessed 6 August 2009).

53. See WHO, "Avian Influenza Frequently Asked Questions," 5 December 2005, available at www.who.int/csr/disease/avian_influenza/avian_faqs/en (accessed 5 May 2008).

54. WHO, "Cumulative Number of Confirmed Human Cases of Avian Influenza A/(H5N1) Reported to WHO," 23 August 2007, available at http://www.who.int/csr/disease/avian_influenza/country/cases_table_2007_08_23/en/index.html (accessed 20 June 2009).

55. Scott Barrett, *Why Cooperate? The Incentive to Supply Global Public Goods* (Oxford: Oxford University Press, 2007), 3.

56. Lindsay Beck, "UN Poverty Goals on Health out of Reach, WHO Says," Reuters, 29 October 2007, available at http://www.reuters.com/article/healthNews/idUSPEK18429920071029 (accessed 27 April 2009). See also Colin I. Bradford, "Reaching the Millennium Development Goals," in *Governing Global Health: Challenge, Response, Innovation,* ed. Andrew F. Cooper, John J. Kirton, and Ted Schrecker (Aldershot, UK: Ashgate, 2007), 79–85.

57. Ann E. Kent, *Beyond Compliance: China, International Organizations, and Global Security* (Stanford, Calif.: Stanford University Press, 2007), 241.

58. "WHO Won't Budge on SARS Travel Warning," *CBC News,* 25 April 2003, available at http://www.cbc.ca/canada/story/2003/04/25/sarstravel_who030425.html (accessed 20 June 2009).

59. WHO, "Strategies to Fight World Health Threats, Such as SARS, Receive International Backing," 28 May 2003, available at http://www.who.int/mediacentre/news/notes/2003/npwha3/en/index.html (accessed 20 June 2009).

60. Kofi A. Annan, *In Larger Freedom: Towards Development, Security and Human Rights for All* (New York: UN, 2005), 39.

10. The Responsibility to Protect

1. Pope Benedict XVI, "Address to the General Assembly of the United Nations," 18 April 2008, available at http://www.un.org/webcast/pdfs/Pope_speech.pdf (accessed 27 April 2009).

2. International Commission on Intervention and State Sovereignty, *The Responsibility to Protect* (Ottawa: International Development Research Centre, 2001).

3. Kofi Annan, "A Progress Report on UN Renewal," *New World* (April–June 2006): 8, available at http://www.una.org.uk/new_world/New%20World%20April-June%202006.pdf (accessed 9 July 2009).

4. Parts of this chapter appeared in Ramesh Thakur and Thomas G. Weiss, "R2P: From Idea to Norm—and Action?" *Global Responsibility to Protect* 1, no. 1 (2009): 22–53. The appearance of this journal devoted entirely to the issue of preventing mass atrocities is an indicator of the extent to which R2P is moving from the margins to the mainstream.

5. Pope Benedict XVI, "Address to the General Assembly of the United Nations."

6. See Kalevi J. Holsti, *War, the State, and the State of War* (Cambridge: Cambridge University Press, 1996).

7. See Roger Normand and Sarah Zaidi, *Human Rights at the UN: The Political History of Universal Justice* (Bloomington: Indiana University Press, 2008).

8. Raphael Lemkin, *Axis Rule in Occupied Europe: Laws of Occupation, Analysis of Government, Proposals for Redress* (1944; repr., Clark, N.J.: The Lawbook Exchange, 2005).

9. See Ben Kiernan, *Blood and Soil: A World History of Genocide and Extermination from Sparta to Darfur* (New Haven, Conn.: Yale University Press, 2007), 10.

10. "In Message Honouring Raphael Lemkin, Secretary-General Calls His Lifework 'An Inspiring Example of Moral Engagement,'" UN Press Release SG/SM/7842, 13 June 2001.

11. Michael Ignatieff, "The Legacy of Raphael Lemkin," lecture delivered at the U.S. Holocaust Memorial Museum, Washington, D.C., 13 December 2000, available at http://www.ushmm.org/genocide/analysis/details.php?content=2000-12-13 (accessed 16 June 2009).

12. For details, see Thomas G. Weiss and David A. Korn, *Internal Displacement: Conceptualization and Its Consequences* (London: Routledge, 2006). Deng is currently the special representative of the secretary-general for prevention of genocide; at the time the 2001 report was being drafted, he was the special representative on internally displaced persons.

13. The examples are drawn from Ramesh Thakur, *The Government and Politics of India* (London: Macmillan, 1995).

14. Weiss and Korn, *Internal Displacement*, 55–70, 103–126.

15. Lloyd Axworthy, *Navigating a New World: Canada's Global Future* (Toronto: Alfred A. Knopf, 2003), 414. Gareth Evans has made this historical link clear in *The Responsibility to Protect: Ending Mass Atrocity Crimes Once and for All* (Washington, D.C.:

Brookings Institution Press, 2008). See also Alex J. Bellamy, *Responsibility to Protect: The Global Effort to End Mass Atrocities* (Cambridge: Polity Press, 2009).

16. See, for example, Francis M. Deng and I. William Zartman, eds., *Conflict Resolution in Africa* (Washington, D.C.: Brookings Institution Press, 1991); Francis M. Deng and Terrence Lyons, eds., *African Reckoning: A Quest for Good Governance* (Washington, D.C.: Brookings Institution Press, 1998); and Francis M. Deng, "Reconciling Sovereignty with Responsibility: A Basis for International Humanitarian Action," in *Africa in World Politics: Post–Cold War Challenges,* ed. John W. Harbeson and Donald Rothschild (Boulder, Colo.: Westview, 1995), 295–310.

17. Roberta Cohen, *Human Rights Protection for Internally Displaced Persons* (Washington, D.C.: Refugee Policy Group, 1991), 1.

18. See Brian D. Lepard, *Rethinking Humanitarian Intervention* (University Park: Pennsylvania State University Press, 2002), 7–23.

19. See Mary Kaldor, *New and Old Wars: Organized Violence in a Global Era* (Stanford, Calif.: Stanford University Press, 1999). For a discussion of the nature of humanitarian action in these armed conflicts, see Peter J. Hoffman and Thomas G. Weiss, *Sword & Salve: Confronting New Wars and Humanitarian Crises* (Lanham, Md.: Rowman & Littlefield, 2006); and David Keen, *Complex Emergencies* (Cambridge: Polity Press, 2008).

20. See Ramesh Thakur and Carlyle A. Thayer, eds., *A Crisis of Expectations: UN Peacekeeping in the 1990s* (Boulder, Colo.: Westview, 1995).

21. *Report of the Panel on United Nations Peace Operations,* General Assembly document A/55/305-S/2000/809, 21 August 2000, para. 50, available at http://www .un.org/peace/reports/peace_operations/ (accessed 27 April 2009).

22. For further details, see Thomas G. Weiss, *Military-Civilian Interactions: Humanitarian Crises and the Responsibility to Protect,* 2nd ed. (Lanham, Md.: Rowman & Littlefield, 2004), 191–214; Pamela R. Aall, Daniel T. Miltenberger, and Thomas G. Weiss, *IGOs, NGOs, and the Military in Peace and Relief Operations* (Washington, D.C., United States Institute of Peace Press, 2000); and Michael V. Bhatia, *War and Intervention: A Global Survey of Peace Operations* (West Hartford, Conn.: Kumarian Press, 2003).

23. In August 2008, Russia deliberately couched its justifications of military action against Georgia in South Ossetia to echo NATO actions and discourse from the Balkans in 1999; see Ramesh Thakur, "Payback Time for Russia," *Japan Times,* 23 August 2008.

24. Greenberg Research, *The People on War Report* (Geneva: ICRC, 1999), xvi.

25. Antonio Donini, Larry Minear, Ian Smillie, Ted van Baarda, and Anthony C. Welch, *Mapping the Security Environment: Understanding the Perceptions of Local Communities, Peace Support Operations, and Assistance Agencies* (Medford, Mass: Feinstein International Famine Center, 2005), 53.

26. See Ramesh Thakur, *The United Nations, Peace and Security: From Collective Security to the Responsibility to Protect* (Cambridge: Cambridge University Press, 2006), 320–342; and Simon Chesterman, ed., *Secretary or General? The UN Secretary-General in World Politics* (Cambridge: Cambridge University Press, 2007).

27. Ramesh Thakur's notes from that event.

28. Kofi A. Annan, *The Question of Intervention: Statements by the Secretary-General* (New York: UN, 1999), 7.

29. Kofi A. Annan, *We the Peoples: The United Nations in the 21st Century* (New York: UN, 2000). For a discussion of the controversy surrounding the speech in September 1999, see Thomas G. Weiss, "The Politics of Humanitarian Ideas," *Security Dialogue* 31, no. 1 (2000): 11–23.

30. For skeptical views, see Mohammed Ayoob, "Humanitarian Intervention and International Society," *Global Governance* 7, no. 3 (2001): 225–230; Robert Jackson, *The Global Covenant: Human Conduct in a World of States* (Oxford: Oxford University Press, 2000); Christopher Bickerton, Philip Cunliffe, and Alexander Gourevitch, eds., *Politics Without Sovereignty* (New York: Routledge, 2007); and Simon Chesterman, *Just War? Just Peace? Humanitarian Intervention and International Law* (Oxford: Oxford University Press, 2001).

31. For elaboration, see Thakur, *The United Nations, Peace and Security,* 264–289.

32. Thomas G. Weiss, Tatiana Carayannis, Louis Emmerij, and Richard Jolly, *UN Voices: The Struggle for Development and Social Justice* (Bloomington: Indiana University Press, 2005), 378.

33. *Report of the Secretary-General on the Work of the Organization,* General Assembly document A/54/1 (1999), 48.

34. Commission meetings were held in Ottawa (November 2000), Maputo (March 2001), New Delhi (June 2001), Wakefield, Canada (August 2000), and Brussels (September 2001). Roundtables and consultative meetings were held in in Ottawa January 2001), Geneva (January 2001), London (February 2001), Maputo (March 2001), Washington, D.C. (May 2001), Santiago (May 2001), Cairo (May 2001), Paris (May 2001), New Delhi (June 2001), Beijing (June 2001), and St. Petersburg (July 2001).

35. They are reflected in Thomas G. Weiss and Don Hubert, *The Responsibility to Protect: Research, Bibliography, and Background* (Ottawa: International Development Research Centre, 2001), 27–46.

36. Richard Haass, "When Nations Forfeit Their Sovereign Privileges," *International Herald Tribune,* 7 February 2003. Haass is currently president of the Council on Foreign Relations,

37. Gareth Evans, "Humanity Did Not Justify this War," *Financial Times,* 15 May 2003; Ramesh Thakur, "Chrétien Was Right: It's Time to Redefine a 'Just War,'" *Globe and Mail,* 22 July 2003; and Ramesh Thakur, "Iraq and the Responsibility to Protect," *Behind the Headlines* 62, no. 1 (2004): 1–16. However, one of the commissioners, Michael Ignatieff, now a Member of Parliament in Canada, justified the war; see Michael Ignatieff, "Getting Iraq Wrong," *New York Times Magazine,* 5 August 2007, available at http://query.nytimes.com/gst/fullpage.html?res=9F01E6DD1E31F936A3575BC0A9619 C8B63 (accessed 7 July 2009).

38. The full list of Evans's extensive speeches and writings on R2P can be found at http://www.crisisgroup.org/home/index.cfm?id=4521&l=1 (accessed 7 July 2009).

39. For example, Thakur's writings encompass a wide range of products from newspaper op-ed columns and scholarly articles to his book *The United Nations, Peace and Security.* Weiss's writings are mainly academic; see, for example, *Humanitarian Intervention: Ideas in Action* (Cambridge: Polity Press, 2007).

40. High-level Panel on Threats, Challenges and Change, *A More Secure World: Our Shared Responsibility* (New York: UN, 2004), 65–66, emphasis in original.

41. Ibid., para. 207.

42. "Position Paper of the People's Republic of China on the United Nations Reforms," Beijing, 7 June 2005, available at http://news.xinhuanet.com/english/ 2005-06/08/content_3056817_3.htm (accessed 16 June 2009).

43. *American Interests and UN Reform: Report of the Task Force on the United Nations* (Washington, D.C.: United States Institute of Peace Press, 2005), 15.

44. Kofi A. Annan, *In Larger Freedom: Towards Development, Security and Human Rights for All: Report of the Secretary-General* (New York: UN, 2005), 48–49.

45. For an assessment, see Alexander J. Bellamy, "What Will Become of the Responsibility to Protect?" *Ethics and International Affairs* 20, no. 2 (2006): 143–169.

46. *2005 World Summit Outcome,* General Assembly resolution A/RES/60/1, 24 October 2005, paras. 138–140.

47. Ibid., 30.

48. Russia's misapplication of R2P in August 2008 reinforced the importance of the "precautionary principles" or "legitimacy criteria" of the ICISS and the High-Level Panel respectively; see Global Centre for the Responsibility to Protect, "The Russia-Georgia Crisis and the Responsibility to Protect: Background Note," 19 August 2008, available at globalr2p.org/pdf/related/GeorgiaRussia.pdf (accessed 23 August 2008). Both authors were involved in drafting the background note.

49. International Commission on Intervention and State Sovereignty, *The Responsibility to Protect,* xi.

50. U.S. Committee for Refugees, *World Refugee Survey 2005* (Washington, D.C.: USCR, 2005), 11.

51. Mohammed Ayoob, "Humanitarian Intervention and International Society," *The International Journal of Human Rights* 6, no. 1 (2002): 84. For the context that drives Ayoob's skepticism, see Simon Chesterman, Michael Ignatieff, and Ramesh Thakur, eds., *State Failure and the Crisis of Governance: Making States Work* (Tokyo: UN University Press, 2005).

52. David Rieff, *A Bed for the Night: Humanitarianism in Crisis* (New York: Simon & Schuster, 2002), 15.

53. Alex J. Bellamy, "Responsibility to Protect or Trojan Horse? The Crisis in Darfur and Humanitarian Intervention after Iraq," *Ethics & International Affairs* 19, no. 2 (2005): 53.

54. Paula Banarjee, e-mail to Thomas G. Weiss, 11 October 2005.

55. Thomas G. Weiss, "The Sunset of Humanitarian Intervention? The Responsibility to Protect in a Unipolar World," *Security Dialogue* 35, no. 2 (2004): 135–153.

56. See Ramesh Thakur, "Humanitarian Intervention," in *Handbook of the United Nations,* ed. Thomas G. Weiss and Sam Daws (Oxford: Oxford University Press, 2007), 387–403; and Weiss and Hubert, *The Responsibility to Protect,* 57–63.

57. UN Documents S/PV.3977 and S/PV.3978, 12 February 1999.

58. Security Council resolutions 1265 (17 September 1999), 1296 (19 April 2000), 1674 (28 April 2006), and 1738 (23 December 2006); reports of the Secretary-General were on 18 September 1999 (UN document S/1999/957), 30 March 2001 (S/2001/331), 30 November 2002 (S/2002/1300), 28 May 2004 (S/2004/431), 28 November 2005 (S/2005/740), and 28 October 2007 (S/2007/643).

59. Anthony Lewis, "The Challenge of Global Justice Now," *Dædalus* 132, no. 1 (2003): 8.

60. See Ramesh Thakur and Vesselin Popovski, "The Responsibility to Protect and Prosecute: The Parallel Erosion of Sovereignty and Impunity," in *Yearbook of International Law and Jurisprudence,* ed Giuliana Ziccardi Capaldo (Oxford: Oxford University Press, 2008), 39–61.

61. See Ramesh Thakur and Peter Malcontent, eds., *From Sovereign Impunity to International Accountability: The Search for Justice in a World of States* (Tokyo: UN University Press, 2004); and Edel Hughes, William A. Schabas, and Ramesh Thakur,

eds., *Atrocities and International Accountability: Beyond Transitional Justice* (Tokyo: UN University Press, 2007).

62. See Robert Gellately and Ben Kiernan, eds., *The Spectre of Genocide: Mass Murder in Historical Perspective* (Cambridge: Cambridge University Press, 2003); and Martin Shaw, *War and Genocide: Organized Killing in Modern Society* (Cambridge: Polity Press, 2003).

63. "In Message Honouring Raphael Lemkin, Secretary-General Calls His Lifework 'An Inspiring Example of Moral Engagement.'"

64. See Kingsley Chiedu Moghalu, *The Politics of Justice for Rwanda's Genocide* (New York: Palgrave Macmillan, 2005); and Kingsley Chiedu Moghalu, *Global Justice: The Politics of War Crimes Trials* (Westport, Conn.: Praeger International, 2006).

65. See Roger S. Clark and Madeleine Sann, eds., *The Prosecution of International Crimes: A Critical Study of the International Tribunal for the Former Yugoslavia* (New Brunswick, N.J.: Transaction, 1996).

66. See William A. Schabas, *An Introduction to the International Criminal Court* (Cambridge: Cambridge University Press, 2001); and Bruce Broomhall, *International Justice and the International Criminal Court: Between State Consent and the Rule of Law* (Oxford: Oxford University Press, 2003).

67. Gary Jonathan Bass, *Stay the Hand of Vengeance: The Politics of War Crimes Tribunals* (Princeton, N.J.: Princeton University Press, 2000), 283.

68. Julie Flint and Alex de Waal, "Case Closed: A Prosecutor without Borders," *World Affairs* (Spring 2009), available at http://www.worldaffairsjournal.org/2009%20-%20Spring/full-DeWaalFlint.html.

69. See Richard Goldstone and Adam Smith, *International Judicial Institutions: The Architecture of International Justice at Home and Abroad* (London: Routledge, 2008).

70. Gary J. Bass, *Freedom's Battle: The Origins of Humanitarian Intervention* (New York: Alfred A. Knopf, 2008), 382.

71. See the discussion in the Fifth Committee of the General Assembly at its 28th meeting on 4 March 2008 ("United Nations Human Resources Structures Must Be Adapted to Meet Growing Demands of Peacekeeping, Other Field Operations, Budget Committee Told," General Assembly document GA/AB/3837, 4 March 2008, available at http://www.un.org/News/Press/docs/2008/gaab3837.doc.htm [accessed 30 May 2009]). This discussion took place in the context of the publicly announced intention of the Secretary-General to appoint Edward C. Luck as his special adviser with a focus on R2P.

72. Quoted in Gareth Evans, "The Responsibility to Protect: An Idea Whose Time Has Come . . . and Gone?" *International Relations* 22, no. 3 (2008): 289.

73. Quoted in Gareth Evans, "Delivering on the Responsibility to Protect: Four Misunderstandings, Three Challenges and How to Overcome Them," address to SEF Symposium 2007, Bonn, 30 November 2007. See also "Int'l Diplomatic Coup to Erode SL's Sovereignty?" *The Nation on Sunday* (Colombo), 27 January 2008, available at http://www.nation.lk/2008/01/27/newsfe5.htm (accessed 16 June 2009).

74. H. L. D. Mahindapala, "Peace Secretariat Calls for UN inquiry into Radhika Coomaraswamy, UN Under-Secretary-General, Stuck in NGO Scandal," *Lanka Times*, 29 January 2008, available at www.lankatimes.com/fullstory.php?id=7218 (accessed 16 June 2009).

75. See Ramesh Thakur, "The Responsibility to Protect and the War on Saddam Hussein," in *The Iraq Crisis and World Order: Structural, Institutional and Normative*

Challenges, ed. Ramesh Thakur and Waheguru Pal Singh Sidhu (Tokyo: UN University Press, 2006), 464–478.

76. Weiss and Hubert, *The Responsibility to Protect,* 49–77. See also Stephen Krasner, *Sovereignty: Organized Hypocrisy* (Princeton, N.J.: Princeton University Press, 1999).

77. Weiss and Hubert, *The Responsibility to Protect,* 79–126.

78. Klaus Naumann, John Shalikashvili, Lord Inge, Jacques Lanxade, and Henk van den Breemen, *Towards a Grand Strategy for an Uncertain World: Renewing Transatlantic Partnership* (Lunteren, Germany: Noaber Foundation, 2007).

79. See Aung Zaw, "Ballot for a Tyrant," *The Guardian* (London), 12 May 2008.

80. International Commission on Intervention and State Sovereignty, *The Responsibility to Protect,* 33.

81. "Forcing Aid to Burma 'Incendiary,'" *BBC News,* 9 May 2008, available at news. bbc.co.uk/go/pr/fr/-/2/hi/uk_news/7391492.stm (accessed 9 May 2008).

82. Julian Borger and Ian MacKinnon, "Bypass Junta's Permission for Aid, US and France Urge," *The Guardian,* 9 May 2008.

83. Washington saw the sense of this, and Secretary of State Condoleezza Rice called her Chinese and Indian counterparts, foreign ministers Yang Jeichi and Pranab Mukherjee, seeking their good offices in persuading Myanmar to adopt a more liberal approach toward foreign aid. "Myanmar: U.S. Seeks India's Help," *Hindu,* 11 May 2008. It should be noted that Japan also rejected outside help after the Kobe earthquake, as did India after the tsunami. And Washington rejected Cuban offers of help after Hurricane Katrina.

84. *Implementing the Responsibility to Protect: Report of the Secretary-General,* General Assembly document A/63/677, 12 January 2009.

85. Ibid., para. 50.

86. Ibid., para. 11.

87. Ibid., para. 12.

88. *Report of the Panel on United Nations Peace Operations,* General Assembly document A/55305 and Security Council document S/200/809, 21 August 2000.

89. Jennifer Welsh, "Implementing the 'Responsibility to Protect,'" Policy Brief 1/2009, Oxford Institute for Ethics, Law and Armed Conflict, available at http://www.elac.ox.ac.uk/downloads/R2P_policybrief_180209.pdf (accessed 6 August 2009).

90. Victoria K. Holt and Tobias C. Berkman, *The Impossible Mandate? Military Preparedness, the Responsibility to Protect and Modern Peace Operations* (Washington, D.C.: Stimson Center, 2006). See also Taylor B. Seybolt, *Humanitarian Military Intervention: The Conditions for Success and Failure* (Oxford: Oxford University Press, 2007); and Charlotte Ku and Harold K. Jacobson, eds. . *Democratic Accountability and the Use of Force in International Law* (Cambridge: Cambridge University Press, 2003).

91. See Jaya Murthy, "Mandating the Protection Cluster with the Responsibility to Protect: A Policy Recommendation Based on the Protection Cluster's Implementation in South Kivu, DRC," *Journal of Humanitarian Assistance,* 5 October 2008, available at http://jha.ac/2007/10/05/mandating-the-protection-cluster-with-the-responsibility-to-protect-a-policy-recommendation-based-on-the-protection-cluster%e2%80%99s-implementation-in-south-kivu-drc/ (accessed 16 June 2009).

92. Annan, *We the Peoples,* 48.

93. See http://globalr2p.org/.

94. "Secretary-General, in Message to New York Conference, Says Prevention of Mass Atrocities 'A Sacred Calling' of International Community," UN document SG/

SM/11212, 10 October 2007, available at http://www.un.org/News/Press/docs/2007/sgsm11212.doc.htm (accessed 7 July 2009).

95. "Daily Press Briefing by the Office of the Spokesperson for the Secretary-General, 28 January 2008," available at www.un.org/News/briefings/docs/2008/db080128.doc.htm.

96. Desmond Tutu, "Taking the Responsibility to Protect," *International Herald Tribune,* 19 February 2008.

97. See UNICEF, "UNICEF Kenya: Post-Election Violence Monthly Situation Report—Jan 2008," 21 January 2008, available at http://www.reliefweb.int/rw/RWB.NSF/db900SID/SHIG-7C7F2U?OpenDocument (accessed 16 June 2009).

98. Edward C. Luck, "The United Nations and the Responsibility to Protect," *The Stanley Foundation Policy Analysis Brief,* August 2008, 6, available at http://www.stanley-foundation.org/publications/pab/LuckPAB808.pdf (accessed 16 June 2009).

99. Roger Cohen, "How Kofi Annan Rescued Kenya," *New York Review of Books* 55, no. 13, 14 August 2008. See also Tutu, "Taking the Responsibility to Protect."

100. Weiss, Carayannis, Emmerij, and Jolly, *UN Voices,* 410.

101. Daniel Philpott, *Revolutions in Sovereignty: How Ideas Shaped Modern International Relations* (Princeton, N.J.: Princeton University Press, 2001).

102. Evans, *The Responsibility to Protect,* 7.

INDEX

Italicized page numbers refer to illustrations and tables.

ABOUT THE AUTHORS

THOMAS G. WEISS is Presidential Professor of Political Science at The Graduate Center of the City University of New York and Director of the Ralph Bunche Institute for International Studies, where he is co-director of the United Nations Intellectual History Project. He is President of the International Studies Association (2009–2010) and Chair of the Academic Council on the UN System (2006–2009). He was editor of *Global Governance*, Research Director of the International Commission on Intervention and State Sovereignty, Research Professor at Brown University's Watson Institute for International Studies, Executive Director of the Academic Council on the UN System and of the International Peace Academy, a member of the UN secretariat, and a consultant to several public and private agencies. He has written or edited some 35 books and 150 articles and book chapters about multilateral approaches to international peace and security, humanitarian action, and sustainable development. His latest books include *What's Wrong with the United Nations and How to Fix It* and *Humanitarian Intervention: Ideas in Action*.

RAMESH THAKUR is the inaugural Director of the Balsillie School of International Affairs, Distinguished Fellow of the Centre for International Governance Innovation, and Professor of Political Science at the University of Waterloo, Ontario. Educated in India and Canada, he was formerly Professor of International Relations at the University of Otago in New Zealand, Professor and Head of the Peace Research Centre of the Australian National University, Senior Vice Rector of the United Nations University, and UN Assistant Secretary-General. He was a Commissioner on the International Commission on Intervention and State Sovereignty, principal writer of UN Secretary-General Kofi Annan's second reform report, and advisor to the Australian and New Zealand governments on international peace and security issues. He has written or edited more than 30 books and 300 articles and book chapters and also writes regularly for several major newspapers around the world. His most recent books include *War in Our Time: Reflections on Iraq, Terrorism and Weapons of*

Mass Destruction and *The United Nations, Peace and Security: From Collective Security to the Responsibility to Protect,* winner of the ACUNS 2008 Award for the best recent book on the UN system.

JOHN GERARD RUGGIE is Kirkpatrick Professor of International Affairs at Harvard's Kennedy School of Government and Affiliated Professor in International Legal Studies at Harvard Law School. He also serves as the United Nations Secretary-General's Special Representative for Business and Human Rights and was UN Assistant Secretary-General for Strategic Planning from 1997 to 2001.

ABOUT THE UNITED NATIONS INTELLECTUAL HISTORY PROJECT

Ideas and concepts are a main driving force in human progress, and they are arguably the most important contribution of the United Nations. Yet there has been little historical study of the origins and evolution of the history of economic and social ideas cultivated within the world organization and of their impact on wider thinking and international action. The United Nations Intellectual History Project (UNIHP) is filling this gap in knowledge about the UN by tracing the origin and analyzing the evolution of key ideas and concepts about international economic and social development born or nurtured under UN auspices. UNIHP began operations in mid-1999 when its secretariat, the hub of a worldwide network of specialists on the UN, was established at the Ralph Bunche Institute for International Studies of The CUNY Graduate Center.

UNIHP has two main components: oral history interviews and a series of books on specific topics. The seventy-nine in-depth oral history interviews with leading contributors to crucial ideas and concepts within the UN system provide the raw material for this volume and other volumes. In addition, complete and indexed transcripts are available to researchers and the general public in an electronic book format on CD-ROM available through the secretariat.

The project has commissioned fifteen studies about the major economic and social ideas or concepts that are central to UN activity, which are being published by Indiana University Press.

- *Ahead of the Curve? UN Ideas and Global Challenges,* by Louis Emmerij, Richard Jolly, and Thomas G. Weiss (2001)
- *Unity and Diversity in Development Ideas: Perspectives from the UN Regional Commissions,* edited by Yves Berthelot with contributions from Adebayo Adedeji, Yves Berthelot, Leelananda de Silva, Paul Rayment, Gert Rosenthal, and Blandine Destremeau (2003)
- *Quantifying the World: UN Contributions to Statistics,* by Michael Ward (2004)
- *UN Contributions to Development Thinking and Practice,* by Richard Jolly, Louis Emmerij, Dharam Ghai, and Frédéric Lapeyre (2004)

- *The UN and Global Political Economy: Trade, Finance, and Development,* by John Toye and Richard Toye (2004)
- *UN Voices: The Struggle for Development and Social Justice,* by Thomas G. Weiss, Tatiana Carayannis, Louis Emmerij, and Richard Jolly (2005)
- *Women, Development and the United Nations: A Sixty-Year Quest for Equality and Justice,* by Devaki Jain (2005)
- *Human Security and the UN: A Critical History,* by S. Neil MacFarlane and Yuen Foong Khong (2006)
- *Human Rights at the UN: The Political History of Universal Justice,* Roger Normand and Sarah Zaidi (2008)
- *Preventive Diplomacy at the UN,* by Bertrand G. Ramcharan (2008)
- *The UN and Transnational Corporations: From Code of Conduct to Global Compact,* by Tagi Sagafi-nejad in collaboration with John Dunning (2009)
- *The UN and Development: From Aid to Cooperation,* by Olav Stokke (2009)
- *UN Ideas That Changed the World,* by Richard Jolly, Louis Emmerij, and Thomas G. Weiss (2009)
- *Global Governance and the UN: An Unfinished Journey,* by Thomas G. Weiss and Ramesh Thakur (2010)

Forthcoming Titles:

- *Development without Destruction: The UN and Global Resource Management,* by Nico Schrijver

The project also collaborated on *The Oxford Handbook on the United Nations,* edited by Thomas G. Weiss and Sam Daws, published by Oxford University Press in 2007.

For further information, the interested reader should contact:

UN Intellectual History Project
The CUNY Graduate Center
365 Fifth Avenue, Suite 5203
New York, New York 10016-4309
212-817-1920 Tel
212-817-1565 Fax
UNHistory@gc.cuny.edu
www.unhistory.org